A Widow's Story

A Widow's Story

A MEMOIR

Joyce Carol Oates

ecco

An Imprint of HarperCollinsPublishers

HarperCollins books may be purchased for educational, business, or sales promotional use. For information, please write: Special Markets Department, HarperCollins Publishers, 10 East 53rd Street, New York, NY 10022.

FIRST EDITION

Designed by Suet Yee Chong

Library of Congress Cataloging-in-Publication Data has been applied for.

ISBN: 978-0-06-201553-2

11   12   13   14   15   OV/RRD   10 9 8 7 6 5 4 3 2 1

In memory of my husband
Raymond Smith

ACKNOWLEDGMENTS

Excerpts from this memoir have appeared in *The Atlantic Monthly* and in *Conjunctions*.

Oh God—you are going to be so unhappy.

—Gail Godwin

I am very sorry to learn that Ray died a couple of weeks ago. When someone I loved died I found it helpful to remind myself that this person was not less real because she wasn't real now, just as people in New Zealand aren't less real because they aren't real here.

—Derek Parfit

When my mother died I adopted the Gestalt technique of saying to myself, whenever there was a surge of grief, "I choose to have a mother who is dead."

—T. D., a former colleague at the University of Windsor

One breath at a time, Joyce. One breath at a time.

—Gloria Vanderbilt

CONTENTS

EPILOGUE

I

THE VIGIL

"My husband died, my life collapsed."

THE MESSAGE

February 15, 2008. Returning to our car that has been haphazardly parked—by me—on a narrow side street near the Princeton Medical Center—I see, thrust beneath a windshield wiper, what appears to be a sheet of stiff paper. At once my heart clenches in dismay, guilty apprehension—a ticket? A parking ticket? At such a time? Earlier that afternoon I'd parked here on my way—hurried, harried—a jangle of admonitions running through my head like shrieking cicadas—if you'd happened to see me you might have thought pityingly *That woman is in a desperate hurry—as if that will do any good*—to visit my husband in the Telemetry Unit of the medical center where he'd been admitted several days previously for pneumonia; now I need to return home for a few hours preparatory to returning to the medical center in the early evening—anxious, dry-mouthed and head-aching yet in an aroused state that might be called *hopeful*—for since his admission into the medical center Ray has been steadily improving, he has looked and felt better, and his oxygen intake, measured by numerals that fluctuate with literally each breath—*90, 87, 91, 85, 89, 92*—is steadily gaining, arrangements are being made for his discharge into a rehab clinic close by the medical center—(*hopeful* is our solace in the face of mortality); and now, in the late afternoon of another of these interminable and exhausting hospital-days—can it be that our car has been ticketed?—in my distraction I'd parked illegally?—the time limit for parking on this street is only two hours, I've been in the medical center for longer than two hours, and see with embarrassment that our 2007 Honda Accord—eerily glaring-white in February dusk like some strange phosphorescent creature in the depths of the sea—is inexpertly, still more inelegantly parked, at a slant to the curb, left rear tire over the white line in the street by several inches, front bumper nearly touching the SUV in the space ahead. But now—if this is a parking ticket—at once the thought comes to me *I won't tell Ray, I will pay the fine in secret.*

Except the sheet of paper isn't a ticket from the Princeton Police Department after all but a piece of ordinary paper—opened and smoothed out by my shaky hand it's revealed as a private message in aggressively large block-printed letters which with stunned staring eyes I read several times like one faltering on the brink of an abyss—

LEARN TO PARK STUPPID BITCH

In this way as in that parable of Franz Kafka in which the most profound and devastating truth of the individual's life is revealed to him by a passer-by in the street, as if accidentally, casually, so the Widow-to-Be, like the Widow, is made to realize that her situation however unhappy, despairing or fraught with anxiety, doesn't give her the right to overstep the boundaries of others, especially strangers who know nothing of her—"Left rear tire over the white line in the street."

Car Wreck

We were in a car wreck. My husband died but I survived.

This is not (factually) true. But in all other ways, it is true.

January 2007. A little more than a year before my husband was stricken with a severe case of pneumonia, and brought by his anxious wife to the ER of the Princeton Medical Center in blissful ignorance of the fact—the terrible and irrefutable fact—that the reverse journey would never occur bearing him back home—we were in a serious car accident, the first of our married life.

It would seem ironic in retrospect, that this accident in which Ray might easily have been killed, but was not killed, occurred hardly more than a mile from the Princeton Medical Center at the intersection of Elm Road and Rosedale Road; this was an intersection we drove through invariably on our way to Princeton, and on our way home; it is an intersection I must drive through as in a dream of nightmare repetition in which my very grief is rebuked *You might have died here! You have no right to grieve, your life is a gift.*

The accident occurred on a weeknight as we entered the intersection: out of nowhere—on the driver's side—there came a hellish glare of headlights, a screeching of brakes and a tremendous crash as the front of our car was demolished, windshields shattered and air bags detonated.

In the immediate aftermath of the crash we were too confused to gauge how extraordinarily lucky we'd been—in the days, weeks, months to follow we would try to fathom this elusive fact—that the other vehicle had struck only the front of our car, the engine, hood, front wheels; a few inches back and Ray would have been killed or seriously injured, crushed in the wreck. It was beyond our capacity to grasp how close we'd come to a horrific accident—if for instance the other vehicle had sped into the intersection even a half-second later . . .

Inside the wreck of our car there was a gritty smoldering odor. Our air bags had exploded with remarkable rigor. If you have never been in a vehicle in which air bags have exploded you will have a difficult time imagining how violent, how forceful, how *bellicose* air bags are.

Vaguely you might expect something cushiony, even balloon-like—no.

You might expect something that will not injure you in the service of protecting you from injury—*no*. In the instant of the air bag explosion Ray's face, shoulders, chest and arms had been battered as if he'd been the hapless sparring partner of a heavyweight boxer; his hands gripping the steering wheel were splattered with acid, leaving coin-sized burn marks that would sting for weeks. Beside him I was too rattled to comprehend how powerfully I'd been hit by the air bag—I'd thought that this was the dashboard buckling in, all but crushing me in the passenger's seat so that I could barely breathe. (For the next two months my bruised chest, ribs, and arms would be so painful that I could barely move without wincing and dared not laugh heedlessly.) But in our wrecked car in the euphoria of cortical adrenaline we had little awareness of having been so battered and bruised as we managed to force our car doors open and step out onto the pavement. A wave of relief swept over us—*We are alive! We are unharmed!*

Princeton police officers arrived at the accident scene. An ambulance arrived bearing emergency medical workers. I recalled that one of my Princeton undergraduate students, a young woman, was a volunteer for the Princeton Emergency Medical Unit and I hoped very much that this young woman would not be among the medical workers at the scene. I hoped very much that this episode would not be reported excitedly back and circulated among my students *Guess who was in a car crash last night—Prof. Oates!*

Strongly it was recommended that "Raymond Smith" and "Joyce

Smith" be taken by ambulance to the ER to be examined—especially it was important to be X-rayed—but we declined, saying that we were all right, we were certain we were all right. Yet in the *faux*-euphoric aftermath of the crash in which there was no pain nor hardly an awareness of the very concept of pain we insisted that we were fine and wanted to go home.

Standing in the cold, shivering and shaky and our car pulverized as if a playful giant had twisted it in his hands and let it drop—there was nothing we wanted so badly as to go home.

We were asked if we were "refusing" medical treatment and we protested we weren't *refusing* medical treatment—we just didn't think that we needed it.

Refused then, the officer noted, filling out his report.

Two police officers drove us home in their cruiser. They were kindly, courteous. Near midnight we entered our darkened house. It seemed that we'd been gone for far longer than just an evening and that we'd been on a long journey. Our nerves were jangled like broken electric wires in the street. I'd begun to shiver, convulsively. I was dry-eyed but exhausted and depleted as if I'd been weeping. I saw that Ray was *all right*—as he insisted—we were both *all right*. It was true that we'd come close to catastrophe—but it hadn't happened. Somehow, that fact was difficult to comprehend, like trying to fit a large and unwieldy thought into a small area of the brain.

I began to feel the first twinges of pain in my chest. When I lifted my arm. When I laughed, or coughed.

Ray discovered reddened splotches on his hands—"I've been burnt? How the hell have I been burnt?" He ran cold water onto his hands. He took Bufferin, for pain.

I took Bufferin, for pain. I had no wish to go to bed anticipating a miserable insomniac night, but by 2 A.M. we'd gone to bed and were sleeping, to a degree. Glaring headlights, screeching brakes, that moment of astonishing impact. . . . The sharp chemical smell, the air bags striking like crazed aliens in a science-fiction horror film . . .

"I'll go to get us a new car. Tomorrow."

Calmly Ray spoke in the dark. There was comfort in his words that suggested routine, custom.

Comfort in that Ray would supervise the aftermath of the wreck.

Raymond—"wise protector."

He was eight years older than I was, most of the calendar year. Born on March 12, 1930. I was born on June 16, 1938.

How long ago, these births! And how long we'd been married, since January 23, 1961! At the time of the car wreck we would celebrate our forty-seventh wedding anniversary in a few weeks. You would not think, reading this, if you are younger than we were, that to us these dates were unreal, or surreal; we'd felt, through our long marriage, as if we'd only just met a few years before, as if we were "new" to each other, still "becoming acquainted" with each other; often we were "shy" with each other; there were many things we did not wish to tell each other, or to "share" with each other, in the way of individuals who are only just becoming intimately acquainted and don't want to risk offending, or surprising.

Most of my novels and short stories were never read by my husband. He did read my non-fiction essays and my reviews for such publications as the *New York Review of Books* and the *New Yorker*—Ray was an excellent editor, sharp-eyed and informed, as countless writers published in *Ontario Review* have said—but he did not read most of my fiction and in this sense it might be argued that Ray didn't know me entirely—or even, to a significant degree, partially.

Why was this?—there are numerous reasons.

I regret it, I think. Maybe I do.

For writing is a solitary occupation, and one of its hazards is loneliness.

But an advantage of loneliness is privacy, autonomy, freedom.

Thinking then, that night of the car wreck, and subsequent nights and days as phantom pains stabbed in my chest and ribs, and I despaired that the ugly yellowish purple bruises would ever fade, that, if Ray died, I would be utterly bereft; far better for me to die with him, than to survive alone. At such times I did not think of myself as a writer primarily, or even as a writer, but as a wife.

A wife who dreaded any thought of becoming a *widow*.

In the morning our lives would be returned to us but subtly altered, strange to us as others' lives that bore only a superficial resemblance to our own but were not our own. It would have been a time to say *Look—* *we might have been killed last night! I love you, I'm so grateful that I am* *married to you* . . . but the words didn't quite come.

So much to say in a marriage, so much unsaid. You reason that there will be other times, other occasions. Years!

That morning Ray called the Honda dealer from whom he'd bought the car and arranged to be picked up and brought to the showroom on State Road, to buy a replacement—a Honda Accord LX, 2007 model (with sunroof) which he drove into our driveway in the late afternoon, gleaming white like its predecessor.

"Do you like our new car?"

"I always love our new car."

And so I would think *He might have died then. Both of us. January* *4, 2007. It might have happened so easily. A year and six weeks—what re-* *mained to us—was a gift. Be grateful!*

The First Wrong Things

February 11, 2008. There is an hour, a minute—you will remember it forever—when you know instinctively on the basis of the most inconsequential evidence, that *something is wrong.*

You don't know—can't know—that it is the first of a series of "wrongful" events that will culminate in the utter devastation of your life as you have known it. For after all it may not be the first in a series but only an isolated event and your life not set to be devastated but only just altered, remade.

So you want to think. So you are desperate to think.

The first *wrong thing* on this ordinary Monday morning in February is—Ray has gotten out of bed in the wintry dark before dawn.

By the time I discover him in a farther corner of the house it's only just 6:15 A.M. and he has been up, by his account, since 5 A.M.

He has taken a shower, dressed, and fed the cats breakfast at an unnaturally early hour; he has brought in the *New York Times* in its transparent blue wrapper; he has made himself a spare little breakfast of fruit and cottage cheese and is eating—trying to eat—seated at our long white Parsons table; through our glass-walled gallery I can see him, across the courtyard, a lone figure haloed in light amid the shadowy room behind him. If he were to glance up, as he has not done, he would see me watching him, and he would see our dogwood tree in the courtyard transformed in the night, clumps of wet snow on the branches like blossoms.

In fact this is a white-blossoming dogwood Ray planted himself several years ago.

This little tree Ray takes a special pride in, and feels a special tenderness for, for it hadn't thrived initially, it had required extra care and so its survival is a significant part of its meaning to us, and its beauty.

If in wifely fashion I want to praise my husband, or to cheer him if he requires cheering, I have only to speak of the dogwood tree—this will evoke a smile. Usually!

For Ray is the gardener of our household, not me. As Ray is an editor of literary writing beloved by writers whose books he has edited and published—so Ray is an editor of living things. He doesn't create them or cause them to live but he tends them, cares for them and allows them to thrive—to blossom, to yield fruit. Like editing, gardening requires infinite patience; it requires an essential selflessness, and optimism. Though I love gardens—especially, I love Ray's garden in the summer and early fall—it's as an observer and not as a connoisseur of growing things that to me send cruelly paradoxical signals: the exquisitely blooming orchid that, brought home, soon loses its petals, and never again regains them; the thriving squash vines that, mysteriously, as if devoured from within, shrivel and die overnight. Ray is of an age to recall "victory gardens" in the early 1940s in Milwaukee, Wisconsin—in his telling, there is an echo of childhood romance about such gardens, which everyone kept as in a communal civilian war-effort. Ray's garden is a way of evoking these idyllic memories. How happy he has always been, outdoors! Driving to the nursery, to buy plants! And how eager for winter to end, that he might have the garden plowed and dare to set in early things like lettuce, arugula despite the risk of a heavy frost.

The gardener is the quintessential optimist: not only does he believe that the future will bear out the fruits of his efforts, he believes in the future.

You would see that all the growing things Ray has planted on our two-acre property, like the dogwood tree, forsythia bushes, peonies, "bleeding hearts," tulips, hillsides of crocuses, daffodils and jonquils, are utterly commonplace; yet, to us, these are living talismans suffused with meaning. *Thoughtfulness, tenderness. Patience. An imagining of a (shared) future.*

A memory comes to me: in our shabby-stylish rented Chelsea duplex, in the belated and chilly spring of our sabbatical year in London 1971–1972, Ray is tending a bedraggled little clump of brightly colored nasturtiums on our small terrace. The potted soil is probably very poor, there are rapacious insects devouring their leaves, but Ray is determined to nurse the nasturtiums along and through a window I observe him, unseen by him; I feel a sudden faintness, a rush of love for him, and also the futility of such love—as my then-young husband was determined to keep the bedraggled nasturtiums alive, so we are determined to keep alive those whom we love, we yearn to protect them, shield them from harm. To be *mortal* is to know that you can't do this, yet you must try.

Our sabbatical year in London was a mixed experience, for me. I was homesick, rootless. Unaccustomed to not working—that is, to not teaching—I felt useless, idle; my only solace was my writing, into which I poured enormous concentration—re-creating, with an obsessiveness that swerved between elation and compulsion, the vividly haunting oneiric cityscape of Detroit, in the novel *Do With Me What You Will.* Ray, however, thoroughly enjoyed the sabbatical year—as Ray thoroughly enjoyed London, our long, long walks in the beautiful damply green parks of London of which our favorite was Regent's Park, and those parts of the U.K.—Cornwall, Wessex—we saw on driving trips. My husband has a capacity for enjoying life that isn't possible for me, somehow.

There are those—a blessed lot—who can experience life without the slightest glimmer of a need to add anything to it—any sort of "creative" effort; and there are those—an accursed lot?—for whom the activities of their own brains and imaginations are paramount. The world for these individuals may be infinitely rich, rewarding and seductive—but it is not paramount. The world may be interpreted as a gift, earned only if one has created something over and above the world.

To this, Ray would respond with a bemused smile. *You take yourself so seriously. Why?*

Always Ray has been the repository of common sense in our household. The spouse who, with a gentle tug, holds in place the recklessly soaring kite, that would career into the stratosphere and be lost, shattered to bits.

On this Monday morning in mid-February 2008 the sun hasn't yet risen. The sky looks steely, opaque. Approaching my husband I feel a tinge of unease, apprehension. Sitting at the table Ray appears hunched over the newspaper, his shoulders slumped as if he's very tired; when I ask him if something is wrong quickly he says no—no!—except he has been feeling "strange"—he woke before 5 A.M. and was unable to get back to sleep; he was having trouble breathing, lying down; now he's uncomfortably warm, sweaty, and seems short of breath . . .

These symptoms he tells me in a matter-of-fact voice. So the husband shifts to the wife the puzzle of what to make of such things, if anything; like certain emotions, too raw to be defined, such information can only be transferred to the other, the cautious, caring, and hyper-vigilant spouse.

More often, the wife is the custodian of such things. I think this is so. The wife is the one elected to express alarm, fear, concern; the wife is the one to weep.

Shocking to see, the smooth white countertop which is always kept spotless is strewn now with used tissues. Something in the way in which these wet wadded tissues are scattered, the slovenliness of it, the indifference, is not in Ray's character and *not-right*.

Another wrong thing, Ray tells me that he has already called our family doctor in Pennington and left a message saying he'd like to see the doctor that day.

Now this is serious! For Ray is the kind of husband who by nature resists seeing a doctor, stubborn and stoic, even when obviously ill the kind of husband with whom a wife must plead to make an appointment with a doctor.

The kind of person whose pain threshold is so high, often he tells our dentist not to inject his gums with Novocain.

Ray flinches when I touch him, as if my touch is painful. His forehead is both feverish and clammy, damp. His breath is hoarse. Close up I see that his face is sickly pale yet flushed; his eyes are finely bloodshot and don't seem to be entirely in focus.

In a panic the thought comes to me *Has he had a stroke?*

A friend of ours had a stroke recently. A friend at least a decade younger than Ray, and in very fit condition. The stroke hadn't been severe but our friend was shaken, we were all shaken, that so evidently fit a man had had a stroke and was exposed as *mortal*, as he had not previously seemed, swaggering and luminous in our midst. And Ray, never quite so swaggering or luminous, never so visibly fit, is taking medication for "hypertension"—high blood pressure—which medication is supposed to have helped him considerably; yet now he's looking flushed, he's looking somewhat dazed, distressed, he hasn't finished his breakfast, nor has he read more than the first sprawling section of the *New York Times* in whose ever more Goyaesque war photos and columns of somber newsprint an ennui of such gravity resides, the sensitive soul may be smothered if unwary.

Post 9/11 America! The war in Iraq! The coolly calibrated manipulation of the credulous American public, by an administration bent upon stoking paranoid patriotism! Avidly reading the *New York Times*, the *New York Review of Books*, the *New Yorker* and *Harper's*, like so many of our Princeton friends and colleagues Ray is one of those choked with indignation, alarm; a despiser of the war crimes of the Bush administration as of its cunning, hypocrisy, and cynicism; its skill at manipulating the large percentage of the population that seems immune to logic as to common sense, and history. Ray's natural optimism—his optimist-gardener soul—has been blunted to a degree by months, years, of this active and largely frustrated dislike of all that George W. Bush represents. I have learned not to stir his indignation, but to soothe it. Or to avoid it. Thinking now *Maybe it's something in the news. Something terrible in the news. Don't ask!*

But Ray is too sick to be upset about the latest suicide bombing in Iraq, or the latest atrocity in Afghanistan, or the Gaza Strip. The newspaper pages are scattered, like wadded tissues. His breathing is forced, labored—an eerie rasping sound like a strip of plastic fibrillating in the wind.

Calmly I tell him I want to take him to the ER. Immediately. He tells me no—"That's not necessary."

I tell him yes, it is necessary. "We'll go now. We can't wait for—"

naming our Pennington physician whose office wouldn't open for another hour or more, and who probably couldn't see Ray until the afternoon.

Ray protests he doesn't want to go to the ER—he isn't that sick—he has much work to do this morning, on the upcoming issue of *Ontario Review*, that can't be put off—the deadline for the May issue is soon. But on his feet he moves unsteadily, as if the floor were tilting beneath him. I slip my arm around his waist and help him walk and the thought comes to me *This is not right. This is terribly wrong* for a man's pride will rarely allow him to lean on any woman even a wife of forty-seven years. A man's pride will rarely allow him to concede that yes, he is seriously ill. And the ER—"emergency room"—the very concession of helplessness, powerlessness—is the place to which he should be taken.

He's coughing, wincing. His skin exudes an air of sickly heat. Yet the previous night Ray had seemed fine for most of the evening—he'd even prepared a light meal for us, for dinner; I had been away and had returned home at about 8 P.M. (This, our final meal together in our house, the final meal Ray would prepare for us, was Ray's specialty: fried eggs, whole grain bread, Campbell's soup—chicken with wild rice. I would call him from the airport—Philadelphia or Newark—when my plane arrived and he would prepare our meal for my arrival home an hour later. If the season was right he would also place on my desk a vase with a single flower from his garden . . .) At dinner he'd been in good spirits but shortly afterward with disconcerting swiftness at about 10:30 P.M. he began coughing fitfully; he'd become very tired, and went to bed early.

Forever afterward I would think: I was away for two days. I was a "visiting writer" at U-C Riverside at the invitation of the distinguished American studies critic and scholar Emory Elliot, formerly a Princeton colleague. In these two days my husband had gotten sick. Ray would acknowledge, yes, probably he'd been outside without a jacket or a cap and possibly he'd gotten a cold in this way though we are told that this isn't so—*scientific tests have proved*—that cold air, even wet, doesn't cause colds; colds are caused by viruses; bad colds, by virulent viruses; you don't "catch" a cold by running out to the mailbox without a jacket, or hauling recycling cans to the curb; unless of course you are exhausted, or your immune system has been weakened. In these ways you may "catch" a cold but it is not likely to be a fatal cold, possibly just a "bad cold" which is what my husband seems suddenly to have, that has spiraled out of control.

Yet another wrong thing—I will recall this, later—as I reason with my husband now in the kitchen where our two cats are staring at us wide-tawny-eyed, for how incongruous our behavior, at this twilit hour before dawn when we are usually in another part of the house—suddenly he gives in and says yes, all right—"If you think so. If you want to drive me."

"Of course I want to drive you! Let's go."

So long as the ER is the wife's suggestion, and the wife's decision, maybe it's all right. The husband will consent, as a way of humoring her. Is this it? Also, as Ray says, with a shrug to indicate how time-wasting all this is, our Pennington doctor will probably want him to have tests and he will have to go to the Princeton Medical Center anyway.

Without my help—though I've offered to help—Ray prepares for the trip to the ER. He doesn't want me to fuss over him, even to touch him, as if his skin hurts. (This is a flu symptom—isn't it? Our Pennington physician makes me uneasy at times, so readily does he prescribe antibiotics for Ray when a "bad cold" is interfering with Ray's work; I worry that an excess of antibiotics will affect Ray's immune system.)

The cats stare after us as we leave the house. Still so early in the morning, scarcely dawn! Something in our manner has made them wary, suspicious. And then how strange it seems, to be driving our car with my husband beside me. Rarely do I drive our car—we have just the single car, the Honda—with Ray beside me, not driving; unless we are on a trip, then we share the driving; still, Ray does most of it, and always difficult driving in urban areas and on congested roads. I am less anxious now, for we've made a good decision, obviously; I am in control, I think. Though our Princeton friends without exception insist that only in Manhattan and (possibly) in Philadelphia can one find competent medical treatment, this ER is the closest by many miles, and the most convenient; there Ray will be given immediate treatment, and he will be all right, I'm sure.

He isn't taking anything with him to suggest that he expects even to stay overnight.

On the drive into Princeton Ray gives me instructions about work he needs to have me do: calls to make, book orders to process, his typesetter in Michigan to contact. Though he's ill he is also—he is primarily—concerned with his work. (It has been a matter of concern to Ray in the past year, a cause of both anxiety and hurt, that in our declining American economy, in which libraries have been cutting budgets, fewer small-press books are being bought and subscriptions to *Ontario Review* are not increasing.) His breathing is hoarse and his throat sounds raw and when he falls silent I wonder—what is he thinking? I reach out to touch his arm—I'm moved to see that he took time to shave. Even in physical distress he hadn't wanted to appear in the ER unshaven, disheveled.

I am thinking that this is the right thing to do of course. And I am thinking that it's a minor episode—just a visit to the local ER.

I love him, I will protect him. I will take care of him.

Ray has been to the Princeton ER before. A few years ago his heartbeat had become erratic—"fibrillating"—and he'd stayed overnight for what seemed to be a commonplace non-invasive cardiac procedure. Then, everything had gone well. He'd come home with a fully restored "normal" heartbeat. I knew that Ray was well when I'd entered his hospital room to see him scowling over the *New York Times* Op-Ed page and his first remark was a sardonic complaint about the hospital food.

This was a good sign! When a husband complains about food, his wife knows that he has nothing serious to complain of.

And so today's ER visit will turn out well also. I am sure. Driving on Rosedale Road in early-morning traffic—to State Road/Route 206—to Witherspoon Street—with no way of knowing how familiar, how dismayingly familiar, this route would shortly become—I am certain that I am doing the right thing; I am a shrewd and thoughtful wife, if an unexceptional wife—for surely this is the only reasonable thing to do.

Knowing of my dislike of high-rise parking garages—these ascending and descending labyrinths with their threat of humiliating cul-de-sacs and no-way-out—Ray offers to park the car for me. No, no!—I bring the car around to the ER entrance so that Ray can get out here; I will park the car and join him inside a few minutes later. It is just 8 A.M. How long Ray will be in the ER, I estimate a few hours probably. He will be home for dinner—I hope.

What relief to find a parking place on a narrow side street where the limit is two hours. I think, I may have to come outside and move the car, then. At least once.

In this way unwittingly the Widow-to-Be is assuring her husband's death—his doom. Even as she believes she is behaving intelligently—"shrewdly" and "reasonably"—she is taking him to a teeming petri dish of lethal bacteria where within a week he will succumb to a virulent staph infection—a "hospital" infection acquired in the course of his treatment for pneumonia.

Even as she is fantasizing that he will be home for dinner she is assuring that he will never return home. How unwitting, all Widows-to-Be who imagine that they are doing the right thing, in innocence and ignorance!

4

"Pneumonia"

This is unexpected!

The first response of the afflicted man—"I've never had pneumonia before."

The first response of the wife—"Pneumonia! We should have known."

Naively thinking *This is a relief. Not a stroke, not an embolism, not a cardiac condition—nothing life-threatening.*

Quickly Ray is checked into the ER. Quickly assigned a cubicle—Cubicle 1. Now he is partly disrobed, now he is officially a *patient*. The essence of that word has to be *patience*. For the experience of the patient, like that of the patient's wife, is to wait.

How long we must wait, how many hours isn't clear in my memory. For while Ray is being examined—interviewed—his blood taken—re-examined—re-interviewed—another sample of his blood taken—I am sometimes close by his side and sometimes I am not.

The minutiae of our lives! Telephone calls, errands, appointments. None of these is of the slightest significance to others and but fleetingly to us yet they constitute such a portion of our lives, it might be argued that our lives are a concatenation of minutiae interrupted at unpredictable times by significant events.

If I'd known that my husband had less than a week to live—how would I behave in these circumstances? Is it better not to know? Life can't be lived at a fever-pitch of intensity. Even anxiety burns out. For now after the urgency of the drive into Princeton it has come to seem in the ER—in the cubicle assigned to "Raymond Smith"—that time has so slowed, it might be running backward. Waiting, and waiting—for test results—for a doctor-specialist—for a *real doctor*, with authority—until at last the diagnosis is announced—"Pneumonia."

Pneumonia! The mystery is solved. The solution is a good one. Pneumonia is both commonplace and treatable—isn't it?

Though we're both disappointed—Ray won't be discharged today after all. He'll be transferred into the general hospital where it's expected he will stay "at least overnight."

Of this, I seem to hear just *overnight*.

If I have occasion to speak with friends I will tell them *Ray is in the Medical Center with pneumonia—overnight.*

Or, with an air of incredulity, as if this were entirely out of my husband's character—*You'll never guess where Ray is! In the Medical Center—with pneumonia—overnight.*

Why the diagnosis of pneumonia is so surprising to us, I have no idea. In retrospect it doesn't seem surprising at all. Ray reacts by questioning the medical workers about pneumonia—asking them about themselves—speaking in such a way to suggest that he isn't fearful, and has infinite trust in them. Like many another hospital patients wishing to be thought a *good sport, a nice guy, fun!* he jokes with nurses and attendants; through his stay in the Princeton Medical Center he will be *well liked, a real gentleman, sweet, fun!*—as if this will save him.

So much of our behavior—our "personalities"—is so constructed. The survival of the individual, in the service of the species.

Our great American philosopher William James has said—*We have as many personalities as there are people who know us.*

To which I would add *We have no personalities unless there are people who know us. Unless there are people we hope to convince that we deserve to exist.*

"I love you! I'll be back as soon as I can."

Yet what relief—at mid-afternoon—to leave the ER at last—to escape the indescribable but unmistakable disinfectant smell of the medical center if only to step outside into a cold cheerless February day!

I feel so sorry for Ray, trapped inside. My poor husband stricken with pneumonia—obliged to stay overnight in the hospital.

A multitude of tasks await me—telephone calls, errands—at home I sort Ray's mail to bring to him that evening—Ray tries to answer *Ontario Review* mail as soon as he can, he has a dread of mail piling up on his desk—as a Catholic schoolboy in Milwaukee he'd been inculcated with an exaggerated sense of responsibility to what might be defined loosely as *the world*—repeatedly I call the medical center—again, and again—until early evening—to learn if Ray has been yet transferred to the general hospital and always the answer is *No. No! Not yet.*

At about 6:30 P.M. as I am about to leave for the medical center, bringing things for Ray—bathrobe, toiletries, books—at his end of our living room coffee table are the books he is currently reading or wants to read—as well as manuscripts submitted to the magazine and the press, a burgeoning stack of these with self-addressed stamped envelopes for return—the phone rings and I hurry to answer it assuming that it's the medical center, telling me the number of the room Ray has been moved to—at first I can't comprehend what I am being told *Your husband's heartbeat has accelerated—we haven't been able to stabilize it—in the event that his heart stops do you want extraordinary measures to be used to keep him alive?*—

I am so stunned that I can't reply, the stranger at the other end of the line repeats his astonishing words—I hear myself stammering *Yes! Yes of course!*—gripped by disbelief, panic—stammering *Yes anything you can do! Save him! I will be right there*—for this is the first unmistakable sign of horror, of helplessness—impending doom—blindly I'm fumbling to replace the phone receiver, on our kitchen wall-phone—a sickening sense of vertigo overcomes me—the strength drains out of my legs, my knees buckle and I fall at a slant, through the doorway into the dining room and against the table a few feet away—the sensation is eerie—as if liquid were rushing out of a container—the edge of the table strikes against my legs just above my knees, for in my fall I have knocked the table askew—heavily, gracelessly I have fallen onto the hardwood floor—I can't believe that this is happening to me, as I can't believe what is happening to my husband; behind me the lightweight plastic receiver is swinging on its elastic band just beyond my grasp as I lie sprawled on the floor trying to control my panicked breathing, instructing myself *You will be all right. You are not going to faint. You will be all right. You have to leave now, to see Ray. He is waiting for you. In another minute—you will be all right!*

Yet: my brain is extinguished, like a flame blown out. My legs—my thighs—are throbbing with pain and it's this pain that wakes me—how much time has passed, I can't gauge—a few seconds perhaps—I am able to breathe again—I am too weak to move but in another moment, my strength will return—I am sure that this is so—sprawled on the dining room floor stunned as if a horse had kicked me and the realization comes to me

I must have fainted after all. So this is what fainting is!

Six o'clock in the evening of February 11, 2008. The Siege—not yet identified, not yet named, nor even suspected—has begun.

Strangely, the Widow-to-Be will forget this telephone call. Or rather, she will forget its specific contents. She will recall—with embarrassment, chagrin— some small worry—that she "fainted"—in fact, she "fell heavily onto the dining room table, and the floor"—"but just for a minute. Less than a minute." An ugly bruise of the hue of rotted eggplant and of a shape resembling the state of Florida will discolor her upper legs, her thighs and part of her belly—she will wince with pain—sharp pains—from crashing to the hardwood floor without cushioning the fall with her hands—but she will forget this terrible call, or nearly. For soon there will be so much more to recall. Soon there will be so much more to recall, from which mere fainting onto a hardwood floor will be no reprieve.

5

TELEMETRY

Now into my life—as into my vocabulary—there has come a new, harrowing term: Telemetry.

For Ray hasn't been moved into the general hospital but into a unit adjacent to Intensive Care.

Telemetry!—my first visit to the fifth floor of the medical center—to this corridor I will come to know intimately over a period of six days—imprinted indelibly in my brain like a silent film continually playing—rewinding, replaying—rewinding, replaying.

These places through which we pass. These places that outlive us.

Vast memory-pools, accumulating—of which we are unaware.

Telemetry means machines—machines processing data—machines monitoring a patient's condition—and I am shocked to see my husband in a hospital bed, in an oxygen mask—IV fluids dripping into his arm. Both his heartbeat and his breathing are monitored—through a device like a clothespin clipped to his forefinger a machine ingeniously translates his oxygen intake into numerals in perpetual flux—76, 74, 73, 77, 80—on a scale of 100.

(When a day or two later I experiment by placing the device on my own forefinger, the numeral rises to 98—"normal.")

It's upsetting to see Ray looking so pale, and so tired. So groggy.

As if already he has been on a long journey. As if already I've begun to lose him . . .

Despite the oxygen mask and the machines, Ray is reading, or trying to read. Seeing me he smiles wanly—"Hi honey." The oxygen mask gives his slender face an inappropriately jaunty air as if he were wearing a costume. I am trying not to cry—I hold his hand, stroke his forehead—which doesn't seem over-warm though I've been told that he still has a dangerously high temperature—101.1° F.

"How are you feeling, honey? Oh honey . . ."

Honey. This is our mutual—interchangeable—name for each other. The only name I call Ray, as it is the only name Ray calls me. When we'd first met in Madison, Wisconsin, in the fall of 1960—as graduate students in English at the University of Wisconsin—(Ray, an "older" man, completing his Ph.D. dissertation on Jonathan Swift; I, newly graduated from Syracuse University, enrolled in the master's degree program)—we must have called each other by our names—of course—but quickly shifted to *Honey.*

The logic being: anyone in the world can call us by our proper names but no one except us—except the other—can call us by this intimate name.

(Also—I can't explain—a kind of shyness set in. I was shy calling my husband "Ray"—as if this man of near-thirty, when I'd first met him, represented for me an adulthood of masculine confidence and ease to which at twenty-two, and a very young, inexperienced twenty-two, I didn't have access. As in dreams I would sometimes conflate my father Frederic Oates and my husband Raymond Smith—the elder man whom I could not call by his first name but only *Daddy,* the younger man whom I could not call by his first name but only *Honey.*)

Is the cardiac crisis past? Ray's heartbeat is slightly fast and slightly erratic but his condition isn't life threatening any longer, evidently.

Otherwise, he would be in Intensive Care. Telemetry is not Intensive Care.

Unfortunately room 541 is at the farther end of the Telemetry corridor and to get to it one must pass by rooms with part-opened doors into which it's not a good idea to glance—mostly elderly patients seem to be here, diminutive in their beds, connected to humming machines.

A kind of visceral terror overcomes me—*This can't be happening. This is too soon!*

I want to protest, Ray is nothing like these patients. Though seventy-seven he is not *old*.

He's lean—hard-muscled—works out three times a week at a fitness center in Hopewell. He hasn't smoked in thirty years and he eats carefully, and drinks sparingly—until two or three years ago he'd risen at 7 A.M. each morning, in all vicissitudes of weather, to run—jog—along country roads near our house for forty minutes to an hour. (While I lay in bed too exhausted in the aftermath of turbulent dreams—or, it may have been, simply too lazy—to get up and accompany him.)

How nice the nurses are, in Telemetry! At least, those we've met.

An older nurse named Shannon explains carefully to me, as she has explained to Ray: it's very important that he breathe through the oxygen mask—through his nose—and not through his mouth, in order to inhale pure oxygen. When Ray does this the numerals in the monitoring gauge rise immediately.

There is the possibility—the promise—that the patient holds his own fate in his hands. In his lungs.

Once we're alone Ray tells me that he feels "much better." He's sure he will be discharged from the hospital in a few days. He asks me to bring work for him in the morning—he doesn't want to "fall behind."

An anxiety about *falling behind.* An anxiety about *losing control, losing one's place, losing one's life.* Always at the periphery of our vision these icy-blue flames shimmer, beaten back by our resolute American sunniness. *Yes I am in control, yes I will take care of it. Yes I am equal to it— whatever it is.*

Ray clasps my hand tight. Ray's fingers are surprisingly cool for a man said to be running a fever. How like my protective husband, at such a crucial time to wish to comfort *me.*

A young Indian doctor comes into the room, introduces himself with a brisk handshake—he's an ID man—"infectious disease"—he tells us that a culture has been taken from my husband's right lung—it's being tested to determine the exact strain of bacteria that has infected the lung—as soon as they identify the bacteria they will be able to fight the infection more effectively.

In a warm rapid liquidy voice Dr. I___ speaks to us. Formally he addresses us as *Mr. Smith, Mrs. Smith*. Some of what he says I comprehend, and some of it I don't comprehend. I am so grateful for Dr. I___'s very existence, I could kiss his hand. I think *Here is a man who knows! Here is an expert.*

But is the Widow-to-Be misguided? Is her faith in this stranger in a white coat who walks into her husband's hospital room misplaced? Would there have been another, happier ending to this story, if she had transferred her husband from the provincial New Jersey medical center to a hospital in Manhattan, or Philadelphia? If she'd been less credulous? More skeptical?

As if she too has been invaded—infected—by a swarm of lethal bacteria riotously breeding not in her lungs but in that part of her brain in which rational thought is said to reside.

6

E-mail Record

February 12, 2008.
To Richard Ford
    At this moment, Ray is recovering from a nasty cold that morphed into pneumonia without our somehow noticing . . .
    Much love to both,
    Joyce

To Leigh Bienen
    Ray is recovering—slowly—from a severe pneumonia that began as a bad cold . . .
    Much love to both,
    Joyce

February 14, 2008.
To Gloria Vanderbilt
    Ray's condition improves—worsens—improves—worsens—I have almost given up having responses to it. But the doctors say that over all

he is definitely improving—it's just that the pneumonia is so virulent, through most of one lung.

(I know little of infectious diseases, but am learning rapidly.)

Love

Joyce

E. COLI

February 13, 2008. The bacterial infection in Ray's right lung has been identified: E. coli.

"E. coli! But isn't that associated with . . ."

"Gastro-intestinal infections? Not always."

So we learn from Dr. I___ . Again we're astonished, naively—there is something naive about astonishment in such circumstances—for like most people we'd thought that the dread E. coli bacteria is associated exclusively with gastro-intestinal infections: sewage leaking into water supplies—fecal matter in food—insufficiently cooked food—hamburger raw at the core—contaminated lettuce, spinach—the stern admonition above sinks in restaurant restrooms *Restaurant employees must wash their hands before returning to work.*

But no, we were mistaken. Even as, invisibly, a colony of rapacious E. coli bacteria is struggling to prevail in Ray's right lung with the intention of swarming into his left lung and from there into his bloodstream to claim him, their warm-breathing host, totally—as totally as a predator-beast like a lion, an alligator, would wish to devour him—so we are learning, we are being forced to learn, that many—most?—of our assumptions about medical issues are inadequate, like the notions of children.

It's liquidy-voiced Dr. I___ —or another of Dr. I___'s white-coated colleagues—(for in his scant six days in the Telemetry Unit of the Princeton Medical Center Ray will be examined or at least *looked at* by a considerable number of specialists as itemized by the hospital bill his widow will receive weeks later)—who explain to us that E. coli infections, far from being limited to the stomach, can also occur in the urinary tract and in the lungs. *Escherichia coli* are found everywhere, the doctor tells us—in the environment, in water—"In the interior of your mouth."

Most of the time—we're assured—our immune systems fight these invasions. But sometimes . . .

Patients with E. coli pneumonia usually present with fever, shortness of breath, increased respiratory rate, increased respiratory secretions, and "crackles" upon auscultation.

(Why do medical people say "present" in this context? Do you find it as annoying as I do? As if one "presents" symptoms in some sort of garish exhibition—*Patient Ray Smith presents fever, shortness of breath, increased respiratory rate . . .*)

Now the exact strain of bacteria has been identified, a more precise antibiotic is being used, mixed with IV fluids dripping into Ray's arm. This is a relief! This is good news. Impossible not to think of the antibiotic treatment as a kind of war—warfare—as in a medieval allegory of Good and Evil: our side is "good" and the other side is "evil." Impossible not to think of the current war—wars—our country is waging in Iraq and Afghanistan in these crude theological terms.

As Spinoza observed *All creatures yearn to persist in their being.*

In nature there is no "good"—no "evil." Only just life warring against life. Life consuming life. But human life, we want to believe, is more valuable than other forms of life—certainly, such primitive life-forms as bacteria.

Exhausted from my vigil—this vigil that has hardly begun!—I slip into a kind of waking sleep at Ray's bedside as he dozes fitfully inside the oxygen mask and in my dream there are no recognizable figures only just primitive bacterial forms, a feverish swilling and rushing, a sensation of menace, unease—those hallucinatory patterns of wriggling light obscuring vision that are said to be symptomatic of migraine, though I've never had migraine headaches. My mouth has gone dry, sour. My mouth feels like the interior of a stranger's mouth and is loathsome to me. The jeering thought comes to me *You must have been infected too. But you have been spared this time.*

Waking I'm not sure at first where I am. The sensation of unease has followed me. And there in the hospital bed—my husband?—some sort of disfiguring helmet, or mask, obscuring his face that has always seemed to me so handsome, so youthful, so *good* . . .

Something of the derangement of Widowhood is beginning here. For in dreams our future selves are being prepared. In denial that her husband is seriously ill the Widow-to-Be will not, when she returns home that evening, research E. coli on the Internet. Not for nearly eighteen months after her husband's death will she look up this common bacterial strain to discover the blunt statement she'd instinctively feared at the time and could not have risked discovering: pneumonia due to *Escherichia coli* has a reported mortality rate of up to 70 percent.

Hospital Vigil(s)

There are two categories of hospital vigils.

The vigil with the happy ending, and the other.

Embarked upon the hospital vigil as in a small canoe on a churning white-water river you can have no clear idea which vigil you are embarked upon—the vigil with the happy ending, or the other—until it has come to an end.

Until the patient has been discharged from the hospital and brought safely home. Or not discharged, and never brought home.

JASMINE

February 14, 2008. Today in room 541 there is Jasmine—dark-skinned, Haitian, lives with relatives in Trenton and hates the "nasty" New Jersey winter—a nurse's aide assigned to Raymond Smith who will bathe the patient behind a screen, change bedclothes and adjust his bed, assist him walking into the bathroom, chattering all the while at him, now at me—*Mz. Smith h'lo? Mz. Smith howya doing?*—voice high-pitched as the cry of a tropical bird. Initially Jasmine is a cheery presence in the room—like the flowers several friends have sent, in vases on Ray's bedside table—she's warm, friendly, eager to please—eager to be liked—eager to be *very well liked*—a squat sturdy young woman with cornrowed hair, fleshy cheeks and shiny dark eyes behind thick-lensed red plastic glasses—but as the minutes pass and Jasmine continues to chatter at us, and to bustle about the room, sighing, laughing, muttering to herself—her presence becomes a distraction, an irritant.

Propped up in bed, breathing now through a nasal inhaler, Ray is gamely trying to sort through some of the mail he's asked me to bring him—here are financial statements, letters from *Ontario Review* writers, poetry and short story submissions—at his bedside I am trying to prepare my next-day's fiction workshop at Princeton University—still Jasmine chatters, and chatters—our lack of response doesn't seem to discourage her, or perhaps she hasn't noticed—until abruptly she makes a hissing sound through her teeth as if in disgust—like a petulant child she takes up the TV remote control and switches on the TV—loud—we ask her please turn it off, we are trying to work—Jasmine stares at us as if she has never heard such a request—she tells us that she *always watches TV in these rooms*—with exaggerated politeness verging upon hostility she asks if she can keep the TV on—*Turned low?*—in her white nylon uniform that strains at her fleshy hips and thighs sitting now in a chair beneath the TV gazing upward at the screen rapt in concentration at antic darting images as if these images were of paramount importance to her provoking her to suck at her lips, murmur and laugh to herself, draw in her breath sharply—*Ohhhh man! Uhhhh!*—until after some time—twenty minutes, twenty-five—as if the magical screen suddenly loses its attraction Jasmine turns back to us with renewed enthusiasm— as the TV crackles and drones she resumes the bright-chattering bird-shriek that makes me want to press my hands over my ears even as I am smiling—smiling so hard my face aches—not wanting Jasmine to be insulted by some lapse in my attention or some failure to respect her personality which in some quarters has surely been praised, en-couraged—as Ray shuts his eyes in misery—trapped in the hospital bed by the IV tube in a vein in the crook of his bruised right arm, nasal in-haler clamped to his head—forced as in an anteroom of Hell to listen as Jasmine begins to repeat her monologue of a former patient who'd been really nice to her—really really nice to her—and his wife as well—they'd given her *real special* presents—sent her a postcard *Dear Jasmine!* from the Southwest—really really nice generous people—an older couple— *really* nice—as I listen to these boastful yet accusatory words a wave of dismay washes over me—a stab of fear—is this nurse's aide employed by the Princeton Medical Center retarded? Is she mentally unstable? Dis-turbed? *Deranged?*

None of the other, older nurses resemble Jasmine in any way— Jasmine seems to have wandered in from another dimension, a Comedy Central TV program perhaps, except Jasmine isn't funny—Jasmine is deadly serious—I try to explain that my husband is tired and would like to rest—trying to smile—trying to speak politely—in dread of upsetting the excitable young woman—finally saying in a forceful voice *Excuse me—Jasmine—my husband is tired, he would like to sleep*—provoking

Jasmine to stare at us in astonishment—for a beat unable to speak, she's so stunned—insulted—a look of exaggerated shock contorting her face as in a children's cartoon—*Ma'am!—You are telling me to be* quiet? *To* stop talking? *Is that what you are telling me Ma'am—to* stop talking? Jasmine's shiny eyes bulge behind the thick lenses of her glasses. The whites of her eyes glare. I tell Jasmine that my husband tires easily, he has pneumonia she must know—he doesn't sleep well at night and should try to rest during the day and if he isn't able to sleep at least he could close his eyes and rest—as Jasmine continues to glare at me and when my voice trails off she retorts by repeating her account of the really nice older couple for whom she'd worked recently—really nice, generous—*Liked me real well sayin Jasmine you a breath of fresh air always smiling—sent me a postcard sayin Jasmine howya doin*—until at last I cry *Please! Please just stop!*

Now Jasmine's jaw drops, she is so insulted.

Jasmine sits heavily in her chair beneath the TV. Jasmine sighs loudly, muttering to herself. Her fleshy face darkens with blood, her eyes glare whitely. She is sulky, sullen as a furious child. There is no subtlety in her hatred of us who have insulted her by failing to adore her. The thought comes to me *I have made an enemy. She could kill my husband in the night.*

My heart begins to beat quickly, in panic. I have brought my husband to this terrible place, now I can't protect him. How can I protect him?

Whatever happens, I am to blame. I am the one who has arranged this.

Outside the room's single window, it's night. I think that very likely it has been night for a long time for night falls early in this perpetual winter dusk. I tell Jasmine that she can leave now for her supper break, if she wants to—a little early—this is a good time since I'll be here for another hour or more.

Jasmine has been rummaging through a large cloth bag on her knees, panting with exasperation. At first she doesn't seem to hear me—in the friendliest tone I can manage I repeat what I've said—Jasmine frowns, glances up—Jasmine pouts and glares—then Jasmine smiles.

Jasmine shuts the large cloth bag with a snap and smiles.

Ma'am thank you! Ma'am that is real nice.

10

Vigil

February 14, 2008—February 16, 2008.

Those days!—nights!—a Möbius strip continuously winding, unwinding.

This nightmare week of my life—*and yet*—during this week Ray is still alive.

"Don't worry about that, honey! I'll take care of that when I get home."

And: "Just put it on my desk. Next week will be soon enough—I should be home by then."

At his bedside. Breathing through the nasal inhaler Ray is reading, trying to read—one of the books I've brought him from home—I am reading, trying to read—with what fractured concentration I can summon—the bound galley of a book on the cultural history of boxing which I am reviewing for the New York Review of Books. *It's a mealtime—but Ray isn't hungry for hospital food. It's time for his blood to be drawn—but the nurse has difficulty finding a vein, Ray's arms are bruised, discolored.*

The air in the hospital room smells stale, used up. Outside is a wintrydusk February day. This afternoon there is a reading at the University sponsored by the Creative Writing Department—readers are Phillip Lopate and a visiting Israeli writer—of course I can't attend, nor can I attend the dinner afterward with my writing colleagues. A hospital vigil is mostly slow time. Stalled time. In such stasis dread breeds like virulent bacteria.

And then—this happens—Ray begins talking about something I can't follow, in a slow drawling voice—a confused tale of needing to get something from home—to bring to "Shannon's house"—Shannon is a favorite nurse—Shannon has been friendly with Ray—somehow, in the way of dream-delirium logic, Ray thinks that he isn't in the hospital but in a "house" belonging to Shannon—he is her guest, and I am, too.

So quickly this has happened, I'm not prepared. When I'd brought Ray to the ER a few days before he'd said a few things that were baffling to me, that didn't quite make sense, but now he's speaking to me as a sleepwalker might speak and this sudden change in his condition is shocking to me, frightening. Quickly I tell Ray no: he isn't in Shannon's house. He's in the hospital—in the Princeton Medical Center.

Ray doesn't seem to hear this. Or, hearing, discounts it.

His concern is something I am to bring for him, from home—to use here in Shannon's house. He has an "apartment" in Shannon's house.

Calmly I tell Ray no: he is not in Shannon's house, he's in the hospital where Shannon is a nurse.

"Honey, you've been very sick. You're still sick. You have—"

But Ray is irritated with me. Ray will have to argue with me to convince me, yes we are in Shannon's house.

"Honey, no. Shannon is a nurse. You're in the Medical Center. You have pneumonia—you've been very sick. But you're getting better—the doctor says you might be able to come home next week."

How long we discuss this absurd issue, I can't recall afterward. I am shaken, disoriented. This man—this slow-speaking stubborn childish man!— is no one I know.

At the nurses' station I seek out Shannon—I ask her what has happened to my husband and she tells me not to be alarmed, this sort of thing happens sometimes, it's common, it will pass. I ask her where on earth Ray has gotten the idea that he's in her house—in an "apartment" in her house—and Shannon laughs and says yes, "your husband who is such a sweet man" has been saying that to me, too—it's better not to upset him, just humor him for the time being.

Humor him. For the time being.

How embarrassed Ray would be, to know that he is being "humored"—
this is very upsetting.

I seek out one of Ray's doctors—Dr. B____.

Dr. B____ is Ray's admitting physician. Dr. B____ is better known to Ray
than to me, a very nice cordial man of early middle age. Dr. B____ will be the
Certifying Physician *on my husband's death certificate.*

Dr. B____ too tells me not to be alarmed—"delusional thinking" isn't
uncommon when a patient's brain isn't receiving quite enough oxygen.

My husband, Dr. B____ assures me, is only "mildly delusional"—the
nasal inhaler isn't working or he's breathing through his mouth and not his
nose as he's been instructed. That's why it's good for me to remain with him
as long as I can, Dr. B____ says, to "anchor" him to reality.

I am relieved—Ray is only "mildly delusional."

I am relieved—Dr. B____ is so matter-of-fact, even a bit bemused. As if,
if he had but the time, he could entertain me with any number of comical
delusions of patients he has known—very possibly, previous patients in room
541 being treated for pneumonia.

Dr. B____ tells me the condition is reversible.

Reversible?

How casually this crucial term is uttered. Reversible!

Yes, Mrs. Smith. Reversible, usually.

Dr. B____ orders the nasal inhaler to be removed, the oxygen mask to be
resumed. Within a short while—it's a miracle for which I will hide away in
a hospital women's room, to weep in gratitude—my husband has returned
to normal—to himself.

Days, nights in giddy succession—like a roller coaster—at the hospital,
at home—at the hospital, at home—driving into Princeton, driving out
into the country from Princeton—this February has been a cheerless
month yet this week—the final week of our lives together—our life—
overcast mornings are suffused with a strange sourceless sunshine.

This mysterious radiance *from within.*

I am relieved—more relieved than I wish to acknowledge—that
Ray's *mildly delusional* state has faded.

Not in a mood to ponder *reversible, irreversible*—nor in a mood to consider what is *normal*, what is *self.* Harrowing to think that our identities—the selves people believe they recognize in us: our "person-alities"—are a matter of oxygen, water and food and sleep—deprived of just one of these our physical beings begin to alter almost immediately—soon, to others we are no longer "ourselves"—and yet, who else are we?

Is the self the physical body, or is the body but the repository of *self*?

It's the most ancient of all philosophical—metaphysical—paradoxes. You do not see a *self* without a body to contain it, yet you do not see a body without a *self* to activate it.

When my mother died at the age of eighty-six she had lost a good deal of her memory—her "mind." Yet she had not lost her self, not quite.

She'd become severely forgetful, you might say a dimmer and less animated version of herself, as a monotype fades with repeated strik-ings, its subtleties lost. Yet Mom was never entirely *lost.* In a garden at her assisted living facility in Clarence, New York, we were sitting with her—my brother Fred and me—and Fred asked her if she remembered me—and Mom said, "I could never forget Joyce!"—and in that instant, this was so.

I loved my mother very much. Friends who knew us both have said how much of my mother resides in me—mannerisms, voice inflections, a way of smiling, laughing. I know that my father resides in me also. (Daddy died two years before Mom. Her *mild delusion* was that Daddy was living in a farther wing of the facility: "Over there," Mom would say, pointing at a specific building. "Fred is over there.")

Loving our parents, we bring them into us. They inhabit us. For a long time I believed that I could not bear to live without Mom and Dad—I could not bear to "outlive" them—for to be a daughter without parents did not seem possible to me.

Now, I feel differently. Now, I have no option.

Returning home!

What happiness—what relief—returning home!

As if I've been gone for days not hours.

As if I've traveled many miles not just a few.

Behind a ten-foot fence so faded you would not identify it as red-wood—behind a part-acre of deciduous and evergreen trees—our house hovers ghost-white in the darkness—no lights within—but I thought I'd left at least one light on, that morning—I am so very very tired, I am so eager to *get inside* this place of refuge, I feel faint with yearning, I could weep with relief, exhaustion.

This nightmare vigil! The smell of the hospital clings to me—that distinctive smell as of something faintly rotted, sweetly rotted beneath the masking odor of disinfectant—as soon as you push through the slow-revolving front door and into the foyer you smell it—the smell of hospital-elevators, hospital-restrooms, hospital-corridors—the smell of Ray's room—(what a quaint sort of usage, *Ray's room*—until it is va-cated and *Ray's bed* filled by another)—this smell is in my hair, on my skin, my clothing. I am eager to get inside the house and tear off my contaminated clothing—I am eager to take a shower—to scrub my face, my hands—my hair that feels snarled, clotted—*But no first: phone*—I must check phone calls on Ray's phone, and on my own—*No first: cats*—I must feed the cats, let them outdoors—skittish and distrustful they prefer to be let outside than to eat in their corner of the kitchen—*No first: mail*—but I am too tired to run outside to the mailbox, the very thought whirls in my brain shrinking to the size of a dot, and vanishes—*No first: lights*—for the house is so very dark—a cave—a sepulcher—like a crazed woman who has thrown off her manacles I run through the rooms of the house switching on lights—living room lights! dining room lights! hall lights! bedroom lights! Ray's study lights!—I turn on the radio in the kitchen—I turn on the television in our bedroom—can't bear this silence—you would think possibly I am rehearsing Ray's homecoming—the entire house lighted as if a party were taking place within—*No first: clean* with manic energy I will vacuum the rooms of the house, lingering over the carpets, of all household tasks it is vacuum-ing I most enjoy for its brainless thumping and the immediate gratifica-tion it yields—there is something especially gratifying about late-night vacuuming—vacuuming into the early hours of the morning which one could not do, surely, if one's spouse were home and trying to sleep—inspired then I will polish a selection of the household furniture—though it doesn't really need polishing, I am eager to polish the dining room table for it's at this table that Ray will eat his homecoming meal in a few days—I am not sure which of his favored meals I will prepare— must discuss this tomorrow—what a pleasure to polish the dining room table which can be polished to a ravishing sheen though it's but mahogany veneer—*No first*: *Ray's desk*—this is crucial!—I will remove the accumulation of mail from Ray's desk—both Ray's desks—I will polish both desks with lemon polish, to surprise him—I will straighten the items on Ray's windowsills which include such curiosities as semi-used Post-its, ballpoint pens whose ink has long dried up, small boxes of paper clips, coiled-together rubber bands, a small digital clock with red-flashing numerals like demon-eyes glowering in the dark—charged with the urgency of my mission I will gather Ray's scattered pens and pencils—as an editor, Ray indulges in crimson, orange, purple, green pencils!—and arrange them in some sort of unobtrusive order on his desks; I will Windex his windows, what a pleasure to swab at the glass with paper towels, as beyond the glass-surface there hovers a ghost-woman whose features are lost in shadow—it is very dark outside—moonless— somehow, it has come to be 1:20 A.M.—no more am I inclined to lie down in that bed in that bedroom than I would lie down in a field in glaring sunshine—as a traveler in even quiet surroundings I am wracked by insomnia—the slightest alteration of my life, I am wracked by insomnia— impossible to sleep while Ray is in the hospital, and distasteful somehow—for *What if the phone rings? What if*—but housecleaning is an antidote to such thoughts, next I will peruse Ray's closets, bureau drawers—or maybe I should sort books in the guest room, which have begun to spill over the white Parsons table—*No first*: *flowers*—as Ray welcomes me back home from a trip with flowers on my desk so I should welcome Ray back from the hospital with flowers on his desk, must remember to buy flowers at a florist—potted begonias? Cyclamen?—but which florist?—you can buy flowers at the Medical Center but—maybe not a good idea, what if they are suffused with the dread *hospital-smell*—thinking such thoughts, plotting such stratagems drifting through the rooms of the brightly lighted house singing to myself—humming loudly—talking to myself—giving detailed instructions to myself—for when there is no one to whom one can reasonably speak except two wary and distrustful cats, one must address one*self*—in my heightened mood of anxiety commingled with relief—the relief of being *home*—my uplifted sparkly voice reminds me of no one's so much as Jasmine's—now I remember *Mail!*—it's urgent to place Ray's mail in rows, neatly—for a magazine editor receives many items of mail daily—this mail I will sort: personal, business, important, not-important—all advertisements discarded—like a diligent secretary I open envelopes, unfold letters so that at a glance Ray can absorb their contents; since Ray entered the hospital I've been paying bills, a household task Ray usually does, and these bill stubs I will set out for Ray to see, and to record; for Ray keeps assiduous financial records; you will say *But it isn't necessary to pay bills immediately when they arrive—you can wait—you can wait for weeks!*—but in waiting there is the threat of forgetting, there is the threat of chaos—there is the threat of totally losing control; now in the snowy courtyard there are shadowy hulks like crouching animals, these are UPS and FedEx deliveries for *Raymond Smith, Ontario Review, Inc.* which I haven't noticed until now—2:20 A.M.—it seems to me urgent to haul these packages inside the house, struggle to open them—several are deliveries Ray has been asking about, and so tomorrow I must bring them to the hospital—page proofs, galleys—proofs of book jackets—there is a special pleasure in bringing Ray something he has requested—something attractive, striking—page proofs for the May issue of the *Ontario Review* cover feature on the artist Matthew Daub whose watercolors of small Pennsylvania towns and rural landscapes Ray so admires—something that will be cheering to Ray in his grim hospital room, something we can share—as for more than thirty years we have shared planning issues of *Ontario Review* and books published by Ontario Review Press—in my dreamy state staring at reproductions of Matthew Daub's watercolors—thinking how much happier visual artists must be, than writers—writers and poets—we whose connections to the world are purely verbal, linear—through language we are beseeching others who are strangers to us not merely to read what we have written but to absorb it, be moved by it, to *feel*—then with a jolt I remember—*Postpone trip!*—this is urgent—I must postpone our upcoming trip to the University of Nevada at Las Vegas where our writer-friend Doug Unger has invited Ray and me to speak to graduate writing students—this trip, long-planned, is within two weeks—impossible so soon; maybe later in the spring, or maybe in the fall, Ray has suggested—*Tell Doug I'm really sorry, this damned pneumonia has really knocked me out*—I will send Doug an e-mail for I can't force myself to telephone anyone, even friends, especially friends—abruptly then another thought intrudes—even as I am preparing to write to Doug on my computer—*No: "Vespers"*—at 2:40 A.M. I am moved to play a CD—Rachmaninoff's "Vespers"—one of Ray's favorite pieces of music—sonorous choral music of surpassing beauty which Ray and I heard together at a concert years ago—it might have been in Madison, Wisconsin—when we were newly married—when the great adventure of accumulating a *record collection* together had just begun—beautiful haunting wave-like "Vespers" which a few months ago I'd heard, returning home from a trip climbing out of the limousine in the driveway and smiling to hear this thrilling music from inside the house where Ray has turned the volume up high, to hear in his study, and thinking *Yes. I'm home.*

11

E-mail Record

February 16, 2008.
To Richard Ford

   Ray is definitely feeling better but I am not going to tempt fate by going on too long optimistically. Thanks, Richard, for your moral support. It is greatly appreciated . . . Maybe you could (come down from Maine) and drive all the Princeton afflicted around. That could be your "new phase." Biographers would be thrilled. How much easier than writing . . .

   Much love to both,
   Joyce

(Richard Ford, hearing that Ray was hospitalized, very gallantly offered to fly down to Princeton and "drive me around"—an offer of such generosity, I was deeply moved even as common sense advised me to decline.)

February 17, 2008, 4:08 A.M.
To Emily Mann

   Ray is said to be improving—and I think that this is so—but he has such a long way to go & is so weak & prone to fevers, I'm dreading the future; somehow I don't think that he will ever be "well" again—this experience has been so ravishing. And in any case I have to see it as a presentiment of what lies ahead, unavoidably. I can't sleep for thinking of all that there is to do, that I doubt I can do . . .

However, you did get through a worse and more protracted experience so I suppose that I will, too. Night thoughts are not productive but—how to avoid them?

I put together a little packet of snapshots to bring to Ray, to cheer him up, and came across the most beautiful photo of you and Gary, taken some years ago by Ray at one of our parties. . . . I'm sure that I'd given you a copy at the time.

Much love,

Joyce

(Emily Mann's husband, Gary Mailman, stricken by a virulent infection following a medical procedure by a physician associated with the Hospital for Special Surgery in New York City, was hospitalized for ten days at about the time Ray was in the Princeton Medical Center—Emily's and my hospital vigils overlapped by a few days. Gary nearly died and recovered slowly afterward at home, over a period of several months. But he did recover.)

12

Memory Pools

Forever after you will recognize those places—previously invisible, indiscernible—where memory pools accumulate.

All waiting areas of hospitals—hospital rooms—and in particular those regions of the hospital reserved for the very ill: Telemetry, Intensive Care. You will not wish to return to these places where memory pools lie underfoot treacherous as acid. In the corners of such places, in the shadows. In stairwells. In elevators. In corridors and in restrooms, you have memorized without your knowing. In the hospital gift shop, at the newsstand. Where you linger staring at news headlines already passing into oblivion as you peruse them while upstairs in your sick husband's hospital room an attendant is changing bedclothes, or sponge bathing the patient behind a gauze screen, unless the patient has been taken to Radiology for further X rays shivering and awaiting his turn in another corridor, on another floor. Memory pools accumulate beneath chairs in waiting areas adjacent to Telemetry. It may be that actual tears have stained the tile floors or soaked into the carpets of such places. It may be that these tears can never be removed. And everywhere the odor of melancholy, that is the very odor of memory.

Nowhere in a hospital can you walk without blundering into the memory pools of strangers—their dread of what was imminent in their lives, their false hopes, the wild elation of their hopes, their sudden terrible and irrefutable knowledge; you would not wish to hear echoes of their whispered exchanges—*But he was looking so well yesterday, what has happened to him overnight—*

You would not wish to blunder into another's sorrow. You will have all that you can do to resist your own.

13

"I'm Not Crying for Any Reason"

February 17, 2008. This morning at 7:50 A.M. arriving at the hospital—ascending in the elevator—at the fifth floor turn left, to Telemetry—breathless/hurrying/eager to see my husband—(for always the first glimpse of a hospital patient, in his room in his bed unobserved, is fraught with meaning)—carrying the hefty Sunday *New York Times* for us to read together—and at the farther end of the now-familiar corridor—past the now-familiar nurses' station—there is room 541—there is Ray's bed—empty—just the stripped, bare mattress.

"Mrs. Smith?—your husband is in room five thirty-nine. Just this morning he was moved. We tried to call you but you must have left home . . ."

And so entering this room—which evidently I'd passed a moment ago without glancing inside—I am trembling so visibly that Ray wonders what is wrong with me—the blood has drained from my face—I am trembling in the aftermath of a shock as profound as any I've ever experienced, or am I trembling in the aftermath of relief—for here is Ray in the new bed, in the new room—a room identical to the previous room, with the identical bedside table and on this table the vase of flowers from friends—Ray is no longer wearing the oxygen mask, nor even the nasal inhaler—since his oxygen intake has improved, and there is the possibility of his being discharged from the hospital this Tuesday—he smiles at me, greets me—"Hi honey"—but when I lean over the bed to kiss him a wave of faintness sweeps over me, suddenly I begin to cry—uncontrollably crying—for the first time since bringing Ray to the hospital—my face is contorted like a child's, in the throes of an agonizing weeping—"I'm not crying for any reason, but only because I love you"—so I manage to stammer, to Ray, "—because I love you so much"—and Ray's eyes well with tears too, he murmurs what sounds like, "Something like this—I'll be knocked out for two months—"

Like drowning swimmers we are clutching at each other. Someone passing in the corridor outside sees us, and looks quickly away. Never have I cried so hard, so helplessly. Never in my adult life. And why am I crying, is it purely out of a sense of *relief* . . .

Something like this. Knocked out two months.

Always I will remember these words. For this is how Ray assesses the situation: pneumonia has interrupted his life. These days in the hospital and his weakened state will result in his editing-work being slowed, delayed.

He isn't thinking of the future in the way that I have been thinking of the future—he's thinking of the May issue of *Ontario Review*, the responsibility he bears to the writers whose work he's publishing. Meeting a deadline. Paying his printer. Paying his contributors. Mailing, distribution. He isn't thinking of anything so petty as *himself.*

Maybe Ray isn't capable of thinking of himself, in the terms in which I can think of him.

Maybe no man is capable of thinking of himself, in the terms in which a woman can think of him.

"Lean on me, Mr. Smith. That's good. Good!"

A physical therapist named Rhoda, very nice woman, is walking with Ray in the corridor outside his room, in the effort of exercising his leg muscles. Lying in bed for several days has weakened Ray's legs—it's astonishing how quickly muscles begin to *atrophy.* Earlier this morning I'd been encouraging Ray to push hard against my hand, with his foot—

to exercise his leg muscles in this way—and he'd pushed hard, very hard
it seemed to me; but Rhoda is telling Ray that when he's discharged from
the hospital it won't be to his home but to Merwick Rehab Center, not far
from the Medical Center. Not only must Ray regain his ability to walk
normally, he must regain his ability to *breathe.*

How bizarre all this would have seemed to us, a week ago! This
shuffling man in hospital pajamas, trying not to wince with pain, leaning heavily on a young woman therapist's arm, an IV gurney tugged in
his wake.

As Ray is walking—unsteadily, leaning on Rhoda—but he is walking—I am thinking *Don't fall! Don't fall please.*

In the hospital corridors it isn't uncommon to see patients walking
slowly with or without therapists—tugging IV gurneys in their wake.
All these days, hours—the IV line has been embedded in the crook of
Ray's bruised right arm—dripping in the antibiotic that, like a magic
potion in a Grimm's fairy tale, has the power to save his life.

An attendant arrives, to take Ray to Radiology for X rays.

It seems that a "secondary infection"—"of mysterious origin"—
"nothing to worry about"—has appeared in Ray's left lung—which is to
say, in Ray's (previously) uninfected lung.

"But—is this bacterial, too?"

(How matter-of-factly this adjective rolls off my tongue—*bacterial.*

As one might say *infinity, light-year, a trillion trillion stars*—in the
naive speech of the non-scientist.)

The smiling young attendant—female, dark-skinned, cheery and
sturdy-bodied—her name tag is Rhoda—says with the bright smile she
lavishes on all patients and patients' relatives who ask such naive questions of her—"Ma'am, I don't know! The doctor will tell you."

Which doctor, I wonder—Dr. I___, or Dr. B___?

Bacterial. One thing that I have come to know—the nightmare-vigil has
so impressed me, for life—we are not so much surrounded by invisible
and very greedy life-forms as enveloped by them—at every instant of
our lives—and before our births, in the womb—we are flesh-vessels for
these microscopic life-forms that require us for warmth—for warmth

and nourishment—those bacteria that benefit us we call, with anthropo-morphic instinct, *good*; those bacteria that seek to ravage us, and destroy us, we call *bad*.

It is utterly naive, futile, uninformed—to think that our species is *exceptional*. So designated to master the beasts of the Earth, as in the Book of Genesis!

"Infection"—another problematic term. For by definition any infec-tion is *bad*—but some are *not-so-bad* as others.

"Mr. Smith, can you tilt your head this way?—that's great."

One of the nurses is shaving Ray's jaws, that have grown stubbly. This is a task I might have done for Ray myself—or, if we'd thought of it, I could have brought him the right sort of mirror and Ray could have shaved himself.

"Your husband is very handsome, Mrs. Smith. But you know that."

Without his glasses, eyes closed, Ray does look handsome—his cheeks are lean, and remarkably unlined for a man of his age—his forehead is marred by the faintest frown lines, scarcely visible in this light. As the nurse deftly shaves him, wipes away lather—I feel a sense of unease, that Ray is becoming adjusted to the hospital setting, ever more comfortable with the eerie passivity such a setting evokes—as in Thomas Mann's *The Magic Mountain* in which the young German Hans Castorp arrives as a visitor at the tuberculosis sanitarium in Davos, in the Swiss Alps, in the decade before the outbreak of World War I, and as if in fairy-tale enchantment remains for seven years.

After Ray is shaved he returns to the *New York Times* scattered across his bed. The visit to Radiology—he was gone for forty minutes—seems to have had no discernible effect upon him—one in a succession of hos-pital tests—at least not so invasive as others.

Both his arms are bruised, discolored from blood-drawing. Even for a stoic the constant blood-drawing is becoming painful but he doesn't complain, Ray isn't one to complain.

He seems not to recall his *mildly delusional* state of the other day, nor am I likely to remind him.

A room in a nurse's house! How convinced Ray was, that this was

where he'd been situated, for what reason he could not have said. I want
to think that one day—maybe—when he's well, and home—and the
hospital vigil is but a memory—I will tell him about this notion of his,
and we might laugh about it together.

And how does the remainder of this Sunday pass?—languidly reading,
talking, listening to choral music played on a Sunday arts channel on
TV. By coincidence this is the identical Sunday-afternoon classical music
program that is broadcast on the radio, to which we often listen at home.

Once listening to a recording of Mozart's *Requiem Mass* Ray had remarked in that bravado way in which, when you're young, you might
speak of dying, death as if you had not the slightest fear of it—"Promise
me you'll play that at my funeral."

"But you said the same thing about Verdi's *Requiem Mass.*"

"I did? I *did?*"

This was years ago. This was another lifetime. We were living on
Sherbourne Road in Detroit, Michigan. We were living then in the aftermath of the so-called Detroit riot of July 1967—fires, gunshots and looting only two blocks away on Livernois Avenue—a nightmare cacophony
of fire sirens, police sirens, random shouts and cries—National Guards-
men deployed to protect municipal property with rifles—an acrid smell
of smoke, smoldering fires that lingered for days—this *racial tinderbox*
of an American city as cliché-speech described it that was at the same
time our home.

In the hospital, on this February afternoon in 2008, decades later I
don't want to think of this. Of our innocence, ignorance.

We'd been very happy in that house on Sherbourne Road where in
an upstairs room—a former child's room pink-walled and unfurnished
except for a desk, a straight-back chair and a single bookcase—I would
write my novel *them* while Ray commuted to the University of Windsor,
Ontario, across the Detroit River in Canada.

I was teaching English at that time at the University of Detroit, a
Jesuit-run institution at Six Mile Road, about a mile from our Sherbourne Road house. I loved my classes at U.D. and I was very friendly
with most of my (mostly male) colleagues but within a year I would leave

to teach, with Ray, at the University of Windsor where we remained from 1968 to 1978 in a single-storey brick house on the Detroit River across from Belle Isle . . .

Hospital vigils inspire us to such nostalgia. Hospital vigils take place in slow-time during which the mind floats free, a frail balloon drifting into the sky as into *infinity*.

In the late afternoon of Sunday, February 17, 2008—as dusk comes on, and deepens to night—it's decided between us that I will go home early today, and return early in the morning. How exhausted I am suddenly!—though this has been Ray's best day in the hospital so far, and we are feeling—almost—exhilarated.

Discharged to the rehab clinic on Tuesday?—a few days in rehab and then—home. By next Friday? Next weekend?

I kiss my husband good night. My very nice husband with his smooth-shaven jaws. It is not an extraordinary leave-taking for it feels so very temporary—I will be returning to this room so soon.

"Good night! I love you."

14

THE CALL

February 18, 2008. The call comes at 12:38 A.M.

Waking me from sleep—a phone ringing *at the wrong time.*

There had long been the dread, when my parents were alive, and elderly, and their health crises escalating, of the phone ringing late—*at the wrong time.*

We all know this dread. There is no escape from this dread.

For finally I'd been able to sleep—in our bed, and with the light out—we'd been feeling so hopeful when I left the hospital in the early evening—the first time since Monday, I was able to shut my eyes, to *sleep*—and now this feels like punishment—my punishment for being complacent, unguarded—for leaving the hospital early—stunned and dry-mouthed I stumble from bed, into the next room—which is Ray's darkened study—where the phone is ringing. And when I lift the receiver—"Hello? Hello?"—the caller has hung up.

A wrong number? Desperately I want to think so.

Almost immediately the phone rings again. When I pick it up it's to hear the words, if not the voice—the voice is a stranger's voice, male, urgent-sounding—that I have been dreading since the nightmare-vigil began—informing me that "your husband"—"Raymond Smith"—is in "critical condition"—his blood pressure has "plummeted"—his heartbeat has "accelerated"—the voice is asking if I want "extraordinary measures" in the event that my husband's heart stops—I am crying, "Yes! I've told you! I've said yes! Save him! Do anything you can!"

The voice instructs me to come quickly to the hospital.

I ask, "Is he still alive? Is my husband still alive?"

"Yes. Your husband is still alive."

And now I am driving into Princeton in the dark of night—along Elm Ridge Road—onto Carter Road, and left onto Rosedale—Rosedale, which will lead straight into the Borough of Princeton several miles away—these country roads so well traveled by day are deserted by night—there are no streetlights—no oncoming headlights—the roads are dark, snow-edged—I am thinking *This can't be happening. This is not real*—this, the very summons I'd been dreading, I'd wished to think with a child's faith in magical thinking that if I'd dreaded the call, if I'd imagined the very words of the call, surely then the call could not come—that would not be impossible!—though I am desperate to get into Princeton and to the hospital, I force myself to drive at no more than the speed limit—as I'd been careful to drive slowly and with as much concentration as I could summon, during this past week—for it would be ironic, it would be disastrous if I have an accident at such a time—when Ray is waiting for me—through a roaring in my ears the telephone voice has acquired a more urgent tone—almost, a chiding tone *Still alive. Your husband is still alive.* Aloud I say, "He is still alive. My husband is still alive"—in a voice of wonder, terror, defiance—"Ray is still alive"—such pathos in *still*, so provisional and desperate—this past week I've fallen into the habit of talking to myself, instructing myself—encouraging myself as one might encourage a stumbling child *You can do it. You will be all right, you can do it. You will be all right!* When I'd thrown on clothes in the bedroom, to prepare for this frantic journey, this admonishing voice had lifted in a semblance of bemused calm—*Be careful what you wear, you may be wearing it for a long time.*

In the ghost-white Honda I am veering over the yellow line into the other lane, for some reason I am having difficulty gripping the steering wheel—my hands are bare, the wheel is cold yet the palms of my hands are slick with sweat. I am having difficulty seeing, too—the road ahead, in the Honda's headlights, looks smudged. I think that there is something wrong with my vision—it's as if I am peering through a tunnel—in the periphery of my vision there are shadowy figures—beyond the snow-edged road—I'm afraid of being struck by a deer—in this area it isn't uncommon for deer to wander out into the road and even at times to leap into the path of a vehicle as if hypnotized by headlights. Now my voice lifts frightened, thin—"Is Ray going to die? Is Ray going to—" I am not able to acknowledge the possibility as I am not able to acknowledge the terror I feel, and the helplessness—such frustration as I enter Princeton Borough and the speed limit drops to twenty-five miles an hour—here, I must wait for a very long time—how long, how long!—a nightmare of lost time!—waiting for the red light to change at the intersection of Hodge Road and Route 206—which is called State Road in Princeton—there is no traffic on State Road as there is no traffic on Hodge Road—no traffic anywhere in sight—yet I am obliged to wait at the light, I am too fearful of driving through a red light, too conditioned to "obey" the law and at such a time especially—at last the light changes—I drive to Witherspoon Street, turn left and drive several blocks to the hospital—past darkened houses—I am able to park in front of the hospital, at the curb—only one other vehicle is parked here, at this time of night—desperate I run to the front door of the hospital which of course is locked—the interior of the hospital, semi-darkened—yet more desperate I run to the ER entrance which is around the corner—my breath is steaming, panicked—I am pleading with a security guard to let me into the hospital—I identify myself as the wife of a man "in critical condition" in the Telemetry unit—several times I give my husband's name—*Raymond Smith!—Raymond Smith!*—thinking how astonished Ray would be, how embarrassed, in the hospital *too much is made of things* he'd said the other day—the security guard listens to me politely—he is middle-aged, dark-skinned, sympathetic—but can't let me inside before making a call—this takes some time—precious seconds, minutes—like butterflies with frayed wings thoughts fly at me in random and frantic succession *He is still alive. It's all right. He is waiting for me, I will see him, he is still alive.* How frustrating this is, how strange, whoever called to summon me to the hospital hasn't made any arrangement for me to be allowed inside—maybe there is some mistake?—the wife of *Raymond Smith* isn't supposed to be summoned to the hospital?—someone else is expected?—but then the security guard informs me that yes, Mrs. Smith is expected on the fifth floor, I can enter through a door he opens—blindly I run through this door and find myself in the hospital lobby—at first not recognizing the familiar surroundings, twilit and deserted—how eerie it seems, no one is around—the foyer is empty, the information desk darkened—the coffee shop darkened—my panicked heart is beating like a frantic fist as I run to the elevator—ascend to the fifth floor—now stepping out of the elevator I am terribly frightened, turning left for Telemetry as usual I taste cold at the back of my mouth *This is not happening, this is not real—of course, Ray will be all right.* In Telemetry there is no one around—except at the nurses' station—lights, white-clad figures—in my distraction I don't see any nurses I know—by the way they regard me, with impassive faces, they know—must know—why I am here, at this time of night when no visitors are allowed in the hospital; and now—at the farther end of the corridor outside my husband's room I see a sight that terrifies me—five or six figures—medical workers–standing quietly outside the opened door—as if they have been awaiting me—as I approach one of them steps forward—a young woman doctor—a very young-looking woman, a stranger to me—silently she points into the room and in that instant, I know—I know that, for all my frantic hurrying, I have come too late—for all my scrupulosity in driving at the speed limit, waiting for the light to change like a programmed robot, I have come too late—in a trance I enter the room—this room I'd left only a few hours before in utter naivete, ignorance—kissing my smooth-cheeked husband *Good night!*—our plans were for me to arrive early tomorrow morning—that is, this morning—I was to bring page proofs for the upcoming *Ontario Review*—but now Ray is not sitting up in his bed awaiting me—he is not awaiting me at all but lying on his back motionless in the hospital bed, which has been lowered—I am shocked to see that there is something *not-right* here—Ray's eyes are closed, his ashen face is slack, the IV tube has been removed from the crook of his bruised right arm, there is no oxygen monitor, there is no cardiac monitor, the room is utterly still—Ray's eyelids don't flutter as I enter, his lips don't twitch in a smile—I don't hear his words *Hi honey!*—numbly I come to the bed, I am speaking his name, I am pleading with him as a child might—"Oh honey what has happened to you!—what has happened to you!—Honey? *Honey?*" For Ray seems so very life-like, there is no anguish or even strain in his face; his face is relaxed, unlined; his hair is not disheveled; it is true that he has lost weight this past week, his cheeks are thinner, there are hollows beneath his eyes which are beautiful eyes, gray-blue, slate-blue, I am leaning over him as he lies motionless beneath a sheet, I hold him, I am frantic holding him, kissing him, I am crying for him—urging him to wake up, this is me—this is Joyce—this is your wife I am pleading with him for Ray is one to be coaxed, persuaded—he is not a stubborn man—he is not an inflexible man—if he could he would open his eyes and greet me, I know; he would murmur something amusing and ironic, I know; I hold him for as long as I can, I am crying, his skin is still warm but beginning to cool; I am thinking *This is not possible. This is a mistake*; I am tempted to shake Ray, to laugh at him—*This is not possible! Wake up! Stop this!*—for never in our lives together has anything so extraordinary happened, between us; never has anything in our lives together so divided us; I am telling him that I love him, I love him so much, I have always loved him; now the young woman doctor has entered the room, quietly; the others remain in the hall, looking in; in a lowered voice in which each word is enunciated with precision the young woman doctor whose name has flown past me, whose name I will never know, explains to me that *everything possible* had been done to save my husband, who had died just minutes ago—he'd gone into unexpected *cardiac arrest*—his blood pressure had *plummeted*, his heartbeat had *accelerated*—it was a *secondary infection* and not the original E. coli infection that had driven up his fever—within just the past few hours—his left lung was invaded, his bloodstream was invaded—though they tried very hard there was *nothing more to be done.*

I am too stunned to reply. I am too confused to know whether I am meant to reply. It is very difficult to hear the woman's voice through this roaring in my ears. I think that I must look distraught, crazed—the blood has drained from my face, my eyes are leaking tears—but I am not crying, not in any normal way am I crying—with what frayed remnant remains of my sense of social decorum I am trying to determine what is the proper response in this situation, what it is that I must say, or do;

what is expected of *me*? It won't be until later—days later—that I realize
that Ray died among strangers—all of these medical workers gathered
in the corridor outside his room, strangers—Dr. I___ is not here, Dr.
B___ is not here, Dr. S___ —Ray's cardiologist for several years—is not
here; none of the other ID specialists who'd dropped by to examine Ray
and to speak with me is here; smiling Nurse Shannon of whom Ray was
so fond is not here, nor even chattery Jasmine.

It is 1:08 A.M. Late Sunday night. None of the senior medical staff is
on duty at such an hour. No one of these medical workers including the
young woman doctor is more than thirty years old.

I will not hear from any of the staff who'd become acquainted with
Ray this past week in Telemetry. Not even Dr. B___ who was the admitting physician and whose signature I will discover on the death certificate
noting that *Raymond J. Smith* died of *cardiopulmonary arrest, complications following pneumonia. 12:50 A.M. February 18, 2008.*

It is the most horrific thought—my husband died among strangers.
I was not with him, to comfort him, to touch him or hold him—I was
asleep, miles away. Asleep! The enormity of this fact is too much to
comprehend, I feel that I will spend the remainder of my life trying to
grasp it.

"Mrs. Smith?"—the young woman doctor touches my arm. She is
telling me that if I want to stay longer with my husband, she will leave me.

In the corridor, the others have dispersed. I am staring at Ray who
has not moved, not even his eyelids have fluttered since I've entered the
room. The young woman doctor repeats what she has said to me and
from a long distance I manage to hear her, and to reply.

"Thank you. I will. Thank you so much."

II

FREE FALL

Oh Life, begun in fluent Blood,
And consummated dull!
—Emily Dickinson, 1130

15

"The Golden Vanity"

Please gather and take away your husband's belongings before you leave.

It is my task—my first task as a *widow*—to clear the hospital room of my husband's things.

Only just today—that is, yesterday morning—which was Sunday morning—I had brought the enormous *New York Times*, mail, page proofs for the magazine, and several other items my husband had requested from his office. Now, I will dispose of the *Times* and I will bring the other things back home with me.

Not yet have I realized—this will take time—that as a widow I will be reduced to a world of *things*. And these *things* retain but the faintest glimmer of their original identity and meaning as in a dead and desiccated husk of something once organic there might be discerned a glimmer of its original identity and meaning.

The wristwatch on the table beside my husband's hospital bed— where my husband is lying, very still, as in a mimicry of the most deep and peaceful sleep—this item, an *Acqua Quartz* watch of no special distinction which very likely Ray bought in our Pennington drugstore, with a dark brown leather band, a digital clock-face pronouncing the time 1:21 A.M.—which, even as I stare at it, turns to 1:22 A.M.—has no identity and no meaning except *It is Ray's wristwatch* and except *Because it is his, I will take it with me. That is my responsibility.*

In this very early stage of Widowhood—these first few minutes, hours—you might almost call it Pre-Widowhood for the Widow hasn't yet "got it"—what it will mean to inhabit a free-fall world from which meaning has been drained—the Widow takes comfort in such small tasks, rituals; the perimeters of the Death-protocol in which experienced others will guide her as one might guide a stunned and doomed animal out of a pen and into a chute by the use of a ten-foot pole.

Mrs. Smith? Do you have someone to call?

Quickly I reply—Yes.

Would you like any assistance in calling?

Quickly I reply—No.

These seem to be correct answers. It is not a correct answer to reply *But I don't want to call anyone. I want to go home now, and die.*

As we'd fantasized—neither of us wished to outlive the other.

Though Ray had a horror of suicide—he did not think of suicide as any sort of romantic option—now he is *dead*, he would surely wish to return to *life*.

These thoughts rush through my head like deranged hornets. I make no effort to deflect them, still less to slow and examine them. It is strange to be so assailed by rushing thoughts when I am moving so slowly—speaking so slowly—like one who has been slammed over the head with a sledgehammer.

Already the time on Ray's watch is 1:24 A.M.

This hospital room is so cold—my teeth have begun to chatter.

In the small windowless bathroom in the medicine cabinet— behind the mirror— in the unflattering fluorescent glare—my fingers close numbly upon a toothbrush—Ray's toothbrush?—a badly twisted tube of toothpaste—mouthwash—deodorant—a man's roll-on deodorant—*clear-glide invisible-solid powder-soft scentless anti-perspirant deodorant for men*—shaving cream, in a small aerosol container—how slowly I am moving, as if undersea—gathering my husband's *belongings* to take home.

Someone must have instructed me to undertake this task. I am not certain that I would have thought of it myself. The word *belongings* is not my word, I think it is a curious word that sticks to me like a burr.

Belongings. To take home.

And *home*, too—this is a curious word.

Strange to consider that there would be a *home*, now—without my husband—a *home* to which to take his *belongings*.

Here is Ray's comb—a small black plastic comb—I have glimpsed amid his things, sometimes. When we've traveled together—staying in a single hotel room—a kind of intimacy more marked than the intimacy of daily life, which has acquired its own subtle protocol; at such times, I would see my husband's *toiletries kit* and in it such articles as toothbrush, toothpaste, deodorant etc. But also nail clippers, after-shave cologne, prescription pills. It would seem to me touching, it would provoke a smile, that a man, any man, should take such care to groom himself, as women take such care.

That a man, any man, should groom himself *to be attractive, loved*—this seems wonderful to me.

That a man, any man, should seem in this way to require another, a woman, to be attracted to him, and to love him—what a mystery this is! For to a woman, the quintessential male is unknowable, elusive.

Even the domestic male, the husband—always there is something unknowable and elusive in him. As in Ray's life, or perhaps in Ray's personality, there has always been, for all our intimacy of forty-seven years—for the record, forty-seven years, twenty-five days of our marriage—a hidden chamber, a region to which he might retreat, to which I don't have access.

Now, Ray has retreated to a place where I can't follow. Just behind his shut eyes.

These toiletry things—that they were *his*, but are now no longer *his*, seems to me very strange.

Now, they are *belongings*.

Your husband's belongings.

One of the reasons that I am moving slowly—perhaps it has nothing to do with being struck on the head by a sledgehammer—is that, with these *belongings*, I have nowhere to go except *home*. This *home*—without my husband—is not possible for me to consider.

The tile floor seems to be shifting beneath my feet. Hurriedly I'd dressed and left the house, I am not even sure what shoes these are—my vision is blurred—could be, I am wearing two left shoes—or have switched right and left shoes—recall that, in the history of civilization, the designation *right* and *left shoe* is relatively recent, not so very long ago individuals counted themselves fortunate to wear just *shoes*—this is the sort of random, pointless and yet intriguing information Ray would tell me, or read out to me from a magazine—*Did you know this? Not so very long ago . . .*

The impulse comes over me, to rush into the other room, to tell whoever it is, or was—a woman—a stranger to me, as to Ray—about *shoes*, the history of *right and left*—except I understand that this is not the time; and that Ray, in any case, for whose benefit I might have mentioned it, will not hear.

This past week I've become astonishingly clumsy, inept—forgetful—to pack Ray's bathroom things I should have brought in a bag of some kind, but I didn't—awkwardly I am holding them in my hands, my arms—one of the objects slips and falls—the aerosol-can shaving cream, that clatters loudly on the floor—as I stoop to retrieve it blood rushes into my head, there is a tearing sensation in my chest—*Shaving cream! In this terrible place!*

It would be a time to cry, now. Ray's shaving cream in his widow's sweaty hand.

Vanity of shaving cream, mouthwash, *powder-soft scentless deodorant for men.*

Vanity of our lives. Vanity of our love for each other, and our marriage.

Vanity of believing that somehow we own our lives.

Lines from a Scottish ballad—"The Golden Vanity"—rush into my head. For my brain is unnervingly porous, I have no defense against such invasions—

> There once was a ship
> And she sailed upon the sea.
> And the name of our ship was
> The Golden Vanity.

There is something faintly taunting, even mocking about these words. I am transfixed listening to them as if under a spell. The words are familiar to me though I have not heard them—I have not thought of them—in a very long time.

There once was a ship
And she sailed upon the sea. . . .

Long ago—as a graduate student at the University of Wisconsin at Madison, in 1961—it was my task—it was my pleasurable task—to write a paper on the English and Scottish traditional ballads for a medieval seminar taught by marvelous Helen White, one of only two female professors of English in that largely Harvard-educated, highly conservative department; subsequently, for years of our married life, Ray and I listened to records of ballads, in particular those sung by Richard Dyer-Bennet. It is this singer's voice that I hear now. Never had it occurred to me—until now—clutching a can of aerosol shaving cream in my hand—that this plainspoken, plaintive Scots ballad has been the very poetry of our lives.

There once was a ship
And she sailed upon the sea. . . .

(Now that "The Golden Vanity" has invaded my thoughts I will not be able to expel it from my mind for days, or weeks; I am helpless to expel such invasions of songs, sometimes a random stanza of poetry, by any conscious effort.)

Again I think—that is, the thought comes to me—that vague fantasy in which masochism masks fear, horror, terror—how frequently in the past I had consoled myself that, should *something happen to Ray*, I would not want to outlive him. I could not bear to outlive him! I would take a fatal dose of sleeping pills, or . . .

How common is this fantasy, I wonder. How many women console themselves with the thought that, should their husbands die, they too might die—somehow?

It's a consolation to wives not-yet-widows. It's a way of stating *I love him so much. I am one who loves so very much.*

When he'd been just middle-aged, and not yet an aging, ailing man himself, my father would say in that way of masculine bravado: *If I ever get bad as*—(referring to an elderly chronically ill and complaining relative)—*put me out of my misery!*

But when Daddy grew older he would live for years with myriad illnesses—emphysema, prostate cancer, macular degeneration—and he did not express any desire to die, still less any desire to be *put out of my misery.*

For this is the fallacy of such wishes, made in "good health"—truly they will not apply to the person who has uttered them, at a later time.

So too the prospect of *taking sleeping pills* at this time is unthinkable. No more than I would escape the cold by flying to Miami tomorrow morning. My responsibility to my husband would not allow such impulsive behavior.

"Honey? What should I do with these things?"

Not quite aloud, in a murmur not to be overheard these words are uttered. Of course I know, I know perfectly well that my husband is dead, and will not hear me, still less reply.

Another habit begun this past week—talking to myself, querying myself. Animated conversations with myself while driving the car. If at home, talking to the cats—in a bright ebullient voice intended to assure the frightened animals that all is well. (It is always allowable, to talk to pets. One may be eccentric *but not crazy* talking to pets.)

Here is a fact, I think—I think it is a fact—not once in our forty-seven years, twenty-five days of marriage did I overhear Ray *talking to himself.* It was rare that Ray muttered to himself—swore, cursed.

When I return to the hospital room—to Ray's bedside—I am relieved that no one else is there. I think that there was a nurse here just a moment ago. I think that she told me something, or asked me something, though I don't remember what it was. I want to cry with relief, she has gone. We are alone.

Outside Ray's room in the hospital corridor there is no one. Those five or six medical workers, strangers to me, as to Ray, including the very nice soft-spoken Indian-American woman doctor, have vanished utterly.

Were these individuals united in their effort—a failed effort, a futile effort—to save my husband's life? Is there some term for what they are, or were—not a *Death Team*—though in this case their effort ended in death—a *Life-Rescue Team?*

Badly I want to speak with them. I want to ask them what Ray might have said, nearing the end of his life. If he'd been delirious, or—deluded—

This rash thought, like others, rushes into my head and out of my head and is lost.

There is something that I must do: make a call. Calls.

But first, I must gather together Ray's *belongings*.

"Honey? Tell me—what should I do?"

I am feeling very light-headed. The phone ringing and waking me from that frothy-thin sleep is confused with a ringing in my ears and the taunting lines of the ballad—*And she sailed upon the sea and the name of our ship was*—I am thinking that Ray so much admired Richard Dyer-Bennet—strange how we'd stopped listening to folk songs, which in the 1960s we'd loved.

Though there is no one in the hall yet I am conscious of being observed. Very likely, all the nurses on the floor have been alerted—*There is a woman in 539. Ray Smith's wife. Smith died, the wife has come to take away his belongings.*

I have been watching Ray—I have been staring at Ray—I am transfixed, staring at Ray—I am memorizing Ray as he lies on his back beneath a thin sheet, his eyes shut, his recently shaved face smooth and unlined and handsome—and I am thinking—that is, the thought comes to me—that Ray is in fact breathing—but very faintly—or he is about to breathe; his eyelids are quivering, or about to quiver. As in sleep our eyeballs sometimes move as jerkily as in waking life—if we are dreaming, and *seeing* in the dream—so it seems to me that Ray's eyeballs are moving, beneath the shut eyelids; it seems to me *He is dreaming something. I shouldn't wake him.*

It's an instinct you quickly acquire during the hospital vigil, not to disturb a sleeping patient. For in such a place, sleep is precious.

I shouldn't disturb Ray of course. Yet—I have to tell him that I'm sorry—I can't leave this room without trying to explain why I'd come too late—though there is no explanation—"Honey, I'm so sorry. I was just—at home. I was just home, I could have been with you, I—don't know why. . . . I was asleep. It was a mistake. I don't understand how—it happened."

How faltering my words are, how banal and inane. As I've become physically clumsy this past week—there are mysterious bumps, bruises and small cuts on my legs and arms—no mystery about the bumps on my head, which I've repeatedly struck while getting into and out of our car—so too I can't seem to speak without faltering, or stammering, or losing the thread of my concentration so that I can't remember what I've been saying, or why it had seemed urgent to say it. Most of what I'd talked about with Ray had been his work, his mail, household matters of the most ordinary sort. Nothing that I'd said to him expressed what I'd wanted to say. And now I can't comprehend—I can barely remember, though it was only a few hours ago—why I'd gone to bed hours earlier than I usually did, why I'd imagined that tonight had been a "safe" time to sleep.

That I was *sleeping* at a time when my husband was *dying* is so horrible a thought, I can't confront it.

Eating—I'd eaten a meal when I'd returned home. For the first time in days I had prepared an actual meal—a heated meal—and not eaten just a bowl of yogurt and fruit while working at my computer. And so I'd been *eating* when my husband had succumbed to the terrible fever that precipitated his death—the thought is repulsive to me, obscene.

Inexplicable actions, behavior. The murderer who swears that he doesn't remember what he did, he'd blacked out, no memory, not the faintest idea, and no reason, no motive—such behavior makes sense to me now.

What is becoming rapidly mysterious is orderly life, coherence.

Knowing what must be done, and doing it.

This hospital room is so cold that I'm shivering convulsively. Though I have not removed my coat. My red quilted coat I'd been wearing when the speeding driver slammed into the front of our car and the air bags exploded pinning us in our seats.

Soon, it will seem to me that Ray died in this car crash. Ray died, and I survived. Is that it?

The two crashes will conflate in my mind. The crash at the intersection of Rosedale Road and Elm Road, the crash at the Princeton Medical Center.

After the one, we'd walked away giddy with relief. In our relief we'd kissed, clutched at each other for the pain hadn't yet started.

In this room Ray had complained of the cold, especially at night, and when he had to wait in Radiology to be X-rayed. Despite the fever he was running, yet he'd been cold. Yet I can remember when Ray went outdoors in winter without a coat, in Windsor. Frigid wind blowing from the Detroit River, the massive lake beyond—Lake Michigan.

Younger then, not so susceptible to colds.

I am frightened—I don't remember that person. I am losing that person—my husband—in that long-ago time before the wreck.

My instinct now is—to locate a blanket, to pull a blanket up to Ray's chin. He is lying beneath just a thin white cotton sheet.

I know—I know!—my husband is *no longer living*. He doesn't require a blanket, nor even a sheet. I know this and yet—I am not able to understand that he is *dead*.

Which is why I seem to be waiting for some sign from him, some signal—a private signal—for we've always been so close, a single thought can pass between us, like a glance—I'm waiting for Ray to forgive me —*It's all right. What you are doing is all right and not a mistake.*

And even if it was a mistake, I love you.

Just yesterday I was able to cry. In this room at this bedside leaning over my husband who was surprised by my tears I was able to cry but now I am not able to cry, I am dry-eyed, my mouth is dry as sandpaper. Now for the first time I see that Ray isn't wearing his glasses— how strange this is, that I hadn't noticed before. And on the bedside table, there are his glasses, which are relatively new, wire-rimmed and rather stylish glasses on which he wears clip-on dark lenses in bright sunshine. Very slowly I take up these glasses though I have nothing to put them in, for safekeeping; and here is Ray's wristwatch—the time is now 1:29 A.M.

And here are Ray's colored pencils, that will need sharpening.

These items, I place carefully in my black tote bag. Beautiful cut flowers—white and yellow mums, red carnations, purple iris—in vases, from friends—these I will leave behind.

(Have I thanked our friends for these flowers? I don't think so—I don't remember. So many messages on our answering machine at home—I haven't answered. And many messages deleted by accident, or in haste.)

The beautiful large Valentine card, signed by our friends—for Ray—
to cheer him up—this, I should have brought to him, yesterday.

On this Valentine the heartfelt wishes of our friends—I am staring
at the words in a sort of trance—*Dear Ray wish you were here. Ray—be
well soon! Ray you must come back to us soon, we love you and miss you so
much. Ray here's to sausage in our future! Ray please rest and rest and rest!
It takes time. And we want to see you soon. Ray heal well! We all miss you
tonight. Come home soon! Ray—I'm glad to hear you're feeling better and
hope you will be entirely recovered very soon. Dear Ray—I once knew a
man named Ray, who I thought was very okay, he liked to read, while drinking mead, the wonderful man who was Ray . . .*

It seems horrible to me, unconscionable—how could I have been so
stupid, selfish, neglectful—I hadn't brought this Valentine for Ray to see.
Naively thinking I would keep it for him, to give to him at home.

"And now it's too late."

So many mistakes I've made, and am making. This is new to me, as
if I have crossed over to another place where continually I will be making mistakes, stupid mistakes, contemptible mistakes. Soon I will learn
that a widow is one who *makes mistakes.*

In the closet are Ray's clothes, shoes. A laundry bag into which Ray
has put soiled underwear and socks. There is his jacket—the one he'd
worn on Monday morning. There, the striped blue flannel shirt, and
the trousers. I am fumbling to remove Ray's clothes from the hangers,
the blue striped shirt falls to the floor . . . In a panic I am thinking *I will
have to make two trips to the car. I will have to make two trips to the car.*

If I leave this room, I will never be able to return. I will never be able
to force myself to return.

I should call someone, a friend. I should call for help. I can't carry
these things by myself! Not in one trip.

Yet, I feel shy about calling friends. It is 1:30 A.M.—a terrible shock to
be awakened by a ringing phone, and news of a friend's death.

Better not. Better just go home.

In the morning will be soon enough. And call Ray's sister who lives
in Connecticut, whom I have never met.

And my brother, and sister-in-law.

Ray has died. He was in the hospital for not quite a week with pneumonia, he was getting better but—he died.

Instead of leaving the hospital room, I lift the phone receiver. I must have decided to call a friend, friends—this seems to be what I am doing, after all.

And the ringing in the distance, invading another's sleep.

In this way, at this moment, the Widow acts instinctively—she does not drive home alone as perhaps she'd fantasized and she does not do harm to herself as perhaps she'd fantasized—she calls friends.

But only friends whose telephone numbers she seems to have memorized.

16

Yellow Pages

You made my life possible. I owe my life to you.

I can't do this alone.

And yet—what is the option? The Widow is one who has discovered that there is no option.

There is a plastic bag provided for me, into which I can put my husband's smaller things. I am determined to carry everything in one trip and somehow, I will manage.

This determination to *manage*—to *cope*—to *do as much unassisted as possible*—is the Widow's prerogative. You might argue that it's a sign of her wish to appear to be—which is not the same as being—self-sufficient; or you might argue that it is a symptom of her derangement.

But then, in the early minutes/hours/days of Widowhood—what is not, if examined closely, a symptom of derangement?

These books Ray has been reading—which he'd asked me to bring from home—and his shoes—in the plastic bag these objects are strangely heavy, and unwieldy. One of the books is a bound galley in which I'd been reading intermittently at Ray's bedside, and from time to time reading aloud to him an interesting passage from it—a book about the human brain by a Princeton neuroscientist whom I have met—the jaunty title is *Welcome to Your Brain*. The sight of the galley fills me with a sick, sinking sensation. . . .

I will take it home. I will hide it on a shelf. Never can I bring myself to look into it again.

"Honey? I think they want me to go now . . ."

My voice is thin, wavering. Perhaps it isn't a voice but a faintly articulated thought.

Staring at Ray on the bed. It is not natural—instinctively you grasp that this is *not-right*—to see a person so composed, unmoving.

Yet there is the sensation—visceral, uncanny—that the person who is lying so still, not breathing, or breathing so faintly that it's undetected, is well aware of being observed, and observing you through shut eyes.

Helplessly I am standing here, thinking—the thought comes to me—*There will never be a right time.*

Meaning, a time to leave the hospital room.

Meaning, a time to turn my back, and walk away.

To turn my back on Ray—my husband. How is this possible!

Awkwardly, and very slowly, in small steps like a blind person I back my way out of the room. Very clumsily, for my arms are full.

I am trying to carry too many things. So frequently lately I've been dropping things, surely I will drop something now. I am in dread of calling attention to myself. I am in dread of losing control in a public place. Suddenly it seems to me—I've left my handbag behind—I can't quite see what I am carrying, in my arms. A wave of panic sweeps over me—though how trivial is this!—how ridiculous—at the possibility of losing my handbag, my car key, house key.

This is the terror: I will lose crucial keys. I will be stranded, marooned. I see myself at the side of a highway—in the dark—frantically signaling for—what?—headlights rush past, blinding. Or maybe this is a dream. Recurring dreams of being lost from my husband are my most frightening dreams but this too is very frightening, for it is so very plausible. Ray is likely to be in charge of keys—to know where a spare key might be kept, outdoors—but now I am obsessed with keys, searching through my handbag for keys a dozen times daily. The relief of finding a key, which might have been lost!

In fact I will lose some things. I will discover that a pair of dark-tinted glasses is missing out of my handbag. They must have fallen out when . . .

I will leave behind Ray's glasses! I will be utterly unable to comprehend how I could have overlooked them, hadn't I held them in my hand . . .

Ray's wristwatch—this, I haven't left behind.

At the brightly lit nurses' station—near-deserted at the hour of 1:43 A.M.—I tell one of the nurses that my husband is in room 539, and he has died, and what do I do now? It is the height of naivete, or absurdity, to imagine that the nurses are not well aware of the fact that a patient has just died in Telemetry, a few yards away; yet, I am trying to be helpful, I am even asking with a faint smile, "Do I—call a funeral home? Can you recommend a funeral home?"

The woman to whom I'm speaking—a stranger to me—looks up with a frown. I don't see in her face the sympathy I've seen in the faces of some others. She says, "Your husband's body will be taken down to the morgue. In the morning, you can call a funeral home to arrange to pick it up."

This is so shocking to me—so stunning—it's as if the woman has reached over the counter and slapped my face.

It! So quickly Raymond has ceased being *he*, now is *it*.

I feel that I might faint. I can't allow myself to faint. I lick my lips that are horribly dry, the skin is cracking. Though I can see that the nurse would far rather return to whatever she's doing at a computer, than speak with me, hesitantly I ask if she can recommend a funeral home and she says, with a fleeting smile, perhaps it's an exasperated smile, that she could not recommend any funeral home: "You can look them up in the Yellow Pages."

"The 'Yellow Pages'?"—I cling to this phrase, that is so commonplace. Yet I seem not to know what to do next.

Another time I ask if she can recommend a funeral home—or if she could call one for me—(such a request, such audacity, I must be desperate by this point)—and she shakes her head, no.

"In the morning, you can call. You have time. You should go home now. You can call a funeral home in the morning."

Deliberately, it seems, the woman does not call me by name. It is possible that, though the Telemetry unit is not very large, she doesn't know my name, and doesn't know Ray's name; it is entirely possible that she never set foot in Raymond Smith's room.

"Thank you. 'Yellow Pages'—I will. In the morning."

How strange it is, to be *walking away*. Is it possible that I am really going to leave Ray—here? Is it possible that he won't be coming home with me in another day or two, as we'd planned? Such a thought is too profound for me to grasp. It's like fitting a large unwieldy object in a small space. My brain hurts, trying to contain it.

The nurse has returned to her computer but others at the brightly lit station watch me walk away, in silence. How many others—"survivors"—have they observed walking away in this direction, toward the elevators, in exhaustion, stunned defeat. How many others clutching at *belongings*.

In the elevator descending to the lobby I am seized with the need to return to Ray—it is a terrible thing that I have left him—I am filled with horror, that I have left him—for *what if?*—*some mistake*—but sobriety prevails, common sense—the elevator continues *down*.

17

The Arrow

Returning to the lightless house beyond Princeton I feel like an arrow that has been shot—where?

The front door is not only unlocked but ajar. A single light is burning in an interior room—Ray's study. When I push open the door to step into the darkened hallway it's to the surprise of a sharp lemony smell—furniture polish. In a trance of anticipation I'd not only polished the tops of Ray's desks until they shone but the dining room table and other tables through the house; on my hands and knees, with paper towels, I polished areas of the hardwood floor that were looking worn. Humming loudly and brightly I had done these things not many hours ago.

So happy you're back home, honey! We missed you here.

By *we*, I meant the cats and me. But where are the cats?

Since Ray's departure—since I drove Ray to the ER—both the cats have been wary of me, and have kept their distance even when I feed them. The younger, Cherie, has been mewing piteously—but when I approach her, she retreats. The elder cat, Reynard, by nature more suspicious, is silent, tawny-eyed. It's clear that these animals are thinking that whatever has happened to disrupt the household, I am to blame.

In a brave cheery voice I call to the cats—though I am an arrow shot into space I am determined to convince them that there is nothing wrong really, and there is nothing for them to fear.

You will be all right. You will be all right. Nothing will happen to you. I will take care of you.

I seem to be forgetting why at near 2 A.M. I am not in bed but still awake and in a state of heightened excitement. My brain is a hive of rushing and incoherent thoughts. Stranger yet—friends are coming in a few minutes. At this hour! There is that slight jab of apprehension—the social responsibility of entertaining others, in one's house—*why?*—and where is Ray, to help greet them? Numbly I am putting on lights—in the guest room, which is where we usually have visitors—an addition to our house built for my parents when they came to visit us several times a year—along one wall overlooking the courtyard there is the white Parsons table at which Ray frequently had breakfast and spread out the *New York Times* to read—now the shock hits me—*But Ray is dead. Ray has died. Ray is not here. I am seeing our friends by myself. That is why they are coming.*

In Ray's hospital room I called three parties of whom one was asleep and didn't pick up the phone and another, an insomniac, answered on the first ring; still another, also awake, picked up the phone and answered warily *Yes? Hello?*—knowing that any call, at such an hour, is likely to be bad news.

It is a terrible thing to be the bearer of terrible news!

It is a terrible thing to invade another's sleep, to hear a friend murmur to his wife *It's Joyce, Ray has died* and to overhear his wife exclaim *Oh God.*

This is what I did, this is what a widow does, though perhaps not all widows call friends, or even relatives, perhaps I am exceptionally lucky, I think this must be so.

My plaintive pleading voice. I'd left a message for the friend who hadn't answered the phone—*Jane? This is Joyce. I'm at the hospital, Ray has died. About an hour ago—I think it was. I'm at the hospital and I don't know what to do next.*

And now like a dream it's unfolding—whatever is happening, that seems to have little to do with me—as the dreamer does not invent her dream but is in a sense being dreamt by it—helpless, stunned. Though my mind is racing and my heart is racing yet my movements are slow, uncoordinated. The sound of car tires in the gritty snow in

our driveway is shocking to me, though I know that our friends are due
to arrive at any minute. A flash of headlights across a ceiling makes me
cringe. I am concerned that the house isn't clean—that I've left things
lying about—the wadded tissues that Ray had scattered on the Parsons
table—did I throw them away?—(teeming with E. coli bacteria?)—I
am uneasy at seeing our friends, and Ray not with me—they will feel
so very sorry for me—it will cost them emotion, to *feel sorry* for me—
the practical idea comes to me to set books out on a coffee table—the
books I'd brought back home from the hospital. These are Ayaan Hirsi
Ali's *Infidel*, Paul Krugman's *The Great Unraveling*, the bound galleys of
Richard A. Clarke's *Your Government Failed You* which our friend Dan
Halpern is publishing.

These books—on the coffee table—we can talk about them—is that
a good idea?

Also, the book on the cultural history of boxing which I've been
reading to review. Which I've been working on this past week in the
interstices of the vigil. Returning home from the hospital and trying to
write for an hour or two before going to bed and trying to sleep. As if
I must allow my friends to know *Joyce is all right, Joyce is working even
now. Don't worry about Joyce!*

I am not thinking clearly. But I am thinking. I am trying to think.

Our friends arrive shortly after 2 A.M., in one car. Susan and Ron,
Jeanne and Dan and their fourteen-year-old daughter Lily whom Ray
and I have known since her birth. When they step inside, and embrace
me—it's as if I have stepped into a violent surf.

Though our friends remain with me until 4 A.M. most of what we
said to one another has vanished from my memory. Our friends will tell
me that I behaved calmly and yet it was clear that I was in a state of
shock. I can remember Jeanne on the phone, in the kitchen, making calls
to funeral homes. I can remember my astonishment that a funeral home
might be open at such an hour of the night. I can remember explaining
to my friends how Ray died—why Ray died—the *secondary infection*,
the fact that *his blood pressure plummeted, his heartbeat accelerated*—
these gruesome words which I have memorized and which even now, at
any hour of the day, along with my final vision of Ray in the hospital bed,
run through my mind like flashes of heat lightning.

My friends are extraordinary, I think. To come to me so quickly in the middle of the night as they've done.

For the widow inhabits a tale not of her own telling. The widow inhabits a nightmare-tale and yet it is likely that the widow inhabits a benign fairy tale out of the Brothers Grimm in which friends come forward to help. *We loved Ray, and we love you.*

Let us help you. Ray would want this.

18

E-mail Record

February 18, 2008, 9:26 A.M.
To Elaine Pagels

I was about to write to you to say that quite suddenly Ray passed away last night at about 1 A.M.

I am too exhausted now to speak but Jeannie is coming to go with me to a Pennington funeral home to make arrangements.

I have been thinking of you as a young—very young—widow and mother. I have seen in you the transcendence of this unspeakable wound and yet the shadow of it, which can never be forgotten.

Much love,

Joyce

February 18, 2008.
To Mary Morris

Ray died at 1 A.M. this morning in the medical center of a terrible pneumonia. I am utterly dazed and will get back to you [regarding an interview for the Italian Storie*] some other time.*

Much love,

Joyce

February 19, 2008.

To Richard Ford

Thanks, Richard. Much of my trouble—"trouble"?—is physical/emotional—I just feel exhausted, groggy around people and want to crawl away somewhere and sleep.

But I know that you are right. I am trying.

Love,

Joyce

February 19, 2008.

To Sandra Gilbert

I was thinking of you, and your wonderful lost husband . . . It was something similar—though not a "wrongful death" I'm sure—Ray had been hospitalized for pneumonia—an e-coli infection which is one of the worst—and was definitely "improving" day by day—due to be released to rehab soon—then suddenly, I had a call at 12:30 A.M. to come quickly to the hospital—where he had just been pronounced dead. A secondary infection had caused cardiopulmonary arrest, and he was gone.

It is just utterly unbelievable. I feel so completely alone.

Though surrounded by the most wonderful friends.

Thank you for writing. Much love,

Joyce

February 19, 2008.

To Gary Mailman

I have here the document "Last Will & Testament" of Raymond Smith . . . What does one do with the will, as a document? Do I present it somewhere? I've been told that I have to take "death certificates" to something called a surrogate court (?) in Trenton soon. Jeanne Halpern has offered to accompany me which is astonishingly wonderful of her.

How grateful we are that you came through your hospital siege. . . . I truly did think that Ray was, too. Even after death he looked not ill at all, quite handsome, his face unlined and peaceful. In the hospital room, all the staff had left, and he was alone in the bed without the IV fluids and the oxygen mask, and the beautiful vase of flowers that you and Emily had sent was on a table just beside him. It is the most haunting memory I will ever have.

Any [legal] advice you can give will be so much appreciated,
Joyce

February 19, 2008.
To Gloria Vanderbilt

[Ray] passed away at 1 A.M. of February 18—just yesterday! It is so hard to comprehend.

I will write to you later. I would love to see you. I am inundated with tasks to be done—like a zombie plodding through the interminable day—yesterday was a nightmare that went on—and on—and on. There does not seem to be much purpose to my life now except these meaningless but necessary tasks (like speaking with a funeral director, buying a cemetery plot, looking for the Last Will & Testament.)

But you are a solace just by existing, vividly in my thoughts if not here before me.

Much love,
Joyce

February 19, 2008.
To Eleanor Bergstein

Eleanor, I am not good on the phone right now. I am overwhelmed and stunned and trying to keep sane by doing a multiplicity—an infinity—of small necessary tasks. Ray died only yesterday morning—so much has happened since then, it seems unbelievable.

I know that you lost your mother and father long ago. What a raw terrible wound that must have been. Losing a spouse of 47 years is like losing a part of yourself—the most valuable part. What is left behind seems so depleted, broken.

Thank you so much for your love and your friendship.
Joyce

February 20, 2008.

To Dan Halpern

There are bouts of utter loneliness and a sense of purposelessness. But I had a lovely evening with Ron and Susan, though it was strange that Ray wasn't there, and Jeanne called this morning, and tomorrow I will be at your house with Emily & Gary & (evidently) Gloria.

Jeanne and Gary are giving me helpful advice re. a lawyer and the "probate" about which I know nothing.

This house is so lonely! It's almost unbearable. But I will bear it . . .

I am so grateful for your and Jeanne's friendship and for other friends who have been so supportive.

Much love,

Joyce

February 19, 2008.

To Jeanne Halpern

I like and need your presence when I am with people, I feel so easily breakable and I think that you can gauge these matters. I am so devastated, I'd just been listening to old messages—"old" meaning today and yesterday—since I rarely pick up the phone—there must have been fifteen calls and the last message (which was the earliest recorded, on Sunday afternoon) was from Ray, when I'd been en route to the hospital. I was stunned to hear his voice . . . now it is on the tape, the last I will ever hear of his voice. It is so utterly shattering. He sounded so good on the phone and was looking forward to seeing me. It is unbelievable that about 8 hours later he was dead.

Much love,

Joyce

Last Words

It is astonishing to discover, amid a number of telephone messages from the previous two days, these words of Ray's which are the last words of his I will hear.

This call made early Sunday morning when I was en route to the hospital, which I hadn't known he had made.

Ray hadn't mentioned the call to me—it was of so little consequence, or seemed so—and so what a shock to hear this so-familiar voice on the tape, intimate as if he were in the room with me.

Honey? This is your honey calling . . . If you want to talk can you call? Lots of love to my honey and kitties.

"You've Said Good-bye"

Many times on our walks in Pennington—a small "historic" town about two miles from our house—Ray and I took note of the Blackwell Memorial Home at 21 North Main Street—a white Colonial with blue shutters built close to the sidewalk.

The Blackwell Memorial Home has the comforting look of a watercolor by a gifted amateur—the kind celebrating small-town America of another era.

More frequently, we walked in the Pennington Cemetery in which, in the oldest section, nearest Main Street, and beside the Pennington Presbyterian Church, there are grave markers from the late 1700s—so aged and weatherworn their inscriptions are no longer readable.

The local legend is, Hessian soldiers exercised their horses by jumping over the stone wall that separates the old section of the cemetery from the street.

Always I will see us walking in Pennington, holding hands: Ray and Joyce of another era.

"If Ray saw us here in Pennington—at this time—he'd be curious what we're doing. He'd say, 'Let's have lunch. I could do with a drink.'"

Why I am inspired to say this, I have no idea. Lately I have heard myself say bizarre unscripted remarks. Ray might have been consumed with curiosity to know what Jeanne, Jane, and I are doing in Pennington in Jeanne's car as she parks in front of the Blackwell Memorial Home— but it's hardly likely that Ray would have suggested lunch at this early hour, mid-morning.

A widow is compelled to say marginally "witty" remarks as a widow is compelled to speak of her husband, to utter his name as frequently as possible, in terror lest his name be lost.

My friends Jeanne and Jane have come to my house to pick me up this morning. I am weak with gratitude, dry-mouthed and excited in anticipation—a funeral home! The very funeral home past which we'd walked so frequently, which it was my idea to call instead of a funeral home in Princeton, early this morning.

"But Ray would like this. In Pennington. Closer to our house. It's only about two miles away . . ."

How eager I am to believe that, in the parlor of the Blackwell Memorial Home, making these astonishing arrangements for the "disposal" of my husband's remains, I am behaving normally, or near-normally. I want to think that my concentration—broken and scattered like a cheap mirror when I'm alone—is flawless here, like the concentration of one inching across a tightrope, high above the ground.

Neither Jeanne nor Jane is a widow—of course. Though neither is a stranger to death within the family—Jane's mother died not long ago— neither woman is a widow and so I am thinking *They are better able to humor me. Another widow would be less patient. She would think—Of course, what did you expect? This is what it is to lose your husband. You never knew, and now you know.*

The widow's terror is that, her mind being broken, as her spine is broken, and her heart is broken, she will break down utterly. She will be carried off by wild careening banshee thoughts like these.

In the Blackwell Memorial Home in Pennington, New Jersey, my friends and I are seated in comfortable cushioned chairs in a small room looking out toward Main Street, and on the wood-plank floor are attractive thin-worn carpets. Panes of glass in the tall narrow windows have that distinct look of age. Almost, this might be one of those museum-homes attached to parks—furnishings are spare—"antique"-looking—a

large fieldstone fireplace takes up most of a wall—on the mantel is a
tarnished-looking but impressive Civil War sword once the property of
an ancestor of the proprietor Elizabeth Blackwell Davis—"Betty."

Betty has a cat, she tells us. The cat is elusive, in hiding. But on the
narrow staircase is a cloth catnip-toy.

In this domestic setting that reminds me of the wood-frame farm-
houses of my childhood—though the houses of my childhood in upstate
New York were austere, even grim, more resembling the black-and-white
realism of Depression-era photographs than watercolors of small-town
America—it's being explained to us by Betty Davis that the Blackwell
Memorial Home has been the Blackwell family business for genera-
tions. Betty has lived in this house most of her life and lives here now—
upstairs—with her (adult) son—and the cat; Betty, too, is a widow. I am
thinking *Ray would like her, I think.*

It's a sign of the widow's derangement, though a mild sign, that frequently the widow will think *My husband would like this.*

Others will conspire in this derangement eagerly. *Your husband would
like this. This is a good decision!*

But how strange it is, to be making such a decision by myself, without
Ray.

I have not made any "major" decision in my life, I think, by myself—
without my parents to consult, or Ray.

As my friends talk with Betty Davis—how much more sociable my
friends are, than I am!—I am grateful for them, as I sit staring at a form,
yet another form, a series of questions to which I must provide answers.
I am thinking how much I yearn to lie down beside Ray in the hospital
bed, and shut my eyes to all of this.

Too late. Now it's too late.

You had your opportunity, now it's too late.

Betty is explaining the services she will provide. She will arrange for
the cremation, in Ewing—it was Ray's wish to be cremated—she will
pick up the death certificate and make duplicates and bring them to me
at my house—"You will need them. Plenty of them."

Strange it seems to me, in my groggy slow-time, that already a *death
certificate* has been prepared.

And little will I know, how frequently the *death certificate* will be

required, in succeeding weeks, months—even years! For there is a bizarre suspicion among an entire category of strangers—bank officers,
investment brokers, bureaucrats of all kinds—that the deceased may not
in fact be deceased but the victim of some sort of prank on the part of
his survivors.

Yet more strange, to find myself inside the Blackwell House, on Main
Street. To have stepped into a kind of storybook looking-glass world
only a few doors from the house in which our genial longtime dentist
Dr. Sternberg shares his practice with another dentist, Dr. Goodman;
scarcely a block from the Village Hair Salon where both Ray and I have
our hair cut; a quarter-mile from the Pennington Food Market where
we've shopped for thirty years. Countless times we'd seen the facade of
the Blackwell Memorial Home in passing and perhaps we'd commented
on it but not once had either of us remarked that this "historic" structure
might one day be a place one of us might enter, on the occasion of the
other's death.

Never. Not once. Nor did we envision the Pennington Cemetery as a
place where one of us might "bury" the other.

There are plots available in the Pennington Cemetery at the rear, in
the newer section—so Betty is informing me. Older parts of the cemetery, long the possession of local families, are virtually closed now.

A small marker—"Aluminum, in good taste"—will be provided by
the funeral home and later, if I want something larger, at a later time, I
can buy it.

And would I like a second plot? I am asked.

"In fact the two plots together—a 'double plot'—won't be any larger
than the standard single plot. You see, with ashes, in just a container,
the space doesn't need to be so large. It's very economical to purchase a
double plot right now, Mrs. Smith."

Economical! This is important.

"Yes. Thank you. I will."

Intimate as a double bed, I am thinking.

Ray would like this—would he? No one wants to be alone in the
grave for longer than necessary.

"You will be purchasing a double plot from the 'Pennington Cemetery Association,' Mrs. Smith. You will be issued a certificate of own-

ership as well as a document from the 'Ewing Cemetery Association' and you will have to sign just a few more papers—for instance, do your husband's remains contain a pacemaker, radioactive implant, prosthetic devices or any other device that would be harmful to the crematory?—if *no*, sign here."

Harmful to the crematory? This is a sobering thought.

In any case I seem to be signing documents. Contracts. I seem to have agreed to purchase the "double plot" for the surviving spouse of Raymond Smith: "Joyce Carol Smith."

Numbly, I make out a check. Three thousand two hundred and eighty-one dollars. I have been making out checks lately, and will continue to make out checks, on our joint checking account. For death is not inexpensive, should you wonder.

Trained as a lawyer, my friend Jeanne reads through the documents before I sign them. From their remarks both Jeanne and Jane seem to think it's a reasonable decision, at this time, to purchase the double plot from the Pennington Cemetery Association.

This is good! I have not behaved rashly or insanely. I have demonstrated *common sense*.

All this while it has been my hazy unexamined idea that Ray is still at the hospital, in the hospital bed where I'd left him. In my vision of Ray he is always, forever, in the hospital bed in room 539 of the Princeton Medical Center, he is "sleeping"—he is "at peace"—his eyes are closed, his face unlined and smooth shaven, he is very still, I am leaning over him to kiss him—and so when Betty informs me that "your husband's remains" are in an adjoining room and will have to be identified, I am taken by surprise; I am stunned; I am utterly shocked.

Of course I must know—I *know*—that Ray's body was picked up this morning at the medical center by a driver for the Pennington funeral home. I know this, since I arranged for it. I know that Ray's body was delivered in a coffin, transported in an inconspicuous vehicle to the rear of 21 North Main Street, Pennington, in order to be "identified."

All this I know, yet somehow I have forgotten.

All this I know, yet somehow I am overwhelmed by the fact that *Ray is in the next room. Ray is dead, Ray is in the next room. Ray is here . . .*

Until now I have been behaving normally—I think. I have been

talking—even smiling—in the company of Betty Davis, Jeanne and
Jane—but now I begin to panic, to hyperventilate; I am light-headed,
terrified. Quickly Jeanne says that she and Jane will identify Ray. "You
stay here."

I am too weak to protest. I am too frightened. I can't bear the thought
of seeing Ray now. Why this is, I don't know. I will regret this moment.
I will regret this decision. I will never understand why at this crucial
moment I behave in so childish a way, as if my husband whom I love has
become physically repulsive to me.

How ashamed I will be, at this decision! Like a child shrinking away,
hiding her eyes.

Always I will think: as I'd exercised such poor judgment, bringing
Ray to the regional Princeton hospital, and keeping him there when he
would surely have received superior treatment elsewhere, so my judgment is faulty now, inexplicable.

"You don't have to see Ray now," Jeanne tells me. "You saw him last
night. You've said good-bye."

*The Widow has entered the stage of primitive thinking in which she imagines
that some small, trivial gesture of hers might have meaning in relationship
to her husband's death. As if being "good"—"responsible"—she might undo
her personal catastrophe. She will come slowly to realize that there is nothing
to be done now.*

*"Identifying" her husband's body, or not—seeing his body one final time,
or not—none of this will make the slightest difference. Her husband has died,
he has gone and is not coming back.*

Double Plot

What my friend Jeanne has said is both true and not-true.

You don't really—ever—say good-bye.

In the Pennington Cemetery at the intersection of Delaware Avenue and Main Street, a short distance behind the Pennington Presbyterian Church, there is a relatively new, grassy section in which, in a space identified as #551 West Center, a small marker reads

RAYMOND J. SMITH, JR.

1930–2008

Oddly, there are few other grave markers in this section. Except, a near-neighbor, an attractive large grave marker made of granite—KATHERINE GREEF AUSTIN 1944–1997, WILLIAM J. O'CONNELL 1944–1996. I stare at these words, these numerals, and conclude—*A widow, who died of grief.*

The contingencies of death have made SMITH and O'CONNELL neighbors, who had not known each other in life.

How strange it is, to see Ray's name in such a place! It's very difficult for me to comprehend that, in the most literal way, the "remains" of the individual who'd been Raymond J. Smith are buried, in an urn, beneath the surface of the earth here.

"Oh honey! What has happened. . . ."

In dreams sometimes it is revealed that what you'd believed to be so is not so after all. In life it is not often revealed that what you'd believed to be so is not so after all—yet there is always the possibility, the hope.

Because my mind is not functioning normally every moment is predicated upon the infantile hope *This is not-right. But maybe it will become right if I am good.*

No one is visiting the cemetery this morning except me. This is a relief! Though I am anxious when I am alone, yet I yearn to be alone; the empty house is terrifying to me yet when I am away from it, I yearn to return to it. Except now, in the cemetery where my husband's remains—"cremains" (hideous word)—are buried, I am both alone and not-alone.

I am almost late for an appointment, I think. Maybe it's probate court—Jeanne will be taking me—since Ray's death my life has become a concatenation of appointments, duties—"death-duties"—making of each day a Sahara stretching to the horizon, and beyond—a robot-life, a zombie-life—from which (this is my most delicious thought, when I am alone) I am thinking of departing. When I have time.

Where some may be frightened by the thought, the temptation, of suicide, the widow is consoled by the temptation of suicide. For suicide promises *A good night's sleep—with no interruptions! And no next-day.*

"I shouldn't have left you. I'm so sorry . . ."

It's a sunny-gusty day. Snow lies in part-melted skeins and heaps amid the grave markers which are of very different sizes. How terrible it is, Ray is *here*—it seems incomprehensible, *here.*

I tell myself with childish logic that if Ray were alive but not with me, that absence would be identical with this absence.

Which day this is, how many hours after Ray's death, I am not sure—much of my mental effort is taken up with such pointless calculations—it is a mental effort exerted against the ceaseless buzz of word-incursions—fragments of music, songs—how best to describe my mind, perhaps it's the quintessential novelist's mind, other than a drain that has captured all variety of rubble—when my life is most shaken, the drain is heaped with rubble as after a rainstorm—there is little distinction between anything in the drain except most of it is to no purpose, futile and exhausting; nothing of what I "hear" is exactly audible, as it would be, I assume, in a person afflicted with schizophrenia; these distractions are merely annoying, when not cruelly mocking.

> *There once was a ship . . .*
> *The name of our ship was*
> *The Golden Vanity.*

Like a metronome set at too quick a rhythm a pulse begins to beat in my head. It's the beat, beat, beat of mockery—a sense that our life together was in vain—now it has ended—sunken into the *Low-Land Sea* as in the ballad's melancholy refrain.

Most of the words of the ballad are lost to me. Only a few words recur with maddening frequency.

Sometimes seeing Ray with a faraway or a distracted look in his eye I would ask him what he was thinking and Ray would reply *Nothing.*

But how can you be thinking about nothing?

I don't know. But I was.

How funny Ray could be! Though there was always this other side of him, as if in eclipse.

He would be so very touched, to know how our friends are missing him. How stricken they are, that he has died. A kind of family has come into being . . . It is horrible to think that Ray's last hours were passed among strangers.

If he'd been conscious at the time, of what was he conscious?

What were his final thoughts, what were his final words?

Suddenly I am gripped by a need to seek out the young woman doctor who spoke to me in Ray's room. I don't even know her name—I will have to find out her name—I will ask her what Ray said—what she remembers—

Except of course she won't remember. Or, if she remembers, she won't tell me.

Better not to know. Better not to pursue this.

From the time of our first meeting in Madison, Wisconsin, it was Ray who was the more elusive of the two of us, the more secretive, elliptical. Some residue of his puritanical Irish Catholic upbringing remained with him through the decades, long after he'd dropped out of the Church at the age of eighteen; he disliked religion, in all its forms, but particularly the dogmatic; he disliked theology, particularly the morbidly arcane and exacting theology of Thomas Aquinas which he'd had to study at the Jesuit-run Marquette High School in Milwaukee.

The Jesuit motto—*I do what I am doing.*

Meaning *What I am doing is justified because I am doing it.*

Because I am in the service of God.

There was a side of Ray unknowable to me—kept at a little distance from me. As—I suppose—there was a side of myself kept at a distance from Ray, who knew so little of my writing.

What is frightening is, maybe I never knew him. In some essential way, I never knew my husband.

For I had known *my husband*—as he'd allowed himself to be known. But the man who'd been my husband—*Ray Smith, Raymond Smith, Raymond J. Smith*—has eluded me.

Or is it inevitable—no wife really knows her husband? To be a *wife* is an intimacy so close, one can't see; as, close up to a mirror, one can't see one's reflection.

The male is elusive, to the female. The male is the *other*, the one to be *domesticated*; the female *is* domestication.

There's a sudden trickle of liquid—blood?—on my wrist. Without knowing, I've been digging at my skin.

Rashes, welts, tiny hot pimples like poison ivy have erupted on the tender skin of the insides of my arms especially, and on the underside of my jaw; striations like exposed nerves have emerged across my back. Staring at these configurations in the mirror of my bathroom this morning as if they were a message in an unknown language.

Also in my bathroom arranging pill-containers on the rim of the sink counter. Painkillers, sleeping pills, an accumulation of years. Did such drugs lose their efficacy? Would their power be diminished?

I am thinking now *I am so tired, I could sleep forever.*

But there is no time. Already it is 10:20 A.M.—it is February 20, 2008—I must put together a packet of documents for probate court in Trenton.

"Good-bye, honey!"

*   *   *

The Widow is consoling herself with a desperate stratagem. But then, all the widow's stratagems are desperate right now. She will speculate that she didn't fully know her husband—this will give her leverage to seek him, to come to know him. It will keep her husband "alive" in her memory—elusive, teasing. For the fact is, the widow cannot accept it, that her husband is gone from her life irrevocably. She cannot accept it—she cannot even comprehend it—that she has no relationship with Raymond J. Smith except as his widow—the "executrix" of his estate.

A Widow's actions might be defined as rational/irrational alternatives to suicide. Any act a Widow performs, or contemplates performing, is an alternative to suicide and is in this desirable however naive, foolish, or futile.

22

Cat Pee

"Oh Reynard! How could you."

It seems that our elder tiger cat Reynard has urinated on a swath of documents which in my desperation not to misplace anything crucial among Ray's many papers I'd spread out on the floor of his study.

A dozen or more manila folders, spread out on Ray's desk and spilling over onto the floor—in block letters carefully designated MEDICAL INSURANCE, CAR INSURANCE, HOUSE INSURANCE, IRS DOCUMENTS (2007), BANK/FINANCES, SOCIAL SECURITY, BIRTH CERTIFICATES, WILL etc.—and sometime within the past several hours Reynard has surreptitiously defiled a copy of the death certificate and the IRS folder so that I must A) wipe the pages dry B) spray Windex on them C) wipe them dry again D) place them in our (unheated) solarium in the hope that by morning they will have A) dried B) ceased smelling so unmistakably pungent.

"Reynard! Bad cat."

My vexed/raised voice provokes both cats to run in that panicked way in which domestic pets will run from irate masters on a hardwood floor—skidding, sliding and slithering—toenails scraping like cartoon animals. I feel a sudden fury for the cats—both Reynard and the younger long-haired gray Cherie—that they have ceased to care for me. In this matter of Ray's disappearance they blame *me*.

You would think that, with Ray missing, they would be more affectionate with me, and want to sleep with me—but *no*.

Barely they condescend to allow themselves to be fed by me. Eagerly they run outside, to escape me. Reluctantly they return when I call them for meals and for the night.

The defiled IRS papers are not the first evidence that the cats are taking a particular sort of feline revenge on me since Ray's disappearance, but this is the most serious.

Where grief couldn't provoke me to tears, cat pee on these documents does. It's the weeping of sheer despair, self-loathing—*This is what I am, this is what I've become. This is my life now.*

23

PROBATE

"Mrs. Smith? You can wait here."

And here too—Mercer County Surrogate's Court, Trenton, New Jersey—is a place where memory has accumulated in small stagnant pools of tears. Almost, you can smell grief here, an acrid bitter odor.

This high-ceilinged waiting room, inexpressibly dour! Rows of badly stained and uncomfortable vinyl chairs in which individuals sit impassively as in an anteroom of the damned.

Unlike the waiting rooms at the hospital, this waiting room holds not even the delusion of a happy ending. For these individuals, the death vigil has ended. We here are survivors, "beneficiaries."

It's evident that there are other widows here this morning. Several appear to be accompanied by adult children. Mostly these are black or Hispanic citizens, for this is Trenton, New Jersey. In their midst my friend Jeanne—in oversized designer sunglasses, shoulder-length blond hair spilling over the collar of her stylish winter coat—is a vivid and incongruous presence, drawing eyes.

Jeanne has explained what we are doing here, what "probate" is—of course, I know some of this, or would know except I seem to be operating in a mist of incomprehension. Very tired, yet alert and excited—sorting through the documents I'd been instructed to bring which include the photocopied pages now only just faintly smelling of cat pee—in this new compulsion of mine, which began when I'd been visiting Ray in the hospital, of ceaselessly rummaging through a handbag or a tote bag to see if somehow I'd lost something crucial like car keys, or my wallet, or a death certificate.

In fact, I have not misplaced the death certificate. Of several copies hand-delivered to me by Elizabeth Davis of the Blackwell Memorial Home—a gesture of kindness which I will not forget—just one was defiled by Reynard, and has been disposed of.

(Though later, I will retrieve this copy of the death certificate from the trash. For I am fearful of running out of copies—so many parties seem to want one, as if doubtful that Raymond Smith is deceased. That one of the copies exudes a sour cat-smell is unfortunate.)

Many times in a curious breathless trance I have read this *Certificate of Death* issued by the *State of New Jersey Department of Health and Senior Services.* You would think from my concentrated interest that I might be expecting to learn something new, to be surprised. Like one digging at a wound to make it bleed I am drawn to reading the sparse information again and again, to no purpose since I have memorized it—

Cause of Death
Immediate Cause
Cardiopulmonary Arrest
Due to (or as a consequence of)
Pneumonia

A minimalist poem by William Carlos Williams!

Now in the dour waiting room of the surrogate court as I reread the death certificate it occurs to me to wonder—*is* this true? Did Ray die simply of *pneumonia*, or were other factors involved?

A *secondary infection*, I'd been told. There is no mention of a *secondary infection* in the document.

I think that I remember having been asked at the medical center if I wanted Ray's body autopsied. In whatever haze of confusion at the time quickly I'd said no.

No! No.

Could not bear it. The thought of Ray's body being mutilated.

I know!—the body is not the man. Not "Ray."

And yet—where else had "Ray" resided, except in that body?

It was a body I knew intimately, and loved. And so I did not want it mutilated.

Now, I will never know if these "causes" of his death are accurate, or complete. I will never know with certainty.

For it's clear—*widow* trumps all other identities, including *rational individual*.

All that one believes of the "rational"—"reasonable"—"scientific-minded" life is jettisoned, when one becomes a widow.

My wish was for my husband's body not to be examined—opened and eviscerated like an animal being gutted. I think that there is something dignified in cremation—or I want to think this—something primal, even "holy."

Of course, I can't bear to think of the circumstances of the cremation in the Ewing Crematorium. I was not there, I was not a witness.

I had been advised not to attend. And so, I had not attended.

My opportunity to see Ray for the final time had been at the Blackwell Memorial Home—in this, I had failed. I will not soon forget this failure.

Ray's wish had been for cremation, as he'd indicated in the document quaintly titled "living will." As Ray had indicated in his remarks over the years.

How casually people speak of such things!—*Promise that at my funeral you'll play Mozart's* Requiem Mass.

In my e-mail to my friend Sandra Gilbert whose husband Eliot had died a *wrongful death* at the U.C. Davis Medical Center, as a result of negligent nursing care, I'd said that Ray's death was not *wrongful death*—but why?

Why had I said this? How would I have known?

What a widow says, a widow will often regret. Yet a widow must speak. A widow must *say something.*

As a widow must *smile*, to assure others that she is all right.

In the waiting room of the surrogate court, time passes with excruciating slowness. The widow will discover that often she is *waiting in public places*—this is her punishment, for having been a wife.

In this new—posthumous—phase of my life such (questionable) epiphanies come to me frequently. *Widowhood is the punishment for having been a wife.*

Vicious reviews, opprobrium of all sorts are the writer's punishment for being a writer.

When you sign on to be a wife, you are signing on to being a widow one day, possibly. When you sign on to being a writer you are signing on to any and all responses to your work.

So we should tell ourselves, when we are hurt, devastated.

When we regret our lives, that seem to us in moments of raw bleak unsparing illumination, to have been lived in vain.

Grief will bring us epiphanies of various degrees of worth. But grief will not bring us much else.

My brain is a snarl of such thoughts. A near-broken radio flooded with static. I am rummaging through my papers for—what?—can't remember what I am looking for—oh yes, Ray's will—for a moment I am panicked *Did I leave the will behind at the house?*—though Jeanne looked through the documents before we left my driveway; and here it is, always a smaller document than I think it will be—pale blue folded-over LAST WILL AND TESTAMENT OF RAYMOND J. SMITH AND LETTERS TESTAMENTARY.

No one could guess why I'm surreptitiously lifting this crucial document to sniff at it. In my bag with the other papers, it has acquired a faint, very faint odor of cat pee.

Suddenly I'm worried—that the will isn't valid, or that my identity will be doubted. In my state of exhaustion I'm not able to think clearly, and could not defend myself or my interests.

In this state of mind one can acquiesce to any sort of charge. The state of mind in which innocent individuals sign "confessions"—sickened with guilt, you surmise that you must be guilty of a criminal act.

It is wrong to have outlived Ray. This is the fact you know, you have not acknowledged.

A widow is susceptible to the most extraordinary thoughts. A widow cannot defend herself against the most extraordinary thoughts.

For a widow has learned that the ordinary can so quickly turn extraordinary, and the extraordinary ordinary.

My punishment began during the vigil. Now that Ray has died, the punishment will escalate. This seems only logical.

What a desperate time I'd had, searching for Ray's will! It wasn't in the place I'd expected it to be—so I thought; so I looked elsewhere, through the house, with mounting panic, until finally I looked again in the first, most obvious place—in the file in Ray's office in which I had looked initially—and there it was.

How to explain this? Is my brain deteriorating, is this a particularly cruel form of the widow's punishment?—losing things in plain sight, not being able to find things, always in a panic? I think in this case I'd expected the will to be an enormous document, and not so small, so—ordinary.

Ray's will—this usage is strange to me. Like *Ray's body, Ray's remains.*

Our wills, drawn up some time ago, had been updated in May 2002. I think this had been a joint decision, but at the time, I'd been stricken with sorrow at the prospect of signing them as if foreseeing—but of course I could not foresee—a day to come like this bleak day in the Mercer County Surrogate Court.

Ray had said *Don't be silly, we have to do this.*

But I don't want to outlive you!

That has nothing to do with it. Just sign, get it over with.

And so I did.

Not anticipating on May 10, 2002 how on February 21, 2008 I would be clutching this document in my hand, in a vinyl chair in the waiting area of the Mercer County Surrogate Court.

"Mrs. Smith? Come with me."

I am led into an interior office. Jeanne accompanies me. A woman—her title is "surrogate court officer"—takes up my case, that seems to me overwhelming in its magnitude, to her utterly perfunctory.

I am required to present numerous documents to the surrogate court in this matter of the "probating" of my husband's will. *Last Will and Testament of Raymond J. Smith and Letters Testamentary*—Ray's and my birth certificates—our wedding certificate—our passports—driver's licenses—Social Security cards—2007 tax records establishing our residence at 9 Honey Brook Drive, Princeton, New Jersey.

It can't be taken for granted—of course, this is only reasonable—that I am truly the person I claim to be, the widow of the deceased Raymond Smith; nor can it be taken for granted that Raymond Smith is, in fact, deceased. (The sourly aromatic *Certificate of Death* is examined closely, as if the surrogate court officer has never seen such a document before.)

The surrogate officer has questions to ask me. Some of them—how long had my husband and I resided at 9 Honey Brook Drive?—are upsetting to answer. As the interview continues, I become increasingly depressed. I am thinking *How futile! What vanity!* My friend Jeanne has been so very kind to accompany me on this errand of futility as she has accompanied me on other similarly futile errands since my husband's death; for Jeanne's sake, I am not going to break down. Yet, how I yearn to run from this terrible place and return to our house—the very house from which, that morning, early, after another sleepless night, I'd been so eager to leave. When I'm away from our house my consoling fantasy is that when I return home, I can swallow as many pills as seem feasible, to put myself to sleep; that is, to sleep forever; for truly I want to die, I am so very tired; it hasn't been more than a few days yet already I've been made sick by widowhood, and I am sick of it; the prospect of another few weeks of this, let alone years, is overwhelming!

Yet when I return home, I am so relieved—I think *This is my home. This is ours.* In defiance of all logic it is possible in this place to think *Ray might be in the next room, or in his office—he might have stepped out of the house.* When you're living in a house with someone it is often the case that he isn't *in the same room with you*—and so, when I am home, I am free to imagine that Ray *is* on the premises.

In my study, at my desk overlooking a stand of trees, a birdbath (not in use, in winter), a holly tree with red berries in which cardinals, chickadees and titmice bustle cheerily about, I am free to tell myself *Ray would not be in this room with you anyway. Your experience at this moment is not a widow's experience.*

"Mrs. Smith? Sign these."

My signature is notarized. I sign—*Joyce Carol Smith.* For this is the widow's identity.

"Sympathy Gift Basket"

"Mrs. Smith? Sign here, please."

My heart contracts at these syllables. *Miss-us Smi-th*. The name, in the mouths of strangers, stings like mockery.

For there is no *Mr. Smith*. And how then *Mrs. Smith*?

The sympathy-siege!

As in a silent film accelerated for crudely comic purposes there appear in the courtyard of our house in the days following Ray's death a disorganized army of delivery men bearing floral displays, crates of fruit, hefty "sympathy gift baskets" stuffed to bursting with gourmet foods—chocolate-covered truffles, Brazil nuts, honey-roasted cashews; smoked salmon, pickled herring, smoked pepperoni sausage; lemon cake, Key West Lime Pie, fruit tarts, chocolate-pecan fudge; "gourmet" popcorn, "gourmet" pretzels, "gourmet" mixed nuts; Vermont cheddar cheese, and Vermont jack cheese; "drunken" goat cheese; jars of peach butter, Russian caviar and pâtés of the most lurid kinds. "Mrs. Smith? Sign here, please"—on his way out of the courtyard the UPS man nearly collides with the FedEx man on his way in; both are followed by a clumsily waddling gigantic plant or small tree in a massive ceramic container—behind it, a harried delivery man from a local Princeton florist—"Mrs. Smith? Sign here, please." Seeing my stunned and exhausted face the delivery men aren't certain how to greet me—*Congratulations!* isn't appropriate for possibly this isn't a festive occasion, but the parody of a festive occasion—*Have a good day!* isn't appropriate for clearly this is not going to be a good day.

Possibly, the UPS man and the FedEx man, who come often to our house, have begun to notice the absence of *Raymond Smith.*

So often in these days—a nightmare of days—in my trance of misery in Ray's office where I am seeking (yet another) misplaced or lost document—United Health, IRS, bank—I am interrupted by the doorbell ringing—propelled into a greater misery at the front door where I am obliged to smile at the delivery man and thank him for having brought me yet another massive floral display, fifty-pound potted plant, "Deluxe Sympathy Gift Basket"—useless, unwanted, invariably heavy vases, pots, baskets, boxes, cartons to be carried in my aching arms, shoved, kicked skidding along the floor into the dining room where wilted petals fallen from the floral displays of previous days lie amid Styrofoam packing pellets, torn wrapping paper, cellophane. On the dining room table is a mad jumble of things—vases of beautiful flowers, baskets of beautiful flowers and fruits, "gourmet sympathy baskets" adorned with special velvet "sympathy ribbons" in tasteful dark colors. *What, have we won the Kentucky Derby?*—Ray's droll voice sounds in my ear.

There does seem to be an element of mockery in all this—sympathy. Almost, one might mistake the siege for a celebration.

Of all deliveries I have come to most dread those from Harry & David those ubiquitous entrepreneurs of fateful occasions—Sympathy Gift Boxes adorned with Sympathy Ribbons hurtled in all directions across the continent. Why are people sending me these things? Do they imagine that grief will be assuaged by chocolate-covered truffles, pâté de foie gras, pepperoni sausages? Do they imagine that assistants shield me from the labor of dealing with such a quantity of trash? This morning I am eager to forestall another delivery of sympathy baskets for I have dragged out all the trash cans I can find in the hope that the trash will be hauled away, I have just emptied the mailbox—so stuffed, I could barely yank out its contents—and this mail I am "sorting" by way of throwing most of it into the trash can—there arrives the UPS delivery truck—another Harry & David monstrosity?—"Mrs. Smith? Sign here, please"—crying bitter tears as I tear open the carton—tear open the cellophane wrapper—tear at the basket cramming into the trash can packages of chocolate-covered truffles, bags of gourmet popcorn, here is a Gourmet Riviera Pear—unnaturally large, tasteless, stately as a waxen fruit in a nineteenth-century still life—here is a jar of gourmet mustard, and here a jar of gourmet olives—whoever has sent me this, I have no idea—the card is lost—the label is lost—I am frantic to get rid of this party food—I am infuriated, disgusted, ashamed—for of course I should be grateful, I should be writing thank-you notes like a proper widow, I should not be weeping and muttering to myself in icy rain at the end of our driveway bare-headed and shivering in a rage of futility accusing my husband *You did this!—you went outside in the freezing cold, I know you did, this is exactly what you did, when I was away in Riverside you did this very thing, you were careless with your life, you threw away both our lives with your carelessness contracting a cold, a cold that became pneumonia, pneumonia that became cardiopulmonary collapse*—and here as if in rebuke to my raging despair is a Harry & David Miniature Rose—a delicate little rosebush that measures about five inches in height—which I think that I will keep—though, back inside the house in better lighting, pried out of its packing-case and set on the kitchen counter, the Miniature Rose appears to be already wilting, near-dead.

I will water it, however! I will follow directions for its care and tending.

Noting on the instruction sheet, at the bottom:

Important: *Decorative plant mosses should not be eaten.*

A widow may be deranged, but a widow is not that deranged!

In the interstices of the monster gifts are practical things from friends—a trolley for the trash cans, now that trash has become a central concern of my life, from Jeanne and Dan; a bag of Odwalla blended fruit-drinks, which will be a food staple for months, from Jean Korelitz; still-warm casserole dishes from several friends—women-friends—left in the courtyard, on our front porch, which, too ambitious in scale for me to attempt to eat alone, I will store in the freezer for use in some vague future time. How deeply moved Ray would be, by this outpouring of grief among our friends. For Ray was so self-effacing, modest . . .

Still, I am angry with him. I am very angry with him. With my poor dead defenseless husband, I am furious as I was rarely—perhaps never—furious with him, in life. *How can I forgive you, you've ruined both our lives.*

The phone is ringing—unanswered. Since the night of the call from the hospital, a ringing phone is hateful to me. Even with caller ID, I don't answer it. Sometimes I walk quickly away, hands over my ears. Many of the calls are from friends—acquaintances—people with whom I should speak—but I can't. I can't bring myself to speak with them. My world has shrunk to a very few friends.

Many phone messages are lost, erased. Only the phone message from Ray remains, through the end of the month, and two weeks beyond. This message, I listen to frequently.

Hello this is your honey calling.

Love to my honey and kitties.

I listen to this message in the hope that I will hear a word or two that I hadn't heard before. Or—an entirely new intonation to my husband's voice.

So often have I listened to this call, the syllables of Ray's words are starting to sound frayed.

"My husband died ten years ago. It doesn't get any easier."

A woman at Mercer County Services addresses me in a no-nonsense voice. In desperation I'd called to get information about the recycling pickup schedule in our neighborhood.

Why I seemed to know so little about the recycling schedule, I explained that my husband had always taken care of the recycling, and that he'd died recently.

To a stranger, I could say this. I could say these words. I could utter the word *die* which I could not have uttered to anyone whom we knew.

Driving then on the Pennington-Titusville Road. In icy rain determined to acquire more recycling cans—both yellow (bottles) and green (paper)—free cans, provided by the township!—since the two cans I have are nowhere sufficient for the siege of trash.

Yet much of this new trash—the "sympathy gift baskets" with their spiraling handles, large enough to hold twin joeys—the unwanted food items themselves—is not *recyclable*. For this trash, which includes *garbage*, a commercial service is required.

It's good for the widow to be told—I think—that there are other widows in the world. Plenty of other widows. Like the no-nonsense woman at Mercer County Services who doesn't offer sympathy so much as a nudge in the ribs. *Get used to it.*

And now returning home on the Pennington-Titusville Road I feel my triumph at acquiring the several recycling cans—for free!—begin to deflate. I am thinking how odd this is, that I am driving here in the country—I am driving here alone—not once in our life in this part of New Jersey had I ever driven on this highway without Ray, and usually Ray was driving; we'd be returning from a trip to the Delaware River, or to Bucks County; an outing on the Delaware & Raritan Canal towpath, that runs along the river; we'd have been walking, running, or bicycling; for these were our favorite things to do together. I am thinking that never have I been alone so much, so *starkly unmitigatedly alone*, as I have been since Ray has died; never, since our marriage in January 1961.

There is a terror in *aloneness*. Beyond even *loneliness*.

And now, this is my life. This is what my life will be. This aloneness, this anxiety, this dread of the next hour and of the upcoming night and of the morning to follow, this dread of a vast avalanche of trash, useless unwanted trash spilling over me, filling my mouth, suffocating, smothering trash for which I am (perversely) expected to express gratitude, thanks; this will be the rest of my life, without my husband; this, unbelievable, impossible to believe, and yet—of course it is true: there is the *Certificate of Death*, as proof.

When you are not alone, you are shielded. You are shielded from the stark implacable unspeakable indescribable terror of aloneness. You are shielded from the knowledge of your own insignificance, your trash-soul. When you are loved, you are blind to your own worth; or, you are indifferent to such thoughts. You have no time for such thoughts. You have no inclination to think *Why am I here, why am I left behind, what am I doing here, why in the car driving on this highway, why trash cans rattling in the rear of the car and in the trunk of the car, why not turn the steering wheel sharply to the right, there are trees, there is the promise of quick oblivion—or—maybe not?*

That is the dilemma: maybe not. Maybe things would be worse. Actual pain, agony, brain damage, hospital, Telemetry—you don't die in the car wreck but survive in a mutilated and disfigured state—a single eye remaining, swollen and near-blind and you open it to see Jasmine hovering over your bed, chattering in your face.

The widow-life of low-grade misery is preferable to *that*.

No hiding! Back from the Pennington-Titusville Road—back in Ray's study trying to make sense of a morass of papers—ignore the ringing phone—ignore the doorbell ringing—but no, I can't ignore the doorbell ringing—I must answer the doorbell ringing—I must put aside my misery out of courtesy for the delivery man on my doorstep—I must not scream at him *Go away! Leave me alone!*

I must smile and graciously accept from him whatever it is—perhaps not a monster-package but something small, that will fit on the dining room table as a token of a friend's sympathy and love, but even if it is a monster package I must accept it, reasoning that the sympathy-siege must end, soon—there is a finite quantity of *sympathy* in the world, and it is rapidly being used up.

"Mrs. Smith? Sign here, please."

Advice to the Widow: Do not think that grief is pure, solemn, austere and "elevated"—this is not Mozart's Requiem Mass. *Think instead Spike Jones, those unfunny "classical" musical jokes involving tubas and bassoons.*

Think of crude coarse gravel that hurts to walk on. Think of splotched mirrors in public lavatories. Think of towel dispensers when they have broken and there is nothing to wipe your hands on except already-used badly soiled towels.

The Betrayal

And one morning I am unable to bear it: the sight of the *New York Times* in its transparent blue wrapper lying at the end of the driveway. Through a break in foliage I can see it from a window in my study and even if only a glisten of the transparent blue wrapper is visible this glisten is enough to make me feel very weak, very bad. I am thinking of Ray reading the newspaper each morning of his life without fail. I am thinking of how surprised Ray would be to see how copies of the paper are accumulating unread. I am thinking *What futility, what vanity! He cared so much for—what?*

Unable to make my exhausted way outside to pick up the newspaper(s) as I am unable to remove the newspaper(s) from the transparent blue wrapper as I am unable to read this incontestably great newspaper nor am I able to glance at its front page, its headlines which had the power to so absorb Ray as he returned to the house he would sometimes pause in the courtyard frowning over the front page until I called to him— *Honey! For heaven's sake come inside.*

The green recycling trash-container is already packed with "mixed paper and cardboard"—many pages of newsprint—magazines, bound galleys, wrapping paper, discarded mail. Too much newsprint! Too much heartbreak!

Within a week of Ray's death I have canceled our thirty-year subscription to the *New York Times.*

The Artisans

Months ago in another lifetime it had been my suggestion to invite George Saunders to Princeton, to give a reading in our creative writing program series, and I would introduce him. Unfortunately this reading was scheduled for February 20.

When Ray was first hospitalized, on February 11, I'd thought that perhaps someone else should introduce George because very likely I would be at the hospital at that time; then, as days passed, and Ray's condition was "improving," I told our reading series coordinator that yes, I could introduce George after all. But then, when Ray died so suddenly, the next day I had to contact our program coordinator to tell her that after all I couldn't introduce George, though I'd prepared an introduction.

Yet thinking perversely *Maybe I can do it! I should try.*

I called our program director Paul Muldoon. I heard myself tell Paul in a calm voice that I would teach my fiction workshops that week, and that I would introduce George. I thought that I should do this. I wanted to behave "professionally"—I did not want to betray myself as weak, "feminine." This seemed important. Like hauling trash cans out to the street and hauling them back again emptied, in order to be filled and again emptied, an effort of virtually no consequence or significance, an expression of Sisyphean futility. I thought *If I can do such things, I am not crazy. I am not in pieces. I am not this new, different, shattered person, I am the person I have always been.*

Paul listened politely to me. Paul said, "I will take it upon myself, Joyce, to cancel your workshops. And Tracey will find someone else to introduce George."

George Saunders came, and read one of his eerie unsettling stories; the bleakest and blackest of humor, stark drop-dead dead-end humor, and the audience laughed, especially the undergraduates laughed—they who imagine that the bleakest and blackest of humor expresses a mode of existence in which, if put to the test, they themselves would be perfectly comfortable; and afterward at dinner, in conversation with my writing colleagues C. K. Williams, Jeffrey Eugenides, and me, George remarked that literary writers in the twenty-first century are artisans who have fashioned elegant friezes on walls, beauty of a kind to be appreciated by a very small percentage of people, and of course by one another; not noticing that the roof of the building is sinking in, about to collapse on our heads.

Bleakly, blackly, we laughed. I laughed.

Why?

27

E-MAIL RECORD

February 21, 2008.

To Edmund White

   The days are not too bad, it's the nights and the empty house that fill me with panic. Not continuously, more in waves that come unexpectedly. It is just so hard to believe that I can't hear Ray's voice again, or see him, in another part of the house . . .

   Did you say you were bringing work with you? What a good idea . . . I can try to "work" too . . . though it seems somewhat futile now, and fruitless. But just typing this letter is satisfying somehow. We are addicted to language for its sanity-providing . . .

   Much love,

   Joyce

February 22, 2008.

To Michael Bergstein (managing editor, Conjunctions*)*

   Ray has died—of pneumonia, after a week in the hospital. Our publishing is coming to an end—I am heartbroken and stunned.

   Joyce

February 22, 2008.

To Robert Silvers (editor of New York Review of Books*)*

Thanks so much for your lovely letter. You have offered "anything you can do"—just keep publishing NYRB. That is a solace to me. During the tumultuous week of Ray's hospitalization last week as his condition was said to be "improving," I gamely came home and worked on the review of Boxing: A Cultural History *for you until late in the night since I could not sleep anyway . . . And now I am trying to get back to the review, amid so many distractions, because, as Barbara Epstein felt also, in the end it is our work that matters, and our work that can be a solace and a lifeline.*

Much love, and continued admiration—

Joyce

February 22, 2008.

To Richard Ford and Kristina Ford

Dear Richard, and dear Kristina—

I am doing all right. Jeanne & Dan have been wonderful. Dan checks on me via his cell phone/email—and Jeanne is giving very helpful advice re. a lawyer/will/probate court, etc., to minimize anxiety there. I had dinner with Jeanne & Gary Mailman last night. So long as I have one meal a day with people—at an actual table—with the social protocol of courses—the logic of "eating" makes perfect sense; alone, with no spouse, with no wish to sit at the familiar table, it seems faintly repellent . . . My favorite time now is sleeping—but it doesn't last long enough.

I feel so sad that so many little gestures Ray did—like planting dozens of beautiful tulips in the courtyard, taking such care with the art-work in the magazine—will outlive him, and maybe not mean so much to others . . .

Much love to both,

Joyce

February 24, 2008.
To Edmund White

Just got back from a two-mile hike in the snow through the woods & around a lake! Except for Ron & Susan, I would never have done this . . .

The night of Ray's death, I took out all my painkiller pills—assembled over the years since I'd never used most of them—plus now I have my "sleeping pills"—and feel that I can use these if things become unworkable. Nietzsche said, "The thought of suicide can get one through many a long night." But I feel such an affectionate tug for my friends—for just a few friends—that I would not seriously do this of course. It is more of a theoretical option . . .

Some of my anxiety has lessened in fact since "the worst" has happened. I had worried terribly about my parents, too, for years. But they lived full lives and died at the right time, quite merciful deaths. Ray died too young. I just can't grasp it.

Thank you for being here yesterday. You are such a solace just by existing. I feel such love for you, I am infinitely grateful.

Joyce

February 24, 2008.
To Gloria Vanderbilt

The beautiful icon [of St. Theresa] is now on my dresser facing my bed . . . Each night I get through is a small triumph.

Love,
Joyce

III

THE BASILISK

Yes, it is a physical and emotional test of endurance.
We shall speak further when we are sitting down
face to face. In the meantime, my only advice is
to sleep all you can and eat when and if you can.
Grief is exhausting and requires the strength of
an Olympic athlete. Just at a time when you can
neither sleep nor eat. I wish you didn't have to go
through this. My heart is in your corner.

—Barbara Ascher

Suffer, Joyce. Ray was worth it.

—Gail Godwin

28

"Beady Dead Eyes Like Gems"

At first—glimpsed at the periphery of my vision, or shimmering against my eyelids when I shut my eyes—not an actual object to be *seen*—it's confused with the flood of new, dreaded things that has entered my life since my husband's death as a virulent infection enters a bloodstream—it is both *there*, and *not-there*.

Sometimes the optical nerve generates patches of light resembling jagged wings, sparkly zigzag figures that soar and float about in your vision but gradually fade. (If you're lucky and don't have a brain lesion.) And there are the hallucinatory migrainous images—"fortifications"— "scintillating scotomata"—"scrolls"—"whorls"—"spirals"—"topological misperceptions"—about which Oliver Sacks has written an entire book titled *Migraine*. But this thing—if it's a *thing*, exactly—seems different, more personal, more pointedly directed at *me*.

At times it appears to be sheerly light, luminous. But it's a dark-luminous like ebony. Yet not a smooth beautiful ebony, more a rough-textured ebony. Something glimpsed at the bottom of the sea? It is covered with a rough shell, or scaly armor. Shimmering eyes—not-living eyes—beady dead eyes like gems.

What does it want with me?—I wonder.

If I shake my head, the dark-shimmering thing disappears. If I rub my eyes, that are nearly always watering.

Unmistakably, my vision has deteriorated in the brief period of time since Ray was hospitalized. Driving in the dark home from the hospital, I'd begun to notice a softening of objects, a kind of haze.

Often my eyes are so flooded with moisture—tears perversely caused by overly dry eyes—that I have to blink repeatedly, but even then I can't see clearly. A few years ago following Lasik surgery the vision in both my eyes was highly precise for distances, remarkable for one who'd been myopic for most of her life, now suddenly all that astounding vision is lost, corroding. A wave of panic—not the first of the morning, or even the hour—sweeps over me *But if I go blind? How can I take care of this household? What will become of us?*

Vaguely it seems to me—when I am not thinking coherently—that Ray will be coming home from the hospital, eventually. After the car wreck, after a stay in Telemetry—I will be responsible for him, his well-being. I am eager for this opportunity to prove myself, as I'd failed so miserably just recently . . . In this vague fantasy, Ray is not fully aware that I'd abandoned him, in any case Ray is not one to criticize or rebuke.

Ray is not one to accuse *Where were you! When I needed you where were you! Why did you stay away so long! What did you think would happen to me, if you left me alone in that terrible place?*

29

THE LOST HUSBAND

And then, I am beginning to think *He will be lost to me. He will disappear.*

I am beginning to think *Maybe I never knew him, really. Maybe I knew him only superficially—his deeper self was hidden from me.*

In our marriage it was our practice not to share anything that was upsetting, depressing, demoralizing, tedious—unless it was unavoidable. Because so much in a writer's life can be distressing—negative reviews, rejections by magazines, difficulties with editors, publishers, book designers—disappointment with one's own work, on a daily/hourly basis!—it seemed to me a very good idea to shield Ray from this side of my life as much as I could. For what is the purpose of sharing your misery with another person, except to make that person miserable, too?

In this way, I walled off from my husband the part of my life that is "Joyce Carol Oates"—which is to say, my writing career.

As he handled our finances generally, so Ray handled the finances generated by this career. As he didn't read most of what I wrote so he didn't read most reviews of this work, whether good, bad, or indifferent. Always it has astonished me that writers married to each other—for instance Joan Didion and John Gregory Dunne—should share virtually every page they write; my friends Richard Ford and his wife, Kristina, not only share each page they write but read their work to each other—

a test of marital love which one as "prolific" as JCO is said to be would dare not risk.

Perhaps it was naive, to wish to share only good news with a husband. I have always dreaded being the bearer of bad news to anyone—I take no pleasure in seeing another person pained, or distressed—especially not anyone for whom I feel affection.

Nor do I like being told upsetting news—unless there is a good reason. I can't help but feel that there is an element of cruelty, if not sadism, in friends telling one another upsetting things for no reason except to observe their reactions.

On his side, Ray shielded me from the more burdensome side of *Ontario Review* and our—to me—hopelessly complicated financial situation; he oversaw the household—does the roof need repairing? Does the house need repainting? Does the driveway need repaving?—somehow, Ray had access to this knowledge, that totally eluded me. While I oversaw housecleaning, Ray oversaw the outdoor care of the property. Once, in Detroit, when the subject of husbands came up, my women friends were incredulous to hear that, if something awful happened to me, I would be reluctant to tell Ray; still less could they believe that Ray would shield me from his problems. One of the women said enviously that her husband would never "let her get away" with not knowing his problems even if there was nothing she could do to help him.

But why? I asked.

Out of spite, she said.

And I'd thought *Then he can't love you. If he wants to upset you.*

Ray would never wish to upset me. Very likely Ray shielded from me all sorts of things I never knew, and will never know.

Maybe in fact Ray was very frightened in the hospital. Maybe he had a premonition that he would never return home—if he had, he would not have told me.

I don't think that this is so. I think that he had no idea that he would die, any more than his doctors seemed to have known. But if it had been the case, Ray would not have told me.

Maybe our way of "shielding" each other from distress was inadvertently a way of eluding each other. Maybe there was something cowardly about my reluctance to acknowledge to my husband, the person to whom I was closest, that all was not perfect in my life—far from it, much of the time.

But then, I have walled myself off from "Joyce Carol Oates" as well. I can't think that this has been a mistaken strategy.

In any case it isn't one I can modify, at this point in my life.

But now I am thinking—obviously Ray revealed only a part of himself to me. Obviously, he kept much to himself. If he had not a "secret" life—(though possibly he had)—still there was an eclipsed side to his personality, of which I had no clue.

Where have you gone?
    What has happened to us?
    How can I reach you?—is there no way, not ever?

As in a dream of forbidden knowledge I am drawn to Ray's things. Most rooms of our house are beginning to be difficult to enter but none more than Ray's study—his "office"—for his presence is so strong here, I'm left breathless. *Maybe he has stepped out for a minute. In the bathroom maybe. Getting the mail.* Yet I am drawn to Ray's desk, his files, the shelves of his closets stacked with manuscripts, documents, page proofs and cover designs of bygone seasons. Repeatedly I study Ray's calendar as if in the hope of discovering something new, mysterious—it's fascinating to me how assiduously Ray marked the days of his life, and how full most of the days were; and then, each day is crossed off with a triumphant black X. As if Ray had taken particular satisfaction in crossing off his days when they were completed. As if he'd had no idea that these days would be finite; that these Xs made with a Magic Marker pen were accumulating into what would be his recent past; as if, beyond the next months— March, April, May—those wonderfully open, empty, blank days would never be filled.

I think with horror of the future, in which Ray will not exist.

Already it has been a week since his death. (How is this possible! Each minute has seemed excruciating.)

It isn't just for emotional reasons that I must contemplate Ray's calendar, of course. So much *Ontario Review* business is tied to the calendar—there is the deadline for paying the Hopewell Township property tax—a notation for a Culligan delivery—an appointment with Dr. S___—a dentist's appointment—and (of course!) recycling days—trash pickup days. I begin to feel such sadness, such sorrow, I have to put the calendar aside.

The phone on Ray's desk—Ray's business line—begins to ring. Never would I pick up this receiver, for the caller will say *Is Ray Smith there?*

Or *Hi Joyce. Can I speak to Ray please?*

Sometime later, I'll check the voice mail. Maybe. If I can force myself. Or maybe not.

It occurs to me now, I will search through Ray's personal papers. I will read—(re)read—all his published work—what I can find of his writing projects. When we'd moved to Princeton from Windsor, in August 1978, Ray had brought a cache of writing projects with him, some of which he'd completed—an essay on the poetry of Ted Hughes, for instance. And other things—notes, sketches, a draft of a novel—parts of which I'd seen. Ray had lost interest in writing, very much preferring to be an editor and publisher, and had ceased thinking about these things, so far as I knew. But I am excited, for once—I am feeling hopeful. I think *I will get to know my husband better. It isn't too late!*

"How Are You?"

This query has always been baffling to me! For I have no idea how I *am*, usually.

Far more logical to reply *How do I appear to you? That's how I am.*

For truly, my "self" is a swirl of atoms not unlike the more disintegrated paintings of J. M. W. Turner—almost, if you peer closely, you can see *something* amid the atoms, perhaps on the brink of coalescing into a *figure*—but maybe not.

Even when Ray was alive, and I was Ray Smith's wife and not yet Ray Smith's widow, I found it difficult to respond to this totally innocent, totally conventional social query.

"How am I? I'm fine! And how are you?"

From time to time, in a social situation, an individual will acknowledge that things aren't so good, maybe he/she isn't so fine, which will derail the conversation in a more personal, pointed direction. But this is rare, and must be handled with extreme delicacy. For it's in violation of social decorum and people will be sympathetic initially—but finally, maybe not.

Now, when people see me, when they ask, often with tender solicitude, *How are you, Joyce?*—I assume that they mean *How are you managing, after Ray's death?* Usually I tell them that I am doing very well. For I am, I think—doing very well.

Interminable days have passed, and interminable nights—and *I am still here*. This is amazing to me.

More and more it seems to me, I may have made a wrong decision at the time of Ray's death. Picking up the phone, calling my friends—making of my plight their concern. Making them feel that they are responsible for me.

A nobler gesture would have been to erase myself. For there is something terribly wrong in remaining here—in our house, in our old life—talking and laughing with friends—when Ray is gone.

I feel that others might think this way about me, too. For there *is* something ignoble, selfish, in continuing to live as if nothing has been altered.

But I am not strong enough, I think.

And then—so I tell myself!—I had—I have—many responsibilities to which Ray would have entrusted me. And in the terms of Ray's will, he has entrusted me.

Though Ray has left me, it is not so easy for me to leave *him*.

"What do you want with me!"

The thing with the beady dead gem-like eyes—that thing, which now more clearly resembles an ugly lizard of some kind, or a Gila monster, than a sea creature—is ever more frequent now in the corner of my eye, alone here in the house.

Erase yourself—of course!

What a hypocrite you are, to pretend not to know this.

So, it's good not to be alone! Except, when I am not-alone, I am in the company of other people, and aware of the fact that the one person I wish might be there is not there.

Thinking always of yourself. Only of yourself. Hypocrite!

This is true. I am obsessed with my "self" now—whatever it is, it seems to be about to break and be scattered by the wind, like milkweed pollen. Though the "self" has no core yet it is a nexus of random sounds, voices—some of them tender, and some of them jeering, accusatory—

Love to my honey and my kitties.

Hypocrite!

Really, I have no idea how I *am*. I have become a sort of wraith, or zombie—I know that I am *here* but have a very vague idea of what *here* is.

I have been observed laughing, with friends. My laughter is not forced but seems natural, spontaneous.

I have been observed staring into space, in the company of friends. Though I am aware of being observed—I try to shake myself, into wakefulness—sometimes it isn't so easy, to haul myself back.

Talk at Princeton gatherings is of politics, mainly. America has become a rabidly politicized nation since the election of George W. Bush— since 9/11, ever more a virulently divided nation—it is quite natural that the personal life is submerged in the public life but how lonely, how empty, how spiritually depleted it seems, to one on the outside.

And so, often I leave for home early. Where Ray and I often stayed late—and were among the last to leave a party—I am now the first person to leave.

When I am departed, my friends talk about me, I suppose.

I hope that they are saying *Joyce is doing very well isn't she!*

I hope that they are saying *There's no need to worry about Joyce.*

I can't bear it, if they are saying *How tired Joyce looks!*

If they are saying *How thin Joyce looks!*

Poor Joyce!

Often when I am driving our car, I begin to cry for no clear reason. Often it's night, I am dreading my return to the (empty, deserted) house in which, on the dining room table, "sympathy baskets" and "floral displays" are still crammed together, and wilted petals are strewn underfoot like tiny bruised faces. Only a light or two will be burning—no longer is the house lit up as if for a festive occasion—the first instant, of unlocking the door—(unless it's unlocked, I'd forgotten to lock it)—is the hardest, a horrible moment—then, if I can manage, I will slip into the bedroom without having to pass through most of the house—though I can't avoid passing by Ray's (darkened, deserted) study where, on his telephone, a red light will be blinking—new messages! Unanswered messages!— these responsibilities clawing at me, I am too exhausted to contemplate.

But in the car—there's a kind of free-fall no-man's-land inside a car—in which one is neither *here* nor *there* but *in transit*.

If I am in tears while driving, by the time I reach my destination I am no longer crying—I am *fine*.

A widow's emotions—I think this must be generally true—resemble the "lake effect" of the Great Lakes. One moment, a clear sky and sunshine; minutes later, enormous dark thunderheads moving like battalions across the sky; soon after, a lightning storm, churning waves, danger . . . You learn that you can't predict the weather from visible evidence. You learn to be cautious. The "lake effect" is ordinary time, speeded up.

But I have become so—*sad*. I have become one of those blighted/ wounded/limping/sinister malcontents in Elizabethan-Jacobean drama— an observer who glances about seeing, not happily smiling individuals, not friends whom I love but individuals destined for terrible, tragic ends—the women to lose their husbands, sooner than they would expect; the men to become ill, to age, to vanish within a few years. I feel a kind of sick terror for my friends, who have been so kind to me—what, one day, will happen to *them*?

Of all malcontents, Hamlet is the most eloquent.

> *How weary, stale, flat and unprofitable,*
> *Seem to me the uses of this world!* . . .

This is the very voice of paralysis, depression—yet it seems to me in my zombie-state an utterly astute reading of the human condition.

Still, one must not say so. One must *try*.

Asked how she is it is a good idea for the widow to say, brightly, like everyone else, "How am I?—fine."

Back home, I am likely to replay Ray's final message—the one he'd made from his hospital bed just a few hours before he died.

Though sometimes, I call our home number from my cell phone, to hear Ray's recorded voice that is so comforting, and which, when they call this number, our friends will hear for a very long time.

Neither Joyce nor I can come to the phone right now but if you leave a detailed message and your phone number . . . we will get back to you soon. Thank you for calling.

31

"Bells for John Whiteside's Daughter"

In Detroit, in the mid-1960s, when Ray taught English at Wayne State University, one of his courses was "Introduction to Literature" and among the poems he assigned his students was the elegy "Bells for John Whiteside's Daughter" by John Crowe Ransom.

This beautiful short poem, Ray read to me with such feeling, in his deep, subtly modulated voice, I am moved to tears recalling it. Reading the poem, which I haven't looked at in years, I realize that I've memorized it, and I've memorized it in my husband's voice.

> *There was such speed in her little body,*
> *And such lightness in her footfall,*
> *It is no wonder that her brown study*
> *Astonishes us all.*

Was this Ray's favorite poem? When I'd first met him in Madison, Wisconsin, Ray could recite a number of classic poems—sonnets by Shakespeare, John Donne, and Milton ("When I Consider How My Light Is Spent"); and he was much admiring of Whitman, Hopkins, Frost, and William Carlos Williams, as well as poetry by a number of our contemporaries whom he was to publish in *Ontario Review*—but no poem moved him as deeply as "Bells for John Whiteside's Daughter."

It is his reading aloud of this poem that is imprinted in my memory—
my handsome young husband, his voice quavering with emotion, in our
house on Sherbourne Road in the small room at the front of the house,
a kind of sunroom, where we sat most evenings to read or prepare our
classes for the next day.

How I wish I could remember what Ray and I said to each other, on
one of our ordinary evenings! In that little room, one of the few comfortable rooms in that not very comfortable house, where for so many nights
after dinner we sat together on a dark blue sofa facing a window.

Outside, our lawn, a sidewalk, the street and a facing beige-brick
house—this, too, is vividly imprinted in my memory, though I have not
thought of it, still less seen it, in decades.

What could have so absorbed us, in those days? I know that we talked
a good deal about our teaching, our classes and colleagues—Ray at Wayne
State, me at the University of Detroit—but all this is vanished now. What
was urgent, crucial in our lives, even upsetting—all is vanished. Virtually no friends remain from that time. We'd given parties in our large
brick Colonial house—almost, I can see our living room with its oddly
dark-blue walls, crowded with people—enlivened with laughter—but
the faces are blurred, indistinct.

Some have died—my closest woman friend, prematurely. Others
have moved away, altered their lives—our closest Jesuit friend, a colleague at the University of Detroit who'd been a prominent member of
the English Department, now no longer a Jesuit, married and living in
Texas . . . *Tom Porter has left the Church! My God.*

Many evenings we'd spent in the company of our Detroit friends
and colleagues and of all those evenings, scarcely a shred of memory
remains. Of all the evenings Ray and I spent together, the meals we prepared together, the house we kept together, the shopping excursions we
went on together—on Livernois Avenue, and at the Northland Shopping Center; the countless times we walked together in our residential
neighborhood and in nearby Palmer Park, holding hands—I can remember so few.

This is terrifying to me—so much of our lives, lost.

Except, there is "Bells for John Whiteside's Daughter"—

There was such speed in her little body,
And such lightness in her footfall,
It is no wonder her brown study
Astonishes us all.

Her wars were bruited in our high window.
We looked among orchard trees and beyond
Where she took arms against her shadow,
Or harried unto the pond

The lazy geese, like a snow cloud
Dripping their snow on the green grass,
Tricking and stopping, sleepy and proud,
Who cried in goose, Alas,

For the tireless heart within the little
Lady with rod that made them rise
From their noon apple-dreams and scuttle
Goose-fashion under the skies!

But now go the bells, and we are ready,
In one house we are sternly stopped
To say we are vexed at her brown study,
Lying so primly propped.

Now John Crowe Ransom has been dropped from the American poetry canon. No one younger than sixty, probably, has even heard of this poem. Greatly admired in his time, and a figure of considerable influence, Ransom is a casualty of the academic-literary culture wars of the late twentieth century—a Caucasian male poet like Delmore Schwartz, Howard Nemerov, James Dickey, James Wright.

All of them, casualties of time.

32

THE NEST

Nothing is so wonderful in my posthumous life as retiring to my nest!

Even to die here—*especially* to die here—will be wonderful, I think.

This "nest"—in our bed—on my side of the bed—is a swirl of pillows, bedclothes, a rainbow-hued quilt crocheted by my mother—books, bound galleys, copyedited manuscripts and page proofs, drafts of things I am working on—whatever I am working on, or trying to work on, each night. And now, in the nest, I am reading—rereading—all that I can find of Ray's published work.

When we were alive—when Ray was alive—I did not read in bed, ever. I did not have a "nest" in bed. I would have considered working in bed, especially, clumsy and messy and not very efficient—excusable if one were ill, or an invalid. Our evenings at home were spent in the living room, on our sofa, where at opposite ends of the sofa we read—or Ray copyedited manuscripts, or read page proofs—or I took notes on whatever it was I was writing at the time, or trying to write—the effort of "Joyce Carol Oates" to compose something of more than fleeting value out of our—(unknown to us at the time)—rapidly fleeting lives.

Now, I have to wonder if I'd spent too much time in that other world—the world of my/the imagination—and not enough time with my husband.

This nest, that draws me to it like water swirling down a drain, is my respite from the day, and from thoughts like this; my reward for having gotten through the day. It is a place where I am not "Joyce Carol Oates"—still less "Joyce Carol Smith"—whose primary worth has been to sign legal documents multiple times, a smile clamped in her face like a steel trap. In the nest, there is anonymity. There is peace, solitude, ease. There is not the likelihood of being asked *How are you, Joyce?*—still less the likelihood of being asked, as I am beginning to be asked *Will you keep your house, or stay in it?*—a question that makes me quiver with rage and indignation though it is a perfectly reasonable question to put to a widow; as one might reasonably ask of a terminally ill cancer patient *Is your will in order? Have you made peace with your Maker?*

In the vicinity of the nest no voice intrudes. In the vicinity of the nest, except for, sometimes, the TV—turned to one or the other of the classical music channels on cable TV—there is a reliable silence. The nest is a warm-lighted space amid darkness, for the rest of the house is darkened at night. In a belated effort to save on fuel—for I have been careless about leaving the furnace on too high, without Ray to monitor the thermostat—as I've been careless about leaving doors unlocked, even at times ajar—and worse—I make it a point now to turn down the furnace at night—I know that Ray would approve of this—and so much of the house is chilly, and forbidding.

I don't undress, entirely. Partly because I am so very cold—sometimes my teeth chatter convulsively—unless I am feeling feverish, and my skin is sweaty-clammy—but mostly because I want to be prepared for leaving the bed quickly—running from the house if summoned. Never will I forget—I hear the voice often—as I see the lizard-creature with the beady dead gem-like eyes—*Mrs. Smith? You'd better come to the hospital as soon as you can—your husband is still alive.* Especially, I wear warm socks.

If you are likely to be summoned unexpectedly from bed, it is a very good idea not to go to bed barefoot.

Precious minutes are wasted pulling on socks! In a time of desperation, nothing is more awkward.

And so I have become, even in the nest-sanctuary, *incapable of removing my clothes* at night, and wearing what is called *night-wear* as I'd used to wear, in my former life.

In fact it has come to seem to me utterly brazen, reckless, and plain ignorant, that one would even consider *undressing*, and making oneself needlessly *vulnerable*, like a turtle slipping out of its shell.

Is he still alive? Is my husband still alive?

Yes. Your husband is still alive.

Though the nest is very comforting, and very welcoming—though *the nest* has become the (emotional, intellectual, spiritual) core of the widow's life—yet it should be acknowledged that the nest is not an antidote for insomnia.

When I can't sleep—which would be every night unless I take a sleeping pill—or a capsule of something called Lorazepam ("for anxiety") which our family doctor has prescribed for me—the nest is my place of great solace and comfort and though I am awake, I am not the desperate person I am during the day. Here, to the extent to which I can concentrate, I am able to mimic my old self to a degree, by taking a sort of pleasure—"pleasure" might be an exaggeration, but let it stand—in going through page proofs for an upcoming review, or working on a draft of a short story abandoned at the start of Ray's hospitalization; there are myriad scattered notes for a novel, which I will not be able to write, but there is a completed novel which I'd intended to revise, and may soon begin revising; this novel, about loss, grief, and mourning, in a mythical upstate New York river-city called Sparta, will come to be primary in my life, if not indeed a lifeline; but at the present time, I am not able to concentrate on even rereading it, let alone undertaking a revision.

How frail a vessel, prose fiction! How fleeting and insubstantial, the "life of the mind"! I must fight against the terrible lethargy, despair and self-contempt so many of us felt after the catastrophe of 9/11 when the very act of writing seemed of so little consequence as to be a kind of joke.

Words seem futile. In the face of such catastrophe . . .

Yet, working on short things—reviews, essays, stories—is a solace of a kind. Almost, immersed in work, I can forget the circumstances of my life—almost!—and if I become restless in bed I leave the nest to prowl about in Ray's study, which is the next room; or, I drift into my study, which is on the other side of Ray's, to answer e-mails, which has already come to mean a great deal to me, far more than it had ever meant when Ray was alive; but always my late-night excursions are predicated by the fact that I will return to the nest in a few minutes.

The possibility of remaining awake through the night, outside the nest, is frankly terrifying.

And if I am very lucky our tiger cat Reynard will appear suddenly in the bedroom—with a leap, onto our bed—he will curl up to sleep with me not exactly beside me but at the foot of the bed, on Ray's side, where as if inadvertently—in the feline imagination, such nuances are not accidental—he may press against my leg; but if I speak to him cajolingly—*Nice Reynard! Nice kitty!*—or reach down to stroke his somewhat coarse fur, he may take offense at such a liberty, leap down from the bed and hurry away into another part of the darkened house.

I can't bring myself to recall the summer day ten or eleven years ago when Ray brought Reynard home from a local animal shelter, to surprise me. We'd lost a much-loved older cat—I hadn't thought that I was ready for another so soon—but when Ray brought the tiny tiger kitten home, mewing piteously for his mother, or for food and affection, my heart was completely won.

And how I loved Ray, for these impulsive, seemingly imprudent unilateral gestures that turned out so well.

The other, younger cat Cherie, though the friendlier of the two, and the less anxious, has steadfastly refused to enter this bedroom since Ray's departure and will not enter it no matter how I cajole her. Cherie will not sleep with me, or near me, in this nocturnal nest-life, nor will she enter Ray's study when I am in it, though she might sleep in his desk chair at other times; she refuses to enter my study, where I sit working, or trying to work, at my desk. Only if I sit on the living room sofa—which I must now force myself to do—as I'd done when Ray and I read together in the evening, Cherie will hurry eagerly to me and leap into my lap and remain for a few restless minutes—until she sees that the other individual who shared this sofa with us isn't here, isn't coming, and so Cherie leaps down and departs without a backward glance.

The cats blame me, I know. Animal reproach is not less palpable for being voiceless, illogical.

The nest is my solace for such cruel—such ridiculous—cat-rejections that in the radically diminished household in which I now find myself, a hapless cartoon character marooned on a shrinking island, actually loom large, and have the power to *wound*.

Absurd, to be hurt by an animal's capricious behavior. Yet more absurd, to be so reduced in scale, so less-than-human, to care about an animal's behavior.

A fact of the widow-life: all things are equally profound as all things are equally trivial, futile, pointless.

As all acts—actions—"activities"—are to the widow alternatives to suicide, thus of more or less equal significance.

Except—the widow must not say such things of course. Far better to be reticent in grief, mute and stoic. Far better to hide away in her nest than to venture into the bright peopled world outside her door.

During the week of the hospital vigil, often late at night huddled in the nest I would stare at the television screen a few yards away, entranced—it seemed too much effort for me to concentrate on reading, or on my own work—restlessly I would scroll through the channels—for insomnia makes of us explorers of the most bizarre landscapes: I was fascinated and appalled in equal measure by a rerun of the *X-Files*—a popular television series Ray and I had never seen during its run—in which the intrepid FBI agents pursue a man whose kiss turns women into rotting phosphorescent corpses—the female victims are so physically repulsive, even the FBI agents are stunned, revolted—here is an allegory of sexual contamination worthy of Nathaniel Hawthorne, though somewhat crudely portrayed, and self-consciously sensational. Watching late-night TV, I came quickly to discover, is like trolling through the uncharted deeps of the ocean—a roiling Sargasso Sea of high-decibel melodrama, gunfire, car chases, helicopter pursuits, CNN and FOX News repeats—the collective underside of our culture—the banality of our fetishes. What a lovely silence, switching off the TV to hear wind, rain pelting against a window.

And there was a time, later, shortly after Ray died, when weirdly at 4 A.M. there appeared on the TV screen a replay of the historic *What's My Line?*—the animated ghost-figures of Steve Allen, Dorothy Kilgallen, Arlene Francis, Bennett Cerf, and John Daly of a long-ago decade preceding color TV—suddenly so vivid, so real, familiar to me as long-lost relatives. This low-tech show, allegedly the most popular game show in the history of network television, on the air from 1950 to 1967, was one I'd watched for years with my younger brother Fred and my mother, on our small black-and-white television set, upstairs in our half of the old farmhouse in which we'd lived with my mother's Hungarian step-parents in rural Millersport, New York. How impressed we'd been by the witty repartee of the panelists and their coolly affable moderator John Daly! Yet I don't recall a word we'd said to one another.

Why is so much lost? So much of our spoken language? It's said that distant memories are stored in the brain—far more securely in the brain than recent memories—but so little is accessible to consciousness, of what value is this storage? Our aural memories are weak, unreliable. We have all heard friends repeating fragments of conversations inaccurately—yet emphatically; not only language is lost but the tone, the emphasis, the *meaning*.

My loss is compounded by the unusual fact that Ray and I had no correspondence—not ever. Not once had we written to each other, for we'd rarely been apart more than a night at a time and, for the first fifteen or so years of our marriage, very rarely even one night.

We had had no "courtship"—no interlude of being apart, that would have warranted letter writing. From the first evening we'd met—Sunday, October 23, 1960—at a graduate student gathering in the massive student union at the University of Wisconsin, overlooking Lake Mendota—we'd seen each other every day.

We were engaged on November 23 of that year and, to maintain some small constancy, we were married on January 23, 1961.

It wasn't until years later that as "JCO" I began to be invited to visit colleges and universities, usually just overnight. At first Ray came with me but then, as the invitations increased, I began more often to travel alone, and so we were apart more frequently in recent years.

And so I'd gone to U.C. Riverside. On the eve of Ray's illness.

Of course I think that possibly he might not have become ill, if I'd stayed home. He'd caught a cold—what could be more harmless! Whatever he'd done that he might not have done if I'd been home, I don't know. *You are being ridiculous. This is reasoning too finely!* Difficult not to feel sick with guilt, that a husband has died, and you would seem to have been helpless to prevent it.

And then, Ray hadn't wanted to go to the ER. You'd insisted. Maybe he would have done better at home, untreated.

Always when I was away, I called Ray in the late evening. After my
reading, after a dinner in my "honor"—my hosts are invariably very
nice, very interesting and engaging individuals—most of them academ-
ics, like us—and so I would tell Ray about my reading, about the dinner;
and Ray would tell me what was far more interesting to me, about what
he'd done that day—what had happened in our life, while I was away.

All this, you have lost. The happiness of domestic life, without which the
small—even the colossal— triumphs of a "career" are shallow, mocking.

But this is wrong! In the nest, huddled beneath my mother's quilt,
listening to a Chopin prelude on the classical TV channel, I am supposed
to be shielded from such thoughts.

It is the night of February 26—or, rather, the early morning of February
27—2:40 A.M.—a full week after Ray's death. Earlier this evening I had
dinner with friends—it isn't possible for me to "have dinner" alone in
this house, or anywhere—but with friends, a meal is not only possible
but wonderful—except that Ray is missing . . . In the nest I have spread
out some of Ray's published work, and have been reading an essay on
Coleridge's famous poem "Christabel"—an "enigmatic fragment," Ray
calls it—titled "Christabel and Geraldine: The Marriage of Life and
Death," which appeared in the *Bucknell Review* in 1968. Astonishing to
discover so much in Ray's essay that relates to our shared interests—in
the English and Scottish popular ballads, for instance—and there is the
striking stanza from a poem of Richard Crashaw which Ray quotes:

> *She never undertook to know*
> *What death with love should have to doe;*
> *Nor has she e'er yet understood*
> *Why to show love, she should shed blood*

How powerful these lines are, how vividly they come back to me, like
a half-recalled dream! The Crashaw poem had made such an impression
on me, I'd appropriated the second line for the title of a short story—
"What Death with Love Should Have to Do"—a mordant love story of
sorts, of 1966.

(I should reread this old story of mine, that was reprinted in my second collection of short stories, *Upon the Sweeping Flood*. I know, I should reread it to recapture that time, those emotions. But I can't. In the nest I feel enervated, paralyzed. I just can't.)

As I read Ray's critical essays of this long-ago time, I realize how close we'd been . . . We had shared every detail of our teaching jobs—our classes, our colleagues, the high points and low points and surprises of our lives—we'd discussed the Coleridge poem together and I'd read drafts of Ray's essay—our lives were entwined like the conflicting emotions of love/hate—beauty/a snaky sort of ugliness—in the haunting Coleridge poem.

I am made to think, not for the first time, that in my writing I have plunged ahead—head-on, heedlessly one might say—or "fearlessly"—into my own future: this time of utter raw anguished loss. Though I may have had, since adolescence, a kind of intellectual/literary precocity, I had not *experienced* much; nor would I *experience* much until I was well into middle-age—the illnesses and deaths of my parents, this unexpected death of my husband. *We play at paste till qualified for pearl* says Emily Dickinson. *Playing at paste* is much of our early lives. And then, with the violence of a door slammed shut by wind rushing through a house, life catches up with us.

In 1966, I was twenty-eight years old. I had suffered no losses of any magnitude—not one! I had no actual knowledge—scarcely a glimmering of knowledge—of what Crashaw might have meant by "What death with love should have to doe"—"Why to show love, she should shed blood."

When we'd first met, at a time in my life when I was both very lonely and very excited about the future—my future—as a graduate student in a distinguished English department—Ray entered my life as an "older man"—older by eight years—in his final year at Madison, completing an ambitious Ph.D. dissertation on Jonathan Swift, and undertaking to look for his first academic job. To use the jargon of academic English studies Ray was an "eighteenth-century man"—he seemed to me wonderfully poised, informed, astonishingly well read in the areas in which I'd just begun to read—Old English, Chaucer, pre-Renaissance drama and Renaissance drama excluding Shakespeare—though he was very kind to me, and patient with my naivete in most matters, his humor was markedly sly, sardonic and satiric—his literary idols were Swift, the great master of "savage indignation"; the brilliant satiric/comic poet Alexander Pope, whose masterpiece "The Rape of the Lock" Ray could recite at length; the legendary Samuel Johnson, less in Johnson's own somewhat didactic work than in the great Boswell biography; and the very witty playwrights William Congreve (*The Way of the World*) and Richard Sheridan (*The School for Scandal*). Ray's single book-length critical study is *Charles Churchill* (1977) which he began with initial enthusiasm—Churchill is no Swift, but he is a devastating satirist, at least intermittently—that quickly faded as Ray's interests shifted from academic studies to establishing our literary magazine *Ontario Review*, begun in 1974. By the time Ray finished his book on Churchill he'd come to dislike his subject thoroughly, like so many who undertake in-depth book-length studies of literary figures entwined with biographical material; making of the sardonic political satirist a figure of some depth and intellectual interest was a challenge Ray felt hadn't been worth the effort. By degrees Ray's interests shifted from the eighteenth century to twentieth-century poetry; he would write a series of sharp, insightful, appreciative essays and reviews dealing with H.D., Pablo Neruda, Richard Eberhart, Howard Nemerov, Ted Hughes, James Dickey, William Heyen (whom Ray would later publish in *Ontario Review*).

We'd particularly shared a love of Nemerov's poetry. It's thrilling to come across these lines of Nemerov's at the conclusion of Ray's essay on the poet which appeared in the *Southern Review* in 1974—lines indelibly imprinted in my memory:

> *O swallows, swallows, poems are not*
> *The point. Finding again the world,*
> *That is the point, where loveliness*
> *Adorns intelligible things*
> *Because the mind's eye lit the sun.*
> *—"The Blue Swallows"*

Though now—in this posthumous state—*finding again the world* doesn't seem to me very likely.

In the nest, reading—(re)reading—this material, I am beginning to shiver violently, though I don't think—I am sure—that I'm unhappy. I can't seem to stop trembling, I must go into my bathroom to run hot water on my hands, that have grown icy. How strange this is! I've been thoroughly engrossed in my husband's literary criticism—I'd totally forgotten that he had once reviewed for the journal *Literature and Psychology*, and that he'd ranged far afield to publish a brief piece on Dostoyevsky's *Crime and Punishment*—a novel we'd both taught in the 1970s—yet now this fit of shivering has come over me, even my teeth are chattering.

On my bedside table is Ray's novel manuscript, on which he'd worked for years in the 1960s, but which he'd never completed. I can't recall if I saw the most recent draft, or if for some reason Ray hadn't shown it to me; I think that he'd intended to revise it, but set it aside. I am eager to read this novel which I found in Ray's closet, which has been untouched for years, but I am beginning to feel some apprehension, too. I wonder if Ray would want me to be reading this manuscript, still far from completion; I don't think that, since moving to Princeton in 1978, he'd so much as glanced at it, and had long since ceased alluding to it. I look at the first page—the title is *Black Mass*—the manuscript looks old, worn—very like a manuscript that has been hidden away at the back of a closet, forgotten for decades—and I feel very sad suddenly.

This is a mistake.

You don't want to read it.

What you don't know about your husband has been hidden from you for a purpose.

And in any case your husband is gone, and is not coming back.

You can resolve to be "brave"—"resourceful"—you can cheer yourself up by (re)reading his writing, or trying to—but he is not coming back, he is gone and he is not coming back.

A strange fact of Widowhood: such epiphanies come rushing at odd, unpredictable moments and yet—are forgotten almost at once. For, in the Widow's posthumous world, there is the most primitive sort of time: what has happened, irremediably, has somehow not-yet-happened; if the Widow can but turn back time, the most devastating of epiphanies can be erased.

33

GHOST ROOMS

Ghost rooms! One by one they are overtaking the house.

There is no volition in me, only in the rooms of this house.

During the hospital vigil—which was, for all its anxiety, *hopeful*—the rooms of the house were lighted in anticipation of a homecoming. Outdoor lights were left on—extravagantly, recklessly—through the day. There was a sharp scent of furniture polish, of Windex; a more perfumy scent of candles on the dining room table, newly removed from their cellophane wrappers. *I would make one of Ray's favorite dinners: grilled Scottish salmon with mushrooms, tomatoes, fennel, dill. He will be hungry for something other than hospital food, but—he will probably be tired and want to go to bed early.*

Now, most of the rooms are never lighted. Most of the rooms are off-limits to me, I dare not enter them, nor even glance into them.

But where is Ray? In which room is—my husband?

The outdoor lights are never on any longer. I am not so extravagant now. When these lights burn out, how will I replace them?

One by one, lights expiring.

And even the nest sometimes fails me, and so there is nowhere to hide.

The vigil continues, though there is no hope.

I did not dare to read Ray's novel, after all—I have put it carefully away for the time being.

The basilisk, that knows my heart more intimately than Ray ever knew it, understands my apprehension. It is the basilisk who supplies me with this wisdom.

If he'd wanted you to read it, he would have given it to you. You know this!

And sometimes—*Obviously, you failed him. You should have offered to read this manuscript when you might have helped him with it. Now, it's too late—you know this.*

Now the flurry of death-duties has abated, the siege is taking other forms. As virulent bacteria will mutate, to insure their virulent survival.

One by one regions of the house are becoming ghostly, unoccupied. The living room that was once so welcoming—the sofa, the white piano, the dark rose Chinese rug Ray and I selected for the space, when we'd first moved to Princeton. On the marble-topped coffee table we'd bought together in a furniture store in Detroit, in 1965, are Ray's books which I'd brought home from the hospital, at his end of the sofa—*Infidel, The Great Unraveling, Your Government Failed You.* Back issues of the *New York Review of Books* and the *New Yorker.*

Finally I've taken away the stacks of *Ontario Review* submissions. A scattering of pens and paper clips Ray had accumulated.

(Between the sofa cushions—and beneath the sofa—more pens, paper clips! As I'd once laughed plucking these out to show to Ray, now discovering them will be utterly depressing, like bad, sick jokes.)

But the living room is a ghost room, and the small solarium that opens off the living room where every day Ray and I had lunch—except when we sat outside on our terrace, in warm weather. This glass-walled room with a glass-topped round table and wicker chairs and a red-brick floor that seems, bizarrely, even in winter to attract spiders and, in abundance, the insect-prey of spiders, is an unlikely ghost room, since it is flooded with light on even overcast days—yet so it has become.

I will not enter the solarium for months, not even to sweep away the cobwebs.

I will avoid looking into the solarium. There is too much heartbreak in even a glimpse of the glass-topped table with the pale beige cloth place mats.

The farther wing of the house which we'd designed with such enthusiasm for my parents to stay in has become a ghost region—of course. This is a part of the house I can shut off from the rest—I have turned down the heat—there is no reason for me to step inside this space for days, weeks at a time. It was in this room, at the long white Parsons table, that Ray ate, or tried to eat, his final breakfast at home. Read, or tried to read, the *New York Times* for the final time at home.

We occupied the house often for hours at a time without speaking to each other, or needing to speak.

For this is the most exquisite of intimacies—not needing to speak.

Now, I dare not look across the courtyard at the plate-glass window that runs the length of the room. I think that I am terrified to see no one there. Yet more terrified, to risk seeing a reflection in the glass—for in our house there are myriad reflections of reflections in glass—a kind of vertigo springs from such reflections, like the sharp flash of light that precedes migraine.

Mirrors too have become off-limits, taboo. As if toxic fumes inhabit these ghost mirrors, you dare not draw too close.

Of course, you dare not glance heedlessly into any mirror!

The miniature rose for which I'd had some hope prevailed for a few days but has finally withered, and died—along with the (inedible) moss. Piles of mail—much of it unopened—on the dining room table and a squat pearl-colored ceramic vase festooned with a dazzling-white satin ribbon proclaiming COMFORT COMFORT COMFORT COMFORT at which I find myself staring as if hypnotized.

What are these *things*? Is there nothing in the universe except—*things*?

Sometime soon—in another day or two—I will begin to thank people. This is my resolve.

Except—I seem to have lost many of the cards that accompanied the sympathy gifts.

Except—I seem to be unable to force myself to read many of the cards and letters, which I have been putting away in a green tote bag in my study.

Is a widow expected not only to write thank-you notes for presents, but for sympathy cards and letters as well? My heart sinks at the prospect. What a cruel custom!

Yet I hope to be a conscientious widow. I hope to be a good widow. A Princeton acquaintance who'd lost her husband last year, a very nice woman whom everyone greatly respects, told me how painstaking she was to reply even to sympathy cards, how much pleasure she took in writing letters to the many people who'd written to her. *It was something for me to do. I was grateful.*

Unlike this conscientious Princeton widow I am not lacking for things to do—I am lacking for the time in which to do them, and for the energy with which to do them. I am lacking something essential in my soul—*I don't want to be a widow! Not me.*

As I hadn't wanted to play with dolls when I was a little girl. Breaking my grandmother's heart by blithely giving away an expensive doll she'd given me for my birthday—passing on the doll to a neighbor girl with a gesture of disdain—*I don't want to be a silly little girl! Not me.*

Now, this is adult life. Much more is expected of an adult and certainly of the widow of a good man. Though I am grateful for the kind attention I will probably just continue to hide away the cards and letters in the green bag with the vague resolve *I will read them later. I will answer them later. When I feel a little stronger.*

This may not be for a while. Months, years.

Eventually, I move the green bag into Ray's study. The corner of my room in which it was placed had become a corner from which my eyes shrank.

When I'd returned from the hospital that night, with Ray's toiletries, I'd replaced them in his medicine cabinet and on his sink counter. As I'd replaced his clothes in his closet and put into the laundry his (very mildly) soiled things and when I did the laundry, I put into his bureau his socks, underwear, shirt.

All of his clothes are in place. Not an article of clothing has been discarded. As all of his mail, papers, financial statements etc. are arranged on his desks and on the floor of his study.

His clothes are very nice clothes, I think. A camel's hair sport coat, still in its dry cleaner bag. A coat of soft dark-gray wool. Dress shirts, newly laundered and not yet worn. A blue-striped shirt which is a favorite of mine. Neckties—so many!—dating back to a long-ago era when men wore inch-wide ties—was this the 1970s?—my favorite is a silk tie imprinted with scenes from the Unicorn Tapestry which we'd bought at the Cloisters one giddy spring day when we'd slipped away from the interminable ceremony at the American Academy of Arts and Letters in Upper Manhattan.

Sure was glad to get out of there alive!—this phrase from a song of Bob Dylan—"The Day of the Locust"—(coincidentally, set at Princeton)—often passed between us.

Earlier today I was drawn again to look into the manuscript of *Black Mass*—Ray's unfinished novel. My heart beat so strangely, I could not continue.

There is some secret in Ray's life, I think. Or perhaps "secret" is too strong a term. Things of which he didn't care to speak, and after the early months in which we'd talked of our family backgrounds—as I suppose everyone does, when new to each other—these things passed into a kind of taboo territory about which I could not make inquiries.

Quietly the other evening at her house my poet-friend Alicia Ostriker said to me *I can't imagine what it's like to be you* and I said *I can't, either.*

Friends have been wonderful inviting me to their homes. I think that they are trying to watch over me—I think they must talk about me—I am deeply moved, but also anxious—I can't fail them—I am most fascinated by the absence of ghost rooms in their houses—the unwitting ease with which they speak, smile, laugh, move from room to room as if nothing is threatening to them—they will live forever, there is no *Why?* in their lives.

Sometimes if I fall asleep toward dawn it is very hard for me to wake up in the morning and very hard for me to leave the nest and the thought comes to me *Why?*

I am utterly mystified *why* there is life and not rather the cessation of life. The earliest effort of *life*—single-celled organisms in a sort of seething chemical soup—millions of years before Man—to prevail, not only to prevail but to persevere, not only to persevere but to triumph by way of reproduction—*Why?*

Once in a while when I am feeling a need for exercise, excitement, I run the vacuum cleaner through the rooms. I am always happy vacuuming—the thrumming noise drowns out the noises inside my head and, underfoot, a sudden smoothness in the texture of a carpet has the visceral feel of a spiritual calm, almost a blessing.

Well—not quite a *blessing*.

Ghost rooms! But there are ghost acts as well.

For instance, I can't any longer "prepare" meals in the kitchen. I am not able to eat anything that isn't flung together on the counter, spoonfuls of yogurt into a bowl, some cut-up (rotted?) fruit, a handful of (stale) cereal; maybe in the evening, a can of Campbell's soup (chicken with wild rice) and those Swedish rye-crisp crackers of which Ray was fond.

The prospect of sitting at the dining room table for any meal is repellent. All my "meals" are at my desk while I do e-mail or work or in the bedroom where I might watch TV, read or try to work.

When you live alone, eating a meal carries with it an element of scorn, mockery. For a meal is a social ritual or it is not a meal, it is just a plate heaped with food.

When I traveled, and Ray was home alone, he took advantage of my absence by bringing home a pizza. When I called home I would ask how he'd liked the pizza and he would say *It was all right* in the way of a shoulder shrug and so I would ask what had been wrong with it and Ray would say *It was too big for just one person* and I would say *Well, you didn't have to eat all of it—did you?* And Ray would say *I guess I did. I ate it all.*

Better even than meals hastily dumped into bowls are bottles of Odwalla fruit-blend drinks. These were left for me in the courtyard a day or two after Ray died, a dozen or more in a plastic shopping bag, from a woman friend who is also a novelist. *You have to eat, Joyce* she'd said *and you won't want to eat. So drink this.*

Bottles ideal for gripping while one is driving. The ordeal of eating alone is mitigated by subordinating eating to another activity, like driving a car.

Often I've noticed that friends/acquaintances who live alone seem to be eating when we speak on the phone. I'd assumed that this must be incidental, or that the individual had a nervous habit of eating continuously, hence could not stop just because I'd called; but now, I think that the opposite is the case—eating alone is so terrible, one must subordinate it to something else, like talking on the phone.

If I'm careless, or distracted, I will make a mistake—glancing into one of the ghost rooms unprepared. And stunned seeing—at Ray's end of the sofa—a shadowy figure, or the outline of a figure—what is called an "optical illusion"—which is to say the *idea*—the *memory*—of a figure.

Quickly I turn away. Run away into a "safe" part of the house.

February 27, 2008

Raymond Smith, Founder and Editor of Literary Journal, Dies at 77

Raymond J. Smith, a founder and the longtime editor of *The Ontario Review*, a noted literary journal, died on Feb. 18 in Princeton, N.J. He was 77 and lived in Princeton.

The cause was complications of pneumonia, according to the Blackwell Memorial Home in Pennington, N.J.

With his wife, the novelist Joyce Carol Oates, Mr. Smith founded *The Ontario Review* in 1974. Until his death, he was its editor; Ms. Oates was the associate editor. The journal, which appears twice yearly, has published the work of established writers — including Margaret Atwood, Donald Barthelme, Saul Bellow, Raymond Carver, Nadine Gordimer, Ted Hughes, Doris Lessing, Philip Roth, John Updike and Robert Penn Warren — as well as that of young writers.

Mr. Smith and Ms. Oates also founded and ran Ontario Review Books, a small independent publishing house that began in 1980. Among its titles are *Town Smokes*: *Stories* (1987), by Pinckney Benedict; *Selene of the Spirits* (1998), a novel by Melissa Pritchard; *The Identity Club*: *New and Selected Stories* (2005), by Richard Burgin; and reprints of many of Ms. Oates's books.

Raymond Joseph Smith was born in Milwaukee on March 12, 1930. He earned a bachelor's degree in English from the University of Wisconsin, Milwaukee, followed by a Ph.D. in English from the University of Wisconsin, Madison, in 1960. He later taught at the University of

Windsor in Ontario and at New York University before becoming a full-time editor and publisher.

He was the author of *Charles Churchill* (Twayne, 1977), a study of the 18th-century English poet and satirist.

In addition to Ms. Oates, whom he married in 1961, Mr. Smith is survived by a sister, Mary.

34

E-MAIL RECORD

February 24, 2008.

To Edmund White

. . . lovely to have you visit. Please come back at any time to continue your so-fascinating memoir. In one of those pretentious flourishes of old you can note, at the end of the volume, the various places you'd written it in, for instance Florence, South of France, Honey Brook Drive.

Much love, & I'm glad that you could eat some of my accumulated food here—

Joyce

February 26, 2008.

To Susan Wolfson

Thank you for your kindness in interceding with Verizon!

At the center of grief, I think there are no words. I feel very mute, though hear myself chattering away . . . Tomorrow at school will be a great test.

I have gotten through the day!—revising my review—[for the New York Review]—trying to urge myself that it was worth it—is worth it . . . My days start at 6 A.M. and go on—forever—like driving across

Nebraska/Texas—just on and on, it's amazing. Then they come to an abrupt stop at about midnight with a little white pill.

I have an array of very nice warm-Ray jackets for Ron to choose among.

> *Much love*
> *Joyce*

February 26, 2008.
To Jeanne Halpern

I so appreciate your love and concern. I am overwhelmed with so much happening, I need time to spend just grieving for Ray—just thinking about him, and remembering. So much has been happening of an exterior nature, I am panicked at the thought of losing him. Another "event"—traveling to New York—to modify my own will—is just too much right now. I am trying to resume some part of my old life—concentrating on my work . . . The thought of another appointment—in NYC—just about brought me to the brink of collapse. I'm sorry, I am very shaky. I am trying to concentrate on returning to classes tomorrow. I need to go more slowly . . . I've been agitated through much of the night, I feel that my frail "personality" could shatter into pieces. Though I am trying to keep a professional manner in and around the University.

Cherie was sleeping beside me this morning for a while . . . like old times' sake. Both cats seem to blame me for Ray's having disappeared.

> *Much love,*
> *Joyce*

February 27, 2008.
To Arthur Vanderbilt

Thank you for the Joan Didion memoir, which I'd already read—but will happily reread. I know that there is much melancholy wisdom here.

My "first day" back at school. It seemed . . . long. But Edmund was very kindly & affectionate, and things went well, over all. It is just so hard to return to this empty house where I risk being snubbed by our haughty cats.

Ray's obituary was in the New York Times *this morning. It took me forty minutes to open the paper . . . Ray loved you. We both recall so vividly how you came to our house bearing a lovely large bouquet (from your garden?) . . . At all our gatherings you have been the very compass of good sense/good humor/irony . . . Ray always felt that you had a "handle" on things . . .*

Love

Joyce

February 28, 2008.

To Gary Mailman

Just one query: what would this lawyer do? You'd suggested a minimum of $10,000—for what? "Problems might mount"—what are the problems? Could my property be seized? What is the danger?

I am so confused and upset by this . . . I'd thought that you and Jeanne had concluded that New Jersey law wasn't so complicated as Ohio and New York. I know that you know so much more than I do, but I am demoralized by this and exhausted . . . This is only one of so many things that have been striking me, I can't even mourn for Ray. I am in a total state of exhaustion and agitation much of the day and night. Nothing ever seems to end. Always there is "more discussion." Always some option. How long will this last? What does the law do for us, if such problems follow the execution of a seemingly legal document? Does the law just create situations to generate more law situations, thus more lawyers, and more fees? Any advice you can give will be so much appreciated!

I love you and trust you as a friend and am just so demoralized about this.

Joyce

February 28, 2008.

To Gary Mailman

I've had a time of meditation to think—try to think—more calmly about this. Now I see that you and Jeanne are right. I had conflated the two issues—(Ray's will and a codicil to my will)—had thought the fee

of $10,000 would be just for taking the will to court. But now, I see
that you mean two quite distinct things which would be executed by
the same lawyer. Jeanne has told me many things and perhaps she did
tell me this but it was caught up in such a turmoil, I never grasped it.
If this could be expedited soon, maybe I could (almost) sleep again . . .

    Much love, see you soon,

    Joyce

February 28, 2008.
To Elaine Pagels

    I am often thinking of your early, terrible losses . . . How totally
wounded you have been, which gives you a special empathy with
people. Every so often a wave of pure, freezing horror sweeps over
me—that Ray is gone, that I will never see him again. I have a fantasy
about hurrying to the hospital room as I'd done so many times last
week—and seeing him there, as he'd been in the bed, sitting up and
reading.

    It's amazing to read in today's New York Times *of suicide rates*
rising for the middle-aged. How anyone could throw a life away, when
life is so precious, and precarious, is astonishing.

    Much love,

    Joyce

February 29, 2008.
To Jeanne Halpern

    Today I will be visiting with Ray's cardiologist. I'm anxious already
at what we might discuss . . . I know it's wrong but I can't help but
think that this man might have saved Ray, that something more could
have been done. Of course, he was nowhere near the Medical Center
when Ray died at 12:50 A.M.

    Love,

    Joyce

February 29, 2008.

To Edmund White

. . . at last finished my review for Bob Silvers yesterday. For much of this I was like a dazed deer with her head trapped in wire, so many hours went into this short essay . . . If you can read the attachment, it's at the break of a new section at the bottom of p. 6 that I was writing after Ray had died, the most numbed kind of "concentration" . . . late at night, staring at these words and at pages of notes for a review of a book virtually no one will read, nor even glance into, it's so obscure. Still it was solace of a kind. Barbara Epstein kept working until a few days before she died. "What else is there but work?" she'd once said to me . . . At least the work isn't just our teeming emotions but does cast out to other people.

Today, just a day of "tasks"—can't even start to write anything new—a visit to the doctor who'd been Ray's cardiologist. . . . It will be very strange, seeing Dr. H____ without Ray close by.

Much love,

Joyce

March 11, 2008.

To Ebet Dudley

. . . I remember your lovely party with such gratitude, it did seem to presage a happy ending; and the wonderful Valentine you'd created for Ray, which he never saw, is on display in our "party room" here though there is not likely to be a party for some time. . . .

What a hopeful evening that had seemed, for me at least! I wish that I could live it over again, in utter innocence. I remember what a cold night it was . . . and how unexpectedly social your dogs were, chatting up complete strangers with equanimity.

Much love,

Joyce

As these e-mail excerpts suggest, the memoir is a memoir of loss and grief but also perhaps more significantly a memoir of friendship.

It is to suggest that, for the widow, as for all who are grieving, there is no way to survive except through others. E-mail has replaced written letters— for some of us, it allows for communications which written letters and the telephone could never have accommodated.

How frantic the widow is, sending out these e-mails into the night! Often, in an effort to forestall the inevitable—confronting the empty house, glancing up to see a ghostly reflection in a window, preparing to deal with the night. And how wonderful her friends, replying—whose e-mails I have not represented here for they are the property of the senders whose privacy I would not wish violated.

35

Fury!

Then suddenly, I am so angry.

I am so very very angry, I am furious.

I am sick with fury, like a wounded animal.

A kick of adrenaline to the heart, my heart begins thudding rapid and furious as a fist slamming against an obdurate surface—a locked door, a wall.

"You don't know what you're saying," I tell Dr. H___. "You don't know the first thing about my husband and I think that I will go now. Good-bye!"

February 29, 2008. The final day of this interminable month.

Overcast sky, storm clouds dense as impacted bowels and yet: at intermittent and unpredictable intervals a blinding sun appears—a razor-sharp slashing sun—so the haze through which the widow moves with the uncertainty of a blind woman is occasionally pierced—the most extraordinary anger leaps forth like heat lightning.

Do not think that the widow is all damp dissolving tissue, watery eyes and quavering voice. Do not think that because the widow's backbone has been broken, that the widow can't lash out at her tormentors.

How healthy it would be, to be angry! To be an angry person, who blames others for her misfortune! Better to be angry, than to be depressed.

An angry person would never wish to hurt *herself.* For an angry person suicide is not an option.

But for some of us, anger is rarely possible. Anger is a high C our voices can't reach. Always I've thought *To what purpose? Anger only makes things worse.*

Indignation is the more civilized face of anger. Fury, the savage face.

On this day, I have an appointment with Ray's cardiologist Dr. H____. In his chilly examination room an effervescent young nurse administers an EKG with the equanimity of a masseuse. You would not guess from the nurse's friendly chatter that, in another few minutes, the most terrifying medical facts might be revealed of the patient. Lying on my back, partially undressed, I am conscious of my quickened heartbeat and of my strangely sunken stomach. I know that there are bruised dents beneath my eyes, my clothes feel loose on me, and I can't stop shivering. A dull ache inside my head like a slowing pendulum. The nurse sticks cold little electrodes against my chest, my side, my leg, my arm like miniature sucking mouths all the while talking to me, smiling—of course, I am smiling at her—I am very good at exchanging those friendly quasi-humorous remarks that are the glue of our daily lives among others, making the most storm-tossed days navigable, tolerable.

With relief I think *She doesn't know about Ray. She doesn't know about me. Why should she know, why should I want her to know?*

For the widow it is possible to be "happy"—to be perceived as "happy" by strangers—only in the interstices of our actual lives.

Not unlike a former athlete who, now aching in every bone, easily winded, stooped with cervical spine strain and overweight by thirty pounds, is nevertheless drawn to throw a few basketballs with young guys in a park—just a few!—and performs so well, for this brief interlude, the young guys are truly impressed. This is good!

My meeting with Dr. H____ is awkward. I think that we are about to shake hands in greeting—but then, we don't. (Is it customary to shake hands with one's doctor? In my confusion, I can't recall.) Dr. H____ murmurs how sorry he is about Ray and moves on to speak of my EKG—that is "near-to-normal"—a fact that should bring relief (to me) since some years ago my heartbeat had been irregular from time to time; I've had attacks of tachycardia severe enough to warrant Ray taking me to the ER at the medical center. At the time of the last attack Dr. H___ became my cardiologist, whom I see just once a year.

Dr. H___ visited Ray at the hospital several times and spoke with us briefly, encouragingly. Dr. H___ was not the "attending physician" and had nothing to do with the treatment Ray received for pneumonia of course.

Dr. H___ had nothing to do with the outcome of Ray's treatment. Of course.

Frowning Dr. H___ takes my blood pressure, as I stare into a corner of the room. Blood pressure! The curiosity of this phenomenon strikes me for the first time.

"One hundred over sixty-eight—same as last time."

Is this good? Or not so good? It is difficult for me to believe that anything about myself might be described as *same as last time.*

Next, Dr. H___ weighs me. I am not able to watch the scale as Dr. H___ adjusts the little weight. In his concerned eyes, however, when I step off the scales, I am made to see the taboo-reflection I can't bring myself to confront in the mirrors in our house.

There is a Jewish custom, I think—covering mirrors after a death in the family. How good if mirrors were permanently covered, or turned to the wall. Then, we would not be tempted to glance into them.

A gay male friend once told me, when his lover left him he'd been so devastated, he could not look into a mirror. When he had to see himself in some way, for instance when shaving, he covered parts of his face with his hand.

These stratagems for survival. *I needed a strategy by which to endure and go on—as who doesn't?*

(This line from Philip Roth's new novel which I am reading in a bound galley, in the nest. *Exit Ghost* is the cryptic title.)

Consulting his notes in my folder, Dr. H___ observes that I have lost eight pounds since my last visit in February 2007: my new weight is one hundred three pounds. I feel an urge to apologize but only just murmur something vague and conciliatory, as I would murmur if Dr. H___ had said that I had a rare disease and only a few weeks to live.

Dr. H___ observes that I am looking "strained"—"stressed"—"of course you've been through a terrible ordeal"—and suggests that he prescribe a sleeping pill for me.

For instance Ambien—"an effective drug, with minimal side effects."

For a moment Dr. H___ sounds soothing and hopeful as a TV commercial.

"To get you through these difficult weeks."

Weeks! I can't envision anything shorter than a decade. My nocturnal life has become the Jersey Turnpike of insomnia.

But do I want a prescription for sleeping pills? No!

I am afraid of becoming addicted to sleeping pills. I think that I am deathly afraid.

I envision myself as *the very archetype of the drug addict*—raw trembling need, insomnia raging most nights like wildfire.

And of course I am alone. Who's to know how many pills I take, how late I sleep?—my fantasy, which I have shared with no one, and will share with no one, is to take a pill to sleep, and when waking take another pill to sleep, and when waking take another pill to sleep, and when waking . . . how long this might continue, I have but mild curiosity.

Like a flashlight's beam shining out into the night—you see the length of the beam. Beyond that, you can't know.

Beyond that, better not to know.

It's shocking then that my voice calmly replies yes thank you, Doctor.

For *of course* I want these pills. As one intent upon assembling a cache of powerful pills, I want all the pills I can get.

Dr. M___, our kindly family doctor, who prescribed antibiotics for Ray whenever Ray requested them, for a "bad cold" for instance, prescribed a tranquilizer for me Lorazepam—which has a sudden sedative effect. Two evenings ago at the Halperns' where I'd gone for dinner, having taken a single capsule before arriving, I'd begun to nod off, so abruptly stricken with torpor no one would trust me to drive home by myself . . .

Of course Dr. H___ need not know that I have this prescription from kindly Dr. M___, as Dr. H___need not know that I already have a considerable cache of pills, a lethal quantity of pills, at home.

Many of these old pills were Ray's. A few, mine.

The prescription for Lorazepam, I'd filled immediately. In the drugstore, I swallowed the first of the capsules.

I thought—*Am I doing this of my own volition, or because it's expected of me? Is this the widow's script? The start of the downward spiral.*

Soon then a languid sensation set in. Where there'd been a hive of crazed and inarticulate emotions like something in a wind tunnel now there was a muffled sort of quiet. A Novocain-numbness. How good it felt, to be numb! *Numb*: *dumb*. I thought of the icy numbness creeping up Socrates' legs. Plato doesn't seem to comprehend that such numbness would be a solace, a vast relief, to the aged man. A way of eluding his captors. A way of assuring his dignity, his death.

Why am I thinking of Plato?—that fascist reactionary? Why am I thinking of Socrates?

The flight into the "life of the mind"—the denial of trauma.

A sledgehammer to the brain and the brain feebly tries to function as it is accustomed to functioning—making shrewd connections, establishing circuits that go nowhere, looping about in snarls. This is the human *strategy*.

It's a coincidence, purely—that my annual appointment with Dr. H___ is scheduled for the week following my husband's death.

I'd considered postponing the appointment for a routine cardiac exam. For why should I be concerned about my health, at such a time? I am contemptuous of my own health, my "well-being." I think that I should be punished if only with a bad cold, a savage sore throat. Then thinking *If there is something wrong with my heart, I should know it. I have so very much to do, that must be done.*

There are no obligations of the dead to the living. All obligations are of the living to the dead.

I am the *executrix* of my husband's *estate*.

What a harsh sound—*executrix*. A kind of *dominatrix*.

Often it is said that death is "embarrassing" to doctors. It is said that doctors are reluctant to admit that death is a possibility for their patients as they are reluctant to draw up wills for themselves.

Especially, I should think, the death of a patient whom a doctor has been treating "successfully" is embarrassing—upsetting—to him.

For Dr. H____ had been Ray's cardiologist for years—he'd prescribed medications to reduce Ray's blood pressure and "thin" his blood and Ray had been given to know that these medications had been working very well.

Unlike many of our Princeton friends, Ray was not critical of Princeton medical care. He was not critical of any of his doctors whom in fact he liked, as he liked our Pennington dentist. Returning from an appointment with Dr. H____, Ray would say how much he liked Dr. H____, and trusted him.

Speaking of Ray now, as Dr. H____ can't avoid doing, Dr. H____ seems genuinely sad, and genuinely surprised.

He'd known about the death, I had not had to tell him.

Our family doctor Dr. M____ had been shocked, when I'd seen him a few days ago, and told him about Ray's death. Dr. M____ had not known about Ray's hospitalization for pneumonia and was stunned to hear that Ray had died "so quickly."

Dr. M____ had protested that Ray was "in such good shape"—"so fit"—"watched his diet"—"took care of himself."

It will not occur to the widow for months that no one would say to any widow *I'm not surprised. Of course your husband died. We all expected it.*

Dr. H____ is not alone in his office for this consultation. A young woman medical student is in attendance, taking notes and smiling at me. Now, she ceases smiling. She begins to look embarrassed, chagrined.

I am beginning to be struck by the fact that Dr. H____ has said several times "I can't imagine how this happened"—"I don't understand how this happened"—as if he believes that I have come to him for an explanation, and that an explanation is due, from him. My impulse is to console him, as women are inclined to console men, all women, all men, in all circumstances without discretion; it must be a genetic component, like a reflexive empathy at the sight of an infant, or a reflexive recoiling at the sight of a snake; especially, the widow's instinct, I am discovering, is to provide some sort of consolation, some sort of apology, or anyway sympathy, to those to whom the husband's death has been a disturbing surprise. But I don't say anything, in fact I am chewing my lower lip. I am discovering that I am angry.

I am sad, but I am *angry*.

As he talks to me in his somewhat faltering way, like a man who has lost his mooring, Dr. H____ is too discreet, or too circumspect, to speak more directly, or to suggest the slightest criticism of the staff at the Princeton Medical Center—for of course, Dr. H____ is on this staff himself; yet he seems to be suggesting, in the repetition of key phrases—*Can't imagine how this happened!*—that his patient Ray Smith possibly—probably?—hadn't received the very best medical attention at the hospital, at that hour of the night.

Is this what Dr. H____ is hinting? Or am I imagining it?

It's chilling and horrible—outrageous—that the best physicians are not likely to be on duty at any hospital, at midnight; especially, a Sunday midnight; of course, there was a depleted crew in Telemetry, that night; a ragtag crew, perhaps; the equivalent of a *graveyard shift*.

If Ray had required emergency care in the morning, which was Monday morning, when Dr. H____ might have been on the premises, making his rounds, he might be alive now . . .

I would be here, in Dr. H____'s office. For my appointment was for this time. And Ray would be elsewhere. Probably at home. And I would return home, and Ray would ask me how the exam went, what did Dr. H____ say, and I would tell him—"Same as last time. Nothing has changed."

I can't think this! Don't dare think this.

I will begin to break down, I will begin to grow faint, sick, this is not a line of thought that is productive, not now. Not now. Dr. H____ is asking if I'd had Ray "autopsied" and I say no—no no!—the bizarre word *autopsied* strikes me—*no I did not have Ray autopsied*—maybe it was a mistake, but no I did not. Dr. H____ says, "Ray was getting better all week, he was getting better all week, when I saw him he was looking really . . ." Dr. H____'s voice trails off. I hear myself say with sudden sharpness, "If I were a doctor, I would feel very discouraged about now."

This is not a way in which I have ever spoken to any doctor, I must say here, for the record. And this sharpness in my voice—this is a surprise to me, as to Dr. H____.

The young woman medical student is staring at me, startled. Never has she heard any patient speak critically of any doctor, to the doctor's face. This is a tense moment!

For suddenly I am angry. My voice rises in accusation. "Ray shouldn't have died! He was left to die. They could have done more for him. This 'secondary infection'—how did that happen? From someone's *hands*? Did someone forget to wash *his hands*? They could have done more— sooner—there never seemed to be any actual *doctor* around when I was there—they didn't even call me until it was too late . . ."

How futile, how pathetic, these words—tumbling from me—why should it matter in the slightest when they'd called me, set beside the profound and irrevocable fact of my husband's death?

Another time Dr. H___ mentions *autopsy*.

Is this a rebuke? I think it must be.

Yes of course. If I had wanted to know why Ray died, more exactly, I should have requested an autopsy.

Except of course *I could not request an autopsy*.

Now, Ray's remains have been cremated. Now, it's too late.

This bizarre conversation! I am thinking *How can we be saying such things about Ray!—as if Ray was just a body.*

"Well—I didn't. I didn't. At the time, I—didn't."

I am not speaking coherently. Of all things I dread breaking down in a public place—this office is a semi-public place—and now I am not speaking coherently and tears are welling dangerously in my eyes.

My face feels as if it is about to shatter. My mouth is stiffening in that terrible helpless way that prefigures crying.

Would I have wanted to instigate a "wrongful death" suit against the medical center? A malpractice suit? Even if one were justified, would I have wanted it?

Not revenge, still less financial compensation, is what I want. What I want is my husband returned to me . . .

That is all that I want! And that is all that I can't have.

And now, Dr. H___ says the unforgivable thing.

Why, for what reason I can't grasp, except he, too, isn't speaking very coherently, Dr. H___ says, "Maybe—Ray was just tired. Maybe he gave up . . ." Again Dr. H___'s voice trails off, maddeningly.

Now, I am really angry. For this isn't right! This is so very wrong.

How can Dr. H____ make such an accusation of his own patient, who'd liked him so much? Who'd trusted him? I want to run out of the room, I am so shocked, upset.

"You don't know what you're saying. You don't know the first thing about my husband and I think that I will go now. Good-bye!"

In my hand, the prescription for Ambien.

Three refills.

In the car driving on Harrison Street amid late-afternoon traffic I am borne aloft by fury like a balloon buffeted in the wind and yet—soon— of course, soon—the fury-balloon begins to deflate. Gripping the steering wheel I begin to cry—it's impossible not to cry—I am protesting—I am protesting to Dr. H____ —"Ray didn't give up!—he may have been tired—of course—after a week's hospitalization—but he didn't give up. He was looking forward to coming home, he loved his home, he was *happy* at the prospect of coming home, of course he didn't want to—die. . . ."

Since the first days of Ray's hospitalization, I've fallen into the habit of talking to myself. Sometimes, screaming to myself.

I've fallen into the habit of stereotypical melodramatic gestures— gripping the steering wheel as if it were a neck to be strangled, and shaking it; striking surfaces with my fist, that rebounds harmlessly from the surface, bruised.

This is the way of madness—is it? Such out-of-control behavior? Instead of addressing oneself silently—stoically—one mutters, rages aloud like King Lear on the heath.

Except unlike King Lear on the heath, one lacks the Shakespearean touch.

It is outrageous to me, unconscionable—obscene—that Dr. H____ should have said what he'd said about Ray. I would recall later—this scene, I have replayed dozens of times—I can replay it precisely frame by frame *now*—how Dr. H____ had seemed to be blundering, groping for words. For an *explanation.* As if he had no idea what he was saying, and to whom; as if he hadn't exactly meant what he'd said, and yet . . . I will never forget these words.

Maybe—Ray was tired. Maybe he gave up.

And so, Ray's death was *his own fault*?

How crushed, how hurt, how appalled Ray would be, to hear this. In Dr. H____'s words.

And this, too, it seems to me, is insufferable, unbearable; how the dead are muted. How the dead are silent. All things—any idiotic, cruel and ignorant things—can be said of the dead but the dead can't reply—can't defend themselves.

In my agitation, I must take care to drive carefully. At the start of Ray's hospitalization I told myself *Drive at the speed limit, or lower. Never more!*

On the way home I must stop at a food store. I am that frantic woman hurrying along the aisles. How cold the store is! In the frozen food aisles steam wafts upward like departing wraiths. I am shivering violently inside my red down coat which is the coat I was wearing when the speeding car struck us—when we might have died, at the intersection of Elm Road and Rosedale a year ago. I am thinking how lucky we were, and how in the aftermath of that accident we carried ourselves with care, for weeks, wincing with pain.

I am thinking that I would give anything to have that time back, those six weeks of excruciating muscle-pain in my chest. When I would beg Ray, breathless—*Don't make me laugh. Oh it hurts so!*

Am I murmuring to myself? In the food store? Am I—laughing? Pressing my hand against my chest, as if in pain?

I think that my face must be contorted. Possibly, smudged with tears. Can't bring myself to make eye contact with anyone for fear that they are staring openly at me.

That distraught woman—what's wrong with her?

That distraught woman—who is she? Looks familiar.

In the parking lot, an icy rain. The shopping bags are wet, the bottom of one of the bags tears open, a cottage cheese container falls onto the pavement, cans of cat food, I am squatting in the rain, in my red down coat, I am desperate snatching up things to put into another bag, quickly before someone sees me and offers to help. No one—no one!—

is more vulnerable than when the bottom of her—his—shopping bag tears open, and the pathetic food-items she, or he, has purchased are exposed, on wet pavement. Here is an ontological fact: since the morning I drove Ray to the ER, since the hour when I began, at first unknowingly, to be *a woman alone*, a kind of crude cruel serio-comic monstrousness has been loosed into my life. Think Monty Python in endless skits adapted from William Burroughs. Think Ionesco's "Theater of the Absurd" in which the widow—that is, this widow—has been cast as the lead. It does no good to be angry, as it does no good to be devastated; crying is as reasonable a response as any other, and as futile. My heart is filled with rage, however—at Dr. H___. Never will I forgive Dr. H___ who said such terrible things about my helpless husband, though I know that, whoever may have contributed to my husband's death, it was not Dr. H___.

Struggling to position the grocery bags in the car, in the backseat, in such ways that they won't topple over spilling things onto the floor, I am forced to acknowledge that it is really myself I will never forgive for all that I have failed to do, to save my husband. It is really myself whom I hate, and condemn.

From a short distance—if I shut my eyes, I can see it clearly—the lizard-like creature is regarding me, its flailing prey, that cannot escape; I see now that it's a living thing, an actual stone-colored reptile of the size of a large bullfrog, with remarkable eyes, hypnotic eyes fixed upon me. *You are finished. You are dead and done for, why don't you just give up.*

36

OASIS

At the University it is my task to impersonate "Joyce Carol Oates."

Strictly speaking, I am not impersonating this individual since "Joyce Carol Oates" doesn't exist, except as an author-identification. On the spines of books shelved in certain libraries and bookstores you will see OATES but this is a descriptive term, this is not a noun.

This is not a person. This is not a life.

A writing-life is not a *life*.

It is not invariably the case that a teacher is also a writer, and that, as a teacher, she has been hired to impersonate the writer. But it is the case with me here in Princeton, as it had not been, for instance, in Detroit, where my identification was "Joyce Smith"—"Mrs. Smith."

In the lives of teachers there are *teaching-days*, *teaching-hours* like islands, or oases, amid turbulent seas.

In the immediate days following Ray's death, I did not teach. It was suggested by some colleagues that I take more time off, even the entire semester, but I was eager to return to my fiction workshops the following week, on February 27, in time to attend a joint reading that evening by Honor Moore and Mary Karr in our creative writing reading series.

This "Oates"—this quasi-public self—is scarcely visible to me, as a mirror-reflection, seen up close, is scarcely visible to the viewer. "Oates" is an island, an oasis, to which on this agitated morning I can row, as in an uncertain little skiff, with an unwieldy paddle—the way is arduous not because the water is deep but because the water is shallow and weedy and the bottom of the skiff is endangered by rocks beneath. And yet—once I have rowed to this island, this oasis, this core of calm amid the chaos of my life—once I arrive at the University, check my mail and ascend to the second floor of 185 Nassau where I've had an office since fall 1978—once I am "Joyce Carol Oates" in the eyes of my colleagues and my students—a shivery sort of elation enters my veins. I feel not just confidence but *certainty*—that I am in the right place, and this is the right time. The anxiety, the despair, the anger I've been feeling—that has so transformed my life—immediately fades, as shadows on a wall are dispelled in sunshine.

Always I have felt this way about teaching but more strongly, because more desperately, after Ray's death.

So long as, with reasonable success, I can impersonate "Joyce Carol Oates," it is not the case that I am *dead and done for*—yet.

Now for the first time in what I've grown to think of as my "posthumous life"—my life after Ray—I am feeling almost hopeful, happy. Thinking *Maybe life is navigable. Maybe this will work.*

Then I recall—hope was the predominant emotion I had felt—we had both felt—during the long week of Ray's hospitalization.

Hope, in retrospect, is so often a cruel joke.

Hope is the thing with feathers Emily Dickinson so boldly said. The thing that is ungainly, vulnerable, embarrassing. But there it is.

For some of us, what can hope *mean*? The worst has happened, the spouse has died, the story is ended. And yet—the story is not ended, clearly.

Hope can be outlived. Hope can become tarnished.

Yet, I am hopeful about teaching. Each semester I am hopeful and each semester I become deeply involved with my writing students and each semester has turned out well—in fact, very well—since I first began teaching at Princeton. But now, I am thinking that I will focus even more intensely on my students. I have just twenty-two students this semester—two workshops and two seniors whom I am directing in "creative" theses.

Devote myself to my students, my teaching. This is something that I can do, that is of value.

For writing—*being a writer*—always seems to the writer to be of dubious value.

Being a writer is like being one of those riskily overbred pedigree dogs—a French bulldog, for instance—poorly suited for survival despite their very special attributes.

Being a writer is in defiance of Darwin's observation that the more highly specialized a species, the more likelihood of extinction.

Teaching—even the teaching of writing—is altogether different. Teaching is an act of communication, sympathy—a reaching-out—a wish to share knowledge, skills; a rapport with others, who are students; a way of allowing others into the solitariness of one's soul.

Gladly wolde he lerne and gladly teche—so Chaucer says of his young scholar in the *Canterbury Tales*. When teachers feel good about teaching, this is how we feel.

And so, in this afternoon's "advanced fiction" workshop, in an upstairs, lounge-like room in 185 Nassau, the University's arts building, I am greatly relieved to be teaching! To be back in the presence of undergraduates who know nothing of my private life. For two lively and absorbing hours I am able to forget the radically altered circumstances of this life—none of my students could guess, I am certain, that "Professor Oates" is a sort of raw bleeding stump whose brain, outside the perimeters of the workshop, is in thrall to chaos.

Along with prose pieces by several students we discuss, in detail, rending our way through the story line by line as if it were poetry, that early masterpiece of Ernest Hemingway—"Indian Camp." Four pages long, written when the author was only a few years older than these Princeton undergraduates, the stark and seemingly autobiographical "Indian Camp" never fails to make a strong impression on them.

How strange it is, how strangely comforting, to read great works of literature throughout our lives, at greatly different phases of our lives—my first reading of "Indian Camp" was in high school, when I was fifteen, and younger than the author; each subsequent reading has been revelatory in different ways; now this afternoon, in this new phase of my life, when it seems to me self-evident that my life is over, I am struck anew by the precision of Hemingway's prose, exquisite as the workings of a clock. I am thinking how, of all classic American writers, Hemingway is the one who writes exclusively of death, in its manifold forms; *the perfect man of action is the suicide*, William Carlos Williams once observed, and surely this was true of Hemingway. In a typical Hemingway story foregrounds as well as backgrounds are purposefully blurred, like the contours of his characters' faces, and their pasts, as in those dreams of terrible simplicity in which stark revelation is the point, and there is no time for digressing.

At an Indian camp in Northern Michigan to which Nick Adams's father, a doctor, has been summoned to help with a difficult childbirth, an Indian commits suicide by slashing his throat while lying in the lower bunk of a bunk bed, even as his wife gives birth to their child in the upper bunk. Hemingway's young Nick Adams is a witness to the horror—before his father can usher him from the scene, Nick has seen him examining the Indian's wound by "tipping" the Indian's head back.

Later, rowing back home from the Indian camp, Nick asks his father why the Indian killed himself and his father says, "I don't know, Nick. He couldn't stand things, I guess."

No theory of suicide, no philosophical discourses on the subject are quite so revelatory as these words. *Couldn't stand things, I guess.*

How poignant it is to consider that Hemingway would kill himself several decades later, with a shotgun, at the age of sixty-one.

Suicide, a taboo-subject. In 1925, when "Indian Camp" was first published, in Hemingway's first book *In Our Time*, how much more of a taboo-subject than now.

Suicide is an issue that fascinates undergraduates. Suicide is the subject of a good number of their stories. Sometimes, the suicidal element so saturates the story, it's difficult to discuss the story as a text without considering frankly the subject, and its meaning to the writer.

Not that most of these young writers would "consider" suicide—I'm sure—but all of them know someone who has killed himself.

Sometimes, these suicides have been friends of theirs, contemporaries from high school or college.

These personal issues, I am not likely to bring into workshop discussions, as I never discuss anything personal about myself, or even my writing. Though I came of age in the 1960s when the borderline between "teacher" and "student" became perilously porous, I am not that kind of teacher.

My intention as a teacher is to refine my own personality out of existence, or nearly—my own "self" is never a factor in my teaching, still less my career; I like to think that most of my students haven't read my writing.

(Visiting writers/instructors at Princeton—I'm thinking of Peter Carey, for instance—and seeing the look of quizzical hurt on Peter's face—are invariably astonished/crestfallen to discover that their students are not exactly familiar with their *oeuvres*—but I'm more likely to feel relief.)

It isn't an exaggeration to say that, this semester of Ray's death, my students will be my lifeline. Teaching will be my lifeline.

Along with my friends, a small circle of friends—this will "keep me going." I am sure that my students have no idea of the circumstances of my life, and that they are not curious about it; nor will I ever hint to them what I am feeling, at any time; how I dread the conclusion of the teaching-day, and the return to my diminished life.

It's a matter of pride to me, that, this afternoon in the workshop, I was no different, or seemed no different, than ever in the past. In my exchanges with my students, I have given them no reason to suspect that anything is amiss in my life.

In the doorway of my office stand two of my writing students from last semester. One of them, who'd been a soldier in the Israeli army, slightly older than most Princeton undergraduates, says awkwardly, "Professor Oates? We heard about your husband and want to say how sorry we are. . . . If there's anything we can do . . ."

I am utterly surprised—I had not expected this. Quickly I tell the young men that I'm fine, it's very kind of them but I am fine . . .

When they leave, I shut my office door. I am shaking, I am so deeply moved. But mostly shocked. Thinking *They must have known all along today. They must all know.*

37

Bruised Knees

In the stark unsparing light of 4 A.M. on hands and knees on the chill tile floor of the bathroom sobbing in despair, rage, shame—out of my shaky fingers a little plastic container of capsules has fallen to the floor—capsules have rolled merrily in all directions and I am desperate trying to locate them, groping to locate one that has rolled—has it?—somewhere behind the toilet amid wispy balls of dust like the most forlorn and despised of thoughts—except, *where is it?*—in dread of running out of my prescription for Lorazepam which helps me to sleep for somewhere beyond three hours each night for I have not yet filled the prescription for Ambien out of apprehension of becoming addicted to whatever this state of being is, this groggy half-sleep, this zombie half-life in which the outlines of things have become blurred and textures flattened like plastic and voices echo at a distance murmurous and jeering as in an obscure language *decedent—executrix—fiduciaries—codicil—letters testamentary—residuary estate*—haunted by the vision of a stricken bull fallen to its knees in the ring bleeding from myriad wounds in a stream of hot blood provoking a deranged crowd to roar —here I am stricken on my knees, face pounding with blood, in this life shorn of meaning as trash blown across a befouled pavement is shorn of meaning, or the young dogwood tree in the courtyard ravaged by winter is shorn of meaning.

Without meaning, the world is *things*. And these *things* multiplied to infinity.

Six capsules remaining—one is missing—I can't find—on hands and knees groping, sobbing—thinking *This is what you deserve, who had been protected from such misery for too long. Suffer!*

38

A Dream of Such Happiness!

My parents are asking me *Where is Ray?*

My parents—only just middle-aged, thus "young"—as they'd been when, not so very long ago, they'd come to visit us in our Princeton house, and stayed in the "guest suite" we'd designed for them. And my mother Carolina who loved to cook helped me prepare meals in the kitchen, and my father Fred who loved music played piano in the living room. And the glass house that was usually so still with just Ray and me in it seemed to expand and to glow with life.

Except—in this dream—which is in fact a happy dream—my parents are asking about Ray. For somehow, Ray isn't here. And it has never been the case that my parents came to stay here, and Ray was not here. With childlike earnestness I am assuring them that Ray is all right—*He will join us later.*

In particular my mother is anxious as if not believing me, exactly—but I am able to convince her.

Ray will be here for dinner.

Or maybe I told her *Ray will be home for dinner.*

Here is the situation: my parents loved Ray as if he were their own son and so in the dream, I don't want them to know that Ray is in the hospital. (For this is the dream's secret—Ray is in the hospital now—he is still alive!) Of all things, I dread worrying my parents about anything, most of all about Ray. Or me.

It doesn't seem strange to me that my parents' faces are blurred as if undersea. Nor that the farther walls of our living room have vanished. The room is scarcely furnished—in fact, it doesn't seem to be our living room or any room familiar to me.

Yes—I understand that my parents Carolina and Fred whom I love so much are *not living*. Still, they are here with me, and I am so very happy in their presence, though the happiness is tinged with anxiety for it's my responsibility to keep my parents from suspecting both that they are *not living* and that *Ray is in the hospital.*

The dream communicates the social awkwardness of such a situation: I must shield my parents from this double knowledge that would so upset them.

Yet thinking *It's a good thing that Mom and Daddy can't know what has happened to Ray. That's the only good thing about being where they are.*

39

"We Want to See You Soon"

She's a lovely woman, a colleague at the University, not a close friend but of that nimbus of friendly acquaintances who in the aftermath of Ray's death have sent cards, flowers; she has sent me an e-mail saying that she and her husband, who teaches at another university, want to invite me to dinner at their house soon, and what are some evenings that are possible for me; and so I have responded, for there are many empty evenings indicated in my calendar, in March; in such empty evenings lurks the *horror vacui* that so terrified the ancient Egyptians, this *horror vacui* that seeps from the outer, darkened rooms of the house into the bright-lighted bedroom; and so what better remedy, if a temporary remedy, than a dinner with friends, to dispel this horror.

Yes it's true—often I see my small circle of friends. My friends who are my family, whom I love. Often, very often we speak on the phone, we exchange e-mails. Still there are empty evenings, in the nest trying to concentrate—reading—trying to read—offprints of Ray's literary essays and reviews from twenty years ago—bound galleys which publishers have sent me, requesting blurbs—(a blurb! from *me*!—how like a cruel joke this seems)—my old battered Modern Library edition of Pascal's *Pensées* which falls open at the most frequently read/annotated pages—

The eternal silence of these infinite spaces frightens me. It is a horrible thing to feel all that we possess slipping away. Between us and
heaven or hell there is only life, which is the frailest thing in the
world.

The last act is tragic, however happy all the rest of the play is; at
the last a little earth is thrown upon our head, and that is the end
forever.

We sail within a vast sphere, ever drifting in uncertainty, driven
from end to end. When we think to attach ourselves to any point
and to fasten to it, it wavers and leaves us; and if we follow it, it
eludes our grasp, slips past us, and vanishes forever. Nothing stays
for us. This is our natural condition, and yet most contrary to our
inclination; we burn with desire to find solid ground and an ul-
timate sure foundation whereon to build a tower reaching to the
Infinite. But our whole groundwork cracks, and the earth opens to
abysses. (*Translation by W. F. Trotter*)

Trying to ignore the lizard-thing hovering at the periphery of my vision
regarding me with calm impassive tawny-staring eyes *I am patient, I can
wait. I can outwait you.*

And so what better remedy than a dinner with friends except the
lovely C___ replies to my e-mail saying that, of the dates I've named, not
one is quite right.

For it seems, C___ is hoping to compose a dinner party of heroic
proportions. Where I'd thought the dinner would be just C___ and her
husband and another couple perhaps, it is revealed that C___ wants to
invite X, Y, Z—*All friends of yours, Joyce—who want to see you, too*—but
these others, one of them a university president with a very busy schedule, can't make the dates we've marked in pencil, maybe other dates,
maybe later in the month, or early April—finally, I send C___ an e-mail
suggesting that we have just a small dinner, just her and her husband
and one or two other couples—but C___ insists *So many people want to
see you, Joyce!*—she has ten guests "committed" for a Saturday in early
April—except, R___, a mutual friend, can't make this date—also S___,

who will be in Rome at a conference on international law—and so, could I look at my calendar again; more e-mails are exchanged; at last C___ has invited eighteen people—several of them "friends" whom I have not seen in a very long time—but of these, one or two are "tentative"—and so C___ must change the date another time; the new date suggested isn't a date that I can make; another time, C___ must change the date; I am beginning to realize that though C___ has said that she and her husband are "eager" to see me they are in fact dreading to see me; to that end, C___ is erecting obstacles to our dinner as in an equestrian trial in which each jump must be higher than its predecessor, and more dangerous; I envision a thirty-foot dining room table and at the farther end the widow placed like a leper, as far from the lovely C___ as possible. *I would so much prefer a small dinner, just you and your husband and another couple perhaps, I think that's what I would like best* which pleading e-mail C___ seems never to receive or, receiving, chooses to ignore; abruptly then, our e-mails on the subject cease; the heroic dinner party imagined by the lovely C___ never materializes.

I will not hear from C___ again for a very long time though mutual acquaintances will assure me, *C___ misses you, she says, and wants to see you soon!*

40

MOVING AWAY

"Good afternoon! Is it—Joyce?"

Yes it is Joyce. Steeling herself for the next, inevitable question *Where is your husband, Joyce?*

Or maybe, since everyone is on friendly, first-name terms here at the Hopewell Valley Fitness Center, the cheery blond receptionist will ask *Where is Ray, Joyce?*

But she doesn't ask about Ray. If she's curious—for I've never stepped into the Fitness Center except with Ray—(though Ray sometimes came here without me)—she doesn't let on.

The blond receptionist is unflaggingly sunny, upbeat—as one of the Fitness Center trainers she's professionally obliged to be upbeat—but she isn't naive. For of course husbands must vanish from the rosters of the Fitness Center frequently: separation, divorce, death?

Separation and divorce are more likely than death, among the Fitness Center members. Since really old and/or "unfit" men aren't likely to belong to a health club.

In any case, it wouldn't be diplomatic to ask. And maybe the blond receptionist sees in my face a certain tightening, a tension around the eyes pleading *Don't ask please!*

All fitness centers are places of hope, optimism. Belief in the future as progress. *Every gain is good!*

Ray's trainer never failed to praise him. The more praise, the harder Ray tried. For he'd meant to be "fit"—to "maintain fitness."

We'd come to the Fitness Center, on the average, about three times a week, for the past several years. We came only in the winter months.

It is very strange to be here without him. I have to think—to realize—he isn't behind me on the stairs, or outside at the car. He hasn't gone ahead of me to begin stretching exercises.

When you pass your plastic card through a device here at the check-in counter, a mechanical voice chirps THANK YOU HAVE A GOOD WORKOUT!

I have come to the fitness center for a purpose. I think it must be for exercise—unless it's to terminate my membership.

Physical exercise!—exertion! This will be my solace.

If I can exhaust myself, maybe I can sleep. Maybe I can sleep "normally." Parts of my brain feel as if they're carbonated. The kind of carbonation that fizzes out of the bottle and runs down your hand.

The Fitness Center is about two miles from our home, just off busy Route 31. It's a building of no distinction, windowless, fluorescent-lit, exuding perpetual music—"soft rock"—"pop standards"—in a cheery upbeat tempo.

Sometimes, this music would be intrusive. Loud, bland, persistent, brainless. When I couldn't bear it any longer I would find areas in the building—unoccupied, sometimes darkened—into which the music wasn't piped, and there I would run in place, or sit and take notes on whatever was preoccupying me at the time, while Ray worked out on the machines.

Often I remained outside. I preferred the outdoors, running/jogging/walking along a track, or trails. In a field beside the Fitness Center I would run in a large figure eight, in a trance of happiness—an ordinary/domestic happiness—for running has always been thrilling to me, both invigorating and comforting.

Running for me has always been meditation, contemplation.

Though now such states of mind are fearful to me, for I am not able to control my thoughts.

Sagely Ralph Waldo Emerson observed *A man is what he is thinking all day long.* We can assume that by *man* the philosopher did not exclude *woman*.

If we can control our thoughts, we can control—what? Only our feelings, emotions. Only our thoughts. Of the vast unfathomable world beyond ourselves, we have not the slightest control.

How sad it is to recall, the brilliant Emerson "lost" his mind as he aged. Many years of his later life he existed in a state of consciousness like a light slowly dimming, fading.

This is the dark, ironic, slyly cruel rejoinder to Emerson's sunny optimism. How self-reliance when there is no *self*?

For days—weeks?—I've been intending to come to the Fitness Center. For here, I am not-known, as Ray was not-known—a few of the employees recognized us as *Ray, Joyce*—but nothing more about us.

I am trying now not to imagine an alternative universe—in fact, this would be a universe far more probable, plausible, and recognizable than this universe—in which Ray was with me, as he'd always been. Outside in the car I'd been parked for several minutes without moving from the driver's seat. Staring at the stucco wall of the building waiting for— what? My life now seems to be waiting, waiting for something to happen, waiting for something to be decided, waiting to know what I must do next. Alone in the car—here? But why? Without a companion to say *Well—why are you just sitting there? Let's get out. Here we are.*

Often when I return home to our house—that is, to *my house*—I find myself sitting in the car like this, in a kind of spiritual paralysis. When I am away from the house, I yearn to return to it; when I am in the house, I think that there is danger there, and I should flee; yet, in the car parked outside the house, in a kind of stasis, often I don't move for minutes as if hypnotized. Ray would be astonished at this behavior, which is wholly "unlike" his wife.

The woman he'd known as *his wife*. Now, as *his widow*, she is not performing so very well.

Ray was the guardian of the household, and the house. Already without Ray's guidance the house is beginning to fail. Think of the collapse of the chic future house in Ray Bradbury's beautiful and chilling little parable, "There Will Come Soft Rains."

Away from the house, sitting here—where?—why?—fighting a sensation of mounting panic—I am suddenly convinced that the house is in danger. Yet, I am too lethargic to drive back to the house. And there is something else I am frightened of—more frightened of—this is the Fitness Center.

Weighing the degree of fear/panic: am I more anxious about the house, or about going into the Fitness Center; is it *more practical* to deal with the anxiety about the house or the anxiety about the Fitness Center? . . .

Look. You're here. You must be here for a reason.

So Ray would advise me, exasperated.

Oh but I am so reluctant to leave the (relative) safety of my battered white Honda—to enter the Fitness Center—to make my way to the large workout room, the size of a ballroom, to which Ray always went.

Soon, I will give a name to such places: *sinkholes.*

Places fraught with visceral memory, stirring terror if you approach them.

At this stage of the Siege—this is still early March—I haven't been able to comprehend my experiences in any coherent way, let alone categorize them. Taxonomy is the instinctive response to a world of dismaying fecundity and complexity but I am not strong enough for taxonomy just now.

Much of my life washes over me like a frothy/dirty surf. In this surf are bits of debris—seaweed, broken glass, mud-clumps, rotted fish, nameless things—a kind of spiritual catatonia as if I've been stung by a venomous sea-creature hidden in the surf—a jellyfish, for instance.

On the south Jersey shore once, we'd seen them: hundreds—thousands? —of jellyfish washed up on the beach after a storm.

Transparent, translucent, dying dead. Even if they are dead you would be unwise to touch one of these jellyfish with a bare forefinger.

Ray said *Let's get out of here. We can walk somewhere else.*

(Why am I thinking of jellyfish, in the Hopewell Valley Fitness Center? Why does every thought that pierces my brain seem to come from a source beyond me, and why do these thoughts bring both pain, and pleasure? Frequently we'd spoken of returning to Cape May. We'd never seen the annual bird migration which is supposed to be spectacular, nor the monarch butterfly migration. For years we'd spoken of this trip to south Jersey which was hardly an exotic trip, a matter of a few hours' drive, and in the interim we'd traveled to England and to Europe a number of times but we'd never returned to beautiful Cape May and now the thought taunts me *It's too late for Cape May. You are never going to Cape May.*)

Lisa is greeting someone else at the reception counter. Another plastic card has triggered the chirrupy THANK YOU HAVE A GOOD WORKOUT!

It's been several minutes and I am still lingering in the corridor above the stairs to the workout room.

I am thinking of how coming to the Fitness Center with Ray was fun, or could be fun sometimes.

A dutiful sort of fun. Like grocery shopping.

Once, shopping at one of those massive windowless warehouse-sized stores on Route 1, I said to Ray with an air of actual surprise *It's fun shopping with you when you're in a good mood! It doesn't matter where we are.*

Dryly Ray said *It doesn't?*

Ray's sense of humor!—he was droll, deadpan, often very funny. He never drew the attention of a gathering of friends by telling stories or anecdotes, his manner was to murmur asides, at the margins of a gathering. Sometimes his humor was unexpected, disconcerting. I know that, if Ray could comment on the Hopewell Valley Fitness Center, and on all the hours he'd spent here in the hope of maintaining "fitness," thus prolonging his life, he'd have said with a wry philosophical shrug—*Well, that was a God-damned waste of our time wasn't it!*

I am smiling, hearing this.

But nothing is sadder.

Here is the challenge: to summon all my strength, to descend the steps to the ground floor to the large, open, high-ceilinged space where the treadmills and weight machines are located.

Am I becoming catatonic? *Am I catatonic?*

(What do *catatonics* think about, I wonder. Encased in concrete, maybe they can't think at all. Maybe that's the point of *catatonia*.)

"Just the treadmill. A half hour. I can do this."

Yet—I'm out of breath so frequently now. My heartbeat feels always slightly fast. While Ray moved dutifully from one weight machine to the next usually I just ran on the treadmill—as far from other people as I could manage. I did not want to be distracted by the huffing/puffing/

grunting of red-faced sweaty men at their machines like visions out of Dante's *Inferno* of twisted bodies, contorted faces, popping eyeballs.

(Was Ray one of these diligent, determined males? Not really! There was a certain—hard to describe—*dogged languor* in my husband's fitness workouts that rarely left him sweaty, let alone short of breath. Ray had never been an athlete, nor had he much interest in sports, the lifeblood of the American male and, along with politics, the primary source of *male bonding* in our culture.)

On the treadmill, which I would set at 4.5, then raise, by degrees to 6—(for the uninitiated, this means six miles an hour—not fast for a runner)—I would lapse into a dreamy state—ridding my mind of the myriad distractions of my domestic life—what one might call "real life"—what I would now call my *inexpressibly precious real life*—that I might scroll through pages I'd written that morning—in my head revising, rewriting, "proofreading"—at such times my memory is sharply visual—eidetic?—and running seems to intensify it; my metabolism feels "normal" when I am running . . . But now, I am afraid of what my thoughts will veer toward, if I run on the treadmill. I am afraid that the frothy surf will wash over me, bearing more than I can withstand.

In the bland interior of the gym, I will be at the mercy of the memory-flash which I see almost continuously. No matter where I am, no matter what I am looking at—staring at—in fact I am seeing Ray in the hospital bed—in that moment when I hurried into the room—in the instant when I knew I'd come too late.

His face is so composed! His glasses have been removed from his face as if he were sleeping. The IV fluid drip in his bruised arm, the disfiguring oxygen mask, the heart monitor—all are removed.

They have given up on him. Their machines—they've taken from him, they've abandoned him.

I have come too late. I too abandoned him.

It's as if a scrim has descended over the world. On this scrim, the memory of Ray. My last vision of Ray . . .

Cheery-blond Lisa is surprised, I am alone. Or, I am not greeting her with a bright flash of a smile to mirror her own.

Before the Fitness Center receptionist can inquire if something is

wrong I tell her—the words are blurted out, with a faint stammer—that
my husband and I have decided to "discontinue" our membership.

You would have thought that I'd rushed to the reception counter to
report a fire.

"Oh! Is there any—reason?"

I explain that we're moving away.

We've been very happy with the Fitness Center—"It's been a wonderful place, we will miss it"—but—we're moving away.

Lisa seems personally distressed to hear this. Perhaps there is something in my face—my watery eyes, a tightness in my mouth—that stirs
her concern. Hesitantly she mentions that she hadn't seen Ray in a while—
a few weeks—and quickly I tell her, "Well, no—that isn't quite right. Ray
has been here more recently than that."

Why it seems important to me to correct the receptionist on this utterly trivial point, I have no idea.

Carefully I enunciate our names for Lisa—"Raymond Smith"—
"Joyce Smith." With a somber little smile-frown Lisa removes our cards
from a file. She types into a computer. She is terminating us, I suppose.
Erasing, deleting. Yet—"Your and your husband's membership dues are
paid through March, so you can continue to visit us . . ."

Never! The thought fills me with dread.

"Where are you and Ray moving to, Joyce?"

My mind is blank. I am having trouble remembering why I am here.
And why—alone?

"Just away. We're not sure where."

41

"Won't Be Seeing You for a While"

March 9, 2008. Since taking him to the hospital I have not dreamt of Ray. Since his death, I have not dreamt of Ray. But now, tonight, I dream of Ray.

I can't see him clearly, we're too close together. He's sitting up in a bed—I think—though wearing his familiar blue sweater. His face is close to mine, we are touching. I am leaning over him, and against him. He is showing me two framed pictures—or diagrams—and these, too, I can't see clearly. So many times—countless times!—in our life together Ray would show me material relating to the press, cover designs, photographs, pages of sample fonts—Ray would ask my opinion, we would confer—but now, since I can't see clearly what he's holding, I am not able to say anything; I am both eager and uneasy, for something is expected of me, I think—but what?

Ray's voice is low, matter-of-fact: "I guess I won't be seeing you for a while."

And then the dream ends—I'm awake—I'm stunned, and I'm awake—it's as if Ray had been in this room with me, a moment ago—and now . . .

"Oh God!"

Such a sense of loss comes over me, I can hardly bear it. I seem to be lying partly beneath my mother's quilt, and I am partly dressed.

Always, now, I wear socks to bed—warm wool socks—my toes are icy-cold, even with these socks; I wear a warm blue flannel bathrobe over my nightgown; still, I am often shivering, and try to sleep curled up, embracing my own (thin) sides, tightly. Sometimes the bedside lamp is on through the night, and the TV might be on, muted; if there's a cat sleeping with me near the foot of the bed it will be Reynard, who comes into the bedroom and leaps onto the bed as if surreptitiously in the night, only of his own volition and never—never!—if I call him; he may nudge against my foot or leg with his side but will not acknowledge me if I speak to him, or rub his head.

Tonight—it's almost 5 A.M.—the TV is not turned on, there is no companion-cat, I am alone in bed. Some of Ray's papers are scattered about me—though not the novel manuscript, which I've set aside for the time being. On the bedside table are student manuscripts I'd read, edited, and annotated some hours ago. There's a sound of wind in the trees outside—at a distance, a screech owl—what sounds like a screech owl—for the muffled shriek could be the sound of an owl's prey also.

One of us would say *Listen! Do you hear the screech owl?*

Now, I don't want to hear the screech owl. Whatever those blood-chilling shrieks are, I don't want to hear.

What I want is to return to the dream. That is all that I want. Such yearning, it's like thirst, the most terrible thirst, this yearning to return to the dream of Ray that has been the happiest event of my life, for weeks.

42

"Can't Find You Where Are You"

We were in a foreign city. We were separated from each other. There was a hotel—a large hotel—we had a room in this hotel—but I couldn't seem to find it. I was walking on a street, *alone—I was so anxious, I wouldn't be able to find you—it seemed impossible in the dream that I could ever find you—and there was no way for us to speak with each other . . .*

This recurring dream began a few years after we were married. How many variants of this dream I've had over the decades, I could not guess—hundreds?—thousands?

Ray laughed when I told him this dream. Ray took dreams very lightly, or gave that impression.

In the morning in the kitchen was the time when I would tell Ray of my recurring dream of loss—my loss of *him*. Each time I told the dream it was a slightly different dream but each time I told the dream it was obvious that it was the identical dream.

That dream again! You know I would never leave you.

Well, I know, but . . .

I would never dream about you that way.

In a tone of mild reproach Ray spoke as if this were the issue—some failure of trust of him, on my part—and not rather, what seems obvious, my terror at losing him.

Now since Ray has died, my sole recurring dream seems to have ceased.

In fact, the Widow's recurring dream of decades will have ceased permanently. Which seems to refute the theory that the unconscious has but a primitive sense of time and capriciously confuses past, present, future as if all were one.

43

"I Am Sorry to Inform You"

Thank you for your submission. I am sorry to inform you that, due to the unexpected death of editor Raymond Smith, *Ontario Review* will cease publication after its May 2008 issue.

Several hundred of these little blue slips I had printed up, a few days after Ray's death.

It's a measure of my fractured concentration at the time—my reputation for prolificacy notwithstanding—that numerous drafts were required to compose this melancholy rejection slip.

Originally, I'd written *unexpected death* but then, rereading what I'd written, I thought that it sounded too—melodramatic, or self-pitying. Or subjective.

For, for whom was the death of Raymond Smith *unexpected*; and why should total strangers care? Why should total strangers be informed?

Unexpected was therefore removed, but later, how many hours and drafts later I would be embarrassed to say, *unexpected* was re-inserted.

Sorry to inform you of the unexpected death of Raymond Smith.

Like a mildly deranged large flying insect trapped in a small space these words careened and blundered about inside my skull for an inordinate amount of time.

For I knew—common sense dictated—that I had no choice, I would have to discontinue *Ontario Review* which Ray and I had edited together since 1974. This was heartrending but I saw no alternative—90 percent of the editorial work on the magazine and 100 percent of the publishing/financial work had been my husband's province.

We'd begun the biannual *Ontario Review: A North American Journal of the Arts* while we were living in Windsor, Ontario, and teaching together in the English department at the University of Windsor. I'd had the idea that since "small magazines" had been so integral a part of my writing career, I should help finance one of our own; also, both Ray and I were interested in promoting the work of excellent writers whom we knew in both Canada and the United States. Our intention was to publish Canadian and American writers and to make no distinction between the two, which was the special agenda of *Ontario Review.*

Our first issue, Fall 1974, was greeted with much interest in literary Canada—not because it was an extraordinary gathering of first-rate North American talent (which we believed it was) but because there were, at the time, many more writers and poets than there were reputable outlets for their work in Canada. We were fortunate to publish an interview with Philip Roth—which I'd "conducted"—as well as fiction by Bill Henderson, soon to become the founder of the legendary *Pushcart Prize: Best of the Small Presses*, and Lynne Sharon Schwartz before she'd published her first book of fiction. Like most beginning editors we'd called upon our friends to write for us and our "briefly noted" reviews—of new books by Paul Theroux, Alice Munro, and Beth Harvor—at the time virtually unknown—were signed "JCO."

Starting a literary magazine is an adventure not for the fainthearted or the easily discouraged. Neither Ray nor I knew what to expect. Ray's first experience with a printer was a near disaster—the printer had never printed anything more ambitious than a menu for a local Chinese restaurant—the page proofs were riddled with errors that required hours of Ray's time and patience to correct; and, when the copies were finally printed, for some reason we never understood, a number were smeared with bloody fingerprints.

I wish that I could recall Ray's exact words, when he eagerly opened the box from the printer, and saw the mysterious stains on the covers. I want to think that he'd said something appropriately witty but probably what emerged from his throat more resembled a sob.

And very likely I said uselessly *Oh honey! How on earth did this happen!*

Carefully we examined each of the copies to weed out the soiled ones—another effort that required hours. Exactly how many copies of this premiere issue Ray had had printed up, I can't remember: maybe 1,000?

(If 1,000, most of these were never sold. No doubt, we gave them away. And we paid our contributors partly with three-year subscriptions. It would be years before *OR* had a circulation of 1,000.)

Our second issue went far more smoothly than the first. Through a bit of good luck—I'd written to Saul Bellow whom I scarcely knew, requesting something from him—we had a "self-interview" by Bellow, at about the time of *Humboldt's Gift*. (When Bellow's literary agent discovered that Saul had sent us this little gem, the agent tried to take it back; but too late, we told her—we'd already gone to press.) We published work by the Canadian writer Marian Engel, and poetry by Wendell Berry, David Ignatow, César Vallejo (in translation), and Theodore Weiss (destined to become our close friend after we moved to Princeton in 1978).

In 1984, when we'd been in Princeton for several years, and Ray had resigned from teaching in order to be a full-time editor/publisher, we decided to expand our small-press enterprise to include book publishing. (Why? Out of some "reckless commingling of idealism and masochism" was Ray's droll explanation.) Though neither the magazine nor the press ever made any profit, we were, resolutely, not "non-profit"; our projects were funded privately, by my Princeton University salary and other more random spurts of income.

The 1980s was a time when libraries were still subscribing to literary magazines and buying poetry books, a situation that would change drastically in the late 1990s. In Canadian publishing circles *Ontario Review* soon ascended to the sort of small-press literary eminence belonging, in the States, to *Paris Review, Kenyon Review, Quarterly Review of Literature*, and Ray Smith was a "major" editor/publisher in these quarters.

Ray's Jesuit training in adolescence had instilled in him a predilection for what is called *perfectionism* but which might resemble, to a neutral observer, *obsessive-compulsive disorder*. Thus, Ray was the ideal editor—as well as copyeditor and proofreader; though he sent out page proofs to our authors, he never trusted any eye but his own, and so he did everything except "set type"—in those days when type was still "set"—and no doubt he would have done that, if he'd been able. Apart from our domestic life, Ray's work was his life. Most of all Ray had loved working with writers: there is no relationship quite so intimate and intense, when an editor is truly absorbed in editing, and a writer is willing to be "edited." Enormous sympathy, tact, diplomacy, shrewdness are required—and a sense of humor. Ray took—this does sound rather masochistic, or at least eccentric—genuine pleasure in reading unsolicited submissions which numbered in the thousands, annually; he passed on to me fiction that was "promising" but needed work, so that, if I wished to, I might work with the writer, making editorial suggestions. He took particular pleasure in working with writers one or the other of us had "discovered"—like Pinckney Benedict, my prize-winning Princeton student whose remarkable senior thesis *Town Smokes* (1987) was one of our first OR Press books, and would be one of the most enduring.

When Ray spoke of Pinckney it was with a special—warm, tender—intonation in his voice.

When Ray spoke of a number of writers and poets with whom he'd worked closely over the years, you could see how much they'd meant to him—even those whom we'd never met.

How touching it is, if heartrending—the dedication to the 2009 *Pushcart Prize*: *Best of the Small Presses*, edited by Bill Henderson, reads:

for Raymond Smith (1930–2008)

Now, all this has ended. No one can take Ray's place. Most of all, continuing to bring out *Ontario Review* without Ray could have no meaning, for me—it would be like celebrating someone's birthday *in absentia*.

The May issue was nearly completed, when Ray had to be hospitalized. Just a few more days' work—which I hope I can do, with the assistance of our typesetter in Michigan. I have a dread of letting down Ray's contributors, who are expecting to see their work in his magazine.

I will have to pay them, too—of course. I will have to calculate what they should be paid, write checks and mail them. I will have to package contributors' copies, and mail them. A kind of wildness sweeps over me, almost a kind of elation. *If I can do this, how impressed Ray would be! How he would know, I love him.*

When I called Gail Godwin, to tell her about Ray, Gail's response was immediate—"Oh Joyce—you're going to be so unhappy."

How true this is! It's a blunt fact few would wish to acknowledge.

There are friends whom we see often—and there are friends whom we see rarely. My friendship of more than thirty years with Gail Godwin has been mostly epistolary, writerly. We are like cousins, or sisters, of a bygone era—the long-ago era of the Brontë sisters, perhaps. And Gail's house on a hillside in Woodstock, New York, overlooking, at a distance, the Catskill Mountains, has something of the air of romance and isolation of the fabled Yorkshire moors.

Many times Ray and I had visited Gail and her longtime companion, the distinguished composer Robert Starer, in their Woodstock house. Robert's unexpected death in the spring of 2001 had the sorrowful feel of the end of an era, though I had not dared to think that my husband would be next.

How similar our experiences have been, Gail's and mine! It is uncanny.

Like Ray, Robert had been hospitalized as if "temporarily"—he'd had a heart attack from which he seemed to be recovering; his condition was "stable"; then, early one morning as Gail was preparing to drive to the hospital in Kingston to see him, she received a call from a doctor whom she didn't know—who happened to be on duty at the time: "I'm afraid Robert didn't make it."

Didn't make it! But he had been recovering . . . hadn't he?

So we protest, in disbelief. Clinging to what has seemingly been promised to us, like children. *But, but—! But he was recovering! You'd said—he was still alive.*

Gail too had driven to the hospital in a trance. Gail too had not believed that her husband wouldn't be waiting for her in his hospital room. Driving in the early morning along a darkened highway each of us thinking incredulously *Is my husband dying? Is he dying? He can't be—dying! The doctor has said—he is alive . . .*

Long after hope has vanished, these phantom-words remain.

Alive, he is still . . . alive. He is recovering.

He will be discharged next Tuesday.

Gail has offered me sympathy, counsel. I am so very broken, I find it difficult to speak. Rarely do I speak to anyone on the telephone any longer but I am able to speak with Gail and to tell Gail that I wish we lived closer together, we might commiserate together, but neither of us is likely to move. Who but Gail Godwin would tell me: "Suffer, Joyce. Ray was worth it."

This is so. This is true. But the test is: Am I strong enough to suffer? And for how long?

Did you send the rest of the copy to Doug? What about the cover art which I didn't finish—can you prepare it and send it to him, FedEx?

(Doug Hagley is Ray's excellent typesetter, in Marquette, Michigan.)

I may as well admit it—if Ray could miraculously return from the dead, within a day or two—within a few hours—he would be working again on *Ontario Review.*

He was working in his hospital bed, on the very last day of his life. He'd be terribly concerned now, that the publication date of the May issue will be delayed . . .

I am trying. Honey, I am trying!

Like a desperate individual in a sailboat, a small sailboat foundering in a raging sea, after the sailor has died, swept overboard and drowned and the left-behind companion must try to keep the sailboat from sinking . . . It's ridiculous to think of completing the voyage when the most you can hope for is to stay afloat.

And so, I am trying. I will do what Ray would want me to do—if I can.

At the moment, opening mail. The Sisyphus-task of clipping these little blue rejection slips to manuscripts. Sometimes I fall into an open-eyed trance reading lines of a poem, a short story, until my eyes lose focus.

In the hospital, we'd read submissions together, and discussed them.

I'd brought two short stories for Ray to read which I was recommending for publication—two stories about which I felt very enthusiastic—but now suddenly, all that has ended. I am distressed to think that possibly the manuscripts have been lost, were never brought back from the hospital.

Terrible to think, things are being lost! I had tried so hard yet Ray's glasses are gone.

As the days—weeks—months pass, the effort of responding to *OR* submissions will become increasingly vexing. I'd thought that word should have spread in the literary community—through our *Ontario Review* Web site, and obituaries—that Ray Smith has passed away, that the magazine is discontinued—yet, with clockwork predictability, the submissions keep coming. Of course, most of these are multiply submitted, as if by robot-writers who begin their form letters *Dear Editor* and seem to have no idea what *Ontario Review* is. (More than two years later robot-submissions will continue to arrive in the mailbox, some of them addressed to *Raymond Smith, Editor,* though this beleaguered "associate editor" has ceased returning them, figuring that by now a statute of limitations has been evoked. Enough!)

Yet, in March 2008, I am diligent—if that's the word—about opening mail. Occasionally, there are even book-length manuscripts, unsolicited—which I return to the sender with a little blue slip *Thank you for your submission.* Sometimes I add a few words, and sign my initials. Even in my numbed state I feel an impulse to encourage writers, or anyway a wish not to discourage them. Thinking *It would have meant something to me, years ago.*

Though nothing means much to me, now. The possibility of being "encouraged" has become abstract and theoretical to me—"encouraged" for what purpose?

Your writing will not save you. Managing to be published—by Ontario Review Press!—will not save you. Don't be deluded.

As with the trash, I dare not allow this mail to accumulate; you might (almost) say, the mail *is* the trash. Most dreaded, beyond even the Harry & David sympathy baskets, is that particularly nasty sub-species of ridged cardboard book-package in which a few publishers persist in sending books, bound with metal staplers thick as spikes. To try to open one of these monstrosities is an exercise in masochism—hurriedly I dis-

card them with the dispatch with which one would thrust away a venomous snake.

Pleading *No! No more of this! Please have mercy.*

Each week the trash cans are so filled that their plastic covers fall
off, and clatter to the pavement as I wheel the cans to the road.

Why would Sisyphus push a boulder up a hill?—much more likely
the poor accursed man was hauling trash cans up the hill, day following
day, *in perpetuity.*

Amid all this, what a joke—a cruel joke—that publishers continue to send me galleys and manuscripts requesting blurbs—yet more
mail, packages to be torn open and recycled. In my state of absolute
lucidity—which might be mistaken for commonplace depression—
nothing seems to be so pathetic as these requests. Nothing so sad, so
futile, so ridiculous—a blurb from *me.*

If the name "Joyce Carol Oates" affixed to her own books can't sell
these books, how can the name "Joyce Carol Oates" affixed to another's
book help to sell that book? This is a joke!

My heart beats hard with resentment, despair. Though my effort
seems so futile, like cleaning all the rooms of the house in preparation
for my husband's return from the hospital, turning on all the lights—or,
turning them off—yet I can't seem to stop, and the thought of hiring
someone to help me, or even bringing anyone into the house for this
purpose, is not possible. All I know is—I can't let Ray down. This is my
responsibility as his wife.

I mean, his widow.

I feel trapped. I am trapped. On the far side of our pond once we'd
seen a young deer, a buck, shaking his head violently—his slender horns
were tangled in what looked like wire. This is how I feel—my head is
tangled in wire.

The reptile-thing—the basilisk—has been regarding me all this
time with its glassy-bead stare, the bemused saurian eyes that penetrate
to my very soul. *You know you can end this at any time. Your ridiculous
trash-soul. Why should you outlive your husband? If you love him, as you
claim? Don't you think that everyone is waiting for you to die, to end this
folly? Outliving your husband is a low vile vulgar thing and you do not
deserve to live an hour longer, you are the very trash you need to haul away.*

IV

PURGATORY, HELL

Which way I flie is Hell; my self am Hell.
— Lucifer in Milton's *Paradise Lost*

There is but one truly serious philosophical
problem, and that is suicide. Judging whether life
is or is not worth living amounts to answering the
fundamental question of philosophy.
—Albert Camus, "An Absurd Reasoning"
from *The Myth of Sisyphus*

44

"Neither Joyce Nor I Can Come to the Phone Right Now"

Hello! Neither Joyce nor I can come to the phone right now but if you leave a detailed message and your phone number, we will get back to you soon. Thank you for calling.

This phone message, recorded by Ray several years ago in a somewhat subdued voice, greets everyone who calls, since these days—in the late winter/early spring of 2008—I rarely pick up the phone.

Yes I hear the phone ringing and—can't move to answer it.

The ringing phone paralyzes me, I can barely breathe until it stops.

I have to resist the impulse to run, when the phone rings.

To run away, to hide. Somewhere.

It's true, we have caller ID—Ray installed it, in my desk phone—and so I should be able to screen unwanted calls and speak with my most cherished friends but often I am nowhere near this phone and my instinct is to back away, not hurry forward.

Often I am not in a mood to speak with even my most cherished friends.

Fear of breaking down on the phone.

Fear of draining friends' capacity for sympathy.

Fear of useless behavior, futile & embarrassing.

No one has chided me for continuing to use Ray's phone message, quite yet. Though several individuals have remarked upon it.

One has said it's a "comfort" to hear Ray's voice exactly as it has been in this phone message, for years.

One has said—delicately—it's "a little jarring, distracting."

One has said—"The voice on the answering machine is the uncanniest abstraction to deal with."

To these remarks, I have said nothing.

In time it will be suggested—tactfully, delicately—by my closest friends, that I should change the recorded message. One woman friend has volunteered her husband, to do a re-recording.

This is sensible advice, but I seem not to hear it. I never respond to it, I simply seem not to hear it.

Though in a rage wanting to cry *Would you erase your husband's voice from your phone message? Of course you would not!*

It will be well over a year and a half before Ray's phone message is finally erased, to be replaced by a (female) computer-voice that chills the blood. But through this hurricane-year 2008, Ray's voice will prevail.

At the university, in my office at 185 Nassau I call our home number frequently. First I dial 9 for an outside line, and then the number. A curious sort of solace—that the ringing at the other end of the line is indistinguishable from the ringing I'd heard for years, when I called Ray from this phone. Usually I called my husband at home for no particular reason but to say hello, to murmur *Love you!* and hang up and now that it is futile to call, I am calling the number anyway.

Five or six rings and then a little click—and there is Ray's voice— exactly as I recall it—as it had been in all those years I'd taken the recording for granted as if it were a permanent feature of the very landscape, or the oxygen surrounding me—*Hello! Neither Joyce nor I can come to the phone right now but if you leave a detailed message and your phone number, we will get back to you soon. Thank you for calling.*

Sometimes, I call this number more than once. My fingers move numbly like fingers "saying" a rosary.

Ray's words have become a kind of poetry—the kind of point-blank plain-speech heart-rending American vernacular poetry perfected by William Carlos Williams in simple columnar stanzas. Keenly I attend to the accent of Ray's syllables, the pause between words—almost, I can hear him draw breath, I can envision his facial expression as these several so-precious seconds out of his life of seventy-seven years, eleven months and twenty-two days is recorded—

Hello!
Neither Joyce nor I can come to the phone right now
But if you leave a detailed message
and your phone number
We will get back to you
soon
Thank you for calling

But quietly then, I hang up.
No message.

How many widows have made this futile call—dialed numbers which are their own numbers; how many widows have listened to their dead husband's voices again, again—again . . .
As you will too, one day. If you are the survivor.

45

The Military Order of the Purple Heart

Keep in motion. Don't break promises. Grieving is self-pity, narcissism. Don't give in.

Each day I set myself a modest goal: to get through the day.

Isn't this the fundamental principle of Alcoholics Anonymous? *One day at a time.*

My friend Gloria Vanderbilt has consoled me *One breath at a time, Joyce. One breath at a time.*

Gloria Vanderbilt, whose son Carter died in an unspeakable way, virtually in her presence.

Soon after Ray died Gloria came out to Princeton to spend some time with me—to commiserate, to give hope—and left in my keeping a small statue of St. Theresa which had been left to her by her beloved nanny many years ago when, as in a cruel fairy tale out of the Brothers Grimm, Gloria Vanderbilt was a child-pawn in a luridly publicized custody suit played out in the New York City courts.

This statue of St. Theresa is on our bedroom bureau. On my bedroom bureau. Where I can see it easily, from my nest in my bed.

Jesus! What on earth is a statue of St. Theresa doing in our bedroom? Ray would cry in startled exasperation. *I'm gone a few days and—a statue of St. Theresa in our bedroom?*

Like all permanently lapsed Roman Catholics, Ray much resented any incursion of his old "faith" into his post-religious life.

Yet: like all former Roman Catholics, Ray would know to distinguish between St. Theresa and the Virgin Mary.

How can I explain this statue of St. Theresa in our home, I can't explain. Except that the statue is facing me, in my nest, across a distance of less than six feet.

March 3, 2008.
To Gloria Vanderbilt
    The St. Theresa statue is astonishing in our bedroom. It exudes an air of antique calm and beauty. I can't believe that you have given me such a precious part of your life. I told Elaine (Showalter) and several others who'd come to see it that I did not feel worthy of this gift and one of them said, "It speaks of Gloria's love for you" which left me stricken to the heart.
    Thank you so much,
    Joyce

The basilisk!

Glassy eyes and chill saurian composure. Utterly still, its reptile heart scarcely beats.

Ugly lizard-creature that beckons me *to death, to die.*

If I sleep a drugged sleep, the basilisk vanishes. But when I wake up—when consciousness blasts me like Mace—the thing returns.

Like the Cheshire cat in *Wonderland*—first, Alice sees the maddening grin appearing in mid-air; then, by degrees, the outline of the large graceless cat, that fills in.

So too the basilisk. The dead stare, that comes first; then, the rest of it.

If I take Lorazepam in the doses that have been prescribed for me I am sure that the basilisk will disappear. Or, if the obscene thing is hovering in my vision, I won't be upset by it.

But if I take too much of this powerful tranquilizer—or the sleeping pills that have been prescribed for me—I will lapse into a deep sleep, possibly a coma and in this way, the basilisk will triumph.

So I am determined to *Keep in motion! To keep my promises!*

When Ray was hospitalized, we canceled our visit to the University of Nevada at Las Vegas. But I think that I will honor the rest of my professional commitments and maintain the schedule of my former life so far as I can.

Cleveland, Ohio. Boca Raton, Florida. New York University. Columbia, South Carolina, and Sanibel Island, Florida.

Readings, lectures, visits for which I've been contracted for months. My agent has suggested that she cancel all my obligations for the next half year but I've told her no, I can't do that.

> *Pride in professional integrity.*
> *Wish not to be viewed as weak, broken.*
> *Fear of remaining home, alone.*

> *Fear of being lost away from home.*
> *Fear of breaking down among strangers.*
> *Fear of being "recognized"...*

March 5, 2008.
To Jeanne Halpern

I called you at about 10 P.M. from howling-snowstorm-bound Cleveland last night, after my reading for the Cuyahoga County Library, which went well despite the terrible weather; in my hotel suite at the Ritz—a very grand suite, with flowers—I was overcome with loneliness and dread, that I couldn't call Ray as always I'd done at these times . . . So I called you, and Lily answered; and I am glad that you were out because I would have been very emotional, and as it was I called Edmund White who quickly cheered me up with tales of his life and misadventures . . .

Much love,
Joyce

March 6, 2008.

To Elaine Showalter

Lovely to see you and English! Most of the time I am in a state of anxiety, however, about legal/financial matters, and life is looking quite grim. Even with medication, I just can't sleep—I've taken a dose and a half of the medication prescribed for me, and I couldn't be more awake, and I have to teach tomorrow, take a car to NYC and give a reading. . . . I guess that, without Ray, there doesn't seem much point to anything I do. But it was lovely to see you and English both days. "Daylight" is my good time—the rest of the time, not so good.

Much love,

Joyce

Half-seriously I am thinking of sending an e-mail bulletin to friends *Please don't laugh at me and/or be alarmed but is there any one of you whom I might "hire"—if you could overcome the scruples of friendship and allow me to pay you in some actual way—to keep me alive for a year, at least? Otherwise—*

Of course this is only *half*-serious.

Of course I dare not hint at such desperation, gossip would run like wildfire through our circle of friends, and beyond, terribly beyond, concentric circles of close friends/"good"friends/friendly acquaintances/colleagues strangers to effloresce on the Internet, luridly highlighted for all to see.

March 6, 2008.

To Mike Keeley

Mike, thank you! Ray loved you so. He had no idea that he would never see any of us again—his last words (preserved on my voice-mail service) are so tender and upbeat. It just seems unbelievable to me. I am so yearning for a companion—even a fantasy or ghost companion (like Harvey the invisible rabbit) to dwell in this house, just to suggest not the reality of the man but some glimmering essence of him. Half the time, I think I must be totally out of my mind. At other times, like last

night, I think I am relatively sane. I hope this gets easier. But the legal/
financial side is overwhelming, and may crack me before the emotional
side does . . .

    Much love to both,

    Joyce

My discovery is: each day is livable if divided into segments.

More accurately each day is livable *only if divided into segments.*

The widow soon realizes that an entire day, as others live it—that vast hideous Sahara of tractless time—is not possible to endure.

Thus the widow is advised to divide the day into Morning—Afternoon I—Afternoon II—Evening—Night.

Mornings, one would assume to be the very worst times, are actually not so very bad since the widow is likely to remain in bed longer than "normal" people do. Since the widow is happiest—that is, happy—only when asleep—deeply asleep—in a tar pit-sludge-sleep predating not only any memory of the catastrophe in her life but any memory of the possibility of catastrophe—it's likely that the widow will find it very difficult to get out of bed.

Get out of bed? How about—opening one's eyes?

No one will understand—no one, except the widow—that the act of *opening one's eyes* is an exhausting act, an act requiring reckless abandon, rare courage, imagination; by *opening one's eyes* the widow has committed herself to another day of the ongoing siege, a hurricane of emotions that leaves us broken and battered yet determined to be, or to appear to be, resilient, even "normal." Worst yet, after *opening one's eyes* is the act of *getting out of bed*—requiring, in this weakened state, the fanatic drive and willfulness of the Olympic athlete.

At first, I could not force myself to open my eyes for a very long time, lying in a state approaching the comatose; listening with mounting dread for the sounds of delivery vehicles in the driveway, the footfalls of delivery men bringing (unwanted, invariably bulky and stapled) packages to the front door, and for the ringing of the doorbell; once, or more than once, well-intentioned friends came to see me, making their way into the courtyard and ringing the doorbell; when I failed to answer, cowering in the disheveled nest in my bed, strewn with papers, bound galleys, books from the previous night, the well-intentioned friends would naturally knock on the door—rap their knuckles sharply on the door—call, in voices meant to disguise their alarm: "Joyce? *Joyce?*" Sometimes it happened that I had only just fallen asleep at about dawn, and the intrusion—that is, the visit from the friend—the well-intentioned friend—came at about 9 A.M.; sometimes, in the aftermath of my insomniac haze, when I'd given in at about 5 A.M. and taken half of a capsule of a prescription sleeping pill—not yet Ambien, for I was hoarding Ambien, but Lunesta—the knocking would come even earlier, waking me from the tar pit sleep of utter, so exquisitely yearned-for oblivion with the blow of a sledgehammer to the head and rendering me paralyzed with despair, misery. At such times—and there are many such times in a widow's slapstick-comedy life—it's clear that if I were to actually summon up my courage to swallow down an "overdose" of drugs—if I'd managed at last to marshal all my energies in a reckless bid to "put myself out of my misery"—the gesture would come to a rudely abrupt ending with the unexpected arrival of the friend. "Joyce? *Joyce?*"

How terrible, the sound of my name. At such times. For to be *Joyce* is to be by definition *The one no one else would wish to be.*

Joyce Carol Oates has an even more mocking-melancholy sound, for the pretension of so many syllables. *What a joke!*

Yet, I will behave reasonably, you can count on it. I will try to behave reasonably. In any case what choice do I have but to drag myself from bed scattering papers onto the carpeted floor, a bound galley or two, an offprint or two by Raymond Smith, tattered paperback copies of Pascal, Nietzsche, Spinoza's *Ethics* (consulted as much for its sleep-inducing possibilities as for the thrill of a logician's imagination turned to the challenge of *reducing the chaos of the world to unity, order, sanity, meaning*) and though my brain has become a sodden mass of gauze in which crazed thoughts teem like maggots, and I must have looked like a scarecrow dragged along a rutted road behind a pickup truck, yet I would lean out into the hallway—(in this single-storey house of mostly glass walls there is really nowhere to hide except the bathrooms, the furnace room, and one or two shadowy corners of other rooms)—calling to my friend a random and desperate response—"Hi! Hello! Yes I'm here! I'm all right—I'm fine! I'm *here!*"—adding with a forced little stoic-laugh, "I'm just not able to see you right now, I'm so sorry—I'll call you, later."

The friend responds: "Joyce? *Are* you all right?"

"Yes! Yes I am *all right!* I'll call you later."

Silently pleading *Please go away, for now. Please!*

Thinking *Is there nowhere I can hide? Is there nowhere—except to die?*

Another morning the phone rings—early—after a miserable in-somniac night that has spilled over into the day like feculent water—the phone ringing in the adjacent room that is Ray's study and for some reason instead of cringing beneath the bedclothes pretending not to hear I am moved to answer—for it might be "my" lawyer, or "my" ac-countant—one or another individual whom the endless requirements of *death-duties* have caused to appear in my life—I am suffused with anxiety thinking *I must answer this*—and so I stagger into the next room partly dressed, barefoot and shivering and it's my brother Fred who lives in Clarence, New York, not far from our old, long-razed family farm-house in desolate Millersport, New York—a rural community approx-imately twenty miles north of Buffalo—and of course I am happy to speak with Fred, my younger brother who has been such a solace to me, if but over the phone, and at a distance; my wonderful brother who was so attentive to our parents, in the latter part of their lives when they lived in an assisted-care facility in Amherst; but while I'm on the phone with Fred, a delivery man appears at the front door less than fifteen feet away, ringing the doorbell, rapping with his knuckles, and I am crouched in Ray's study trying to hide, silently pleading *Please just go away! Go away and take whatever it is you have with you please!*

In my tattered paperback *Nietzsche* is the philosopher's famous aphorism— *The thought of suicide is a strong consolation; one can get through many a bad night with it.*

Nietzsche also said *If you stare too long into an abyss, the abyss will gaze back into you.*

And, in the quasi-visionary voice of Zarathustra *Many die too late, and some die too early. Yet strange soundeth the precept: Die at the right time.*

How often these aphorisms run through my mind, like electric shocks! And at unexpected times, like random shocks.

Yet: even in his profound loneliness and the despair of his final, protracted illness/madness, Friedrich Nietzsche did not commit suicide.

Nor did Albert Camus commit suicide. (By his own terms, Camus died a worse death—a "meaningless" death in a car crash, as a passenger. Suicide would have been preferable!)

Do not think—if you are healthy-minded, and the thought of suicide is abhorrent to you—(as it was to Ray)—that suicide is, for others, a "negative" thought—not at all. Suicide is in fact a consoling thought. Suicide is the secret door by which you can exit the world at any time— it's wholly up to you.

For who can prevent you, if suicide is truly your wish? Who has the moral authority, who can know your heart?

The basilisk's stare!—that is the suicide-temptation. That, the very face of deadness, void.

Yet while the thought of suicide is consoling, it's also terrifying. For suicide is the secret door that, once you have opened it and stepped through, swings shut and locks behind you—never can you re-cross that threshold.

The basilisk-stare is accursed. It is a temptation that must be resisted.

In this way, thinking seriously of suicide is a deterrent to suicide. As it is to think of the posthumous consequences of suicide—what its effect would be upon others.

My brother Fred, for instance. For I have recently made him the executor of my estate.

As I am "executrix" of Ray's estate, thus having inherited a matrix of responsibilities not unlike the responsibility one would feel carrying a pyramid of eggs across a lurching floor.

Speaking to my brother I am thinking these thoughts but I would never share my thoughts with my brother, or with anyone; I would never impose such an awkward intimacy upon another. A few days ago I actually asked a friend what she would do in my place, thinking she would say *I would kill myself of course* and instead she said thoughtfully, astonishingly *I think I would move to Paris. I would buy a flat, and live in Paris. Yes—I think that's exactly what I would do.*

How bizarre this seemed to me! Like suggesting to a paraplegic that she take up cross-country skiing, or marathon running.

(The only friend with whom I've spoken openly of such matters is Edmund White who has seen so many friends and lovers die of AIDS, and is, at the time of this writing, the oldest individual diagnosed as HIV-positive; dear Edmund who has, very likely, a cache of powerful pills like mine, accumulated over the years, and an appreciation of Nietzsche's admonition to die at the right time . . .)

The delivery man has gone away. The conversation with my brother has ended. Now I am "up"—the first hurdle of the day successfully mastered—I am feeling almost enlivened. I am thinking of how Ray usually got up between 7 A.M. and 7:30 A.M. He seemed to wake immediately, with no transition; one moment asleep, the next awake; while I woke by degrees, slowly, as if ascending from a deep region of the sea, to the lighted surface far above; leaving a darkly warm region of dreams for the starkness of daylight. Until this final winter when he'd seemed to have less energy Ray had gone running—jogging—for about two miles every morning, in all weathers—in addition to going out with me every afternoon (running, walking, bicycling, Fitness Center); but I'd never had Ray's motivation to get up so early. And to run in the cold, even in the rain sometimes.

Chiding him, fondly—"Your feet are wet! You'll catch pneumonia."

March 7, 2008.

To Jan Perkins and Margery Cuyler

Is there anything like a "grief support group" locally? I may have to try this . . . I'm not sure that I can get through this alone. My personality seems to be falling apart. Especially at night. I am usually all right among other people but begin to fall apart when alone. I guess I can't grasp it somehow, that Ray is really gone. That he isn't just somewhere where I can't see him. It just seems impossible . . .

Perhaps something like an AA group—(sounds so Nabokovian).

Sorry to go on and on about myself! That really is evidence of derangement . . .

Love,

Joyce

Of the many things I did not tell my friends, I did not tell them of how, the day following Ray's death, that night unable to sleep I cleared away approximately one-half of my clothes, from our bedroom closet.

Not Ray's clothes! My own.

In a heap I threw dresses, skirts, slacks, shirts—sweaters—things not worn for a year or more. In some cases, a decade.

Dresses I had worn, with Ray, long ago in Windsor. In Detroit. Dinner parties, festive occasions. There are photographs of the two of us, in our dress-up clothes. Looking so happy.

In a fever to be rid of these clothes—clothes that had once been new— clothes I'd once took pleasure in wearing—on my knees with paper towels and Windex cleaning the dusty floor of the closet.

A kind of rage is smoldering in my heart. Why am I so angry— jeering-angry—*You are alone now. All this is vanity, worthless. What a ridiculous person you are! This is what you deserve.*

Clothes twisted into a heap, stuffed into a garbage bag, to be dragged out to the curb. So crucial it seems to me, to get rid of these things, not to give them a second glance, I don't think to call Good Will, or the Salvation Army—or maybe it seems to me no one would want my clothes, no one would want *me.*

Next day, after the trash has been taken away, and the clothes are gone, and my closet half-empty—I'm stricken with a sense of loss.

Why did I do such a thing? Why, so desperately?

Ray's clothes, I have left untouched. Ray's beautiful gray wool sport coat, his camel's hair coat, his shirts still in the Mayflower laundry wrapper, his khaki shorts neatly folded . . . But there is a bureau drawer stuffed with his socks, I think that I will give away Ray's socks, there is a veterans' service organization I will call—the Military Order of the Purple Heart.

Weeks later, I am staring at the Purple Heart card left in our mail-box. It can only be coincidental, I am thinking.

We need small household items and your usable clothes. We raise funds for service, welfare, and rehabilitation work in connection with the members of the Military Order of the Purple Heart of the U.S.A. Those eligible for membership are any wounded, disabled and/or handicapped veteran, his/her surviving spouse, orphan or other survivor.

Quickly I place Ray's socks—(neatly folded after laundering, by Ray)—in a cloth bag. So many socks!—white cotton socks, black silky socks, checked socks. I can't bring myself to give away Ray's shirts, sweaters, jackets, neckties—but socks are minimal, lacking identity and significance.

In other bags and boxes, more articles of clothing (my own), random household items like plates, glasses, vases, coffee mugs.

None of these needs to be discarded but I think that I must donate more than merely socks to the veterans' service organization. And when mid-morning a van appears at the end of our driveway and the driver comes to load things into his vehicle I feel a flash of terror, the sensation you feel when you realize you're making a terrible mistake but it's too late—too late!

Now, Ray's bureau drawer is empty. I have no idea why I have done what I've done. (Did I think that I *needed* the bureau drawer?) I feel sick, stunned. I could have run after the van and called for him to stop, I could have taken back the socks—(maybe)—but a kind of paralysis had come over me, I simply stood at the window staring helplessly as at Ray's bedside when I'd arrived too late I had stood staring helplessly at Ray, my brain struck empty of even self-loathing, self-recrimination.

The lizard-thing, the basilisk—that wants me to give up, to die—is staring at me, steady and resolute, waiting, from just a few feet away but I don't look. I won't.

46

In Motion!

Keep in motion!—here is salvation.

And so in these hallucinatory weeks following Ray's death I am determined to impersonate "JCO" as flawlessly as in the cult film *Blade Runner* the race of replicants impersonated human beings. I am determined to impersonate "JCO" not merely because I have contracted to do so but because—a fact I am not likely to acknowledge in the Q & A sessions following my readings/lectures—it is the most effective way of eluding the basilisk.

And there is the stark blunt fact *What difference does it make where you are, there is nowhere you will not be alone and all places are equidistant from death.*

Cuyahoga County, Ohio. March 4, 2008. Amid a blizzard—banshee-howling winds—there's an almost festive air—giddiness, gaiety—when the plane bearing sixty or so ghastly-pale passengers westward from Philadelphia in the way of a small boat on a stormy sea lands—slightly lurching, wobbly—but not disastrously—on the snow-whipped runway at the Cleveland airport.

I will try to feel good about this. I will try not to hear the mocking refrain running through my head *There once was a ship, and she sailed upon the sea. And the name of our ship . . .*

Somehow it has happened, against the advice of friends, and my longtime lecture-agent Janet Cosby, that I have come to Cleveland to give a talk—"The Writer's (Secret) Life: Woundedness, Rejection, and Inspiration"—for a fund-raiser evening sponsored by the Cuyahoga County Public Library in a suburb of Cleveland, Ohio. My appearance isn't at the library but in the Ohio Theater, a quaintly restored movie palace of the 1920s with a midnight-blue-felt sky twinkling with stars—vast space is suggested, magical transformations as in a children's storybook—a cavernous space of one thousand seats—of which only about half will be filled, as a result of this terrible weather.

"Miss Oates! Thank you so much for coming! We heard about your husband, we're so very sorry . . ."

My hosts are women: librarians. Very nice people.

Inevitably, everywhere—(yes, I can be quoted on this!)—the very nicest people you meet are likely to be librarians.

How hard this is, however—maintaining my poise as "JCO" when I am being addressed, so bluntly, as a woman whose husband has died—a "widow."

How hard too, to change the subject—to deflect the subject—for I must not break down, not now. I know that these women mean well, of course they mean well, one or another of these women might in fact be widowed herself, but their words leave me stricken and unable to speak, at first. Accepting their condolences I must be courteous, gracious. I must understand that their solicitude is genuine, that they have no idea how desperately I would like not to be reminded of my "loss"—at this time, particularly.

By degrees then "JCO" returns, or resumes—the precarious moment has passed.

I am thinking of having a T-shirt printed:

YES MY HUSBAND DIED.
YES I AM VERY SAD.
YES YOU ARE KIND TO OFFER CONDOLENCES.
NOW CAN WE CHANGE THE SUBJECT?

With eight or ten others, mostly women, I am taken to dinner at a private club close by the Ohio Theater; our hostess—clearly a donor with money—stares at me almost rudely during the course of the dinner as she interrogates me at length about my novel *The Gravedigger's Daughter*, seemingly the only book of mine she has read. There are people for whom a work of fiction presents some sort of obstacle, or challenge—a portrait of lives or life views that differ from their own, and therefore require this sort of sharp interrogation. The situation is compounded by the fact that the woman is evidently hard of hearing, so that my polite-murmured replies draw blank stares, and her voice is raised, strident as she asks why, having been "middle-class" in Germany, did the Jewish family in my novel so quickly "give in" and "become peasants" in the United States? I am so taken aback by this question, and the curious stridency with which it's asked, I have to think carefully how to reply. Because they were traumatized by their experiences in Germany, I say. Because they were made to flee their homes, they were uprooted, terrified—they suffered. The Nazis persecuted the Jews—you must know of this, surely? The woman stares at me. Is she seriously deaf? Is she being contrary, adversarial? Is she a snob? An anti-Semite? Or just obtuse? Yes, she says, with a disdainful expression, but they became poor so quickly, they lived in squalor. The father had been a high school teacher, he should have known better . . . How bizarre this is, how disagreeable, it reminds me of an astonishing remark made to Susan Sontag and me at a literary conference in Warsaw in the early 1980s, by a Polish translator—*The Jews could have saved themselves from the Nazis. But they were too lazy.*

The other guests at dinner—the librarians—are listening in silence. I am wishing that I were alone—anywhere, alone!—even as I try to explain to the skeptical woman that a writer does not present characters as they should be ideally, but as they might be, plausibly; I am not about to tell her that *The Gravedigger's Daughter* is based upon my grandmother's life—my Jewish grandmother, the mother of my father—long before I knew her. The woman plying me with questions is clearly accustomed to being taken very seriously, for soon it's revealed that she and her husband have "dined with the Bushes"—that is, George W. and Laura—at a $25,000-per-plate fund-raiser; her husband is a "staunch Republican"—

an older man. Grudgingly she concedes, "I suppose it wasn't easy to get a job over here. In the 1930s." Yes, I say. That's right. It wasn't easy— "Jacob Schwart became a gravedigger because he had no choice."

Yet she repeats, as if this were the telling blow: "Yes but they gave in so quickly. That's what I don't understand."

I feel furious, wanting to say to her *And how quickly would you have given in? A month, a week? A day?*

The other women seem embarrassed. The subject is changed. For the first time I think that maybe this was a mistake, coming here. Leaving home in a snowstorm, to give a presentation for a public library in Ohio—in a snowstorm. Clearly, I'm not in my right mind. This silly conversation with a stranger, a "staunch Republican"—what do I care about it, or her? What do I care what this woman thinks? I will never see her again, I will never return to Cuyahoga County again.

The dinner continues, on a lighter note. I can tell stories—not about myself, or my fated Jewish ancestors, but of other writers, writer-friends, names familiar to my dinner companions who are eager to be entertained and keep telling me how "grateful" they are that my plane didn't crash in the storm, or that I hadn't canceled at the last minute—"That's what we expected, you know."

Everyone agrees, vehemently. Even the woman who'd so disapproved of my Jewish family. *They* would have canceled in similar circumstances, of course.

I can't tell them that canceling wasn't an option for me. Because if I had, I might have canceled the next engagement. And the next. And one morning, I wouldn't get out of bed at all.

By the end of the dinner I've forgotten the unpleasant exchange with the hard-of-hearing donor and am feeling almost giddy, elated. It's as if Ray were present and were reminding me—*If you were upset by her, you must care. You are not totally defeated, depressed. A depressed person would not become angry. This is good!*

There's an ironic appropriateness to my presentation—"The Writer's 'Secret Life': Woundedness, Rejection, and Inspiration"—with its focus upon *woundedness*—especially in childhood. The writers of whom I speak—

Samuel Beckett, the Brontës, Emily Dickinson, Ernest Hemingway, Sam Clemens, Eugene O'Neill among others—are brilliant examples of individuals who rendered *woundedness* into art; they are not writers of genius because they were *wounded* but because, being *wounded*, they were capable of transmuting their experience into something rich and strange and new and wonderful. Tears spring into my eyes when I quote Ernest Hemingway's stirring remark—it's so profound, I will quote it to the audience twice:

> From things that have happened and from all things that you know and all those you cannot know, you make something through your invention that is not a representation but a whole new thing truer than anything true and alive, and you make it alive, and if you make it well enough, you give it immortality. That is why you write and for no other reason.

(Hemingway was in his late fififties—nearing the end of his life—when he made this passionate statement to the young George Plimpton, interviewing Hemingway for one of the first issues of the fledgling *Paris Review*. The ringing idealism is at odds with Hemingway's deeply wounded if not mutilated self—his twisted soul, his embittered and grudging spirit—yet, how powerful!)

During the presentation I feel buoyed aloft—as always—as if my particular *woundedness* has been left behind, in the wings of the stage; but afterward, alone, after the applause has abated, and the book-signing is ended, and I have been driven back to my hotel—alone—this is the dangerous time.

I would make a joke of it, if I could—"Honey? I'm here in Parma, Ohio. In a snowstorm—and on Snow Road. Don't ask why!"

Or: "There's a gigantic bouquet in the room here—a strong scent of lilies—like a funeral home."

If I were to call Ray as ordinarily I would have called him at this time, this is what I would say to him, to make him laugh. And

Ray would say—

Don't stay up too late working.

Come back soon!

I love you.

It is a fact that I am in Parma, Ohio, but not quite truthful that I am, at the moment, at 2111 Snow Road, which is the address of the Cuyahoga County Library; I am in a very nice hotel in this Cleveland suburb.

Nor is it truthful that I know what Ray might have said. Very likely we'd have spoken of the most mundane things . . . as usually we did.

This is the first engagement away from home since Ray has died and thus the first night away from home when I can't call him.

How relentless, snow blown against the hotel windows! Banshee-howling outside! It was very kind of my librarian-hosts to leave the large beautiful floral display for me with its waxy-white lilies that emit the most exquisite sweetness . . . How sad it seems to me that there is no one with whom I might share these flowers, as there is no one with whom I can share the luxurious hotel suite, the "king-sized" bed the size of a football field.

I am so lonely—I have no one to call back home—no one knows where I am, nor does anyone care; this is the most maudlin sort of self-pity, I know; yet—how to transcend it? I am not Camus's Sisyphus—the "hero of the absurd" who resists the temptation to suicide by a stoic acceptance of his fate. One must imagine Sisyphus happy, says Camus. To which I would say *Really? What would Sisyphus say for himself?*

In the somewhat drafty hotel room—near the tall narrow windows—the basilisk is hovering. If I turn my head, the thing retreats—the glassy stare, that look of terrible patience.

Never would I contemplate "harming myself" away from home—of course. So I am safe here in Parma, Ohio.

Yet so anxious and depressed, I have to call my friend Jeanne—but her daughter Lily answers—Jeanne isn't home; I call Edmund White, who is home, in his apartment in Chelsea, New York City, and doesn't even seem surprised that his writer-friend Joyce is calling him at 11 P.M. from Desperation, Ohio.

How lucky I am, Edmund will talk with me at this hour! If there is a Mozart of friendship, Edmund White is the Mozart of friendship; the most sympathetic of individuals, open emotionally to his friends at any time; Edmund doesn't judge, he who is beyond being judged as he is, by his own admission, beyond shame. In a startling passage in *My Lives* he has said of himself:

> In my pursuit of lightness, I sometimes feel like a spider monkey swinging through the trees in a world that is more and more deforested. If I look hard I can still find moments of frivolity, of silvery silliness, of merry complicity, even of pure cross-eyed joy. Till now I can usually spot the next branch but sometimes it's quite a stretch.

That night lying in the enormous bed in chilly sheets I listen to snow flung against the windows like crazed neutrinos thinking *I did it. I was here. I didn't cancel. And now—next?*

47

In Motion!—"Still Alive"

New York University, NY. March 6, 2008.

Not in a howling blizzard but on a dank chill winter evening.

Not desperately flinging my life into the sky but driven by car on the New Jersey Turnpike, exiting at the Holland Tunnel, a familiar landscape no more than two hours from home.

Home! The thought makes me anxious, breathless. For no sooner am I away from home than I yearn to return to it.

In a sense now, I am homeless. For the home, the place of refuge, solitude, love—where my husband lived—no longer exists.

Where am I, why am I here, I must remind myself—*Where there is nowhere to be, all places are equal.*

My friend Ed Doctorow is my host this evening. I am speaking/reading to a gathering of young writers in a "writers' house" near the NYU campus. Today has been a good day, a "safe" day—earlier, I was teaching at Princeton; now, I am here in the writers' house at NYU; it's an interlude of several hours in which I am not obsessively a widow but another, freer individual—whom these young New York City writers perceive as "Joyce Carol Oates"—and though the identity is something of an imposture it's familiar and comforting like my worn old down-filled quilted red coat that falls nearly to my ankles and has a hood inside which I can hide.

This coat, my old red coat, purchased in Ray's company years ago, reminds me of him, however. For this is the coat I wore daily in the winter, in many winters, as Ray wore one or another of his jackets from L.L. Bean. (These jackets, hanging now in the hall closet at home. Often I stare into the closet, I stroke the sleeves. My mind is utterly blank, baffled.) As being publicly and warmly greeted by Ed Doctorow, hugged and my cheek kissed, reminds me of Ray, so keenly of Ray, for never had I seen Ed Doctorow and his wife Helen except in Ray's company also, over the years.

I am trying to recall when we'd first met Ed and Helen. Possibly, when Ed taught a fiction workshop at Princeton in the late 1970s. We'd driven out to Sag Harbor, on the far, northern shore of Long Island, to visit the Doctorows at their country house.

"It's a pleasure to introduce my friend Joyce Carol Oates—"

So Ed tells the young writers, of whom many are his students. There's a festive air in this crowded space, the kind of excitement and nerviness that young writers—young artists?—exude. I would like to tell them that being an "established" writer—even a "major American writer"—(a designation that seems utterly unreal to me)—doesn't bring with it confidence, security, or even a sense of who/whom one *is*.

Do you know how a novel will end, when you start out?

Do you ever alter the endings you've planned, when you get to the end?

Who has been your greatest influence?

A wild fear comes over me, something will happen to Ray's uncompleted manuscript *Black Mass*—something will happen to the house in my absence.

Vandals trashing the house. A fire . . .

What are you working on now?

How can you tell when something will be a story or a novel?

Did you ever start out writing a story, and it turned into a novel?

Did you ever start out writing a novel, and it turned into a story?

When did you know you wanted to be a . . .

The blunt fact is: to be a writer, you have to be strong enough to write. You have to have emotional strength, and you have to have physical strength. Now that I no longer have this strength, it seems wrong of me to try to answer young writers' questions like some sort of writerly Delphic oracle . . .

(Surely the Delphic oracle knew very well that he was an imposter.

Every oracle knows that he/she is an imposter. Yet—when others are asking you questions, and are eager to believe that you know the answers, who are you to break the spell?)

Where do you get your ideas from?

. . . your inspiration?

Inspiration! Of all people I am singularly ill-equipped to talk about inspiration—I feel like a balloon from which air has leaked—deflated, flat. Yet I manage to answer the question plausibly—

Ideas come from anywhere, everywhere. Personal life, what you've heard from others, newspaper accounts, history. . . .

What is strange and unsettling in my life now, about which I can't tell anyone—it would sound too utterly trivial, for one thing—is that I am overwhelmed by ideas for stories, poems, novels—entire novels!—that flash at me like those hallucinatory images that come to us as we sink into sleep; these ideas appear, flare up and effloresce and vanish within seconds virtually every time I shut my eyes. And I am certain that—if I had time—if I had time, energy, strength, "inspiration"—I could execute them, as I have executed so many story-ideas in the past.

Maybe it's a symptom of insomnia. Maybe it's a symptom of grief. Maybe some sort of neurological fissure in the brain. Amid the clamoring of songs, lines from poems, part-heard voices and music . . . Never before in my life have I felt so "inspired"—and simultaneously so dispirited, exhausted; I haven't even the energy to write down these ideas, let alone plot out ways to execute them.

At the end of the evening Ed Doctorow walks with me to the car that will return me to Princeton. Warmly Ed hugs me, and tells me again how sorry he and Helen are, about Ray. He tells me that they'd expected that I would cancel the engagement and I tell Ed, "Oh but why would I cancel tonight? Where would I be if I weren't here? I mean—where would I rather be . . ."

Thinking *I don't really have a home. It doesn't matter where I am, I am homeless now.*

This is wrong of course, for I have a home. And I am very lucky, as a widow, to have such a home.

Think of the widows who are made truly homeless by the loss of a husband! Those for whom some sort of *suttee* might be the least of their sorrows.

The challenge is, to live in a house from which *meaning* has departed, like air leaking from a balloon. A slow leak, yet lethal. And one day, the balloon is flat: it is not a balloon any longer.

By identifying the books on the coffee table as "Ray's books" I have tried to inject meaning into them, meaning that once inhabited the objects but has since drained out; as I have tried to inject meaning into the jackets, sport coats, shirts and trousers, etc., hanging in closets in the house—men's articles of clothing, but belonging to—whom?

The terror of mere "things" from which meaning has drained—this is a terror that sweeps over the widow at such times, ever more frequently since I've been traveling, and return home to the empty house.

For no things contain *meaning*—we are surrounded by mere things into which *meaning* has been injected, and invested. Things hold us in thrall as in a kind of hypnosis, hallucination

The entire house in which I live—in which I live now alone—each room, each article of furniture, each artwork on the wall, each book—and now, more visibly each day, for spring is approaching inexorably as a locomotive on a track, the snowdrops, crocuses, and tulip-shoots in Ray's courtyard garden—has been drained of *meaning*. These objects, "things"—almost, I feel a tinge of hatred for them—resentment and revulsion. If I stare at something—a mirror, for instance—a scrim of some sort begins to obscure my gaze. Often I am light-headed, dazed and dizzy when stepping inside the house, even as I'm very very relieved—happy to be back: "Honey, hello! Hi! I'm home . . ." If I'm not careful I will collide with a chair, or a table; my legs are (still) covered in bruises; sometimes I am short of breath as if the oxygen in the house has been depleted, or some sort of odorless toxic gas has seeped in; I have difficulty with my balance as if the floor were tilting beneath my feet. The more I stare at a mirror, for instance the mirror in the dining room, on the wall contiguous with the kitchen, the more the reflection inside waves, blurs—is that a face? Or the absence of a face? *For I too am fading. With no one to see me, no one to name me and to love me, I am fast fading.*

The art-works on the walls. The large oil paintings by Wolf Kahn.

These are the most striking objects in our house, the eye moves immediately to them. Visitors invariably comment on the paintings—"So beautiful! Who is the artist?" Sometimes I stand staring, mesmerized. For this is the magic of art—it can pull us out of ourselves, it can mesmerize. Yet—perversely—I have been thinking of removing some of the art-works on our walls because they remind me too painfully of Ray— of how Ray and I purchased them, in New York City soon after we'd moved to Princeton. There are two quite large Wolf Kahn landscapes— a lavender barn, an autumn forest—as well as several pastels, all New England scenes in the artist's striking impressionistic style. The lavender barn we'd bought in a Manhattan gallery, the others we'd bought, or were given, by the artist himself when we'd visited his dazzling-white studio in Chelsea. (Wolf Kahn's studio is flooded with light because the artist is afflicted with macular degeneration and needs as much light as possible when he paints. Seeing immense canvases on the walls, all of them paintings-in-progress and all of them gorgeous pastel colors, dreamlike swirls of color, I was naive enough to ask Wolf Kahn what it was like to work in beauty every day, not to be snarled in prose like writers of fiction, and Wolf replied, with an air of explaining something elemental which I should have known: "The canvases aren't beautiful to me. Beauty has nothing to do with it. I'm solving problems.")

Solving problems. Of course. This is what it means to be human.

What the widow must remember: her husband's death did not happen to her but to her husband. I have no right to appropriate Ray's death. This swirl of emotions, this low-grade fever, nausea, malaise—what has this to do with true grief, mourning? Is any of this true grief, mourning? I must stop dwelling upon the past, which can't be altered. I must stop hearing these teasing, taunting voices—Is my husband alive? Yes! Your husband is alive Mrs. Smith!

I must take a pill tonight, or maybe a half-pill—but leave the other half here on the bedside table, with a glass of water, for 4 A.M. Just in case.

48

In Motion! —"Mouth of the Rat"

Boca Raton, Florida. March 9–10. Following the principle of it scarcely matters where the widow *is*, since there is no longer a place in which the widow is *at home*, I find myself in an utterly unreal—wind-whipped, "beautiful"—as glossy advertisements in *Vanity Fair* are "beautiful"— setting: Boca Raton!

It's the Boca Raton Arts Festival. To which Ray and I had been invited together, months before. Now, Edmund White has been kind enough to accompany me. And my friend former Modern Library editor David Ebershoff is one of the participants. This is an interlude of just two days that will pass in a blur like landscape glimpsed from a speeding vehicle—most memorably, following my reading one evening, guests at a reception are utterly shocked, incredulous and thrilled, wanting to talk about nothing else but the Eliot Spitzer scandal, only that morning headlined in the *New York Times.*

For of course in this upscale Florida resort, populated by what appear to be mostly upscale Manhattanites, everyone reads the *New York Times.*

"We know the family! Spitzer's father—Bernard—such a wonderful man—a *devoted family man!*—he will be *devastated.*"

"We know the wife—the wife's family—"

"How can a man *do such things* to his wife—"

"—his family—"

"—daughters—"

"*My son*—he's the same way! Just like Spitzer! These women—'call girls'—these terrible women—the men can't resist them, it's terrible—*my own son!*—I know, he's doing such things—he's risking his family—what a terrible terrible thing—"

"And him such a hypocrite—Spitzer—"

"No one can stand Spitzer—a bully, a bastard—"

"—snide, sneering—"

"—like Giuliani—"

"—Giuliani? Worse!—"

"No, not worse than Giuliani—Spitzer's policies are good—solid liberal Democrat—"

"He's a crook!—Spitzer. Whatever came of that investigation—his father 'loaning' him money—"

"Campaign money—he spent on 'hookers'—"

"What happened to that?—that investigation—"

"Imagine, the man spent $80,000 on prostitutes! He spent *campaign money* on prostitutes!"

"Poor Bernard. I think of that family—"

"Bernard? The father? He's a crook, too!"

"No, no he is not! He's a good family man, a wonderful man—devoted—"

"*My son*—he refuses to discuss his family life—he has no idea how he is risking his marriage—these 'call girls' are like cocaine—the married men can't *resist*."

Such avid conversations swirl about us, Edmund White and I are fascinated and don't at all mind being side-lined. Especially striking to us—as if Ethel Merman were to have stepped off a Broadway stage in full war-paint makeup, bejeweled and glittering, in expensive designer resort-wear clothes and hair the color and consistency of cotton candy—is the excitable woman so openly, so bizarrely speaking of her son to a gathering of strangers; to Edmund and me, most particularly, as if being "literary" writers, we might offer some special understanding and insight.

"Maybe this will knock some sense into my son's head, what has happened to Spitzer. If anything like this ever happened in our family . . ."

No one notices when Edmund White and I drift away from the reception, having signed as many of our books as we are likely to sign, in fact more copies than we might have predicted in such a setting. For here is a true-life drama beside which the stratagems of fiction are mere shadows. Nothing like another's scandal, the devastation of another's family and the collapse of a public career, to stir the heart.

Almost, I've forgotten why I feel so—bereft.

Why I feel as if I were just recovering from—what?—a nasty case of the flu?

A friend has written to me this poignant letter—

> *I had a nervous breakdown when I was twenty-eight and beside anxiety attacks, I had acute insomnia. It was because I was going through a huge internal sea change, and I remember that the insomnia was hell. It lasted for about six months and it was all I could do to hold onto the threads of sanity during the day. I felt unhinged and wondered if I would ever feel normal again. It was very frightening—and the symptoms sound similar to yours . . . I used to feel it was like a baby's fontanel, where there's a hole that closes up very slowly, and one doesn't feel like one is on solid ground until the plates of the skull have finally grown together. While the hole's still there, one feels as if one is falling into the chasm ALL ALONE. So (I think) it might be helpful to have some of your friends take turns staying in your house with you. I also think a grief group would help . . . You should know our hearts are totally with you and we'd like to support you in whatever way would help.*

Staying in my house with me!—these are haunting words.

I am grateful, yet terribly embarrassed—and ashamed—to think that friends are talking about me—obviously, they are concerned about me—*and I have hardly hinted to them how desperate, how frantic, how unrecognizable to myself I really am.*

Is it therapy of a kind, or is it a coincidence—(but in the mental life, as Freud suggests, there are no coincidences)—that the story I am composing, with such excruciating slowness, that will require literally weeks, months, to complete, is about suicide; a young woman poet abandoned by her lover, driven by depression/fury/madness to kill herself . . .

The romance of suicide, for poets!—the heightened being, the ecstatic expectations that can't be sustained, the engulfing by language, "music"—the terror that the "music" will cease.

Or has ceased, without the poet quite knowing.

But my story isn't about a loss of "music"—or not entirely: it's about a woman abandoned by her lover who is also the father of her child . . . a child whom she is contemplating killing, along with herself . . . and so the situation is very different from my own.

Or at least, I want to think so.

I am not going to commit suicide. I have not even any clear, coherent plan!

For I've been told—warned—by a philosopher-friend that "taking pills" is not a good idea.

You have no idea how many pills to swallow, he said. You become sick to your stomach and vomit, you lapse into a coma and when you wake up you're brain-damaged—and now, you will never have the opportunity to kill yourself.

What a bizarre matter-of-fact conversation this was! And we were in a restaurant, amid cheery convivial fellow-diners.

I hadn't told him about the pill-cache. Somehow he'd seemed to know.

Or maybe—this is a sudden, chilling thought—accumulating pills is utterly commonplace, everyone does it and for the same reason.

Foolproof ways to commit suicide, my philosopher-friend says, are few. A bullet in the brain, you might think—"But then, you might miss—and you need a gun"; inhaling carbon dioxide—"But then, someone might discover you too soon"; taking a few pills prior to affixing a plastic bag over your head which you take care to tie tightly—"But then, it's so laborious and clumsy, you might panic and change your mind."

Suicide may be a taboo subject but speaking of it in such a way has its blackly comic element. One tries for a too-casual air, or a too-somber air. Even hinting at it one is likely to seem insincere, childish, hungry for attention.

Of course I don't mean it! I mean very little of what I say.

Of course, I am a fantasist . . . You can't possibly take me seriously.

There is a philosopher—Leibniz?—who claimed to believe that the universe is continuously collapsing and continuously reassembling itself, through eternity. Whether he believed in God also, I don't recall—I suppose he did, if this is Leibniz, in the late seventeenth century. As bizarre metaphysics go, this isn't the most bizarre. To dismiss it as illogical, arbitrary, and unprovable is beside the point. And so I've come to think of my "self"—my "personality"—as an entity that collapses when I am alone and unperceived by others; but then, as if by magic, when I am with other people, my "personality" reassembles itself.

Like one who must make her way across a tightrope, with no net beneath—quickly, before falling!—but not too quickly.

Walking with Edmund White along the beach—tramping in the damp sand—on the eve of our departure from Boca Raton, Florida, we're talking of Ray, whom Edmund knew well; and we talk of Edmund's French lover Hubert who'd died of AIDS some years ago, of whom he'd written in his novel *The Married Man* with unflinching candor; how it seems to us, who have "survived," that some part of us has died with those we'd loved, and is interred with them, or burnt to ash. Death is the most obvious—common—banal fact of life and yet—how to speak of it, when it has struck so close? When one dies, and another lives, what is this "life" that's left over?—for a long time, Edmund says, it will seem unreal. It *is* unreal—set beside the intensity of the love that has been lost.

And so how wonderful, to have a friend like Edmund, to whom I can speak of these things. And Edmund is the most cheerful of companions, and makes me laugh. And makes me forget the furious voice in my head *This is wrong! You can't enjoy this. If Ray can't be here by the ocean, it isn't right that you can be. You know this!*

Later that evening, we hear the astonishing young Chinese pianist
Lang Lang playing Chopin. Still later, in my hotel suite watching *Lock-
down*—a gritty, grueling cable-TV documentary set in a men's maxi-
mum security prison in Illinois, which neither Edmund nor I has seen
before—"These are people worse off than we are!"

And maybe at 11 P.M. we will switch to CNN to see what the latest
lurid revelations are, in the Eliot Spitzer scandal.

49

IN MOTION!—"THE WONDER WOMAN OF AMERICAN LITERATURE"

Columbia, South Carolina. March 19, 2008.

And now I am in the warm welcoming company of Janette Turner Hospital who has invited me to give a reading at the University of South Carolina in conjunction with her enormous class in contemporary American writers—the novel of mine they've read is *The Falls*, but some have also recently read *The Gravedigger's Daughter*—there's a blur of applause, handshakes and smiling faces—I am feeling elated, afloat—for how easy it is, how *natural* to smile when others are smiling. The widow would have to be clinically depressed/catatonic not to respond.

Miss Oates! You are my favorite writer, the first novel of yours I read was them . . .

Miss Oates! I've read all of your books, my favorite is Blonde . . .

My sister's birthday is Sunday, please will you inscribe Happy Birthday, Sondra!—*sign and date thank you* . . .

A buzz of voices, a roaring in my ears—though I seem to be smiling and in fact I am *very happy to be here*—whatever "Joyce Carol Oates" is, or was—I am *very happy to be her*—if this is the individual to whom such attention has accrued for this warm welcoming fleeting hour at least.

I am trying to recall what it was like—this couldn't have been long ago, a month and a day—to feel that I was *alive*; to feel that I was *an actual person*, and not this simulacrum of a person; to feel that, if I don't retreat soon to my hotel room, I will disintegrate into bits and pieces clattering across the floor. And yet—such is the widow's (secret) vanity, I am thinking that only now in this diminished but utterly lucid state am I allowed *to see things as they really are.*

For when Ray was alive, even when he wasn't with me I was never alone; now that Ray is gone, even when I am with other people, a crowd of other people, I am never not-alone.

The cure for loneliness is solitude—as Marianne Moore has said. But how frightening solitude seems to me, now!

Centuries ago writers hoped to attain a kind of immortality through their writing—Shakespeare's sonnets are suffused with this hope—the last lines of Ovid's *Metamorphoses* are almost defiant in the claim—

> *Now I have done my work. It will endure,*
> *I trust, beyond Jove's anger, fire and sword,*
> *Beyond Time's hunger . . .*
> *Part of me,*
> *The better part, immortal, will be borne*
> *Above the stars; my name will be remembered*
> *Wherever Roman power rules conquered lands,*
> *I will be read, and through all centuries,*
> *If prophecies of bards are ever truthful,*
> *I will be living, always.*
> —*(Ovid,* Metamorphoses,*"Epilogue,"*
>   *translated by Rolfe Humphries)*

In contemporary times—in the West, at least—it isn't just that most writers no longer believe in anything like "immortality"—for either our books, or ourselves; it's rather that such a claim, or even such a wish, has an ironic/comical ring to it. Who could have guessed, in Ovid's time, in the first century B.C., that there would one day be a world in which the very term "Roman power [ruling] conquered lands" would be divested of all meaning, like the god of all gods "Jove." It's a sad comfort—far more sad than comforting—to know that one's books are being translated, sold, and presumably read in many countries, even as one's life lies in tatters; and what a mocking sort of "good news" it is to be informed, via email, on the eve of Ray's birthday last week, that a long-anticipated exhibit of a collection of my books owned by the writer/interviewer Larry Grobel in Los Angeles has just been mounted in the Powell Library at UCLA under the title JOYCE CAROL OATES—THE WONDER WOMAN OF AMERICAN LITERATURE. (" . . . over four decades she has written over 115 books, 55 novels, more than 400 short stories, over a dozen books of essays and nonfiction, eight books of poetry and thirty-plus plays. . . .")

How Ray would have smiled at this—or laughed outright: "The Wonder Woman of American Literature."

What the widow has lost—it would seem a trifling loss, to others—is the possibility of being *teased*.

Of all categories of being, The Widow is the least likely to be *teased*, *laughed-at*.

It's the eve of Ray's birthday, March 11. Tomorrow he would have been seventy-eight years old.

Janette confides in me, she doesn't know how she would manage the loss of her husband—retired academic, Sanskrit scholar, comparative historian and philosopher of world religions who'd been a professor at Queen's University in Kingston, Ontario; she thinks she might "curl into a fetal ball and pull the covers over my head for a couple of months."

I am thinking *Yes! What an appealing image.*

Janette is driving me in her car to an event. Janette is confiding in me in the way that women confide in each other who have not much time together—crucial things must be said, and quickly. She tells me about a close friend of hers who'd lost her husband unexpectedly and has become depressed and agoraphobic.

Agoraphobia! I am thinking *This is something I could try, next.*

The prospect of staying at home, hiding at home—instead of this frantic travel . . . Traveling in the wake of my husband's death has been the outward face of my madness as my madness has been the inward face of my grief. Yet travel is perceived as "professional"—it is respected, as hiding at home would not be respected.

Agoraphobia—fear of open spaces. *Claustrophobia*—fear of closed-in spaces.

How hellish it would be, if the two were conjoined! For there would be some creaturely comfort in agoraphobia, at least. As a wounded or dying animal crawls away to be alone so the stricken person craves aloneness, whether to die of it, or to be healed.

Agoraphobia is more frequently a female affliction than it is a male affliction—three to four times more frequently, in fact. This can't be because men are less neurotic and phobia-prone than women but because men have traditionally had little choice about leaving their homes—"earning a living"—while women, wives and mothers, have traditionally been "house-bound."

In some fundamentalist cultures, women are virtually house-prisoners: prisoners of their/our sex. This is the extreme of which the "housewife" of contemporary American culture is a more liberal, seemingly more liberated example. To be a recluse in our culture is perceived as a choice of a (perverse) kind; to be morbidly "house-bound" requires at least one enabler, very likely a family member. Someone willing to provide an income, shop for groceries, mediate between the agoraphobic and the outside world.

I think of Shirley Jackson—brilliant writer, chilling and funny and "feminist" in an era—the 1950s—before "feminism" began to be established as a new and revolutionary way for women to think of themselves, who ended her life as an acute agoraphobic, unable even to leave the squalid bedroom of her house in North Bennington, Vermont.

Not that Shirley Jackson had "lost" her husband in any literal sense—except that, repeatedly, Stanley Edgar Hyman was openly unfaithful to her, often with his worshipful Bennington undergraduates.

The most hideous of deaths—morbid obesity, amphetamine addiction, alcoholism. Months Shirley Jackson had hidden away in her squalid bedroom—with Hyman's complicity?—certainly he was indifferent to her by this time—before she was found dead, her heart stopped, at the age of forty-nine.

And there was Emily Dickinson, whose withdrawal from the world seems to have been in inverse proportion to the efflorescence of her revolutionary poetry. Secluded—protected?—within the walls of the Dickinson family house in Amherst, Massachusetts, Dickinson was both housebound and "free"—in the interstices of housework and nursing for dying relatives—to create her poetry.

> *I hide myself within my flower,*
> *That, fading from your vase,*
> *You, unsuspecting, feel for me*
> *Almost a loneliness.*
> *(903)*

Dickinson remarked to her niece Mattie that all she needed to do was retire to her bedroom, turn the key and—"There's freedom!" Her gradual withdrawal from the world was perceived by relatives as "only a happening"—not the consequence of any real deficiency or abnormality in her personality.

So strange that I should feel a kinship with Emily Dickinson when, to all neutral observers, I would appear to be so utterly different!

Yet: as the "perfect man of action is the suicide"—in William Carlos Williams's words—so the individual most frantically "in motion" may be resisting the lure of agoraphobia.

When we arrive at Janette's beautiful house overlooking a lake, when I am shown through the sun-filled rooms, and shake her husband's hand—I am stricken to the heart thinking how all this beauty, these carefully chosen pieces of furniture, these colorful carpets, artwork, books—all that makes this house a *home*—will be horrible to Janette, a mockery, as the things in my house have become a mockery, if she should lose Cliff.

Am I insane, to think such thoughts? At such a time?

To the widow, all wives are widows-to-be. Ours is the basilisk stare you will want to avoid.

Tonight in my room in the Inn at USC—in the high, canopied bed that reminds me of an old-fashioned sleigh—phrases of Emily Dickinson career through my mind. I don't know if I am awake or asleep; or partially awake, and partially asleep; that porous state of the soul when poetry is the most natural speech, and the poet speaks for the soul *in extremis*:

> The Brain, within its Groove
> Runs evenly—and true—
> But let a Splinter swerve—
> 'Twere easier for You—
>
> To put a Current back—
> When Floods have slit the Hills—
> And scooped a Turnpike for Themselves—
> And trodden out the Mills—
> (556)

Next morning on the way to the Columbia airport—Cliff is driving, Janette is in the passenger's seat and I am in the backseat of Cliff's car—I hear myself remark that at least I don't have to worry any longer about flying, as I'd always done when Ray was waiting for me back home. "I would think, what if the plane crashes? And I won't ever see Ray again. But now I don't worry about planes crashing. I don't worry at all."

I'd meant to sound upbeat, cheery. I'd meant to make Janette and Cliff laugh. But the awkward silence in the car indicates that I've said an inappropriate thing and made my hosts uncomfortable and suddenly I am desperate to be *home*.

50

In Motion!—"You Can't Sit There"

Sanibel Island, Florida. March 20, 2008.

Windy/sunny Sanibel Island on the Gulf Coast to which I have come as a guest of the Sanibel Island Public Library—surely the most spectacular of small-town American libraries! As soon as I check into my hotel room—a suite—in fact, a small apartment with a compact kitchen and a balcony—windows looking out onto a dazzling vista of beach/ocean/sky—I put on a jacket, a hat, running shoes—jogging in the wake of the chilly spray as epiphanies fly at me as if I have traveled hundreds of miles for these revelations—*Ray was not unhappy, Ray did not experience his death as you are experiencing it, he did not experience the loss you are experiencing, he knew nothing of what was to come and so he did not suffer—Ray was happy in his lifetime—Ray loved his work, his domestic life—Ray loved his garden—he did not suffer the loss of meaning that his survivor feels; he was defined by that meaning, which you provided for him; not for one moment of his life with you was he not-loved, and he knew this; for Ray, his death was no tragedy but a completion.*

This is so! This logic so overwhelms me, I've begun to shiver, almost convulsively shivering with excitement, I think it must be excitement—for I am convinced, this reasoning is so: *Ray was not unhappy, only you are unhappy. Think of Ray, and not of yourself for once . . .*

The widow is one to whom such epiphanies come frequently. The widow is one to whom such nuggets of insight, profound revelations, "truths" rush with disconcerting intensity. When you see the widow staring into space, as if she's listening to something no one else can hear, you can be sure that the widow is receiving these revelations in the way that a sleeping person receives dreams, or a schizophrenic receives hallucinations.

In the days immediately following Ray's death, I felt like inert matter bombarded by radioactive waves—every minute an acute, profound realization—heart-stopping revelations!—except, almost at once they evaporated, vanished.

So this is what life is! Life is—bounded by death!

People die! People die, and disappear! We will all die!

We will all suffer, and we will all . . .

It's unfortunate, you might say it's unfair, that the most heart-rending revelations are utterly banal, commonplace. So the widow must confront the fact that, though she is shaken to the roots of her being, and the clarity of grief washes over her at irregular, frequent, unpredictable intervals, all that she can know about the experience is a familiar set of words.

. . . all suffer, and we will all die. And . . .

Except now, returning to the hotel, the sky now darkened, riddled with goiterous storm clouds of the hue of tarnished pots, and the surf the color of lead, and all conviction has ebbed, and all spurious joy, and the thoughts that now assail me are sneering, deflating—*You! You are so ridiculous! Trying to cheer yourself up when the only significant fact of your life is, you are alone. You are a widow, and you are alone. You are not prepared to be alone for you had thought you would be loved, you would be protected and cared for, forever. But now you are a widow, you have lost all that. Your heart is not broken but shriveled. You are ridiculous flying everywhere giving "talks"—"readings"—because you are terrified of staying home. You are terrified of reading Ray's novel because you are terrified of discovering something in it that will upset you. Too cowardly to stay home, to try to work, to write—terrified that you can't. You are a failure, you are an unloved woman no longer young, you are worthless, you are trash. And you are ridiculous . . .*

*   *   *

" . . . this evening our guest . . . 'Joyce Carol Oates' . . . she has created some of the 'most enduring fiction of our time' . . . born in upstate New York, currently residing in Princeton, New Jersey . . . recipient of National Book Award, Prix Femina . . . author of way too many titles to list . . ."

The very nice librarian who introduces me is not mocking me, I know. Intellectually, I know this. Yet the lavish claims made for "JCO," the lists of prizes and awards, quotations from reviews, such critics as Henry Louis Gates Jr. and Elaine Showalter, have an air of the preposterous; halfway, I expect individuals in the audience to begin laughing, shaking their heads in derision—*You! Do you think for a moment we believe all these preposterous things about* you?

Yet, the audience is very courteous, even enthusiastic. The audience is gratifyingly large. What will I say to them? Read to them? How dismayed these residents of Sanibel Island would be if I were to tell them what my epiphanies on the beach have revealed to me; if I were to say *Yes it's true that I used to be a writer—a writer with a very mixed reputation— "controversial" is the kindest term. But now—I am not a writer now. I am not anything now. Legally I am a "widow"—that is the box I must check. But beyond that—I am not sure that I exist.*

As I address the Sanibel residents in a flawless imitation of my writer-self (I want to think!) I find that I am glancing about the room as if seeking—what? Who? In public places I seem to be searching for someone who is missing—I wonder if for the rest of my life I will be searching for someone who isn't there . . .

I feel as if I'm missing something visible—an arm, a leg. Or that part of my face has been smudged and distorted as in a nightmare painting by Francis Bacon. Like the cruelest and most succinct of prognoses in a Chinese fortune cookie the thought comes to me—*Not one person in this room would want to trade places with you: widow.*

As I speak, my attention is drawn to older, white-haired men in the audience—men of perhaps Ray's age—though Ray didn't have white hair but dark hair laced with silver-gray; in this upscale Florida retirement community there are numerous older, elderly individuals with canes and walkers, in wheelchairs . . . A bizarre fantasy comes over me: I will meet a man, an older man, a man in a wheelchair, and it will be granted to me to be given a second chance, with this man—I had not had the opportunity to bring my husband home from the rehabilitation center—I hadn't "nursed" him for even a day.

But how absurd this is, even in fantasy—no older man in urgent need of a nurse/female companion could have made his way to the Sanibel library unassisted! And indeed, when I look more closely, each elderly/ infirm man is accompanied by a companion.

What could be more ridiculous—casting an envious eye on strangers in wheelchairs! No one can believe what compulsive fantasist the widow is, even the widow herself.

Yes! It has been decided that you will be allowed to have your husband back but in a diminished state. In exchange for his being alive you will have to care for a convalescent, an invalid, a very sick man; a man who has lost his vision, or his hearing; a man on a respirator; a man who must be fed through a tube; you may be called upon to provide blood, bone marrow, a kidney . . .

Later, at the motel, I stand in the darkened living room and stare out at the dark ocean—a stretch of beach, pale sand—vapor-clouds and a glimpse of moon—the conviction comes over me suddenly *Ray can't see this, Ray can't breathe . . .* As I've been thinking, in restaurants, staring at menus, forced to choose something to eat *This is wrong. This is cruel, selfish. If Ray can't eat . . .*

Only a few hours earlier I was running along this beach in dazzling sunshine without seeming to have acknowledged *Ray can't see this sunshine, the ocean, any of this.*

Tightly I draw the blinds! So tightly, the cord cuts into my fingers. If in the morning sunshine floods against the window, I will be spared seeing it.

I draw the blinds shut tight. In the morning if sunshine floods against the window, I will not see.

"Excuse me—you can't sit here."

A row of seats, a broken seat, nowhere to sit in the crowded Char-

lotte, North Carolina, airport and so I have laid my coat over the seat, set
down my bag—awaiting a delayed connecting flight to Philadelphia—
staring into space, thinking. So eager to return home and yet—fearful
of returning home. Again and again, again I see Ray in the hospital bed;
I see myself timidly approaching him; I hear my pleading voice *Honey?*
Honey—? This is the instant before I knew, when it was not possible
that I did not know; before, I had suspected, I had dreaded the worst, as,
at the time of the car crash, I had braced myself for the worst, but now, in
this instant, I would know. This is the pivotal moment of my life: before
this moment there is the possibility of being relieved, happy; after, I am
damned, accursed.

Startled by a harsh male voice—"*He's* sitting there."

"He? Who?"

"My son."

Though the seat is unoccupied as well as broken there is, in fact, a
very young child sitting/crawling on the dirty floor in front of it, oblivious of me and of his father's anger at me. Quickly I snatch up my things
and apologize to the irate man—"I'm so sorry—I didn't see your son
there. I didn't see that anyone was 'sitting' in this seat."

Though the child's father is strangely upset with me, as if I had not
only taken his son's seat but violated the special sanctity of his family, my
stammering apologies and the tears welling in my eyes seem to placate
him for he ceases glaring at me and mumbles, "It's O.K."

Quickly I back away. There is a mother, too—and another young
child—*a family*—inadvertently I have intruded upon *a family*! Keenly I am
aware of my isolated and despised state—*family-less, husband-less*—continuing to apologize even as my face dissolves, my fragile self-control evaporates,
before I can turn and hurry away I am crying abjectly, as a child might
cry, blindly pushing through a crowd jostling for position to board a plane.

Through the congested airport, stumbling. There is nowhere to
hide—strangers glance at me in passing, at my tear-stained face—if one
should recognize the "Wonder Woman of American Literature"—how
embarrassing!—how shameful!

I think *I am breaking apart. I am unraveling. Cracking up. I must get
home. I must never leave home again.*

51

"Never Forget"

The hard part of travel is the return. Where formerly the return was the very best part of travel.

"Honey? Hello—"

In the hospital he'd said, in regard to one or another fussy procedure *They make too much of things, here.*

In fact, he'd been mistaken. In the end "they" had not made enough of things that had mattered crucially.

"Honey. Hello. . . ."

Silly forlorn voice. Even the cats aren't deceived.

Walking through the rooms of the house and in each room there is a likeness of Ray—that is, of the watercolor portrait of Ray which an artist-friend painted after his death, as if it were the cover of the final issue of *Ontario Review.*

The original, which is framed, is kept in the kitchen. Photocopies are placed elsewhere including on the door of Ray's study and on my desk.

In this way, as I walk through the house, I am seeing Ray's face as he would look, more or less, if he were alive this very day. To greet me, to cheer me up. To suggest to me *You are not going to be defeated by this. You can do it!*

Aphorisms drift through my head. It's like trying to stop a dripping faucet with a finger, to try to stop this drift.

For instance, this chilling aphorism of Nietzsche:

What someone *is*, begins to be revealed when his talent abates, when he stops showing what he can *do*.

To this, the widow can add: *What I am, begins to be revealed now that I am alone. In such revelation is terror.*

It was not that, of her own volition, of her own specific wish to do herself harm, nor even of her reasonable wish to annihilate the ceaseless cascade of broken and jeering language in her head Your life is over, you are finished, you are dead and done for and you know it, hypocrite!—*that she began to calculate the ways she might die; rather, it was the wish itself—coolly conceived, pure and inviolable as a Chopin prelude of surpassing beauty* There is a way out, and the way out is death.

On a counter she laid out the pills accumulated over the years by both her husband and herself. These were painkillers prescribed for pains long since vanished and forgotten. These were painkillers of which but one or two had been taken from the container—obviously, pills too powerful to risk taking in ordinary life! There were sleeping pills, there were "muscle relaxants." There were tranquilizers, sedatives. On the counter she spread them, carefully she counted them. Hypnotized by these pills, capsules. Hypnotized by what they contain. A sensation of such security, relief runs through her! Marcus Aurelius counsels The power to take your own life is yours at all times. Never forget.

She never forgot.

The Widow's Secret

I measure every Grief I meet
With narrow, probing, Eyes—
I wonder if it weighs like Mine—
Or has an Easier size.
Emily Dickinson, 561

Congratulations! I

Ringing phone at a distance as if through wads of cotton batting and later this morning an e-mail message—several e-mail messages—CONGRATULATIONS!—not one but two of my books of the past year have been nominated for National Book Critics Circle awards in two categories—fiction, nonfiction. The news leaves me just a little sadder than I'd been for thinking *But there is no one to share this with. There is no one.*

You would not realize, how painful "good" news can be. Who has known this?

"Bad" news—if I were diagnosed with cancer, for instance—would be a relief since Ray would be spared knowing of it. But "good" news that can't be shared—this is painful.

In the bedclothes there is the elder tiger-cat Reynard still sleeping curled in cat-fashion with a single stubby paw over his tight-shut eyes. Almost you would think that Reynard isn't breathing except if you look closely, you can see his sides move. *Reynard* named by me as a kitten for his beautiful bright tiger coat—that has faded and coarsened a bit, with time—as well as for *Raymond.*

Recalling when Ray brought Reynard home, to surprise me. A very small abandoned kitten from a Pennington animal shelter.

How many years ago! I don't want to calculate Reynard's age.

Through the night Reynard slept beside me pressing warmly against my leg which was comforting though also constraining for I dared not move for fear of disturbing him, provoking him into jumping down from the bed and trotting away and so now carefully I make up the bed as always each morning I make up the bed—as if embarrassed of the nest, that must be, to a degree, dismantled—books, manuscripts, etc., removed to a nearby table.

Making up the bed also, quickly to forestall climbing back into the nest. Already I have forgotten why I'd been summoned to be *congratulated*—an ache in the region of the heart is all that remains— thinking of how my father assured me that there was no need for Ray and me to come visit him just yet—"You're busy teaching, there's no rush—you can come later—you can see me any time"—he'd convinced me—of course, I had hoped to be convinced—"I'll be here."

Except he wasn't. I never saw him again.

When Daddy was satisfied that Mom would be well taken care of, in their assisted-care residence in Amherst, New York, he fell asleep, my brother Fred told me, and never woke up.

No one could wake him. Daddy was being treated for emphysema, prostate cancer, a heart condition but he hadn't seemed close to death. Except—a powerful sleep overcame him, and he never woke.

So exhausted! For years he'd been concerned with my mother's health, this had become an obsession with him. Daddy had burnt out, in living.

Now petting Reynard—rubbing his bone-hard head to evoke a low, near-inaudible purr, the barest hum of recognition   I am blinking back tears of grief for my father who died in May 2000.

In that last year of his life we'd spoken frequently on the phone. Since my father was hard of hearing, visiting him had its disadvantages —he would seem to hear, he would smile and nod and you couldn't know if truly he heard what you were saying. But on the phone, Daddy could hear perfectly well. And so we spoke, as we'd never spoken in person.

Saying *I love you* was hard. I think perhaps I never did say *I love you* to my father. Only at the end of a conversation could I murmur something rushed and seemingly casual like *Love you, Daddy! Bye!*

My father, my mother. My husband.

One by one disappearing.

Where?

54

Congratulations! II

The horror is: one of the books which has been nominated for the award is my *Journal: 1973–1982*. Into which—I've just recently discovered—I can't bring myself to look.

For if I do, each page, each paragraph is a mockery. Each entry—most of them breathless, rapidly typed and never revised—a testament of some younger, happier, oblivious time in my life—is a mockery to me in late winter/early spring 2008.

Worse yet are the photographs—the first is particularly heartrending, Ray and me in our little brick house on Riverside Drive East, Windsor, Ontario, seated on a sofa as I am laughingly posed pouring tea into Ray's cup out of (as I recall) an empty teapot; as Ray, hair long, dark, with sideburns in the long-ago style of the era, looks on with an affectionate smile. *We thought we would live forever, then! We never gave a thought to—what awaits.*

Or, if we did, it was cursory, *pro forma*—mortality, death, loss being "themes" in literary works of which we could speak knowledgeably.

Numerous photographs in the *Journal* were taken by Ray himself—the invisible man behind the camera. Joyce in a winter coat on the beach behind our Windsor house, on the Detroit River; Joyce in another winter coat, on a street in Mayfair, London, in 1972; Joyce with a very girlish-looking Margaret Drabble posing in front of Maggie's house in Hampstead Heath, 1972.

Ray had seen the *Journal* of course—at least, portions of it, and all of the photos—but my parents had not. Their photographs, too, are heart-rending to see.

Because of the nomination, I will be obliged to read from this *Journal*, and discuss it, with my lawyer/poet/friend Larry Joseph and John Freeman, the president of the National Book Circle, in a few weeks, in New York City. And because of the other nomination, I will be obliged to read from my novel *The Gravedigger's Daughter* at one or another literary event.

How strange it is to the writer, whose life's-blood would seem to have been drained, in order that works of prose be "animated"—given a semblance of life through printed language—when the writer is obliged to revisit the work, at a later time. Sometimes it's a painful, powerful experience—opening a book, staring down at the lines of print and re-calling—in the helpless, vertiginous way in which one recalls, or half-recalls, a lost dream—the emotional state of being you were in, at the time of the writing.

In my case—a "posthumous" case—the feeling is *But I was alive then! I remember that.*

My friends are lifting their glasses to me. My friends are smiling happily at me. My friends are visibly happy for me. And I am grateful, or seeming-so; I am smiling, and lifting my glass—of sparkling water—shifting my face into a reasonable approximation of cheeriness, anticipation. So long have my friends pitied me, this opportunity to say *Congratulations!* instead of—for instance—*Condolences!* is not to be overlooked.

In this attractive Princeton restaurant my friends are not mocking me, I know. No one is mocking me. Only brash adolescents mock grief, laugh uproariously at death, are drawn to video games simulating violent death—presumably because they've had no experience of death, except as a game.

In this posthumous state my career—all that has to do with "Joyce Carol Oates"—has come to seem remote to me, faintly absurd, or sinister—like a black dirigible drifting across the treeline, some distance away.

John Updike once said that he'd created "Updike" out of the sticks and mud of his Pennsylvania boyhood—so too, I'd created "Joyce Carol Oates" out of the sticks, mud, fields and waterways of my upstate New York girlhood. Both of us—that is, our actual selves—John, Joyce—seem to have been amazed, over all, by the accomplishments of our name-sakes. A shelf of books looks formidable when glimpsed all at once—as if the achievement were all at once, instead of wrought—laboriously, ob-sessively—through years of effort.

When I leave the restaurant to return home, I must drive along Rose-dale Road out into the country—always, this same route—reminding me so sharply of the days and nights of the hospital vigil—*Alive! Still alive!*—the voice on the other end of the phone had sounded so certain, so sincere—hopeful.

Letting people down. Letting friends/editors/agents down. I think that this is a proclivity of "JCO" from which I can't altogether detach myself. *You will just be disappointed again. When my books fail to win. I am so sorry, there is nothing that I can do.*

On February 28, John Updike wrote an eloquent and heartrending letter of condolence. I wish that I could quote it—John's personal correspon-dence is no less beautifully written than his published work—but the provisions of his will forbid publication of his letters. In this brief typed letter John said that he and his wife, Martha, were both "shocked" to read of Ray's death in the *New York Times* obituary. In his "mind's eye," John said, Ray was "still young and a fixture in the literary world." So "calm, gentle, soft-spoken and sane"—Ray scarcely seemed like a "liter-ary man" at all.

Reading this, despite tears, I had to laugh. For how like John Updike this was, a very funny remark embedded in a simple statement of condolence.

John concluded by saying that he and Martha would miss Ray's "re-assuring presence." There was a little more, of course—but this is the essence of the letter.

(Over the years, since April 1977, John Updike and I exchanged per-haps hundreds of letters and cards—cards stamped with John's address in Beverly Farms, Massachusetts, were John's signature mode of com-

munication: he executed them with the flourish of a Renaissance son-
neteer—which I'd once hoped to publish as a little book, after his death.)

This letter from John Updike, I'd read quickly when I first received
it, then put away.

Along with so many other lovely letters and cards, some of which
I could not bring myself to read fully, I put it away in my grass-green
Earthwise Reusable Bag. And now tonight—late tonight—in fact it is
past 2 A.M.—in the interstices of a sudden frenzy of housekeeping—I
am moved to reread it, and to think of the first time Ray and I visited
John and his then-new wife Martha Bernhardt in Georgetown, Massachusetts, in the summer of 1976.

I remember the charming old house on the main road past which
traffic streamed constantly, so that we could barely hear one another
speak, at times. I remember how formidable Martha seemed to me, a
strong-willed blond woman who'd brought three young sons into this
new marriage/household—what a testimony to love!

I remember John saying that Harvard had had a destructive effect
upon him—Harvard was "anti-matter"—and had made of his "hillbilly"
self another personality, an "anti-self." Bizarrely he'd said that he was
"not famous"—but I was.

(By this time, John had had an enormous success with *Couples*—he'd
become not only famous but infamous.)

Of course, John always spoke playfully, provisionally. In his lightness
of tone he was the antithesis of dogmatic, argumentative, assertive; his
natural demeanor was self-deprecatory. The most surprising thing he'd
said to me was that James Joyce's *Ulysses* seemed to him "ugly."

Ulysses!—that most beautiful, rhapsodic, phantasmagoric of novels
from which Updike learned so much.

Some years later we visited John and Martha in their stately hill-
top house in Beverly Farms, north of Boston: the quintessential upper-
middle-class suburb, in which John took a homeowner's pride. By this
time the rural Pennsylvania hillbilly-self had long since been outgrown
and cast aside like old clothes. The Updikes' house was expensive, lavishly furnished, large—John took us on a little tour—we saw the warren
of small rooms at the top of the house in which he worked: a desk and
a typewriter for fiction, another desk and a typewriter for reviews, an-

other space for manuscripts, galleys, books. Of all male American writers John Updike must be the most happily *domestic*, and *domesticated*: not for him the dubious pleasures of such masculine proclivities as hunting, fishing, hiking arduous trails; not for John, who adored and was adored by women, the ecstatic male-bonding of team sports, the army, war.

It has been years now since we've visited the Updikes. And now, Ray and I will never visit them again.

The smell of Drano makes my nostrils pinch—a pungent, powerful odor—more than fifteen minutes have passed since I'd poured Drano into each of three bathtub drains, now I must hurry to the bathrooms to turn on hot water, to "flush" the Drano down.

Not that the drains are blocked, yet. Not that any of this housekeeping needs to be done, just yet. Just now.

This memoir, steeped in the grittiest of details as the bed linens of poor Emma Bovary were steeped in her physical agony, yet fails before the prospect of accurately suggesting how much, how very much, how unendingly much, there is for the widow to do following the death of her husband; so much to do, yet more to ponder, in various stages of anxiety, even when, as in this case, the deceased husband left behind financial records in very good shape, and a will. *A legally executed unambiguous will leaving everything to the surviving spouse!* Yet—still another document is required—"urgently"—and yet another "original" copy of the death certificate—this stiff-parchment document being the one that, to the widow, is most terrible to hold in the hand.

Advice to the widow: MAKE DUPLICATE COPIES OF THE DEATH CERTIFICATE. MANY!

Another time now I am in Ray's office looking through his files. Many of these are now in fact "my" files since I've rearranged the material and placed it in manila folders marked in large block letters to avoid confusion. (The widow is advised: ALWAYS WRITE IN BLOCK LETTERS in such circumstances. As the widow is advised ALWAYS KEEP YOUR KEYS IN EXACTLY THE SAME PLACE.) Belatedly, I have removed all the folders from the floor; it's entirely out of character for poor Reynard to assuage his anxiety by climbing atop a table to urinate on these hateful documents—too much effort for an aging cat.

Until 4:10 A.M. when exhaustion overcomes me I will search for what-ever it is Matt has requested. Diligently I will search though I know—(I think I know)—that I have searched these files numerous times as I have searched Ray's filing cabinets, and Ray's study closet, not finding what I have been assured *has got to be there.*

For Ray Smith left such careful records, it's inconceivable that this document *is not in his office. Somewhere.*

The last time I searched through Ray's things, including desk draw-ers containing mostly office supplies like paperclips, pens, stamps, I'd dis-covered a valentine—*To My Beloved Wife*—which he hadn't yet signed.

Such discoveries, that rend the heart.

Also, caches of old birthday cards, some of them hand-made, and meant to be comical, to Ray from me.

All these precious items I have put away, for safekeeping. With our cache of snapshots and photographs dating back to the fall of 1960 in Madison, Wisconsin.

Prominent on Ray's desk is his calendar for 2008. How essential to all our lives, our calendars!

I am holding Ray's calendar in my hand. I am staring at Ray's calen-dar. This is not the first time that I have stared at Ray's calendar in some bleak hour of the early morning, as if it were a riddle to be decoded. For all that the widow does, the widow has done previously. Quickly the widow has become a ghost haunting her own house.

How ironic it is, and terrible, Ray has X'd out every single day of January 2008; in February he'd X'd out February 1–10—the tenth, a Sunday, which would be the last day he would spend at home.

In his methodical way Ray kept a diary of sorts, in his calendar. Ap-pointments, tasks to be done, magazines and press deadlines. Our social engagements entered, in abbreviations. If I try, I can recall what these engagements were—which dinner parties, evenings in restaurants, at McCarter Theater. New Year's Eve, New Year's Day . . . February 14, Valentine's Day, Ray had marked as for a party, here.

Now I am left with this pattern of X's. If I examine Ray's calendar for 2007, which is still in his desk, I will discover an entire year—365 days!—methodically X'd out.

By slow degrees our lives are a pattern of (ever increasing) X's. With what misplaced satisfaction X'ing out a day, finishing with a week, a month, a year—with never the thought that the supply of days is after all finite, and you are using them up.

Congratulations! I am thinking of, years ago, it might have been ten, or fifteen years ago, we were preparing for bed and the phone rang, past midnight this was, an alarming time for the phone to ring, immediately the thought came to me *Something has happened to Mommy, or Daddy*—the caller would have been my brother, in that case; but when I answered the phone, as Ray looked on, concerned, the caller identified herself as the book review editor at the *Philadelphia Inquirer,* calling to tell me—to "be the first to notify you"—that I was that year's Nobel Prize winner in literature; it was not an altogether new phenomenon in our lives, that such rumors were passed on to me, or to Ray, always with an air of excitement; year after year, such vague wisps of rumor, presumably wafting about the heads of how many dozens, hundreds of possible candidates; tonight this information, or rather mis-information, came to me through a roaring of blood in my ears for I'd been dreading a call about my parents and now—instead—this dazzling if improbable news—to set my heart racing, and to stir my penchant for irony *Any nomination of any book of mine is simultaneously the announcement that the book has not won*—except in this case, as the journalist at the other end of the line emphatically assured me, this was no mere "nomination" that was the subject of her call but the news that Joyce Carol Oates had won the Nobel Prize for Literature. . . .

The call from the *Philadelphia Inquirer* editor was to elicit from me a comment, a response, to this wonderful news, but I could only ask how the journalist knew this, how she knew so definitely; she insisted that she had her "sources"—this was not a mere rumor.

I told her thank you but that I would wait for the official announcement.

But I had won, the caller insisted. In a few hours, I would get a call from Stockholm!

When I hung up the phone and told Ray what the call was he laughed and said, "That! Let's go to bed."

55

E-mail Record

March 17, 2008.

To Edmund White

Thanks so much for your phone call, I just wasn't up to answering the phone at that time . . . Have been trying to get through the night without the drug [Lorazepam] & would prefer to be tired/groggy through tomorrow than "addicted" . . . have been panicky, sweating, anxious but have been determined not to give in . . . have been reading in bed & taking notes, which is somewhat calming . . . The cats are convinced that I am utterly crazy since I am up through the night as Ray & I never were; so they've been going outside, & coming back inside virtually upon demand.

I think that you can tolerate your sleeping pills, obviously—but I am not used to any kinds of drugs, & the "suicidal thoughts" have certainly been powerful . . .

I had a lovely long conversation with Gail Godwin earlier tonight, who'd lost her husband/partner of more than 30 years a few years ago . . .

Much love to my traveling companion,

"sleepless in Princeton"—

Joyce

March 17, 2008.

To Richard Ford

I can't face any sort of commemorative event [for Ray] . . . I'm frightened of picking up the phone and it's an old friend wanting to grieve with me—like tearing at my pathetic thin scabs with their fingers—though they "mean well"—I know!—but I just can't face the prospect of friends coming here, & Ray not here; I would be just sick about it though Jeanne has thought it is a good idea, but I am not up to it, I hope Jeanne understands . . .

What I take from Ray's [phone] message is that he was utterly unaware of what would lie ahead. Maybe a medical crisis of a sudden spike in temperature—Jeanne says these virulent bacteria can sweep through the bloodstream & carry off even a younger person within hours. It's terrifying. But Ray was perhaps spared this. (As Bob Fagles is not being spared . . . There is the true horror and tragedy.)

I like to think that he just fell asleep—didn't even know what was happening. High fevers cause delirium . . . He probably didn't experience pain.

My "writing" these days is mostly e-mails but just to a very few friends. Can't use the telephone. . . .

Isn't Eliot Spitzer something! A welcome change . . .

Much love to you both,

Joyce

March 22, 2008.

To Edmund White

I am so looking forward to you & our party. But such a misery of insomnia tonight, though I've taken the full strength of this drug, & just can't sleep; & can't imagine many more nights like this. There is such a yearning to swallow every pill in the bottle . . . Of course, one has to be a good example to others, including students. I am so worn out with tasks & obligations; I think it was a mistake not to follow Ray immediately, the night that he died. All this aftermath has been crazed with little let-up & meaning. Of course I much appreciate your presence . . . You have kept me going . . . If I could sleep just an hour or two, I'm sure that I would feel differently. It just seems impossible.

These days just go on, on and on without end like that play of Sartre's in which individuals' eyelids have been removed . . .

Much love,

Joyce

March 22, 2008, 4:08 A.M.

To Doug Hagley [typesetter, Marquette, Michigan]

None of these figures is very clear in Ray's handwriting . . . This is all overwhelming . . . This insomnia is ravaging to me—just can't sleep even having taken the full medication—truly I don't know what to do but can't imagine many more days—weeks?—of this. I had not realized that the [Ontario Review] publication would be so very difficult & wonder now at the feasibility of my having continued after Ray's sudden death. I am in over my head, completely.

Much affection,

Joyce

March 23, 2008.

To Doug Hagley

Thanks so much for your advice . . . I have to concentrate on getting through one day at a time, then one night at a time, and trying not to panic at the emptiness/loneliness. Though I am surrounded by friends—I can't seem to get any of my old energy back, and I guess I am what one might call flat-out depressed . . . had no idea what it was like until now. I will be sorry when our collaboration ends . . . You have been a wonderful presence across the miles.

I am meeting with our accountant tomorrow to ask about many things including the future of the OR Press. I suppose he will say as many have said, including you, that I shouldn't make any decisions for a while.

Much affection across the miles,

Joyce

March 23, 2008.

To Gloria Vanderbilt

. . . just came back from a brisk walk, and feel somewhat encouraged. My worst times are nights of course—I am trying different medications—ultimately, it's probably best just to sit up and read or try to take notes . . . I have not been able to write in any formal way but have taken many fevered notes over the past weeks . . . everything dazed and deranged and unreal and seemingly without end. I love the beautiful St. Theresa figure, it suggests such calm and seems to rise above time. I think, It will outlive us all. This is only right.

Today is Easter, and I am hoping to see "newness" in things. The past six weeks have been claustrophobic and leaden, and I am eager for some change!

Love,

Joyce

56

The Cache

Lorazepam—43 one-milligram tablets—"for anxiety"
Methocarbamol—67 two-milligram pills—"for muscle pain"
Citalopram—29 forty-milligram tabs—"for depression, anxiety"
Vicodin Es—29 thirty-milligram tabs—"for pain"
Propoxy—30 thirty-milligram tabs—"for depression, anxiety"
Lunesta—18 three-milligram pills—"for insomnia"
Ambien—30 ten-milligram pills—"for insomnia"
Quinidine—5 two-hundred-milligram tabs—"for rapid heartbeat"
Tylenol P.M.
Benadryl
Bufferin
Advil
Melatonin

The widow's drug cache, spread out on a counter, is a haphazard accumulation of years. Every American household must have such an arsenal of drugs hidden away in medicine cabinets, at the rear of shelves, in drawers. The earliest prescription listed here, quinidine, from a Princeton physician long since retired, is dated 1989. (Would the drug still be effective, after so long? How many would one need to take, to stop a heartbeat altogether?) The pain pills are more recent and the anti-anxiety/anti-depression, anti-insomnia prescriptions are all recent, and all mine.

Such quantities of pills and tablets remain of these prescriptions, because very few of these drugs were ever taken as prescribed. A single Vicodin tablet and you feel as if you've been struck over the head with a sledgehammer—who could dare to take a second tablet?

And so I am left with a rosary of pills. A single decade of this rosary and the subject will have vanished. The widow's misery will have vanished.

So deep a sleep, even the *beady dead eyes like gems* will have vanished.

Otherwise, the widow is AWAKE. Never has there been such WAKEFULNESS as that which inhabits the widow's skull like rapid gunfire. Lying AWAKE through the interminable hours of the night sweaty, frankly scared—not as an adult but as a child is scared—trying not to think of the remainder of my life.

Calculating how long I might have to endure in this posthumous limbo—ten years? Fifteen? *Twenty?*

You have your writing, Joyce. You have your friends. And your students.

Almost, such remarks sound like mockery. But of course no one intends to be mocking.

You know, Ray would not want you to feel this way. Ray would want you to—

But I am angry with Ray! If Ray were to appear in the doorway of this room, I would not speak with him.

It was his carelessness! He let himself get pneumonia, and he let himself die. He left me behind—with this.

The truth is, it was I—the wife, the widow—who left my husband behind.

When you have abandoned the one who trusted you, there can be no solace.

Your punishment is *to be yourself*: *widow*. This is a just punishment.

*   *   *

"I can be strong. I can stop this."

And so tonight, I will not take another pill. Not another half-pill. No more hateful Lorazepam that makes my mouth dry as chalk and my eyes smart with tears. I am curled up in my nest, wool socks, a flannel bathrobe over my nightgown, for I am both shivery and warm, sweaty—the nape of my neck is slick with sweat; propped up in my nest against pillows, as I never did when Ray was alive, I am reasonably comfortable reading, trying to read—this new translation of *The Brothers Karamazov*, or is it the new translation of *Don Quixote*; and there, in the corner of my eye, Ray's novel manuscript on the bedside table, beneath other papers, which impulsively I might read tonight—I might begin to read tonight—for the earnestly typed words are faint, and fading—the pages are at least thirty years old, perhaps forty years old; *Black Mass* was written before my young husband met me, and some years after we were married it was partly revised, or rewritten; the novel is a secret document, I am thinking; as my own writing, in a kind of code, is a secret writing; as all writing is secret, even as it is made public—"published."

I can be strong, I think. *I can stop this.*

Whatever terrible thing is happening to me, inside me—I have the power to stop. If I can concentrate.

Except—I can't concentrate. Not as I used to. As, if I were required to jump out of bed, hurriedly dress and drive to the medical center—I don't think that I could do it. Not now.

Not again.

Perhaps it's a withdrawal symptom—being unable to get out of bed in the morning. (The very concept of "morning" is open to revision when one is depressed—"morning" becomes an elastic term, like "middle-age.") Feeling arms, legs, head heavy as concrete. An effort to breathe—and what a futile effort! Never mind rolling a boulder up a hill like Camus's Sisyphus, what of the futility of *breathing*?

How easy it is, to turn on the TV. Switching through channels, hurriedly, never pausing for more than a few seconds. And how ridiculous life is, viewed as a sequence—a concatenation—of jumbled, random, and unrelated "scenes": especially with the sound muted, these fragments of others' lives—simulated lives—have no more significance than shadows dancing on a wall.

For these, too, are fragments of lives. And many of the actors, in the older films, are no longer living. Ghost-actors, their faces "iconic"—though they themselves have long vanished.

Though I would publicly identify myself as one who reads, and doesn't frequently watch television, yet it's true—I've come to be habituated to late-night TV—switching through channels in a kind of perpetual motion—a lurid Möbius strip of the soul. Court TV with its endless store of documentaries on forensics cases, trials, and celebrity murderers—Animal Planet, Turner Classic Movies, CNN, USA, TNT—you would think that insomnia would have proved fruitful, productive; in the way that, for some of us, fantasies of "sick days" summon the prospect of limitless indulgence in reading, all of *Remembrance of Things Past*, for instance, in the new translation, or a (re)reading of all of Jane Austen, the most delicious sort of escape; or, better yet, jotting down notes for a new project, or "catching up" on correspondence. Then, when you are finally sick, and must retreat to bed, really sick, with flu let's say, you are so terribly weak, so unambiguously *sick*, it is all you can do to hold up your head, or even to rest your head against a pillow. Reading, so long imagined as a much-deserved reward, is suddenly out of the question, like jumping out of bed and dancing—running—to the far end of the house.

And so it has been, with me. Despite my good intentions quickly I lose interest in rereading *The Magic Mountain*, yet more quickly in *War and Peace*—Elias Canetti's *Auto-da-Fé* which I've been meaning to read for years, since Susan Sontag so passionately recommended it to me, proves excruciatingly obscure, and boring; a few pages in a philosopher-friend's book on Wittgenstein, inscribed to me years ago, are all that I can manage. As for *Don Quixote* and *The Brothers Karamazov*—these great works which I'd first read as a teenager now pass overhead like monumental cloud formations, utterly distant from me, unreachable.

The TV remote control, amid the swirl of bedclothes in the nest, is *reachable*.

57

Morbidity Studies

Why is everything so—*bright?*

Even through my eyelids—*blinding-bright?*

Now in the aftermath of my heroic night of sleeplessness—when I'd imagined that I was triumphing over my (presumed) addiction to Lorazepam—this day is so endless, so wracked with headache, dazzling-bright yet splotched with curious lesions like tears in cheap stage scenery—I am thinking *If only! If only I could sleep! I would lie down here, on this floor and I would shut my eyes and sleep for just a few minutes! If only*—in this place where I have never before shopped, Shop-Rite on Route 1, dazedly pushing a balky grocery cart along endless aisles in glaring fluorescent light; my heart is pounding strangely and there is a high ringing in my ears for I'd been able to sleep no more than an hour the previous night sweaty and shivering in the rumpled nest rising several times to stumble through the house to turn down the thermostat . . . It's unbearable to remain awake, yet what alternative?—when I try to sleep my mind races flashing like knives; my brain is a runaway wheel containing nothing, there is no content to my thoughts apart from the obsessive worry *drug-addiction, insomnia—drug-addiction, insomnia*; with true insomniac compulsiveness I'd actually risen from bed one night to look up, in Homer, the encounter of Odysseus and his men with the sea-monsters between whom they must sail:

Scylla lurks inside [a cavern at Erebus]—the yelping horror,
yelping, no louder than any suckling pup
but she's a grisly monster, . . .
She has twelve legs, all writhing, dangling down
and six long swaying necks, a hideous head on each,
each head barbed with a triple row of fangs, thickset,
packed tight—armed to the hilt with black death!
. . . .

beneath it awesome Charybdis gulps the dark water down.
Three times a day she vomits it up, three times she gulps it down,
that terror! Don't be there when the whirlpool swallows down—
not even the earthquake god could save you from disaster.
. . . .

Now wailing in fear, we rowed on up those straits,
Scylla to starboard, dreaded Charybdis off to port. . .
(Homer, The Odyssey, Book 12, *translated by Robert Fagles*)

Where the life-struggle is stark, primitive, elemental—the terror is of being devoured alive.

Where the life-struggle is more "civilized"—the terror is of being driven mad.

If only! But I won't.

This evening, dinner at a friend's house.

This elegant house in Princeton from which my friend E. must soon depart—for her domestic/marital life, too, has collapsed.

House, home, household—these are mysterious words, fraught with meaning. They signal conditions we take for granted until one day when, irrevocably, we can no longer take them for granted.

E. has been one of my intense e-mail correspondents since Ray's death. Late at night—very early in the morning—E. and I exchange our most intimate, inspired, lyric-surreal messages.

Though E. doesn't think of herself in my terms—she doesn't consider herself quite so stricken as a widow—yet I feel a kinship between us. Both of us have lost our closest companions, both of us find ourselves suddenly alone.

Living alone, in houses we'd each shared with another person, for many years.

You could say, each of us has been in a car wreck. Our injuries are not visible, exactly.

Who is to say—which is worse? To lose a husband to death, or to lose a husband because he has chosen to leave, for another woman?

This evening at dinner there are just four people: four women: of whom three have been divorced—(each, more than once)—and one "widowed."

Much of the dinner conversation turns upon E.'s situation—the imminence of her expulsion from her beautiful house—her financial crisis—the ways in which her companion seems to have betrayed her trust.

Where there is betrayal, there can be anger, rage. I am thinking with envy how much healthier, how much more *exhilarating*, such emotions would be, than the heavyheartedness of grief like a sodden overcoat the widow must wear.

One of the—several-times-divorced—women tells us that her most recent husband cheated her of thousands of dollars, but that her lawyer advised her not to sue him: "It wouldn't be worth it."

It's shocking that this man—known to the community as a distinguished research scientist—seems to have been dishonest, duplicitous. From the way in which M. speaks of him, you would be led to believe that she despises him. Yet she'd left a previous husband for this man amid a flurry of Princeton scandal, some years before.

Each had left an unsuspecting spouse. Each had deeply wounded the left-behind spouse.

And E.'s tales of her traitorous companion of seventeen years! Robustly told, and funny.

Wine helps. If one drinks.

Amid this bawdy Wife-of-Bath talk how lonely I feel, how—inexperienced, naive. . . . It's a fact that Ray was the first man in my life, the last man, the only man . . . Despite my reputation as a writer my personal life has been as measured and decorous as Laura Ashley wallpaper.

The women turn their attention upon me. I've been so quiet. I can't tell them *I am so yearning to go home, to crawl into my nest. Even if I can't sleep. I am so unhappy, here . . .*

Though really, I am happy here. I am "having a very good time" here. The women are wonderful company, E. has made a splendid dinner, there is something heartening about our being together—as if the glittering dining room table—candlelight reflected in the fine wood, slender glass vases of white flowers—were a kind of life raft, and we four in the life raft, on a choppy sea.

M. asks if I am sleeping and I tell her that I'm not sleeping very well but that I've stopped taking a prescription drug to which I'd become addicted—just the previous night, I managed not to give in and take this drug; if I'd expected M., a professional woman with a medical degree of some kind, to be impressed with this remark, I am taken aback by the bluntness with which M. speaks, ostensibly to me, but for the benefit of the others: "You could be 'addicted' to that drug for the rest of your life and it wouldn't be nearly so serious as going without sleep. If you don't sleep your immune system will be weakened, you'll be susceptible to illnesses and infections and your life expectancy will be shortened. If you don't sleep, you die."

How like a curse this sounds to me, I sit stunned at the dining table, staring. How helpless I feel, like one about to slip from the life raft out of sheer weakness, exhaustion. *If you don't sleep, you die.*

M. speaks with authority. M. tells us that "morbidity studies have shown . . ."

Morbidity studies! The words strike a chill in me. I'd been so determined to break my addiction to Lorazepam—as if this were equivalent to breaking an addiction to anxiety, depression, insomnia—the condition of *widowhood* itself . . .

Driving home, I feel mounting anxiety, yet a kind of childish relief— *I tried to break the addiction. I tried!*

58

The Intruder

There is someone in the house! There is an intruder in the house! Care-lessly she had not locked all the doors—again. And now, Death has entered through the rear door overlooking the terrace. Frightened and paralyzed she lies in her bed. Footsteps, in the hallway. Silently the door, kept ajar, is pushed open. A figure in the dark—a darkness ten times dark—for she has turned off the bedside light, evidently—and she has fallen asleep—has she?—in a state of anxious exhaustion—in a state of drug withdrawal—"derealization"—unable to move as the intruder approaches her. For Death is always he. *Death is always mute and efficient and the most efficient way is to press a pillow over her face, her nose and mouth. No air! No oxygen! She struggles, panicked. This is not the Death she had fantasized. This is not the Death she had wished for. She will put up a struggle for she is an animal fighting for her life—the physical life, raw animal-life, that knows nothing of the luxury of loss, grief, melancholia. The struggling woman in her sweaty churned bed is unexpectedly strong but Death is stronger.*

V

"YOU LOOKED SO HAPPY"

Though you loved Ray, very much, and could not imagine living without him, you will begin to discover that you are doing things that Ray would not have much been interested in doing, and you are meeting people you would not have met when Ray was alive, and all this will change your life for the better, though you might not think so now.

—Eleanor Bergstein

59

Too Soon!

This is shocking to me—that the unremitting cold of the season of Ray's death—New Jersey sky like a pot carelessly scoured, twilight easing up out of the drab earth by late afternoon—is yielding by slow degrees to *spring.*

The widow doesn't want *change.* The widow wants the world—time—to have *ended.*

As the widow's life—she is certain—has *ended.*

A perverse sort of comfort, solace—that the winter has hung on so long, well into late March, early April.

Standing in the doorway staring into the courtyard. How long I've been standing here, I have no idea. What fascinates me—what fills me with dread—are the small green tender shoots pushing through the snow-crust of the earth: tulips. *Too soon! This is too soon.*

Ray's tulips. Last fall he'd dug up this entire bed, and he'd planted dozens of tulip bulbs. On his knees in the soft dark earth utterly absorbed, contented, *happy.*

A gardener is one for whom the prospect of the future is not threatening but *happy.*

He'd shown me the packages of tulip bulbs, from Holland. Bright red, yellow-striped, purple-striped, white with pale orange strips like lace. He'd bought these tulips at his favorite nursery/garden center which is Kale's Nursery about two miles from our house.

Want to come with me?—I'm going to Kale's after lunch.

Usually, I'd said no. *No thank you, I have work to do.*

Now I am sick at heart, remembering. What stupidity—madness—had blinded me, that I'd imagined there was *work to do* more important than accompanying my husband to Kale's.

In other beds, near the driveway, snowdrops are already in bloom—almost invisible, unobtrusive. Such small delicate bell-like flowers, almost you might mistake them for dollops of snow, or overlook them entirely amid the late-winter accumulation of rotted leaves, storm debris.

And crocuses, which Ray had planted also: lavender, purple-striped, yellow, pale orange . . . *Too soon! This is all too soon.*

These small early-spring flowers I would pick, just a few, to place in small vases on the dining room table, on the kitchen windowsill, sometimes on Ray's desk.

Now, the thought of picking flowers, bringing them into the house, is repulsive to me, obscene.

Like preparing a meal in the kitchen. Sitting at the dining room table, eating.

So much is becoming *obscene*, because it has not *ended*.

"It isn't fair. Ray would want so badly to be . . ."

To be *here*. To be *alive*.

I am thinking of how, that morning in February, I'd found Ray in the guest room, at the white Parsons table, wadded tissues scattered on the tabletop amid the sprawl of the *New York Times*. How I'd insisted upon taking him to the medical center. How I'd believed—we'd both believed—that this was an inconvenience, an annoyance—an interruption of our workday—but that Ray would be home within hours, or maybe by next morning.

By the road to the contagious hospital—this line of William Carlos Williams reverberates in my head like a persistent rattle.

And I am thinking, helplessly I am thinking, how terrible it is, that, when I'd driven Ray into Princeton, it was the *contagious hospital* to which I was delivering him, like a good wife. Taking my husband away from the home in which he'd been so happy, and delivering him—where? He'd trusted me, he'd been weak, sick. He had not the strength to resist, or to question my decision.

And now, the tulips. These tulips from Holland, that will outlive him.

A kind of rage comes over me, almost I want to dig up the tulip bulbs, or cover the shoots with rotted leaves, dirt.

If the widow could *stop time.*

If the widow could *reverse time.*

My mouth is parched, my lips feel chafed. There is the familiar sour taste of morning—the insomniac's *morning-after*—this groggy/head-achey/zombie state that follows an interminable night interrupted by periods of "sleep"—not the powerful Lorazepam which I have ceased taking despite S.'s advice but other medications, spaced through the night: at 11 P.M. maybe a Lunesta half-pill; at 4 A.M. a second half-pill, or, at a friend's recommendation, one or two tablets of Tylenol P.M., or Benadryl—non-prescription drugs said to be *non-habit-forming.*

How I dread being *addicted!*—an *addict!*

Though the rest of my life is in ruins, yet—I am determined not to be an *addict.*

Though I have come to feel enormous sympathy for drug addicts of all kinds, as for alcoholics, the *walking wounded* who surround us—these are ourselves, self-medicated. Their spiritual malaise is such, only powerful medication can assuage it. Otherwise, there is suicide.

Where in my former life I'd seemed to believe, with a schoolgirl sort of moral certitude, that drug addiction, alcoholism, suicide—the general collapse of an individual—suggested some sort of spiritual dereliction, to be avoided by an act of will—now I believe the exact opposite.

What astonishes me is that there are so many who don't succumb. So many people who have not killed themselves . . .

I am not sure if "suicide"—as an idea—was abhorrent to Ray, or whether Ray was indifferent to it. Not once do I recall Ray speaking of suicide as a philosophical issue, still less as a personal issue. Though I recall his having taught the poetry of Sylvia Plath, whose breathless incantatory lines are a summons to nullity, extinction:

Dying
Is an art, like everything else.
I do it exceptionally well.

I do it so it feels like hell.
I do it so it feels real.
I guess you could say I've a call.
—*"Lady Lazarus"*

It is the "almost unnameable lust"—of which Anne Sexton speaks in her poetry, as well—this wish to *self-medicate*, to the point of *self-erasure*.

As if there were a terrible mistake, a fundamental error—that one is alive and the act of suicide is a correction, a "righting" of what is "wrong."

The widow feels in her heart, she should not be *still alive*. She is baffled, frightened—she feels that she is *wrong*.

Standing in the doorway shivering staring into the courtyard at the tiny green tulip-shoots thinking these thoughts like one entranced. If Ray were alive I would not be here, I would not be thinking these thoughts; the fact that I am thinking these thoughts is profound, I must pursue these thoughts further. In the periphery of my vision the lizard-thing glimmers faintly—why should I need *that*?

Now it's late morning, now a stirring of the air, a scent of—spring?—yet the widow is near-catatonic, mesmerized. If the phone rings I will not have the strength to answer it but the ringing will rouse me from this trance. Oh who will call me, who is the friend who will think—*Maybe I should call Joyce to say hello, poor Joyce!*—she won't answer the phone anyway.

60

"Leaving Las Vegas"

These entranced TV nights—remote control in my numbed fingers—
the movie I seem to be seeing often, in fragments like a broken mirror,
is *Leaving Las Vegas.*

This was a movie we'd avoided seeing. Neither Ray nor I had had the
slightest interest in it—the story of a terminal alcoholic. No matter that
it had received very good reviews and people had spoken admiringly of
it—we would not have wanted to see it, ever.

Yet, unexpected, over the past several weeks since Ray's death, it is
Leaving Las Vegas that exerts a curious sort of spell.

Sometimes it's playing on two cable channels, at different times. In
a single week, it is likely to be playing several times. I haven't yet seen
it from start to finish—(but now, I rarely see anything "from start to
finish"—I'm too restless and my attention is too scattered)—but I've
seen fifteen-, twenty-minute intervals, in a jumbled sequence with just
enough continuity for me to make sense of the plot.

As if only in such intervals is *Leaving Las Vegas* bearable.

Things have meanings. All things have meanings. There are no coinci-
dences.

Some of the scenes I've seen several times. Just once, the final wrench-
ing scene. And just once, belatedly, the opening of the film—a sequence

that explains the protagonist's self-destructive behavior even as it distances us from him and undermines our sympathy for him.

Almost against my will I'm caught up in this blackly comic/tender-morbid account of an alcoholic Hollywood screenwriter in his late thirties?—early forties?—who comes to Las Vegas after his wife leaves him, with the intention of drinking himself to death.

Where previously I'd not had the slightest interest in Nicolas Cage's Oscar-winning performance as the alcoholic "Ben Sanderson"—now I am mesmerized by it. Cage is not an actor for whom I've felt an exceptional admiration until now but this performance is riveting, utterly convincing. Still more, I'm drawn to "Sera"—a Vegas prostitute played by Elisabeth Shue who exudes a wan, about-to-be-extinguished sort of beauty. That *Leaving Las Vegas* is a romance despite its subject matter—that one comes to care for the doomed lovers—is unexpected. The devotion of the prostitute Sera for the doomed Ben is both outrageous, as the devotion of certain legendary Christian saints and martyrs is outrageous, and yet convincing. *We don't choose the people with whom we fall in love. The love we feel, is our fate. We don't choose our fate.*

And: *Because we had so little time left . . .*

After I'd seen the film piecemeal, it became evident that Sera has survived Ben and is recounting the story of her love for him. Her hopeless love for him.

At the start of their relationship, Ben warns Sera *Don't ever tell me to stop drinking.*

Sera warns Ben *Don't try to make me change my life.*

Ben would drive Sera away, he's even unfaithful to her—this man so saturated in alcohol that he's barely potent sexually. It's the unmitigated devotion of the woman to the doomed and unrepentant man that makes *Leaving Las Vegas* such a powerful movie.

All that I'd disliked about the film initially, before I'd actually seen it, seems to me now irresistibly attractive. As I had disliked, or disapproved of, the "moral weaknesses" of those who self-medicate, and now feel that I understand them, and sympathize with them—*For I've become one of these myself.*

My interest in *Leaving Las Vegas* increases when I learn that the novelist John O'Brien from whose semi-autobiographical novel the film was adapted was himself alcoholic, suicidal—(of course, who else could have written such an intimate account of this doomed life)—and that he'd committed suicide in the second week of the film production.

What is touching, captivating—that Sera will stay with Ben, to the end. She will not desert him. She will not save herself by abandoning him. She expects nothing more from him than he can give her. *To stay with him, the doomed afflicted man, for as long as possible. To understand that your time together is limited. To expect nothing more than—what is.*

Though we've been more intimate with Ben than with Sera yet it's Sera who has outlived Ben. For the woman is likely to outlive the man—and to be the chronicler of his life/death.

The woman is the elegist. The woman is the repository of memory.

And so the film ends with a reprise of their relationship—Sera's "happy" memories of the doomed Ben. We can see how a woman might be drawn—against her better judgment—to such a man.

In sickness and in health. Till death do us part.

61

"The Unlived . . ."

But isn't one's pain quotient shocking enough without fictional amplification, without giving things an intensity that is ephemeral in life and sometimes even unseen? Not for some. For some very, very few that amplification, evolving uncertainly out of nothing, constitutes their only assurance, and the unlived, the surmise, fully drawn in print on paper, is the life whose meaning comes to matter most.

Philip Roth, *Exit Ghost*

How I wish that I could believe these words!

Brave defiant words that claim, for the writer, a privileged life of meaning, significance, and value beyond that of mere "life"—the claim that art is compensatory for the disappointments of life.

Curled in the nest reading a bound galley of Philip's new novel—which Ray had read shortly before he'd been hospitalized. I wish that I could believe this claim for art but I can't—at any rate, it isn't a possibility for me.

Since Ray has died—*died* is a new word, I am almost able to use it without flinching—I've come to realize that my writing—my "art"—is a part of my life but not the predominant part.

We revere a cult of genius—as if "genius" stood alone, a solitary mountain peak. This is false, preposterous.

My life is my life as a woman, my "human" life you might say, and that "human" life is defined by other people; by the ever-shifting web, weave, waxing of others' emotions; others' states of mind that can't be fixed, as their very existence can't be fixed. Philip Roth's claim is that "print on paper" endures in a way that life can't endure, and maybe this is so, in a manner of speaking—(at least, for those writers whose work isn't permanently out of print)—and yet, what chill, meager comfort!

Here is an American predecessor speaking in a very different idiom, yet in a common language:

> A writer must live and die by his writing. Good for that and good for nothing else. A War; an earthquake, the revival of letters, the new dispensation by Jesus, or by Angels, Heaven, Hell, power, science, the Neant [Nothingness],—exist only for him as strokes for his brush.
>
> Ralph Waldo Emerson, "Experience"

His brush. For this is a masculine stance, I think. The bravado, the futility.

Bravado in the very face of futility.

It is terrifying to consider—maybe, one day, out of loneliness, desperation, and defiance—I, too, will make such a claim.

62

CRUEL CRUDE STUPID "WELL-INTENTIONED"

"Ohhh Joyce—you're wearing *pink*. How nice."

Like a slap in the face, or a kick in the gut—this exclamation from a woman when we meet, in the company of several other women, following the memorial service for Robert Fagles in the Princeton University chapel. The woman is not a close friend of mine—rather more, an old acquaintance—for whom I've felt affection in the past though at the moment I want only to turn away from her, and run.

What should I be wearing? Black?

How dare you speak to me like that!—and how stupid of you, to mistake dark-rose for "pink."

Of course I manage to be civil. I suppose, I manage to smile. Only my friend Jane sees the shock, the hurt, the incredulity in my face.

She means well. She doesn't mean to upset you. She's clumsy, awkward—she doesn't know what to say, and she doesn't know how to not-say it.

Still, as soon as I can, I run.

"Beginning again—like, a divorce—can be *good*."

Such a smile wreathing this man's face, such affable vehemence in his voice—it seems contrary of me, to point out that my husband and I weren't divorced—"I'm a widow. There's a difference."

Still he persists: "Not an actual difference. Not literal. It's 'beginning again'—you can go in any direction."

"Really!"

"The spouse is gone. That's a literal fact. Whether he moved out or—whatever."

He's a contractor whom I've called to the house, for an estimate on repairs. He's a stranger to me though highly recommended by mutual friends. He is not someone whom Ray knew, nor did he know Ray. Hence his affable manner, his sense of certitude, as of a man who'd been divorced—dragged over the rubble, battered and humiliated—but over it, now.

"The house is yours, you can do what you want with it. You can renovate, you can build an addition, you can *sell*. That's the bottom line."

Is this real? This bizarre conversation? Or is it a perfectly ordinary commonsensical conversation, of the kind people have with women who've just recently "lost" their husbands, and I am overly sensitive, like one whose outermost layer of skin has been peeled off? I am trying not to be upset for of course this man, too, is well intentioned—he doesn't mean to be crude, cruel, stupid—his meaning is *Look on the bright side! Why be gloomy! Here's a golden opportunity!*

By the time the contractor leaves, I'm feeling dazed, exhausted. His boastful little business card I tear into bits. His cheery over-loud phone messages I will not return. When, one day, his pickup truck turns into my driveway as if, impulsively, while he's in the neighborhood he has decided to drop by, I run away to the rear of the house, far from the front door, and hide.

"Ohhh Joyce! I was *so sorry* to hear about—"

In the midst of dinner with friends in a Princeton restaurant, in the midst of smiling and laughing with friends, something like a predator-bird has swooped upon us having sighted me across the restaurant—(in fact I'd seen him, this individual, making his way to me)—and this time quickly I say, I hope that I am smiling as I say, a flash of scissors in my heart—"Not right now, please. This isn't the right time, thank you."

* * *

Edmund White reports to me, a mutual acquaintance, a university administrator, regretting to him that she'd "never gotten around to sending Joyce some flowers"—and we laugh together at the remark, all that such a remark entails, as if flowers from this woman, any expression of sympathy or even acknowledgment from this woman, would mean anything.

"I told her not to bother," Edmund said. "I told her that you had all the flowers you want."

Earnestly a (woman) friend consoles me.

"'Grief' is neurological. Eventually the neurons are 're-circuited.' I would think that, if this is so, you could speed up the process by just *knowing*."

"We want to see you, Joyce! It's been so long."

In another Princeton restaurant with friends—three couples, among them our oldest Princeton friends—it somehow happens that one of the men lifts his glass in a toast to marriage—long marriages—for each of the couples has been married more than fifty years; their conversation turns upon old times, old memories, in their marriages; at length they reminisce, one of the men in particular goes on, on and on; and I am miserable with longing to be away from these people, away from their unwittingly cruel talk that so excludes me as if they'd never known Ray, who had been their friend. *How can they not know how they are hurting me? How, when they'd all known Ray well* . . .

"Excuse me. I have to leave."

For the first time since my husband died, I am crying in a public place, and must quickly depart, even as my friends stare after me; one of the men follows me, apologizing, meaning to be kind—but I can't speak with him, I must escape.

The first breakdown in public, and the last.

"And what will you do now? Sell your house?"

"If . . ."

If I take my own life it will not be premeditated but impulsive.

One day—more likely, one night—the loneliness will be overwhelming—more than overwhelming, purposeless—& I will be so tired—bone-marrow-deep tired—& the knowledge that this condition will not change but prevail, or become worse—& I will weaken, or maybe I will feel a surge of strength, a determination to finally *get this over with—like one who has been poised trembling at the end of a high diving board—a very high diving board—and the depth of the water below uncertain—the surface choppy, shiny, plastic-y—& so—the cache of pills will be the solution.*

But how to leave this note? This stumbling note? For it must be clearly stated—

I am not suggesting that life is not rich, wonderful, beautiful, various and ever-surprising, and precious—only that, for me, there is no access to this life any longer. I am not suggesting that the world isn't beautiful—some of the world, that is. Only that, for me, this world has become remote & inaccessible.

On shore, in a tangle of storm debris, & a lighted ferry or sailboat or cruise ship is pulling out—on the shore you stand watching as the boat recedes—sparkling lights, music, voices—laughter. If you wave at the boat, or do not wave at the boat, it comes to the same thing: no one notices, and the boat is pulling out to sea.

"Never, Ever That Again"

Dear Joyce,

Oh please don't think of giving up. Many people who value and need your friendship would miss you terribly. This may seem a little abrupt but I've begun to think that we might be friends, and I surely don't want to lose a friend that I may have just found! And we don't need to lose any more people with your sensibilities . . . I can't imagine that you would want your life's work to be colored by this great sadness. I tried to kill myself once—no one close to me knew or knows about it—many, many years ago when I was an undergraduate at the University of Minnesota. I was under a lot of pressure in school taking advanced classes, working to pay for school, living with my girlfriend. I thought I could do everything—and very well—but I was overwhelmed. I didn't follow the surefire, masculine Hemingway route . . . I took pills, which allow for a period of reflection before it's too late. I did finally make my way to the emergency room where I was treated with shocking cruelty (to teach me a lesson?). And in the end, I wandered out of the hospital unnoticed, in the midst of severe hallucinations! (Which I find equally shocking.) Obviously I survived the attempt, and I will never, ever do that again. Even just seeing the sunlight is worth it . . .

Please take care of yourself.

G.

The "Real World"

Outside the bell jar of the widow's slow-suffocating life is the "real world" at a distance remote and antic in its ever-shifting contortions—glimpsed in newspaper headlines, fragments of television news—avoided by the widow as one might avoid staring at the blinding sun during an eclipse.

Exactly why this is, that the "news" so upsets me, I'm not sure. I don't think it can be just that Ray was so avidly interested in the news, especially in politics. I don't think that this is it, entirely.

Where once I'd scrolled through the cable stations out of curiosity, and spent several months watching Fox News in the late evening, researching a novel set in "tabloid hell"—now I can't bear to hear these monologue rants and "panel discussions" involving shouting and interruptions.

In Princeton, New Jersey—where no one watches Fox News and my interest in such righteous enemies of "secular progressivism"/liberalism/Democrats is considered a quirk of the fiction writer's skewed mentality—the *sole topic of conversation* for months has been the Democratic primary for the presidential candidate in the upcoming election.

For it seems that half of Princeton is rallying for "Hillary"—the other half for "Obama": at social gatherings there are endless discussions of the merits/demerits of "Hillary"/"Obama"—endless discussions of the merits/demerits of the candidates' campaigns—endless discussions

of the political/moral/economic/intellectual/spiritual bankruptcy of the
Bush administration and how an incoming Democratic president might
deal with this terrible legacy.

Often there are sharp, highly vocal disagreements: a number of Princeton people are actively involved in each of the campaigns, fund-raising,
speech writing, "consulting." (One single, singular Princeton individual is
"pro-Iraqi War"—a locally notorious Middle East advisor to Bush/Cheney.)

It is astonishing how virtually the same words are uttered again,
again and again—"Hillary"—"Obama"—with subtle, shifting variants.
One would think that there is nothing in life, nothing of significance in
life, except the Democratic primaries. Nothing except politics!

*Because they are not wounded people. Because they are free to care about
such things—the life of the more-than-personal, the greater-than-personal—
as you are not.*

In these gatherings I am thinking of Ray. I am seeing Ray.

The vision of my husband in his hospital bed—in that last, deathly
hospital bed—superimposed upon this living room, upon the bright-
peopled gathering. I am thinking of how Ray has lost this world, he has
lost his place in this world, he has been expelled from this world, even as,
oblivious to his absence, the world careens on.

If I should take my own life . . . In this setting, how forlorn, silly, sad,
trite these words! In this instant, suicide is not a possibility.

I am thinking of my friend in Minnesota—whom I have not yet
met—who'd written to me so frankly and so kindly about trying to kill
himself as an undergraduate—*I will never, ever do that again.* His calm
caring letter is a rebuke to my desperation.

I must think of grief as an illness. An illness to be overcome.

And yet: how lonely I feel, amid my friends. I could be a paraplegic
observing dancers—it isn't even envy I feel for them, almost a kind of
disbelief, they are so utterly different from me, and so oblivious. These
are the people on the brightly lit ship putting out to sea, I am left behind
on shore. Now wanting to think *But your happiness too is fleeting. It will
last a while, and then it will cease.*

As at dinner in New York City, in an Upper East Side restaurant, my
friend Sean Wilentz and our mutual friend Philip Roth become quickly so
engaged in a discussion—a heated discussion—in fact, an "argument"—

that I am in the position of a hapless spectator at a Ping-Pong match, glancing back and forth between the men. Sean, who happens to be working for Hillary Clinton, is very critical of Obama; Philip, an ardent supporter of Obama, is very critical of Hillary Clinton. You have to be impressed, listening to these two, by the refusal of either to concede to the other's point of view, as by the absence of any gesture of quasi-compromise—*Maybe I'm mistaken, but—*.

I am thinking of how, the last time I saw Philip Roth, Ray was with me—of course. We'd come into the city and had dinner together at another of Philip's favorite restaurants, the Russian Samovar. Philip told us then that he'd begun to feel lonely in his country house in Cornwall Bridge, Connecticut—one by one his old friends were dying—the winters were particularly difficult. How remote to us at that moment, any thought that Ray—an "old friend" of Philip's also though not a close/intimate friend—might be the next to die . . .

It's so, one always thinks that death is elsewhere.

Though death may be imminent, it is imminent *elsewhere.*

How I wish now that I could recall what we'd talked about, with Philip! As the men continue to argue—now the subject has shifted to the ever-iterated conundrum *If Hillary is elected, where will Bill be? In the White House? Telling her what to do?*—I am thinking of how we'd mostly laughed; Philip is very funny, when he isn't passionately engaged in arguing politics; though Ray had strong opinions about politics he wasn't argumentative, and he and Philip shared the same opinions at that time.

Ray and I had never visited Philip in Cornwall Bridge though we'd visited friends/neighbors of Philip's, years ago—Francine du Plessix Gray and her husband the artist Cleve Gray. Cornwall Bridge is a rural, very beautiful and very hilly northwestern corner of the state, not far from the Massachusetts border, an ideal place for a writer who is something of a recluse, or who values his privacy.

I am thinking that I couldn't bear to live alone, as Philip has done since the dissolution of his marriage to Claire Bloom years ago. A life so focused upon writing, and reading; a life of isolation in the interstices of which there are evenings with friends, and (seemingly short-lived) liaisons with younger women; a brave life, a stoic life commensurate with the claim *the unlived, the surmise, fully drawn in print on paper, is the life whose meaning comes to matter most.*

A line of Franz Kafka's comes to my mind. The conclusion of "A Hunger Artist"—*I never found the food I wanted to eat. If I had, I'd have stuffed myself like everyone else.*

For Philip, as for me—Kafka is a predecessor-cousin. Older, remote, iconic, "mythic." Long before I'd known that my father's mother was Jewish, thus I am "Jewish" to a degree, I'd felt this strange kinship with Franz Kafka: every aphorism uttered by Kafka is likely to be one lodged deep in my soul.

No one but you could gain admittance through this door, since this door is intended only for you. Now I am going to shut it.

The horror of the widow's posthumous life washes over me. The door before me, the only door through which I can enter—will be shut to me, soon.

Philip was very kind to have written to me soon after Ray's death. Not once but twice.

For I'd failed to reply, the first time. Philip's letter of sympathy—succinct, very touching—I'd placed on a corner of my desk, where I saw it every time I approached. A plain sheet of white paper, a few typed lines—*The few times we were together I was always impressed by his calm and his kindness . . . Your fortitude is such that you'll go on but it must right now be a stunning loss. I am thinking of you.*

Scattered about my study in the way one might place precious stones in an ordinary setting are such sympathy letters and cards from a number of our friends. But the majority remain in the green tote bag, unopened.

Very few of these letters have I answered. A strange lethargy overcomes me, a dread of the words a widow must write.

Thank you for your condolences. Thank you for thinking of Ray and for thinking of me. . . .

Words of such banality, futility! Like the "suicide note" scrolling in my head much of the day and night, which I assume I will have enough good sense/pride never to share with another person.

If Hillary wins the nomination—

If Obama wins the nomination—

If the Democrats have a majority in Congress, finally—

What a terrible legacy the Bush wars in Iraq, Afghanistan!

When we part on East Eightieth Street, Philip and I hug each other. It's a wordless gesture, as between two battered individuals. If I'd told Philip that Ray read *Exit Ghost* soon before entering the hospital from which he never returned, I did not tell Philip that, for me, the most riveting passages in the novel had little to do with the protagonist but with a Connecticut friend named Larry who, diagnosed with cancer, manages to smuggle one hundred sleeping pills into his hospital room in order to kill himself in a place where professionals are at hand to care for a corpse. In this way the considerate husband and father spares his family "all that he could of the grotesqueries attendant upon suicide."

I'm sure that "Larry" was a Connecticut neighbor of Philip's—but I can't bring myself to ask.

The first time we'd met Philip Roth was in the summer of 1974. I'd interviewed Philip for the first issue of *Ontario Review* in a sequence of questions to which Philip wrote thoughtful answers. We walked in Central Park—dropped by Philip's apartment in the East Eighties not far from the Metropolitan Museum of Art—spent several hours together. I remember the three of us laughing a good deal. I remember Philip's customary wariness, watchfulness. But I'm not sure that I remember what I'd written at the end of the interview, about the interior of Philip's apartment—his study filled with books including the classic Baugh's *A Literary History of England* and, on a wall, a "somber, appealing photograph of Franz Kafka"—the identical photograph which, as an idealistic and literary-minded undergraduate at Syracuse University in the fall of 1956, I'd taped to the blank beige wall above my desk.

66

LITTLE LOVE STORY

At a book signing in New York City, a tall figure in jeans, denim vest, blue cotton shirt with sleeves neatly folded back to the elbows presents me with seven books to sign *for Lisette*. It isn't clear if the person is male or female, relatively young or not-so-young, a baseball cap has been pulled down to obscure part of his/her face.

"'Lisette'! That's an unusual name."

"Yes. I think so." The voice is low, throaty—a woman's voice?

"Are you Lisette?"

"No. Lisette is my girlfriend."

I glance up seeing it's a woman—late thirties, or early forties—lanky-limbed, with short-trimmed sand-colored hair, a strong-boned face and pale eyes. Reticent by nature, perhaps—but something has triggered a sudden urge in her to speak to me, as if in confidence.

"Lisette loves your books, and I love Lisette. So I'm giving her these."

"That's very nice of you."

At these public occasions my voice radiates a kind of warmth that surprises me. Is my widowhood a mirage, is this cheery smiling public-self my true self?

The widow's vow—*If I am not happy, yet I can try to make others happy.*

"And what is your name?"

"My name? M'r'n."

"Marian?"

"Mar'n."

Grudgingly she speaks, in a lowered voice. As if, whatever her name is, it's of little significance to her.

"And what do you do?"

"What do I *do*?—I'm retired."

"You look too young to be retired."

This is so. Now that I think of it, the pale-eyed woman in denim is much too young to be retired. There is something in the way she holds herself, cautiously, tentatively, that suggests the anticipation of pain, and the wish to forestall it; the stronger wish to disguise it. Her lean face is suffused with heat. "I used to drive a truck. Now I don't. Lisette lives in Denver. I'm going to Denver to live with her."

"Denver! That's far away."

Signing the title pages of my books, in the large clear Palmer script of my long-ago schoolgirl self, invariably I feel just slightly giddy, as if, at such moments, the grim facade of life is stripped away and what is revealed is a kind of costume party. I am the Author, the smiling individuals waiting patiently in line to have their books signed are Readers. Our roles provide a kind of childlike contentment like those food trays in which areas are divided from one another, so that foods will not run together. Signing books for readers may be the only times that certain writers smile.

"Not so far. I can drive. I don't fly, but I can drive. I'll fill my truck. It's a one-way trip."

I am signing the next-to-the-last book, a paperback copy of *Blonde*. It seems to me that the mysterious Lisette must be blond. I ask how she and Lisette met and the woman says, "We ran into each other. In a bookstore. I mean, we ran into each other—really! I stepped right into Lisette. Didn't mean to hurt her, but—that was how we met." The woman is speaking in quick terse syllables like one who hasn't spoken in some time. Her voice is eager now, almost giddy. In the aftermath of a crowded reading the atmosphere is often festive; strangers find themselves talking to strangers, waiting for the line to move.

"And what does Lisette do?"

"Lisette don't *do*, Lisette just *is*."

This is so wittily put, we laugh together. The woman in denim is delighted to be queried about the mysterious Lisette.

"Well! Good luck in Denver."

The woman takes up her books, in a crook of her arm. One of the books clatters to the floor and she bends to retrieve it, stiffly. She turns away and murmurs, over her shoulder, "Yeah thanks. I'll be OK. Soon as I get to Denver I'll be OK and when I get over this leukemia, I'll be OK."

Within a few seconds the woman is out of sight. I feel a powerful urge to run after her.

But what would I say? What words? I have not a clue.

I hope you will be happy. You and Lisette, in Denver. I am thinking of you. I will not forget you.

67

Tulips

"Ray's tulips are flourishing—so beautiful."

In the sunny courtyard my friends are admiring a half-dozen vivid-red tulips, some cream-colored tulips, pink-striped . . . I am smiling as if the sight of the tulips—the fact of the tulips, though Ray is gone—is some sort of compensatory magic for the fact that Ray is gone.

Why should Ray's tulips be here, and not Ray? Why should we be standing here, and not Ray?

Bitterness rises in me, like something undigested. It's the bitterness/incredulity of the mad old Lear, after Cordelia has died.

What is the widow—any age, any state—but a variant of the mad old Lear.

Ray's beautiful tulips, Ray's beautiful crocuses, Ray's beautiful daffodils and jonquils planted on a hill behind the house, on the farther side of a meandering little stream that empties into our pond. . . . Ray's beautiful dogwood tree here in the courtyard, soon to burst into bloom.

I am trying not to think *What mockery! This is all so trivial.*

Of course I take care to hide my agitation from my friends who are such special friends, whom I love for their generosity, their kindness, their good sense and their warmth. These are individuals for whom Ray had great affection, if not love. I think yes—love. There is/was an (unspoken) love between them.

In the hospital when I'd suggested that Ray call Susan and Ron, at first Ray thought that he might, then he changed his mind: "It would be too emotional."

Recalling this now, I wonder if Ray had had some awareness that his condition might be serious. That he might not be seeing Susan and Ron again.

"This was Ray's happiest time of year. In a week or two . . . He so much liked . . ."

" . . . his garden was so beautiful."

Terrifying, the way the widow grasps at such things. This familiar metaphor—*grasping at straws*. Or is it rather—*gasping through straws*.

Trying to breathe. Just a little oxygen! Just to keep going.

Why?

How is the issue. *Why* can't be asked.

Last night! Long I will recall last night.

Rarely has the urge to die—to become *extinguished*—been so strong as it was last night. In the home of old friends, who'd known Ray and me for nearly thirty years.

In this setting, that should have been warm, supportive—"safe" and not a "sinkhole."

For somehow, as if they'd planned it beforehand—(which I'm sure they had not)—my friends did not speak of Ray at all. The husband spoke almost exclusively about politics—Hillary/Obama—Bush/Cheney—worse yet Princeton University politics—while I sat staring toward a window—reflections from the dining room table, in this window—trying to recall when Ray and I had been at this table last—when would have been *the last* time Ray was here; it was painful to me, that the husband not only made no mention of Ray but addressed me as he did the several other guests in his jocular-joshing way, as if whatever words tumbled from his mouth, however exaggerated, comical-surreal, provocative, were just a kind of show; an entertainment, a passing-of-time; a kind of academic/intellectual display not unlike the display of the male peacock, staggering beneath the weight of its magnificent full-spread tail. Almost calmly I thought *This is unbearable, I will not miss this*—wanting to flee the house, drive home and swiftly swallow down as many pills from the cache as I could, before I lost my courage—*Anything! Anything but this*—but as soon as I left the house and began driving—as soon as I stepped into this house—the terrible sensation lifted from me, as of a literal weight lifted from my shoulders.

"Honey? Hi. . . ."

For here is the place where Ray awaits. If Ray is anywhere.

When I am with people, an ache consumes me, a yearning to be alone. But when I am alone, an ache consumes me, a feeling that it is dangerous to be alone.

Alone, I am in danger of my life. For the emptiness is close to un-bearable.

With others, I am safe.

Not happy, but *safe.*

The basilisk, for instance, rarely follows me from this house. Amid a babble of people chattering of politics the basilisk seems to have no power, no presence. If we are asked *How are you?* we must not say *Suicidal. And you?*

Yet, my happiness is now other people.

The other day, at the university, I was genuinely happy, I felt a thrill—if short-lived, if pathetic—while reading one of my student-writer's work; revisions by a young woman in one of my workshops. It was a pleasure to see how capably the writer had absorbed our criticism, how she'd revised her story to make it emotionally engaging, compelling . . .

And there are other student-writers this semester. Young writers whose work is significant, "promising". . .

I must have faith in this connection with others. In these "relation-ships"—fleeting as they are.

But these relationships are fleeting. These relationships are not "real"— not intimate. You are deluding yourself, that a professional involvement with others can compensate for the loss of intimacy in your life.

"You should see a therapist"—"grief counselor"—"a local group, people who've lost spouses"—of course this is so, this is admirable advice, and yet—who can be trusted? In this age of memoir, can we trust even professionals not to violate confidentiality?

Recall that psychiatrist who'd treated Anne Sexton in the final years of her life. He'd had no qualms about violating professional ethics by talking of her, revealing a sick woman's most sordid and pathetic fantasies, in interviews with Sexton's biographer.

This is the era of "full disclosure." The memoirist excoriates him-/herself, as in a parody of public penitence, assuming then that the excoriation, exposure, humiliation of others is justified. *I think that this is unethical, immoral. Crude and cruel and unconscionable.*

As the memoir is the most seductive of literary genres, so the memoir is the most dangerous of genres. For the memoir is a repository of truths, as each discrete truth is uttered, but the memoir can't be the repository of Truth which is the very breadth of the sky, too vast to be perceived in a single gaze.

A friend urges—"You should write a memoir. About your life since Ray's death."

A friend urges—"You should not write a memoir. Not about such a subject. And not yet."

Another friend astonishes me by saying, with evident seriousness— "By now, you've probably written the first draft of a novel about Ray. Or—knowing you!—two novels . . ."

Not a friend but a Princeton acquaintance confounds me by saying, with an air of hearty reproach—"Writing up a storm, eh, Joyce?"

It is amazing to me how others wish to believe me so resilient, so— energized . . . Mornings when I can barely force myself out of bed, long days when I am virtually limping with exhaustion, and my head ringing in the aftermath of an insomniac night, yet the joshing-jocular exclamations are cast on me like soiled bits of confetti—how infuriating, the very vocabulary of such taunts—*Writing up a storm, eh?*—since a review of mine has appeared in the *New Yorker*, or the *New York Review of Books*, or a story written long before Ray's death has appeared in a magazine; a newly published book, written more than a year ago, in a more innocent time.

Of course, people want to imagine the widow strong—stronger than she is, or can hope to be. It's pointless—it's just self-pity—to want to explain that the "old" self is gone, and the "old" strength; that sense of one's self that is called *proprioception*—in the words of Oliver Sacks (quoting Sherrington) " 'our secret sense, our sixth sense' "—

that continuous but unconscious sensory flow from the movable parts of our body . . . by which their position and tone and motion are continually monitored and adjusted, but in a way which is hidden from us because it is automatic and unconscious.

Oliver Sacks, "The Disembodied Lady" from
The Man Who Mistook His Wife for a Hat

This is it!—that is, this is what *is-not*, for me, any longer. As one of Sacks's patients tells him, in trying to describe this eerie sense of the crucial self being lost, inaccessible—"It's like the body is blind."

The soul, too, can be "blind." Or what passes for the soul, in the sparking/spiking realm of the brain.

The healthy individual—the "normal" individual—experiences proprioception with no more awareness than he experiences oxygen when he breathes. The wounded individual, the widow, has been disembodied; she must try very hard to summon forth the lost "self"—like one blowing up a large balloon, each morning obliged to blow up the large life-sized balloon, the balloon that is *you*, a most exhausting and depressing effort for it seems to no particular purpose other than to establish a life-sized balloon to inhabit from which, in slow degrees, air will leak, over the course of the next twelve hours until one can collapse in "sleep"—some sort of blessed oblivion. But next morning, the effort must be taken up again.

Again, and again!

For the healthy, no particular effort is involved in being "healthy." For the wounded, so much effort is involved in pretending to be "healthy"—the question hovers continuously, at about arm's length, *Why?*

Our friends have left me with two pots of rosemary—"for remembrance." I will plant one of these in the courtyard beneath the window where often I saw Ray, reading the *New York Times*, or spreading out work sheets, and the other in the Pennington cemetery, beside the marker at Ray's grave.

68

Please Forgive!

"Today. I will."

If I make a kind of ceremony of it, perhaps I can do it. At least, I can begin.

I will sit in the courtyard—on a white wrought-iron bench beside Ray's tulips—in a warm splotch of early-April sunshine—and open letters.

These letters—of sympathy, condolence—commiseration—kept in a green tote bag—a now fairly heavy/bulky tote bag—I have not been able to open. Thinking now calmly and with even an air of expectation, anticipation. *I will do this. Of course I must do this. I am strong enough now.*

> *February 26, 2008*
>
> *I was very, very saddened to hear of Ray's death. I remember him as such a gracious and gentle man. One felt—how can I put it?— safe in his gaze, beheld, and in the wonderful presence of a measured and assessing mind. With his enormous and straightforward integrity he affirmed through his very presence and being a human goodness I will never forget. Though I hardly knew him well, my life is richer for having been in his presence. I cannot begin to comprehend your pain or your loss but please know that you are very much in my thoughts.*

I remember once in Princeton seeing you and Ray by the side of the
road—you had gotten off your bicycles to help a wounded animal—I
think it was a baby deer. Or maybe the mother had been killed and
you were rescuing the fawn. All these years and it still comes back into
my mind . . .

This letter, from a poet-friend who has since moved from Princeton to New York City, is the first letter I've taken out of the Earthwise
tote bag. Reading it leaves me shaken, biting my lips to keep from crying. How disorienting—how *disembodying*—it is, to be sitting here in
the sun, on this morning in April 2008, yet pitched so abruptly into the
past—*you had gotten off your bicycles to help a wounded animal . . .* On
Bayberry Road, this was. Of course I remember. And I am ashamed—I
have not replied to this beautiful letter, so thoughtfully composed. I have
not even read it until now, and I have not replied, and weeks have passed,
and I am ashamed.

So much has unraveled. So much, slipping from my control.

Suddenly I am becoming anxious. I wonder if this is such a good
idea—opening mail. I call to the cats—"Reynard! Cherie!"—to keep
me company. The kitchen door is ajar—one of the cats steps through
hesitantly, warily—this is Reynard, the elder cat who walks stiffly; the
other, Cherie, has become more trusting of me lately, perhaps recognizing, with shrewd feline wisdom, that we have only each other now, Ray
is not going to return to feed her breakfast and allow her to settle on his
New York Times as he tries to read it, ever again.

Both cats appear, blinking as if dazed by the sun. Both stretch out
on the flagstone terrace in the sun. Reynard's tail is twitching, which
means that he's uneasy, suspicious. Cherie basks in the warmth, now
rolling over, showing her pale-gray furry stomach, in luxuriant abandon.
I want to call for Ray, to see the cats in the sun—Cherie would make
him laugh.

Honey? Where are you? Come look.

A young buck outside my study window—wild turkeys making their
way past the window—bright-red cardinals, blue jays and titmice in the
birdbath: *Honey, come look! Hurry.*

Last June I ran to Ray's study, to summon him to mine, to observe, at

a distance of about twenty feet, a doe giving birth to two tiny fawns in a
wooded area outside my window.

We watched in fascination. Here was an astonishing sight—the doe
so calm, the births so seemingly easy, effortless; the tiny cat-sized fawns
almost immediately on their spindly legs, capable of walking, if a bit
unsteadily.

The rapacity of nature is such, newborn deer must be able to walk—
to run—soon after birth. Otherwise, predators will devour them.

In Mercer County, New Jersey, there are no natural predators. In the
fall/winter there is hunting, in designated places. But not in residential
neighborhoods. Not here.

One winter, before such well-intentioned naiveté was outlawed by
Hopewell Township, Ray spread out feed for deer on one of our stone
ledges where we could observe them through the plate-glass walls of our
living room and solarium. At first we'd been delighted by the several
deer, including fawns and a young buck, that came to eat the feed; next
day, the number of deer was doubled; next day, tripled; finally, so many
deer, and so many cantankerous and noisy deer, including one fiercely
aggressive doe who crowded out younger deer, snorting and stamping—
"I guess this wasn't such a great idea," Ray said.

No more feed for the deer. For a while afterward they continued
to show up, staring at our windows with expressions of mute animal
reproach.

The strangest sight I ever called Ray to see, from my study window,
will seem unlikely in the telling: a young fawn was making its way past
my window and close behind it, an aggressive wild turkey was peck-
ing at its heels. We watched in amazement as these two disappeared
around the corner of the house—the fawn hurrying forward, the wild
turkey close behind. Ray said, "If we hadn't seen this, we would never
believe it."

Ray often said, "It's very hard to get anything done in this house, with
so much happening outside our windows."

Now I am trying to recall—when was it that our poet-friend saw
us, "rescuing" the fawn? Five years ago? Ten? We'd been bicycling on
Bayberry Road when we discovered a seemingly abandoned tiny fawn
by the roadside. Naively I brought the fawn home in my bicycle basket,

wrapped in my sweater, and when we called the Hopewell Animal Shelter we were admonished for "interfering"—we should have left the fawn exactly where we'd found it, with the assumption that the doe would return, and would re-unite with her fawn.

"Yes, but what if she doesn't?" Ray asked.

We returned the baby deer, in our car. We left it by the roadside. When we returned some time later, there was no sign of the deer.

The principle seems to be—*Don't interfere with nature!*

The next several letters out of the tote bag are not so upsetting—though very kind, very thoughtful expressions of sympathy. The widow is made to know that the death of her husband is a matter of others' concern, not just her own; this is meant to comfort, to console. *We loved Ray so much. Ray was such a humane, dignified, astute, wise, and gentle man. It is a devastating loss. . . .* And this, from another former Princeton resident, a writer-friend now living in Philadelphia:

> *I am so sad that Ray is gone. I will miss his quick, bright eyes, his humor and his large spirit. When I was around Ray, I felt a sweet comfort from his kindness.*
>
> *Death is so mysterious. When [my partner] died, I felt great solace in searching for words to express what I was experiencing, which felt brand new, a place I'd never been before even with all the death I've seen. Knowing how you write, you may already be completing the first of many novels that will help you explore what you've been experiencing . . .*

At these words, I begin to shake. I am actually shaking with cold, with a kind of choked fury. *Knowing how you write, you may already be completing the first of many novels. . . .*

Of course, this writer-friend doesn't mean to be cruel. She doesn't mean to seem taunting, mocking. I know that she means well—she has written a thoughtful and even profound letter which I must not judge from my own desperate perspective. *Completing a novel! I haven't been able to complete a thank-you note!*

The first several letters have been set aside. I know—I am well aware—that "good manners" oblige the widow to reply to each expression of sympathy—(unless the writer has indicated *Please don't trouble to reply*)—but I am not ready to begin these replies just yet.

Blindly I reach into the tote bag. Mostly there are cards, some of them very beautiful seemingly hand-crafted cards, but there are many letters, both typed and handwritten. How stunned Ray would be, at this outpouring of solicitude!

> *I cannot comprehend that Ray has died. And now that this terrible, sad news can no longer be denied, I do not, and will not, understand the injustice of it. I selfishly think of justice in terms of myself, and Ray was much younger than me. Also, he was unusually trim and handsome. So, I assume he always attended to diet and exercise. And then, if goodness has anything to do with justice, Ray was a good, wise, gentle and extraordinarily courteous man . . . When I think of the quality of "calmness in the face of danger," I would think right off of Ray Smith. Suppose Ray and I were in a little boat in Nantucket and we are about to sink in a Nantucket storm. Without knowing one thing about Ray's knowledge of seamanship, I would bet on Ray to remain calm and to always make a correct decision.*

*   *   *

> *I can't get it into my consciousness that we will never see Ray Smith again. It can't be true. You have both been so kind to us, you were the first people who invited me to dinner when I was in the middle of radiation . . . You welcomed us into your home and made me feel healthy and normal. You probably don't remember that evening but I do. I sat next to Ray and had a happy evening. We didn't talk about illness. Ray was so happy with his birds and his flowers and with you, his beloved.*

*   *   *

> *Kate came by early this morning to tell me that Ray had died in the night, and we sat together in the kitchen, remembering that dear man, and trying to think how we could help you, and knowing we couldn't. Liz said, "Back home we'd bake a ham and carry it round," but that didn't seem right, in Princeton.*

*   *   *

I'm writing to express sorrow for your loss. I know the rare kind of relationship you and Ray had (have) is the only thing that can console even as it is the source of grief. Everyone respected him. In these terribly uncivil times, he was a true gentleman . . . It was actually soothing to talk with him. And I always loved seeing the two of you together. I could see how safe he made you feel. I hope you don't feel unsafe now. If there is or will be some memorial charity in his name please let me know.

* * *

I was so deeply shocked and depressed to hear of Ray's death. It seemed only yesterday that we spoke. I admired him so much—did you know that Ontario Review *published my first memoir/short story . . . ? Over the years Ray's (and yours) support have meant just about everything to me. The next issue of the* Pushcart Prize *will be dedicated to Ray, as will my remarks at Symphony Space on March 26 . . . a small tribute to Ray.*

From a writer-friend who'd recently lost his adult daughter:

You and I know there's nothing to say that does much good in the face of a fathomless sorrow. But I hope you're writing again, or will soon. It's difficult to write when there's no joy. (I haven't gotten started again, myself.) Yet it's our only way out. Isn't it? And you bring so much joy to others. We will crawl out of this, I am certain— eventually reach a point where we can live with a deep sadness, but live nonetheless. Know, meanwhile, that you have our love which will never go away.

From a former colleague at the University of Windsor, now a preeminent Canadian writer:

I remember Ray very fondly, not only because of all the work he did, along with yourself, in bringing out my first American collection but just because he was himself . . . I am sending this Mass card because of something Ray said to me years ago. He said that his father

*was prouder of him when he became an altar boy than when he
received his Ph.D. So this is for the former altar boy who did achieve
a Ph.D. and much more.*

And another Canadian colleague:

*I am so sorry about your loss and hope you can grieve freely and
deeply . . . There is no possible consolation, I know. You were so
completely together for so long. Over 30 years ago people used to
see you together walking holding hands. This can only be very hard
but please do not feel alone . . . When my mother died I adopted the
Gestalt technique of saying to myself, whenever there was a surge of
grief, "I choose to have a mother who is dead," and that helped . . .
After a while it is self-punishing to resist or regret what's real.*

*   *   *

*Ray was a perfect man—a gentle soul and honest and sweet. I
often thought of him as a perfect mate. He seemed so comfortable
as the husband of a . . . woman writer. Few women writers have
had someone like Ray. In counseling students and even my own
daughters, Ray was one of my models for the "right kind of man."
I talked to them about a man who would be able to genuinely,
without jealousy or selfishness, support their attempts and
achievements as his own.*

*   *   *

*I will miss Ray but always feel his presence. He will forever be one
of the threads that have created my personhood . . .*

*   *   *

*I haven't written because I haven't wanted to deal with knowing
Ray won't be on the phone again . . .*

*   *   *

*I realized that I had never seen you alone, without Ray—I have
seen you always together. I cannot picture you apart . . .*

Letters from widows!—these, I read avidly. Here is a special language, I am coming to understand.

You have been constantly in my thoughts knowing as I do the devastation of raw grief over the loss of one's nearest and dearest. What a privilege though in this life to have a marriage like yours combining in perfect harmony love and work. From the very first time I met you and Ray, I admired your rich collaboration and the loving way you treated each other . . . Though it may not help to assuage the sadness of your loss, I pass on to you something [my late husband] said to me in the days before his death: "You will be grief-stricken for the rest of your life, but don't lose your vitality."

*   *   *

There is no easy way to live through what you are experiencing. I know this so well. Nothing anyone says makes the pain go away. I forever and ever miss my life as it was with [my late husband] and to this day it is just as poignant and meaningful and monumental.

*   *   *

After nearly two years my wounds are less raw but I'm constantly reminded of [my late husband] and am beginning to find comfort in letting him live in my heart. I want his memory kept alive . . . I think I was in shock for a long time after he died—barely functional. It's hard for me to imagine how you manage to continue teaching— being your public self . . . Please be kind with yourself. Healing will come in in its own good time. But you do need time for yourself. Oh how I wish we were closer. Please call me any time. I love you Joyce and embrace and kiss you through these miles.

*   *   *

. . . a note to say how often I have thought of you since Ray died—the absolute finality of death is both the most obvious thing about it & the most astonishing—it took me a long time to get beyond being stunned by [my husband's] death, which was in fact quite predictable. (I see now.) I hope you are well & working— writing was at first just another hard part—there was no one to read it. But there is . . .

*   *   *

From the first e-mail you sent me that Monday morning with the shocking news, I noticed this: even though you were in a state of shock, at a time when living without Ray surely seemed unimaginable

(as I would think it still does), when, if your experience was like
mine, you may not have wanted to go on living—even then the
words you chose showed a resilience and intention to live through it
and recover your life. I noticed this, since not everyone has that—it's
quite involuntary, I think: but I felt that way too when widowed so
suddenly. Then, when you were at Jeanne's, I could see that in spite of
the terrible grief you were going through, you were not depressed: you
were alert, noticing, engaging the life around you. I was relieved and
glad to see that. Not that one ever "gets over it." Recently someone
said she was glad I had "gotten over" the grief for my husband and
I immediately asked her, "What makes you think I have gotten over
it?" And [my husband died] twenty years ago.

   Dear Joyce, you know that words break and slip at times like
these . . .

Yes. Words may be "helpless"—yet words are all we have to shore
against our ruin, as we have only one another.

An hour has passed. The sun has shifted. Both cats have left the
courtyard and I am alone and the aloneness weighs upon me like something leaden. It's a measure of my *disembodiment* that I have to think, to
recall where I am; why I am here, outside in the courtyard.

So many letters and cards! So much sympathy, and kindness!

I meant to begin answering the letters. I've brought postcards outside
with me, and Ray's address book as well as my own; but now I am overcome with lethargy, a sick sinking sensation. *This is a mistake. I can't do
this. Not yet.*

In all this time—an hour and a half—I have opened only a fraction
of the letters in the bag. The bag is still heavy with letters and cards and
I am so terribly sorry, I just can't do it.

Please forgive me, if you are one who wrote to me. The person to
whom you wrote isn't here any longer, I am not sure who this is, in her
place.

69

"Happy, and Excited"

Impulsively—naively—we'd gone to live in Beaumont, Texas.

Of all unlikely places—this industrial coastal city in southeastern Texas near the Louisiana border, in the late summer of 1961.

Ray's first teaching job was at Lamar College in Beaumont: an assistant professorship he'd too quickly accepted after we were married in January 1961. He'd thought that he had better have a job, and a reasonably secure job, to "support" a wife. With a Ph.D. in eighteenth-century English literature from the University of Wisconsin Ray had seemed attractive to the Lamar English department as he had to several other English departments that made him early offers of assistant professorships—one I recall was in northern Wisconsin, near the Canadian border.

Somehow, we'd imagined that Texas might be romantic. We did think that Texas would be remote. Insane as it seems in retrospect, we had both wanted to put distance between ourselves and our families. . . . We'd wanted to be "independent."

In subsequent years I would become so very attached to my parents, it seems alien to me now that I ever thought this way. Ray, too, became more attached to his family in Milwaukee, after his father's death.

In the early 1960s, it was expected that a man would "support" a wife. It was not altogether common that a woman, even with a master's degree in English from the University of Wisconsin, would want to work, or could find work; and when I applied to teach freshman English at Lamar College, or, later, with what naiveté I could not have begun to fathom, high schools in Beaumont and vicinity, my applications were turned down.

At Lamar, though he'd suggested to Ray at the time of their interview that, if I completed my master's degree, he might be able to "use Joyce" as a freshman English teacher, the department chair declined to hire me after all—something of a shock, and a disappointment. In the Lamar public schools, only teachers with education degrees, preferably from Texas state colleges, were qualified to teach.

(The public school system was rigorously segregated, like the city of Beaumont. Not much of this was exactly known to Ray and me when we first moved there but we soon caught on that "Ne-gras" were very different from "whites"—so different that they seemed to speak a dialect so foreign as to be near-unintelligible to our northernly ears.)

What humiliating interviews! I recall an "assistant superintendent" of Beaumont public schools staring coldly at me as if, with my degrees from Syracuse University and the University of Wisconsin at Madison, and one or another publication listed on my *vita*, I were some sort of subversive impostor. "Your undergraduate major was English," she said, frowning at my résumé, "and your minor was 'phil-o-soph-y.'" So carefully was *phil-o-soph-y* enunciated, it might have been a rare disease.

Yes, I said hesitantly. That was correct.

"Well!" the woman said, now smiling with a look of triumph, "Did *you* study 'phil-o-soph-y' in high school?"

No, I admitted.

"Then how can you expect to teach it in our high schools?"

There, she had me. My pretensions were utterly exposed.

"We don't teach 'phil-o-soph-y' in our Beaumont public schools, Mrs. Smith."

The woman's triumph was complete. My application was denied.

In my chagrin I had no idea how to reply except to murmur thanks and quickly depart.

In the parking lot Ray was waiting in our black, secondhand Volkswagen. (Our first car!—we'd had to borrow $100 from Ray's brother to help purchase it.) Seeing the stricken look on my face Ray squeezed my hand and said, "Never mind, honey. You can stay home and write."

Meager consolation, I thought, for such jeering professional rejection.

Beaumont, Texas! Forever afterward—for nearly five decades—when Ray and I were faced, as frequently we were, with one or another serio-comic crisis, we would say *But we're not in Beaumont!*

Or, *At least we're not in Beaumont.*

My memory of this East Texas city near the Gulf of Mexico, one of the points of the "Golden Triangle" (Beaumont, Port Arthur, Orange), is vivid, visceral: the air was hazy, fuzzy; the air tasted of rotted oranges, with a harsh chemical taste beneath; at sunset the sky erupted in apocalyptic hues of crimson, flamey-orange, bruised-purple—"Isn't the sky *gor-geous*!" residents would exclaim, as if such sunsets were a sign from God and not rather the consequence of airborne pollution from the then-booming oil refineries along the coast.

Our predominant Beaumont memory, apart from the perpetually hazy air, was of waiting—waiting, and waiting!—in long lines of traffic at train crossings, as freight trains rattled slowly—endlessly—past. Nearly every day there was rain, and sometimes very heavy rain; gale force winds rushing up from the Gulf, a threat of hurricanes; in the aftermath of torrential rain and flash floods the roads were frequently washed away in sections, or impassable; more than once, a line of cars had to maneuver around the bloated corpse of a steer in the road; everywhere were the bodies of snakes—some of them unnervingly long—broken and mashed on the pavement. Another ongoing joke in our marriage—if "joke" is the proper term to recall an incident fraught with alarm, disgust, near hysteria—had to do with the region's "palmetto bugs"—enormous roaches with wings that seemed to be everywhere, and invincible. In the middle of our first night in a furnished rented duplex not far from the Lamar campus I prevailed upon Ray to investigate a sound of scurrying in our bedroom, and with a flashlight Ray discovered a swarm of roaches; by this time, I was standing on a chair, not very helpfully emitting cries of terror; Ray managed to banish the roaches with a broom, afterward claiming that the larger specimens actually "stood up to him" —"glared" at him.

Next morning we discovered to our horror that the duplex was infested—mattress, bedsprings, sofa, chairs—cupboards, closets—the interior of walls; in a panicked flurry we moved out, to an apartment in a more upscale section of Beaumont which, on Ray's modest salary, we could barely afford.

Of such memories, the most intense intimacy is born.

When you're young, your worst blunders can turn into blessings. It was a terrible blunder to have gone to live in Beaumont, Texas—a terrible blunder for my husband to have accepted a teaching position at Lamar College where, at the end of the first semester, Ray Smith caused something of a scandal when he graded his Lamar students as if they were Wisconsin undergraduates, though he'd been hired to "raise standards" at the college; it was a blunder, and would have been a severe strain upon many marriages, for a newly married couple to live in so remote a part of the country where they knew no one, hundreds of miles from their families.

Yet, somehow: our eight or nine months exiled in Beaumont were often idyllic, tenderly intimate, and certainly productive. In these months we became so extremely close, so utterly dependent upon each other, as we had not been while living in Madison, Wisconsin, and attending classes, that we were "wedded" in this way for life, as each other's closest friend and companion.

We established at this time the routine of our domestic lives: work through the day, a late afternoon walk, dinner, reading/work in the evening until bedtime. While Ray taught courses at the college in a great squat cube of a concrete building without windows—so constructed to save on air-conditioning costs, in the pitiless Beaumont climate—I dealt with my newfound solitude by reworking a manuscript of short stories and beginning a new novel, inspired in part by the starkness of the Texas landscape and my sense of being *in extremis* so far from all that was familiar to me. Both the short stories and the novel dealt with "philosophical" subjects—the exploration, in fiction, of ideas of predestination and autonomy, that had so fascinated me as an undergraduate at Syracuse.

Never in my life had I been so isolated, in my attachment to the world by way of a single individual, my husband. Never had I had such uninterrupted time in which to work, for previously I'd been a student, and a student's life is fragmented and driven by schedules; now, alone for hours, I could immerse myself in my writing, like one sinking beneath the surface of the sea. In such isolation I might have drowned—there were mornings, entire days, when I felt a touch of panic, that maybe I was making a mistake, another mistake, in so plunging into what had seemed to me previously far too risky to have considered—*a writer's life.*

Always it had seemed to me, and seems to me still, a kind of boastfulness, or hubris—claiming that one is a *writer,* an *artist.* In the subliterary working-class world of my parents and grandparents, such a claim would have been greeted with disbelief, if not derision. The drollery of the Lamar public schools administrator is exactly the sort of reaction one might have expected in upstate rural New York in those years: " 'Phil-o-soph-y'? "

In our (mostly) roach-free apartment in an outlying Beaumont neighborhood—Sweet Gum Lane was the luridly lyric street name!—I had time to read at length those writers who, in my undergraduate courses, had seemed to me so compelling, beguiling, haunting—Dostoyevsky, Kafka, Pascal, Spinoza, Nietzsche, Mann, Sartre, Camus. As it happened, one of my professors, Donald Dike, had taught the prose works of a writer of whom no one had heard— Samuel Beckett: *Molloy, Malone Dies* and *The Unnameable.* When shortly after we met, Ray learned that I'd been reading Beckett as an undergraduate, and that I'd written an essay on Beckett's prose trilogy which had been published in an academic critical journal, he'd looked at me with some surprise but smiled saying, "Well! You must be serious."

It might be, that I was *serious.* But my *seriousness* was never an impediment in my marriage.

At Madison, and when he'd lived in Milwaukee, before starting graduate school, Ray had wanted to be a "writer," too—it was then he'd begun the manuscript he would title *Black Mass,* upon which he worked intermittently for years. When he gave this novel manuscript to me to read it was piecemeal—some chapters he considered "less incoherent" than others—and some passages he thought might be "fairly good"— but overall, he was doubtful, and did not wish to seek encouragement from me, as his young adoring wife. "Whatever you tell me, it can't be objective. You would want to shield me from criticism."

No, I said. Oh no!

Yet, this was probably true. It is probably always true when we read something written by an individual whom we love, and do not want to hurt. Our wish is for these individuals to be *made happy*—our wish is that we are the means by which they are *made happy*—objective criticism does not flourish in such soil.

For these reasons, and for other more personal reasons, I did not wish to give Ray my fiction. Ray's response to my work was likely to be identical to his response to my cooking: *Honey this is really good!* Or, *Honey this is excellent.*

Though Ray Smith was highly critical elsewhere, a controversial figure in the Lamar English department where in his first semester of teaching he'd failed more students than the rest of his colleagues combined, and gave many more Ds and C minuses, yet Ray was rarely critical of my writing; perhaps in fact he was never critical of the writing I gave him to read, but only just encouraging, enthusiastic. For more than four decades Ray read my nonfiction essays and reviews with the sharp remorseless eye of one trained by the Jesuits to detect grammatical inaccuracies and errors of logic—he was an ideal editor, one whose editorial comments are lightly marked in pencil.

I am thinking now, in writing this—Ray will never see it. . . .

Never again will I see his penciled *unclear*—the subtlety of *?*.

The ideal marriage is of a writer and her/his editor—if the editor is your closest friend and companion.

In the interstices of my long writing days at a card table in our bedroom on Sweet Gum Lane, I decided to begin graduate studies at Rice University—at the time, Rice Institute of Technology—in Houston, some ninety miles away; it must have seemed, to one with a hope of teaching college, a necessary next step. I had no great love of scholarship or the kind of immersion in historical documents that is, or was, the essence of advanced graduate work in English literature, but I was eager to be self-sufficient; I did not want to be *supported by* my husband indefinitely; I thought it unfair, that Ray must work, in such unpleasant circumstances, while I had time to write. Each midweek I would take a bus to Houston, attend two graduate seminars, both with an emphasis upon historical documents—Shakespeare, The Eighteenth Century; Ray would drive in the Volkswagen to meet me, we would have dinner and stay overnight at a hotel, and drive back to Beaumont in the morning. How romantic this was! Simply to escape from Beaumont was a great relief—by contrast Houston was a *city*, and Rice was a beautiful oasis of a campus, a place of such prestige that, when I happened to mention to a faculty wife in Beaumont that I was taking graduate courses at Rice, the woman blinked at me in amazement: "Why, it's real hard to get into Rice—you must be *smart*."

Abruptly I quit the Rice Ph.D. program when I discovered, on the bus trip to Houston one day, that a short story of mine that had been published in a literary magazine was listed in the "honor roll" of *The Best American Short Stories 1962* edited by the renowned Martha Foley.

It is likely that Ray read some, if not all, of the stories collected in my first book *By the North Gate*, since this book was dedicated *to Raymond Smith*. I don't believe that Ray read my first novel *With Shuddering Fall*, most of which was written during our Beaumont exile.

I remember reading to Ray one of Nietzsche's aphorisms, which I would use as an epigraph for *With Shuddering Fall*: " 'Whatever is done out of love always takes place beyond good and evil.' "

Ray asked me to repeat this.

" 'Whatever is done out of love always takes place beyond good and evil.' "

Jesuit-trained, the shrewdest of editors, Ray said: " 'Always'—I would circle 'always,' with a question mark."

And then there was the morning when I called Ray—from a pay phone at a nearby gas station—(we were too poor, in our Sweet Gum Lane apartment, to afford a phone)—to tell him the good news, in fact the unbelievably good news: *By the North Gate* had been accepted for publication by a New York publisher known for its "left-leaning" books—a succession of novels by James T. Farrell, for instance, as well as Saul Bellow's first novel *Dangling Man*. It had been something of a shock to receive a letter—in an envelope—and not a returned manuscript, in a manila package; more than a shock, to read the first line of the letter—*We are happy to inform you . . .* instead of the more common *We are sorry to inform you . . .*

Yet more extraordinary, I would be receiving an advance of $500—to us at that time, the equivalent of at least $5,000.

Writing can be a descent into one's deepest, most hidden and "profound" self, or selves; trying to be published, for a young writer, is not unlike fishing, casting out lines into an utterly murky mysterious stream in the hope of being "accepted"—the more fishing lines you cast out, the more desperation; yet also the more likely that something—something positive!—might happen one day. And so it was, with me.

In the turbulent and pitiless publishing waters of our era, what would be the fate of such a collection of "philosophically"-oriented short stories written by an unknown young woman titled *By the North Gate*, with a return address of Sweet Gum Lane, Beaumont, Texas?

What would be the fate of most "unsolicited" manuscripts sent to a New York publishing house?

Of course, the small independent family-owned Vanguard Press has long since vanished, its considerable backlist acquired by Random House.

That morning, calling Ray at college, my euphoria at such good news was dampened by a sudden rush of physical symptoms—my vision was blotched, my breath was shallow and my heartbeat erratic—my fingers and toes had gone icy-cold—bizarrely, my tongue was *numb!*—"I have good news but also bad news to tell you," I told Ray, my teeth chattering, "—the good news is, my story manuscript has been accepted by Vanguard Press and the bad news is—I think that I am having a s-stroke . . ."

Ray asked me to describe my symptoms. Ray said, "You're just happy, and excited. Congratulations!"

70

Blood in the Water!

Joyce Carol Oates sincerely regrets that she is unable to read, still less comment upon, the many manuscripts, galleys, and books she receives, often of very high quality, which number into the thousands in the course of a year. She sincerely regrets being unable to enter into correspondences with individuals whom, in other circumstances, she would be delighted to know.

Joyce Carol Oates sincerely regrets that she cannot give blurbs, except in exceptional circumstances, for she is overwhelmed with requests.

Joyce Carol Oates sincerely regrets that, her life having unraveled like an old sock, she is unable to aid you in knitting up your own. Sincerely, she regrets!

With the acuity of sharks sensing blood in the water, vulnerable prey thrashing about heedlessly, in the weeks and months following Ray's death many strangers—alas, not only just strangers—write to me with requests that begin with the inevitable/identical/heart-stopping words *I know that you must be terribly busy but . . .*

Now that the volume of sympathy letters and cards has abated—and I have not had a "sympathy gift basket" from Harry & David for weeks—it seems that this other sort of mail, that might be called *supplicatory*, if not *precatory*, is increasing at an alarming rate.

I know that, deranged with grief, no doubt suicidal and in any case exhausted and not in your right mind, you might be prevailed upon to do a favor for me whom you scarcely know—but hurry! The deadline for dust jacket copy blurbs is next Monday.

The unexpected side of widowhood is a lack of patience—a rise in irritability—(as irritability is the first rung on the stepladder of hysteria)—and so I am inclined not only not to reply to most *supplicatory* letters but to dispose of them outside, at the green recycling barrel.

"Leave me alone! Why can't you leave me alone!"

Sometimes I am fooled—"fooled" is the apt term—by a letter that purports to be sympathetic *So sorry to have heard about the death of your husband* but is soon revealed to be a request for one or another favor; several times, these requests have come from individuals whom Ray had published in *Ontario Review.* The most persistent is a New York artist who has asked me to write about his work for an upcoming exhibit catalogue and when I explained—initially, apologetically—that I was so exhausted, so overwhelmed with responsibilities in the wake of Ray's death, and far behind on my own work, that I simply could not do this, he wrote back to say *But the deadline wouldn't be until November.*

How like predator sharks these seem to me! How I resent them! Not just their aggressive callousness but their naiveté in imagining that any publication of theirs, any achievement, will make the slightest difference in their lives, or in the lives of others.

Sometimes I am so upset, I pace through the house striking my fists together lightly, or not-so-lightly. I try very hard to imagine how Ray would react, if he were here to advise me.

Honey, you're just excited. Don't take these people too seriously.

"But—how can I not take them seriously? All this—these people—are taking up most of my life now."

Of course not. You're exaggerating. Don't upset yourself needlessly.

"But—what can I do with all these letters? All these—manuscripts, galleys? I hardly have time to do finances—'death-duties'—you left me so suddenly. How can I live my life, without you?"

Now there is silence. I have spoken heedlessly, hurtfully. In life, I would not have spoken in such a way to my stricken husband.

You will have to. You have no choice.

This will be my new mantra. I hope that it will drown out another recent mantra that has gotten into my head like a moth trapped in a cobweb—a late remark of James Joyce—(is it from Joyce's massive tombstone *Finnegans Wake?*)—*"How small it's all!"*

. . . will have to. Have no choice.

And so, what I think I will do—what I *will do*—is see my Pennington doctor, and acquire from him a prescription for anti-depressants.

Where there is blood in the water, yet there may be a thrashing, desperate-to-survive creature. I will be that creature, I will not give up.

You will have to. You have no choice.

71

WALKING WOUNDED

So near to death—yet still "alive"—the widow's great surprise is that she finds herself in a vast company of what might be called the *walking wounded*.

Of course, Ray and I knew that certain of our friends were taking anti-depressants. These were not secrets but were spoken of openly, conversationally—one or two had even written about their use of anti-depressants which had been both beneficial and not-so-beneficial, on the Internet. (One, a close poet-friend, experienced considerable initial benefits from an anti-depressant called Paxil, but, after a few years, when the drug began to lose its efficacy, terrifying side effects.) But now, in my nocturnal e-mail correspondence especially, I am learning that an unexpectedly high percentage of people I know are in fact "on" anti-depressants.

What a shock! Some of the most accomplished, confident-seeming, healthy-minded and overall *cheerful* individuals of my acquaintance are not only taking anti-depressants but claim that they "could not live without" them; in fact, they are so experienced in psychotropic medications, from years of experimentation, that they provide detailed information for me, lists of medications, benefits and side effects. One of my most accomplished and *cheery* woman friends confides in me that she has become an expert in this area and will tell me exactly what to say to my doctor, so that he will prescribe not only the ideal anti-depressant but a secondary medication to be taken with the anti-depressant. And everyone cautions me—the medication won't begin to have an effect for as long as two weeks, and even then, its effect might be erratic for a while.

Suffer, Joyce! Ray was worth it.

How ashamed I am, to be so weak! For this is the great discovery of my posthumous life—*I am not strong enough to continue a life to no purpose except getting through the day followed by getting through the night. I am not strong enough to believe that so minimal a life is worth the effort to protract it.*

Among the several anti-depressants friends have recommended is "Cymbalta"—a melodic name to suggest a distant planet not yet contaminated by the neuroses of *Homo sapiens.* And so in mid-April at about the time that it has become abundantly clear that a new season is imminent, and the freezing-numbing cold season of Ray's death is rapidly vanishing, I begin, with much hesitation, and some hope, a regimen of one 30-milligram tablet a day.

Added to which, in the night, an improvised assortment of supposed sleep-aids—mostly non-prescription like Benadryl.

Added to which, through the day, a conscious effort to *take on a new non-morbid attitude for instance*: *I have been in a car crash, and I am recovering . . .*

72

Dead Woman Walking

Joyce Carol Oates author of . . .

Rising from my seat—ascending a stage—this eerie muffled sense of language being spoken at a distance—as in a vacuum in which there is no sound only just vibrations to be deciphered by some mechanism in the brain—and blinding light, stage-light, obliterating the audience so that this might be—where?—how strange to be applauded, I know there is no mockery in this applause, as there has been no mockery in the lavishly generous things that have been said of me by the woman who has introduced me; this is not the domain of the ugly lizard-thing sneering *Here is a woman utterly alone. Here is a woman utterly unloved. Here is a woman of no more worth than a pail of garbage. Why are you applauding such a woman, are you mad?*

Somehow it has come to be April—nearly two months since Ray died.

I feel that I should apologize to Ray. I feel stricken with guilt, that I am still here, and still more or less the person I'd been before he died—while his life has ended. All that was *his*, irrevocably lost.

There is something shallow, vulgar—trivial—about this sort of survival, I am thinking.

If you understand what I am saying, then you understand.

If not, not.

You, who are healthy-minded. *You*, imagining yourself safe on a floating island amid a Sargasso Sea of sorrow.

I am not resentful on my own behalf—I am thinking that yes, this is what I deserve. But I am resentful on Ray's behalf.

At so oblique an angle to reason, let alone rationality, the widow speaks a language others can't understand. Like the aptly named black widow spider, the (human) widow is best avoided.

Gently I am being nudged awake—out of my Cymbalta-zombie state by the expectations of an audience here in Camden, New Jersey—on the Rutgers campus like a floating island amid the utterly depressing war-torn slum of this most economically depressed/crime-ridden of American cities.

I am thinking of how, not far from this podium, in the small wood frame house he'd bought for himself, restored now as an arts center, Walt Whitman lived out the final years of what had been a life of surpassing exuberance—you might say, the most exuberant of poet-lives. Our greatest chronicler of the American soul in its expansive, outward mode, as his contemporary Emily Dickinson was the greatest chronicler of the American soul in its withdrawing, inward mode. Oh Walt Whitman—could we only believe you, as we admire you, and yearn to draw you inside us as our best, bravest, most optimistic self:

The smallest sprout shows there is really no death . . .

All goes onward and outward . . . and nothing collapses,
And to die is different from what any one supposed, and luckier.
—*"Song of Myself"*

Earlier this evening, amid a buzz of voices, convivial laughter, a buffet dinner in a Rutgers-Camden dining hall with fellow participants at the festival, I experienced a moment of some distress—a precarious moment when the Cymbalta-daze seemed not to be adequate—finding myself rooted to the spot staring at slabs of blood-leaking meat on trays adorned with wilted lettuce leaves—and staring at the hearty convivial

cheery individuals—as it happened, men—who were spearing this meat
onto their plates, with no more hesitation at its bloody nature than a
lion would feel tearing out the throat of its living prey; but there was a
sister-mourner at the dinner, a poet/memoirist/translator with whom I
could speak intimately and frankly; this woman in the cruel twilit state
of being *not-yet-a-widow*—whose husband has been afflicted with early-
onset Alzheimer's.

Rachel has written about this ordeal. It is not a secret, I am not violating her confidence. Amid the hearty carnivores in the dining hall we
cling to each other like sisters. Terrible as losing a husband is, there is
perhaps a worse predicament in losing the person he was; living with
him on a daily basis as he deteriorates; feeling that you have no choice
finally, as Rachel felt, but to arrange for him to be hospitalized, in the
face of protests from his relatives and friends who have no idea what you
are experiencing . . . Rachel is very thin, her skin is very pale, she too is
one of the *walking wounded*. I would like to comfort her: "You've had a
trauma. You must take care of yourself."

She'd known Ray, as an editor; I'd never met her husband but had
heard of his exemplary career, particularly as a lecturer, at Columbia.

Unvoiced between us is the question—which of us has been less
lucky.

To lose your husband suddenly, or—to lose your husband by slow
excruciating degrees.

To lose your husband amid a flood of sympathy, or—to lose your
husband amid accusations and recriminations.

I wonder—has Rachel glimpsed the basilisk, in the corner of her
eye? In the corner of her soul? Has Rachel heard the basilisk perversely
gifted with language, its cruel jeering voice?

I dare not ask. I am afraid of what Rachel might say.

Nor do I ask her, as I might, if she's taking medication for her anxi-
ety/depression/insomnia.

How sympathetic I feel, for Rachel! Or so I think. For in my
Cymbalta-zombie-state I am never sure if I am actually "feeling" much
of anything or rather just simulating what a normal person might feel
in these circumstances; as I have become adept at impersonating *Joyce*

Carol Oates as some sort of post-Whitman beacon-of-light of exuberance and optimism.

Joyce Carol Oates, author of . . .

But maybe this is a mistake. This evening, in this place.

Maybe this time, I will really break down. Maybe even the Cymbalta-haze will fail me.

For this is—this was—Ray's favorite restaurant in New York City. For we'd come here numerous times, in sunny weather; once or twice with friends, but usually alone. One or another of my birthdays we'd celebrated here, lunch in the Boathouse Restaurant in Central Park, at a table overlooking a pond upon which swans and other waterfowl paddled about companionably; and in the dark water, if you looked closely, you could see turtles just beneath the surface, surprisingly large turtles of a size and archaic appearance to suggest creatures of a primeval era.

The occasion is a fund-raiser for the Autistic Children's Association. I may have been invited to be the featured speaker because I have a younger, autistic sister but perhaps mostly because I am a close friend of a close friend of the organizers, and I am available.

To heighten the air of the *quasi-real*, I am reading a poem I'd written years ago and probably have not read aloud to any audience in the past twenty years—"Autistic Child": a short poem dedicated to my autistic sister Lynn who has been institutionalized in Amherst, New York, since the early 1960s . . . When the audience asks me about the poem, and about my sister, I tell them frankly that, in the 1950s when Lynn was diagnosed as autistic, it was a time when little was known about autism but much was speculated: a Freud-saturated era in which mothers of autistic children, like mothers of homosexuals, were "blamed" for their children's aberrations.

There's a stricken silence when I say this. For *blame* is the most natural of responses, when one's life has shattered.

Blame whoever is closest, and vulnerable—a mother.

This cold wet windy evening! It seems unbelievable that this rain-lashed place is the same Boathouse Restaurant that Ray and I so liked.

It's a pitilessly cold wet windy evening—April 27, 2008. I am thinking of a happier, sunnier time—Ray and me holding hands, at our table
overlooking the pond.

Should we rent a rowboat?

Maybe—some other time.

I am thinking of our own, smaller pond in the woods behind our
house at 9 Honey Brook Drive which Ray stocked with turtles from
a "wild-life pond-supplier" in Wisconsin. These turtles delighted us by
basking luxuriantly in the sunshine on a fallen log Ray had dragged
into the pond at an angle, for that purpose; eagerly I would look for the
turtles to display themselves so that I could call to Ray *Come look! Your
turtles.*

Ray stocked the pond with tadpoles, too—very successfully. (When
you approach the pond, in warm weather, dozens of frogs leap into the
water croaking in alarm.) He had conspicuously less success stocking the
pond with small, beautifully colored koi, that, within weeks, were devoured by a rapacious spindly-legged great blue heron descending upon
their tranquil setting like a heraldic/demonic creature in a Bosch landscape.

One by one the beautiful koi were devoured by the predator bird
until they were all gone—and the bird flew away.

Remember the koi?

Remember the great blue heron?

Remember how shocked we were? How naive?

*Remember how you [Ray] ran down to the pond to chase the heron
away, shouting and waving your arms? How the heron flew into the trees a
few yards away, unalarmed, waiting?*

So sad! Our beautiful fish!

After the fund-raiser, I am told that the evening was a "great success." I am told that it "meant a great deal" for the parents and families
of autistic children to hear me speak so openly about my sister and my
parents and to answer any question they asked me. And I am thinking
of a line of Anne Sexton which the suicide-obsessed poet had adopted as
a kind of mantra—*Live or die but don't spoil the world for others.*

* * *

And now this morning, I am staring into the courtyard.

Dimly I am registering *There is something very wrong here.*

Where, pre-Cymbalta, I would have been anxious and upset now I am dull-anesthetized registering *Ray's tulips have been decapitated* as if the statement were uttered by a computer voice, at a distance.

It's as if someone entered the courtyard with a scythe and cut off the tops of Ray's tulips—you would not be able to identify these raw stunted green plants as tulips any longer.

A long time is required for me to absorb this. Not that I am excited or upset—I am not—but in even my Cymbalta-daze state I understand that something terribly sad has happened here, and it is irrevocable.

Deer entered the courtyard in the night. Deer nudged the gate open—no doubt, I'd failed to shut it tightly—and devoured Ray's beautiful tulips in a matter of seconds chewing and swallowing as negligently and as mechanically as if they were devouring weeds.

I would cry, except I have no tears left.

For the first time thinking—"It's just as well, Ray isn't here to see this. He would be so upset."

Just as well. Ray isn't here.

This bad-headache morning I am at the front door calling for our elder tiger cat—"Reynard? *Reynard!*"

In the night, Reynard seems to have vanished.

Except that I seem to have no "emotions"—in the Cymbalta-daze I can barely remember what "emotions" are—I would be stricken with anxiety, and guilt.

"Reynard? Where are you? Breakfast. . . ."

My voice trails off in mid-air. How foolish and plaintive the word *breakfast.*

Once a sleek young cat with a burnished-orange coat, a winning way of nudging his head against our ankles and cuddling close and purring when we sat together on the sofa, Reynard had been Ray's favorite; Ray had been the one to choose him from a litter of kittens at a shelter and bring him home to surprise me.

This might have been twelve years ago. How quickly those years have passed!

Reynard hadn't recovered from the loss of Ray—a presence he could not have named or defined but whose absence he keenly missed.

In past weeks he'd begun to age visibly. So rapidly all remnants of kittenhood faded from him. His head seemed over-large on his body, his legs had grown spindly. Overnight it seemed he'd lost weight—his ribs showed through his fur, and his spine.

His spine! Petting Reynard, I felt the vertebrae, with a shudder.

The last time the vet had checked Reynard, in the fall, she'd said that Reynard was an "older" cat but "bearing up well"—it isn't likely that she would say this now.

From time to time lately he has seemed to be having difficulty breathing. Last night I carried him to the living room sofa—to Ray's end of the sofa—thinking that he might sink into a deep cat-slumber and expire peacefully in my arms—but he did not.

For a while Reynard lay panting as I tried to comfort him but then he began to struggle to be freed, feebly at first, then more actively, until at last his sharp claws began to scratch me, I had to release him.

It was annoying to me, as it was upsetting, to see how eagerly Reynard wanted to escape from me. At the rear terrace door agitating to be let outdoors though it was a cold night, and raining. And so I slid open the terrace door and Reynard bounded out with surprising swiftness, for an elderly cat, and in the night several times I went to call him, at the rear door, and at the front door; but he never returned; nor was he lying on the front stoop in the morning in his usual position, patiently waiting to be let indoors to be fed.

In the night, groggy in my Cymbalta-daze that never quite translates into actual sleep, I seemed to think that Reynard was lying at the foot of my bed, pressing against my leg.

"Reynard? Where are you . . ."

When I search for Reynard outside, I am horrified to discover him lying just a few yards away from the rear door through which he'd bounded the night before, stretched out against the side of the house in such a position that I could not see him from inside.

As if he'd wanted to come back inside. But the door was shut against him.

Now I am crying, now I am sobbing—"Reynard! Oh Reynard!"

This is a sick sobbing grief like the kind that overcame me in Ray's hospital room, the day before Ray's death. At a time when it had not seemed that Ray would die.

Another horror—Reynard is stiff, like a cat carved of wood. His teeth are bared, his eyes are half-shut, if there can be an expression on a cat's face Reynard's expression is one of extreme anguish, pain.

This was not a peaceful slumber-death. This was an anguished animal-death, suffered alone.

I am stunned by this death, my head reeling. I am so broken up, I think that I must be losing my sanity. Reynard was not a young cat! Reynard was an elderly cat! Yet, I can't stop crying—not a normal sort of grief but ravaged, abandoned. Like a deranged child I am stroking Reynard's coarse cold fur as if I could stroke life back inside him—I am stroking Reynard's head, that feels bony, lumpy. The teeth bared in a snarling look—a fierce angry grin—disconcerting to see. . . .

This too is your fault. You left him outside, in the cold. He has frozen to death. He has died alone.

Carefully I wrap Reynard in one of our large bath towels—a thick green towel that, in the custom of our household, was Ray's towel. With Cherie looking on warily, keeping her distance, I carry Reynard outside beyond the garden, and set him down amid tall grasses. Is this the proper thing to do? Is this a sensible thing to do? I am not feeling strong enough to dig a grave for Reynard, in this hard-packed soil. Somehow I slip and fall onto one knee and Reynard tumbles from my arms, stiff as if frozen.

I am aware of myself as if glimpsed at a distance, a woman who has become a cartoon-figure, as in a Charles Addams drawing, carrying a stiffened cartoon-cat.

Just as well, Ray isn't here. Ray would be so sad.

73

Taboo

It's a taboo subject. How *the dead* are betrayed by the living.

We who are living—we who have survived—understand that our guilt is what links us to the dead. At all times we can hear them calling to us, a growing incredulity in their voices *You will not forget me—will you? How can you forget me? I have no one but you.*

Most days—most hours—the widow dwells in a netherworld of *not-here* and *not-there*. Most hours of the day the widow yearns for the unspeakable oblivion of sleep.

For the widow is a posthumous person passing among the living. When the widow smiles, when the widow laughs, you see the glisten in the widow's eyes, utter madness, an actress desperate to play her role as others would wish her to play her role and only another widow, another woman who has recently lost her husband, can perceive the fraud.

One widow glancing quickly at another—*Is it like this for you? Are you dead, also?*

> *... it took me a long time to get beyond being stunned by [my husband's] death, which was in fact quite predictable. (I see now.)*

Rereading my friend's letter, I am struck by these words which I had not fully processed before.

The author of these words is in fact a very well known writer whose memoir of her husband's death and her own survival a few years ago was a highly acclaimed best seller. Rereading her letter now, I wonder if it was the fact of being "stunned" that propelled my widow-friend into writing the memoir, that so combines the clinical and the poetic—if she had understood at the time of her husband's death that his death was "in fact quite predictable" would she have written the memoir? *Could* she?

Now I am being made to think: is there a perspective from which the widow's grief is sheer vanity; narcissism; the pretense that one's loss is so special, so very special, that there has never been a loss quite like it?

Is there a perspective from which the widow's grief is but a kind of pathological pastime, or hobby—a predilection of the kind diagnosed as OCD—"obsessive-compulsive disorder"—not unlike washing one's hands for hours every day, or hoarding every sort of worthless junk; on hands and knees "waxing" hardwood floors with paper towels and furniture polish, or vacuuming late into the night rugs that are already spotless . . . *If only someone would publicly ridicule the widow, give the widow a good solid kick, slap the widow's face or laugh in her face—the spell might be broken.*

At 4 A.M. such epiphanies rush at me like miniature comets. Such wisdom, that within a few hours will be lost in the groggy aftermath of insomnia and the low-grade nausea of the anti-depressant medication that never allows for full wakefulness as it never allows for full unconsciousness; never allows for any clarity of thought, and muddles even the most urgent of thoughts like radio static. This time, I have looked up my medication on the Internet and am not so surprised at what I find.

Anti-depressant medication is indicated for individuals suffering from obsessive thoughts, insomnia, depression, suicidal fantasies; yet, anti-depressant medication may sometimes exacerbate obsessive thoughts, insomnia, depression, suicidal fantasies.

Unmistakably, anti-depressant medication will cause urine retention, constipation, drowsiness, decrease in appetite and weight loss. In some, paresthesia, blurred vision, vivid nightmares, tremor, anxiety, palpitations of the heart, sweating, depersonalization.

Is this medication helping? Is it—making things worse?

I have no way of knowing. Since Ray's death I have been transformed from a person who rarely thought about her "health" or "state of mind" to an ambulatory assemblage of symptoms like a skeleton rattling about in a loose gunny sack—some days, I can't even imagine what *personalization* might once have been—I can't remember having been a *person*.

My Pennington doctor suggests that I begin to take 60 milligrams of Cymbalta a day, up from 30 milligrams. Since the lower dose "doesn't seem to be helping."

In the Pennington drugstore, like a manic character in a Dostoyevsky novel bent upon self-destruction, I swallow a 60 milligram Cymbalta tablet as soon as the pharmacist hands me the vial. Driving home, I imagine cotton batting clotting my brain, my arteries. It is true—my vision is blurred. And it is true, my heart often leaps and cringes in "palpitations"—but I am no longer obsessively thinking of Ray in the hospital bed, or Ray in the funeral home when I failed to see him one final time. *The medication is a scrim through which objects are viewed but so dimly, you have no clear idea what they are. You have no clear idea why they should mean anything to you, or to anyone.*

74

"Ashamed to Be 'White'"

This was a long time ago, in Detroit, Michigan. In a residential neighborhood one block west of Woodward Avenue and one block south of Eight Mile Road where we'd bought a house—our first house!—on Woodstock Drive.

We'd moved north from Beaumont, Texas, as soon as the academic year 1961–1962 ended. In fact, we'd been so eager to leave that desolate East Texas landscape that Ray mailed in his final grades en route to Detroit where we had teaching jobs for the following year; we'd managed to pack everything we owned into the boot-shaped black Volkswagen that rattled at sixty miles an hour and had no heat except in gusts of hot air that entered from the motor.

In Detroit, we lived for a year in an apartment building on Manderson Road, near Palmer Park; then, we bought a four-bedroom, two-storey Colonial on Woodstock Drive in an area known as Green Acres. The price of our house in May 1963 was $17,900.

Ray's yearly salary as an instructor at Wayne State University was $5,000. My yearly salary as an instructor at the University of Detroit was $4,900. The gentlemanly man who'd hired me—his name, renowned in the area at that time, was Clyde Craine—confided in me that he and the chairman at Wayne State had conferred, to make sure that Ray's salary was just a little higher than mine.

On Woodstock Drive in the spring of 1963 our house shone with newness. White aluminum siding, orange-red brick, dark blue shutters—the
house was ravishingly beautiful to us, we could not stare at it enough.
Repeatedly we drove past our house before we moved in, admiring it,
planning how we would furnish it. Of course, we didn't own the house,
technically speaking—the mortgage company owned it.

I remember being hurt and upset when, at the bank, my modest
salary at the University of Detroit was discounted. Only Ray's salary
counted. I was a married woman, the bank officer told me, with an expression somewhere between disdain and pity. Likely I would quit work
in another few years and have a baby.

"But we're not planning to have a baby."

"I'm sorry. That is our rule."

Together, our two salaries were respectable. But only Ray's salary
would be computed for the thirty-year mortgage.

Thirty years! The expression on Ray's face, as he signed these documents!

"This will take us to 1993. In theory."

Quickly we discovered that Detroit was nearly as segregated racially
as Beaumont had been. The area in which we lived was totally white.
The Detroit *News* and *Free Press* were filled with reports of incidents
one assumed to be "racial"—if you decoded them correctly. But the city
would not explode in racial violence until July 1967.

Before we moved into our new house, before we even had a key to
the house, we drove over in the evenings to work on the lawn—at this
point, just hard-packed bare earth and weeds. We brought over bushels
of topsoil, flats of ground cover, small trees. Earnestly we planted grass
seed. The backyard was deep, bounded by an alley; beyond the alley
was another row of smaller houses, and Eight Mile Road which was a
major thoroughfare. One day when Ray was working in the backyard
and I was raking in the front, a neighbor child approached me to ask—
"Are you eighteen? My mother says you don't look old enough to be
married."

I laughed at this. Not only was I over eighteen, I was twenty-four.
My first book had been accepted for publication—though its publication had been postponed until fall 1963. I was an instructor at the

Jesuit-run University of Detroit where, in the English department, there were but two women—an elderly nun with the impressive title Sister Bonaventure, and me; and my very nice, handsome husband Ray was an instructor at Wayne State—the area's most prominent "institution of higher learning" with a mandate from the state of Michigan to bring education to culturally deprived—i.e., mostly black—students. With his Ph.D. from Wisconsin, Ray was considered a highly respectable academic, with the likelihood of promotion at Wayne, or elsewhere; with my master's degree, and a gathering number of publications, I was what might be called "promising." We were so young, happy and optimistic!—all the world lay before us.

Several months after we moved into the house on Woodstock Drive, neighbors began to complain to us—mostly to Ray, who worked outdoors in the back, laying bricks for a small improvised patio: there was a rumor that "Negroes" were moving in across the street. Residents on both sides of us spoke of the homeowner across the street who'd "betrayed" his neighbors—he'd listed his house with a real estate agent who sold to "Negroes" in an effort to "block-bust."

In our naiveté Ray and I had had no idea of the racial melodrama smoldering in Green Acres, into which we'd moved with such anticipation. We knew little of the notorious history of racial violence in Detroit—a bloody riot on Belle Isle, a city parkland, in 1943, in which thirty-four people were killed, and many injured; the new threat of "block-busting" in white residential neighborhoods through the city— unscrupulous real estate agents arranging for black families to settle in houses in "white" neighborhoods, at low prices, talking anxious homeowners into selling their homes, and so inspiring panic—seemingly overnight, entire blocks of long-settled residential neighborhoods on the west side began to be festooned with FOR SALE signs. Here was a demonic parody of racial integration that would eventually drive the city's white-majority population into the suburbs—Birmingham, Bloomfield Hills, Southfield, Grosse Pointe and St. Claire Shores—and reduce entire neighborhoods to rows of abandoned houses and rubble-strewn vacant lots as in the aftermath of war—though no one could have predicted such a cataclysm, at the time.

In Green Acres in 1963, where the houses were generally newer, better kept and some distance from the inner city, there was no real panic—yet.

In Beaumont, the races had lived so far apart, there wasn't—yet—any discernible tension. In Detroit, in an economy that was booming for some and stagnant for others, tension was evident. Though we never watched television—in fact, we didn't own a set—we were aware of a kind of latent hysteria in the air, and often it was suggested to me—as a "white woman"—that I should be very careful walking alone in any semi-deserted place, or even in my parking lot at the edge of the University of Detroit campus.

Much was made in the local media of a lone woman—a "white woman"—whose car had broken down on the John Lodge Expressway, at night, and who had been harassed, chased, raped and beaten by marauding "black youths."

It may have been at this time, or a year or two later, that much was made of the fact—if it was a fact—that there were more handguns in the Detroit area than there were residents and that, in law enforcement circles, Detroit, Michigan, was known as Murder City, USA.

In Green Acres, a For Sale sign erected across the street in front of a two-storey brick house was knocked down, or removed; soon after, the For Sale sign reappeared, and was knocked down, or removed. Each day we drove along Woodstock Drive we were made uneasily aware of the status of the For Sale sign. "Who's doing that?" one of us might ask, and the other would say, "Who do you think? Our neighbors."

Behind the houses facing us on Woodstock Drive was a city cemetery.

It was believed by certain of our neighbors that "Negroes" are particularly frightened of living near a cemetery and so, stealthily one night, they'd gone to cut down vines and shrubs at the rear of the property that had hidden the cemetery from view. When Ray was told this by the man who lived next-door to us Ray failed to respond as the man might have anticipated and their exchange ended abruptly.

I wasn't there, and so I didn't hear. I have no idea what Ray actually said or what was said to Ray in return. But I know that the exchange was unpleasant, and that Ray was upset and disgusted by our neighbors' behavior.

"It makes you ashamed to be 'white.'"

Milwaukee, too, where Ray was born and had lived until he'd gone away to college, had its segregated white suburbs. But Milwaukee was never so racially fraught as Detroit and had comparable history of racial violence.

It was rare for Ray to speak of his home, or of his family. His father was a "devout" Roman Catholic who'd hoped that Ray might become a priest and had been disappointed when Ray had dropped out of a Jesuit seminary after graduating from the prestigious Jesuit-run Marquette High School in Milwaukee. His mother had been upset when Ray had ceased attending Sunday mass at the age of eighteen but, unlike his father, she had not tried to "reason" with him.

As a wife must respect her husband's family even when—as it sometimes happens—her husband does not entirely respect them, or appears to be somewhat estranged from them, so I did not ever speak of Ray's family in any way other than warmly and positively; if I asked Ray about his father, for instance, some stiffening in his expression, a palpable resistance in his manner, allowed me to know that I was intruding into my husband's privacy, and had better retreat.

My sense was that Ray's parents were politically conservative, like many Catholics; that, in the volatile matter of civil rights for Negroes, and in all matters involving radical or even reasonable social change in the United States in the early 1960s, they were adamant in opposition.

When you think of Bob Dylan's "The Times They Are A-Changin'" you might imagine the provocative singer addressing white Americans like Ray's parents—*Your sons and your daughters are beyond your command.*

No words strike more horror in the hearts of parents—especially, in the hearts of conservative Catholic parents.

(And how Ray admired Bob Dylan in that early, thrilling and iconoclastic phase of Dylan's career!)

Soon then it happened, in Green Acres, that the house across the street from ours was sold, and, yes—to a black family.

An altogether "respectable" black family, it seemed to us.

For we, too, were hyper-aware of our new neighbors. We, too, watched from the front windows of our house as movers carried furniture and packing boxes into the house across the street.

(For how could we not be *aware*, how could we not *look*? Though we had virtually no sense of anyone else living on Woodstock Drive and would probably not have recognized any of our neighbors out of context—yet we were distinctly aware of the new black family. Race makes of us hyper-vigilant in the most primitive and distressing of ways.)

Anxiously we waited for something to happen—some act of petty vandalism, or meanness. If the black family suffered any sort of harassment, we did not know about it, and would not have been informed, in any case. One day Ray said, "Let's go over and say hello."

And so we went across the street, rang the door, shook hands with our new neighbors and introduced ourselves: "Ray Smith"—"Joyce Smith."

I don't recall a word that was exchanged but assume that we "welcomed" the new family into the neighborhood—nor do I remember the black couple except that they were slightly older than they'd appeared at a distance, and that the man was a doctor who'd gone to medical school at Wayne State. I remember the man and his wife looking at us quizzically—smiling—though they didn't invite us to step inside, and had not many questions to ask of us.

We never spoke to the black couple again, nor did they speak to us. Frequently we waved at one another in greeting, driving in our cars or working on our lawns. We smiled, we mimed cheery greetings— "Hello! How are you!" In such ways we might have imagined that we'd contributed to the amelioration of racism in Detroit.

Four years later the city would erupt in racial violence. After years of "police brutality against blacks" a raid by the Detroit police on the United Community League for Civil Action on Sunday, July 23, 1967, would ignite a social cataclysm of arson, looting, rioting and even sniping; both whites and blacks were involved in the rioting, but black fury was predominant, and much publicized; the violence would continue for several days, making of Murder City, USA, a national monument to racial/social American chaos:

Forty-four people would die, 5,000 were left homeless, 1,300 buildings would be destroyed, 2,700 businesses were looted, the smell of smoldering ruins would linger long in the very air, one might say permanently. On the first night of the rioting white homeowners like us would huddle in our houses with doors and windows locked, blinds drawn, listening to the terrifying sound of sirens, angry shouts and sporadic gunfire and waiting for martial law to be declared and the Michigan National Guard to occupy the city.

Ashamed to be "white"—but what alternative?

75

It Made No Difference

" . . . at my old high school in Los Angeles, four since June."

" . . . at my high school in Boston, two since Christmas."

" . . . an eleven-year-old boy, in New Brunswick."

" . . . three high school girls who were close friends, in Toronto."

" . . . at Berkeley."

" . . . at Cornell."

" . . . at NYU."

In the wake of a painfully candid story about suicide by a young Korean-American woman in my advanced fiction workshop who has written about suicide before, the others are discussing suicide in a way to suggest that this is a taboo subject about which, in other circumstances, they would not be speaking; here, in the fiction workshop, the animation with which they speak suggests that this is a subject to which they have given much thought.

" . . . in Tokyo, it's, like, an epidemic."

" . . . in Delhi . . ."

In their other university courses, impersonality is the norm. A scrupulously impersonal mode of speech is the only acceptable means of communication. Our creative writing courses here in the arts building at 185 Nassau provide counter-worlds in which the most upsetting truths can be uttered. Perversely, what is "fiction" is likely to be what is "most real"—in writing of fictitious individuals, the young writer is most likely writing about him-/herself.

Of course, this is "fiction"—in a short story, the suicidal undergraduate who finally hangs himself in the shower of his residential college is not a Princeton student but a Yale student.

Or, a Harvard student.

(It hasn't yet been the case that a student from a non–Ivy League university has hanged himself in any short story in one of my workshops. Even suicidal fantasies are buoyed aloft by a certain residual snobbery.)

" . . . you need to make the Yale campus, like, more believable."

" . . . you need to make him seem like he isn't at Princeton. Reading it, you just keep thinking he *is*."

How distressing this is, that my young writers—the oldest would be twenty or twenty-one, the youngest nineteen—are so obsessed with suicide; or, if not with suicide per se, with the severe depression that precedes suicide. Suicidal fantasies are presented in serio-comic form, sometimes crudely composed, as in a cartoon by R. Crumb. Often the stories are said to be based on an individual whom the writer knew, or knew of—"in prep school"—"my brother's suite-mate, at Stanford"—and if the means of suicide is disputed or criticized in the workshop, the rejoinder is the protest: "But this really happened, like this."

Amid this animated discussion, there are those who sit quietly, listening. Like the Korean-American girl who has written the most intimate and unsettling stories about suicidal fantasies, including unnervingly detailed passages about a high school girl intent upon "cutting" herself as a prelude to slashing her wrists.

These very bright, very talented, very privileged Princeton undergraduates! It is tempting to think *This is their secret subject. This is their bond.*

Of course I would not tell them that a friend of mine, a vice president at Rutgers in New Brunswick, remarked the other evening that suicide among college-age students has become a virtual "epidemic" in parts of the country.

Of course I would not tell them about the basilisk.

(For what if the basilisk is known to one of them? To several of them?)

I would not tell them how Anne Sexton spoke of the wish to die as *the almost unnameable lust.*

Nor would I tell them that I've known at least one suicide up close.

At least one suicide, among the hundreds of students I have taught since Detroit in 1962.

It had seemed almost like happenstance that Richard Wishnetsky wandered into my office at the University of Detroit one afternoon in the spring of 1965—"wandered" is the accurate term for Richard had seemed idly drifting about, though unusually well dressed for a student, with trimmed hair, a white cotton shirt, shining eyeglasses. His greeting was smiling, subtly belligerent: "You are—'Joyce Smith'? I've been told that I should meet you."

At the University of Detroit, I would always be "Joyce Smith." But it was known among some, and written of in the local papers, that I was also "Joyce Carol Oates," a writer. When Richard Wishnetsky uttered the name "Joyce Smith" it was with a wink, or a twitch in his cheek to indicate *But I know who you really are! My soul mate.*

Utterly confident, or confident-seeming, Richard Wishnetsky introduced himself to me, taking it for granted that I had time for him, or would make time for him, though clearly I was busy; without hesitation he extended his hand to grip mine, and shake it, as no previous student at the University of Detroit had ever done. He was twenty-three, and I was twenty-seven.

Was this a contest of wills? In the classroom, I had learned to simulate a sort of playful authority; outside the classroom, to this day I am likely to be shy, even reticent. Powerful personalities roll over me and suck all the oxygen out of the room if I am not alert and able to defend myself.

Here was a young man who thought well of himself: he allowed me to know within minutes of our meeting that he'd graduated with honors from the University of Michigan and, yet more impressively, he was a Woodrow Wilson fellow. (Immediately this seemed strange to me: why would a Woodrow Wilson fellow have elected to come to the University of Detroit for a degree in sociology, in an undistinguished department in an undistinguished university? Woodrow Wilson fellows can study virtually anywhere.) It soon became clear, in this and in subsequent conversations, that Richard's interests ranged far beyond sociology: philosophy, religion, European literature, the Holocaust, Judaism. From the first it was also clear that Richard was both brilliant and unmoored; highly articulate, though often he spoke so rapidly that he almost stuttered, and saliva glittered on his lips; and highly contemptuous of most other people: "They are herd animals" was a frequent—(Nietzschean)—remark. He was scathing in his denunciation of suburban Detroit, in which he'd lived most of his life, except for four years at Ann Arbor—his South-field family, relatives, friends and neighbors—the members of the af-fluent Shaarey Zadek synagogue, in Southfield. In 1965 it was rare for anyone to speak at such length, with such knowledge, of the Holocaust; most Jews, along with most non-Jews, were in a state of denial about the catastrophic Nazi genocidal campaign. Here was a vast cultural sinkhole very few had yet dared to explore. As a university instructor I was too young and inexperienced to recognize that this exciting young graduate student was in the grip of mania—set beside my less exuberant, and far less well-read Catholic undergraduates, Richard shone like a flame.

Though Richard never enrolled formally in any course of mine, often he visited my larger, lecture courses in which I might be discussing Dos-toyevsky's *The Brothers Karamazov* or *The Possessed*—(in those idyllic days of long ago when one could expect undergraduates to read such long novels); Nietzsche's *Beyond Good and Evil* or *Thus Spake Zarathus-tra*; novels and plays by Sartre, Camus, Beckett, and Ionesco; Tolstoy's "The Death of Ivan Ilyich," Kafka's "The Metamorphosis." Impatient with the younger, slower-witted students in the class, Richard had a habit of speaking out, addressing me personally as in an intense, inti-mate dialogue; as the other students listened in astonishment and resent-ment, Richard soared to heights of eloquence evoking Goethe, Aristotle, Heidegger, Nietzsche. Often he was close to disrupting the class, and I would have to ask him to speak more quietly, and to speak with me after class. It is thrilling—dangerously contagious—to be in the presence of mania, if one does not quite recognize what mania is.

Of all the ideas raging in his head, Richard was most obsessed with two: the "disgusting hypocrisy" of "post-Holocaust" Jews in affluent America and the proclamation by Nietzsche's prophet Zarathustra "God is dead."

In subsequent years, "God is dead" has come to be over-familiar as Edvard Munch's *The Scream*—harrowing insights into the psyche of modern man that find their way, in popular culture, into the comic-satiric sensibility of a Woody Allen. Poor Richard Wishnetsky! He would pay a terrible price for living before his time.

Late one afternoon when I returned to my office in the English department, there was Richard Wishnetsky sitting at my desk, brazenly looking through my papers. For all the semblance of egalitarianism between us, in our intellectual discussions, I was brought up short by the sight of Richard sitting at my desk; the violation of the professor-student relationship was startling to me, if petty. And there was something in Richard's eyes that unnerved me.

"Afraid of me, Joyce? Why are you afraid of me?"

Richard's laughter was high pitched, protracted. Perspiration shone on his face. I told him that I was not afraid of him. Though in that instant, alone in the office with Richard, I was afraid.

I had told Ray about Richard Wishnetsky, from time to time. But I did not tell Ray about Richard sitting at my desk. I did not show Ray Richard's carelessly typed diatribes and prophecies in the mode of Zarathustra.

Only once, Ray had met Richard. He'd come to the U. of D. campus to pick me up and there was Richard who'd followed me outside, wanting to talk. Ray said, as we drove away, "I don't think that you should encourage him. I don't think it's a good idea."

"He has no one to talk to but me."

"So he says."

"He's very touching . . ."

"He isn't your student, is he?"

"No, but . . ."

"Whatever he wants from you, you can't give him."

"But . . ."

"You can't."

It wasn't like Ray to disapprove of me, or to tell me what to do. I did not argue with him—it isn't in my nature to argue with anyone who is close to me, whom I respect—and if I discounted his intuition about Richard Wishnetsky, I did not tell him. Not until many years later would I realize that Ray must have recognized, in this tormented young man, some residue of his former adolescent self—not the flamboyance of Richard's ideas, not the messianic contempt for others, but Richard's essential loneliness, his estrangement from his parents, and his obsession with "religion."

It was so, Richard Wishnetsky was not my student. He appeared and disappeared in my life as he was becoming more disturbed, less able to coexist with the contemptible others who surrounded him. It was said that his parents tried to commit him to a mental hospital in Ypsilanti, but without success. Perhaps he was banned from the U. of D. campus for causing disruption in a classroom. There was one other professor to whom he felt a combative sort of kinship, in the German department.

(My story "In the Region of Ice" was written at this time. It's a curious hybrid of "reality" and "imagination"—clearly stimulated by the intrusion of Richard Wishnetsky into my life, though recounted from the point of view of a fictitious Catholic nun, who becomes involved with the brilliant, alienated young Jewish student to a degree to which I was not involved; the young man quarrels with his family, his friends, his professors, leaves his comfortable suburban home and flees across the border into Canada, where he commits suicide. If I'd been asked why I had written this story, I would have said, "Because Richard Wishnetsky is on my mind and this is my effort of exorcism." I'd thought, too, that the story was a cautionary tale I might give to Richard, the next time I saw him.)

I never saw Richard Wishnetsky again.

On the morning of February 12, 1966—less than a year after he'd entered my life—Richard interrupted Sabbath services in the Shaarey Zadek synagogue in Southfield with the intention of committing a murder-suicide. Waving a .32-caliber pistol he'd purchased in Toledo, Ohio, Richard ascended the bimah where fifty-nine-year-old Rabbi Morris Adler had just finished speaking to a congregation of nearly eight hundred people, including Richard's family; like a figure out of Dostoyevsky's *The Possessed* Richard defiantly addressed the congregation with a prepared statement that would long outlive him, being taped on a synagogue recorder:

"This congregation is a travesty and an abomination. It has made a mockery by its hypocrisy of the beauty and spirit of Judaism . . . With this act I protest a humanly horrifying and therefore unacceptable situation."

Calmly then Richard shot Rabbi Adler twice, and then himself. Both men died of their wounds, though not immediately.

It would be noted in the many articles about this tragedy that Richard Wishnetsky had had his bar mitzvah on that very bimah. It would be noted that Rabbi Adler had been a spiritual model in his life and was a friend of the Wishnetsky family.

Why why why why why!

What a loss! What folly! Killing the man he most admired, Rabbi Adler, and killing himself—for the sake of mere ideas.

"In the Region of Ice" has been anthologized frequently, received an O. Henry award, and was made into a starkly dramatic black-and-white short feature film by Peter Werner, that won an Academy Award in 1977 in the category Best Short Subject. When I reread this story written so long ago, immediately I am mesmerized by the dialogue, that so vividly recapitulates Richard's speech, even as it has been severely abbreviated; again I am stricken with sympathy, sorrow, guilt. *I could have done more. I could have done—something.*

To comfort me Ray assured me, it was not my fault. Richard Wishnetsky would have killed Rabbi Adler and then himself if he'd never met me—"He was very sick."

But he had met me, I thought. And it made no difference.

76

Sinkholes

The widow must learn: beware sinkholes!

The terror of the sinkhole isn't that it exists. You understand, sink-holes must exist. The terror of the sinkhole is that you fail to see it, each time you fail to see it, you don't realize you have blundered into the sinkhole until it's too late and you are being pulled down, down. . . .

In the office suite shared by several doctors, on Harrison Street. And a tall slightly stooped gray-haired man, one of the resident doctors, stares at me and smiles—does he know me?—and my heart begins to clench, for often this sort of smile presages words that will hurt, words that will sting, words that will cause my throat to close, though those who utter such words mean only to be kind of course, like this gentle-manly gray-haired man in his sixties who comes forward, who will not be avoided coming forward, extending his hand, soft-spoken, somber, the most sympathetic of smiles, he introduces himself as one of Ray's doctors, the name is familiar to me in a vague way, yes I say, yes of course, he is saying, "I was sorry to hear of your loss. I saw Ray's pic-ture in the paper. Ray was—very"—he pauses, searching for the right words, like a man searching in his pocket for his car keys, which he has misplaced; in the instant before he realizes he has misplaced the keys, frowning, insisting—"exceptionally nice." He pauses again, smil-ing sadly. "I liked Ray—Raymond—very much."

Don't tell me these things, my heart is broken.

Of course I thank Dr. P___ for these words. Though I am stricken as if impaled by a sharpened steel rod, still I thank Dr. P___, blinking tears from my eyes I stagger away, I am not well, I think I will crawl away somewhere, I think I will hide in the women's room or better yet leave, and return home.

On an outdoor bench at the Princeton Junction train depot—wadded tissues.

Someone has left behind a half-dozen damp, wadded tissues.

No one notices except me. For what is there to notice?—just ordinary litter, debris. You might crinkle your nose in disgust. Left-behind tissues in this public place!

I feel something pierce my heart, a sliver of ice, a bit of glass, so suddenly I've become weak, staggering. But I am not *panicked*—in this medicated state it isn't possible to become *panicked*—picture a living creature—"turkey"—"calf"—so boxed into a tiny space in a vast agrifactory that it cannot move—or one of those laboratory monkeys whose vocal cords have been cut so that it cannot scream in pain.

Still, I find myself moving away from the bench. I dare not glance back at the bench. I will hope to forget the bench. I think that I have avoided a treacherous sinkhole, so long as I can forget the bench.

This was the first wrong thing. The scattered damp-wadded tissues.

And I remember—I think—that, the previous night, when Ray had been sitting at his end of the sofa reading, he'd been blowing his nose also, there were scattered damp-wadded tissues on the table beside him which, when he rose to leave, he took with him, and disposed of. And this was the night before—the night before the emergency room. For already he'd been sick. Already it had begun. The wadded tissues were the sign, I did not understand just yet.

Once begun, it cannot be halted. The inexorable plunge to death: the inexorable sinkhole.

*　　*　　*

Depersonalization. Of the many side effects of psychotropic medication, this is surely the most beneficial.

At the end of an evening, the ritual kissing-of-cheeks.

At the edge of the gathering, I can slip away without being seen.

Too late, this is a sinkhole I have blundered into—the kissing, the hugs, the bright exclamatory voices—I am plunged into *a blackness ten times black*—as Melville would have said *the blackness of the soul without hope*—staggering away seeing again with such hallucinatory vividness it's as if I am there, again—I have never left—the Telemetry unit, the room outside which figures are standing so oddly motionless—and in the room there is Ray in the hospital bed so oddly motionless—*This is not happening. This is not real, this cannot be happening* even as I bend over Ray in the bed, bend to kiss his cheek, I am talking to him, I am lost in wonder speaking to him, my husband, I have come too late, for his skin has a waxy pallor and is just beginning to cool.

Just beginning to cool! What can these words mean!

In the sinkhole, time does not budge. In the sinkhole it is always *that time*. Even in my dazed-zombie state I am made to know that, like the roaring of blood in my ears, this is a time that is ever-present, unceasing.

At the Pennington Market where we'd shopped for—can it have been thirty years?—and where Ray had befriended one of the older male cashiers, known to us as "Bob"—in his sixties or early seventies—who'd been retired but when his wife died became so lonely he'd decided to take a job at the local food market in order to meet people, as an antidote to being alone. And once, when I'd shopped at the market alone, before Ray died, Bob had sighted me—alone—and with an anxious expression asked me where Ray was and I said, cheerily—"Oh, Ray is just at home. I'm shopping alone today."

After Ray died, which seems to me like a very long time ago now, but also like the day before yesterday, when I come to the Pennington Market to shop, a task which I put off as long as possible, half-consciously I've avoided Bob—a sudden panicky sensation alerts me to Bob's (innocent, innocuous) presence in the row of cashiers, which my eye has sighted before my brain has quite registered the sighting; as in the deepest core of our brain we react to the approach of danger, a threat to our well-being, mistaking a twisted stick for a venomous snake; I have even pushed my grocery cart to another cashier, to take my place behind other customers, when Bob is free. Of course I have avoided glancing at Bob—I am in terror that Bob will see me. (My assumption is: Bob has certainly noticed me shopping—alone—a number of times now; Bob must certainly know that "something has happened to Ray"—Ray has died. Therefore, I dare not lock eyes with Bob in this public place.) Yet this afternoon, who knows why, distracted by other things, the gauze-scrim less penetrable than usual in my dazed brain, or simple ineptitude, carelessness, stupidity—the basilisk is quick to register *You are so utterly stupid, worthless—you have forgotten the grocery list—you have probably lost your car keys—again*—I seem to have blundered into Bob's checkout line; there is just one customer ahead of me, and Bob has seen me, I can't suddenly push my cart away, certainly I can't go to another checkout line; and so I am—suddenly, without preparation—obliged to meet Bob's inquiring eye, and Bob's friendly smile—(for Bob is the sweetest, most mild-mannered and courteous individual, one would not know the grief in the widower's heart), and when Bob asks me about Ray—"Where's Ray? I haven't seen Ray in a while"—I am stunned that Bob doesn't know, I have no choice but to stammer, "I'm afraid—Ray has died. Ray has—last month—Ray died . . ."

This is wrong: Ray did not die last month. It's late April now, Ray died more than two months ago.

It's as if I have struck Bob in the face. His expression registers shock, incredulity. His eyes clutch at mine, fearfully. "Ray has *died*?"

For nearly two months I have avoided this confrontation. I have anticipated it and now I am overwhelmed with grief despite the 60-milligrams Cymbalta tablet I took this morning. My fingers are gripping the handle of the grocery cart so hard that my knuckles have turned white.

There is no escape. Bob continues to stare at me, stricken. This kindly man had not known Ray, really—they could not have spoken together more than a dozen times, and always briefly—yet Bob is as shocked by this news as an old friend might have been.

"But—how did it happen? When . . . ?"

These are prepared words many times uttered by now. *Pneumonia, Princeton Medical Center, improving, soon to be discharged—infection, died. Infection, died.*

"I wondered why—haven't seen Ray for a—a while . . ." Oblivious of other customers waiting behind me Bob continues to stare at me. My mouth has begun to make that gruesome-twitchy movement which signals danger. Stammering I tell Bob that I can't talk right now, I have to leave—"I'm sorry—I can't t-talk."

Seeing my distress, Bob apologizes. Bob rings up my purchases, frowning. It seems strange to continue with this procedure—credit card swipe, signature—when we are both so shaken. I know—from Ray— that when Bob's wife of many years died—of cancer?—not long ago, Bob had become desperately lonely, and depressed, and physically ill for a while; I know that Bob lives alone in the Pennington area, and his children are grown, and scattered.

This is a sinkhole that might have been avoided. An exhausting and upsetting sinkhole. Pushing the grocery cart out into the parking lot I am observed from a little distance by the ugly lizard-thing jeering at me as clumsily I unload the cart, place the grocery bags in the trunk of the car *Do you think that you can continue like this? Are you so desperate to live, you want to continue like this?*

Loading the car trunk with groceries, unloading the car trunk at home—how strange, how bizarre, how wrong this is to be doing alone, without my husband.

Have you no pride, no shame—to continue to live, like this?

(What has begun to frighten me: the basilisk can sometimes penetrate the Cymbalta-haze, unpredictably. Obviously if one is sufficiently drugged—near-comatose—"self-medicated"—no basilisk has the power to penetrate consciousness; but I am frightened of that degree of sedation, knowing how it must escalate. It's a cruel revelation how little one's public self matters, to the basilisk; definitely, the basilisk is *not impressed* with any sort of literary accomplishment, professional acclaim, Ivy League endowed chair; especially I'm vulnerable when being introduced in a public place, before an audience, when the basilisk-jeering is pitiless, and terribly distracting. With uncanny insight the lizard-thing recognizes that *it is more contemptible for someone of "stature"* to be alone, unloved, left-behind than it would be for others, who might imagine that acquiring "stature" would make them less miserable, thus less vulnerable to the basilisk.)

All of Detroit would be a *sinkhole*, for instance. The house on Woodstock Drive which we'd loved, and the larger house into which we'd moved a few years later, a mile south and closer to the University of Detroit campus, on Sherbourne Road—which we'd loved less, and seemed in retrospect less-happy in; for it was in this house we'd huddled in those terrible crazed hours of the "riot" hearing gunshots on Livernois Avenue and smelling smoke and hoping that we might be spared harm.

And the house in Windsor, at 6000 Riverside Drive East.

Unlocking my office door at the university, sometimes I see—for just an instant—a ghost-figure at my desk, looking through my papers. This is not Ray of course—never once had Ray sat at my office desk, he'd spent little time in my university office over a period of thirty years—but Richard Wishnetsky who has been dead—by his own desperate hand, dead—for more than forty-five years.

The sinkhole *within*.

To a friend in Evanston, Illinois, April 29, 2008.

. . . difficulty in living alone, Leigh. My life is totally changed. Everything takes longer to do & I am not able to concentrate . . . My mind is constantly buzzing/running amok/with useless thoughts. Only with medication can I turn it off for 4–5 hours a night . . . I am taking an anti-depressant which might have some effect . . . I feel utterly changed like one who has been gutted/hollowed out . . . yet when friends see me, they say that I look & behave just as I always have! I don't think that they are just being polite, which makes it so very strange. What I am concerned about is continuing to live in this way . . . it is such an effort,

& of questionable worth. Everyone says that "time heals all" but when
we are a certain age, & alone, there is not likely to be any improvement
in our situations. Friends continue to be wonderful . . .
   Much love,
   Joyce

The blunt truth is: I would (very likely) not be alive except for my friends.

To a poet-friend in Boston, whose mother is dying in a hospice in Virginia, April 30, 2008.

I am thinking of you, Henri . . . We will endure of course and we will
be happy again—sometime—if only taken by surprise—perhaps in
July.
   Much affection,
   Joyce

(My poet-friend's mother exists on a diet of something called *mechanical soft*. I must tell myself that Ray has been spared this, Ray is not slow-dying in a hospice but has died, Ray has died suddenly and seemingly without pain and perhaps without even the consciousness of imminent death. I am not at Ray's bedside at the hospice feeding Ray spoonfuls of *mechanical soft*.)

A way to escape—elude—the *sinkhole of the soul*—is to immerse myself in work. For work is, if not invariably sanity, a counter-insanity.
   You cannot really work if you are crazy; if you are crazy, you cannot really work. This is hopeful!
   In fact, I am not able to write fiction any longer, except haltingly. Like a drunken woman staggering, colliding with walls, stunned . . . For weeks I labored on a single short story, that was finally completed last week. Of the many ideas for stories that assail my brain when the Cymbalta-haze lifts there is not one that I feel I can execute; I am too

exhausted, I have so little concentration. . . . No more could I plan a new novel than I could trek across the Sahara or Antarctica. My principal means of communication in these early posthumous weeks is *e-mail*.

I will take out of a drawer a novel I'd finished before Ray died. To save myself, as a drowning person might seize a rope, a lifeline, to haul herself up—to haul herself *up, up*—I will rewrite this novel entirely: each syllable. I will change the title. I will change the tone, the "voice." In this novel I will mourn my lost husband, as I'd believed I had mourned my lost father, when I'd originally written the novel. In this way, I will try to defeat the basilisk jeering at me—I will "endure."

Returning home after dark and approaching our house I see that the road has become a sort of tunnel, lined with vehicles parked on both sides—is there a party in the neighborhood?—why does this seem so ominous, threatening? My heart begins to beat quickly as I am forced to drive—slowly—through the narrow space between the parked ve-hicles—SUVs and minivans in mostly dark colors, like military vehicles; I am fearful of scraping against the side of one of the vehicles; it seems to take a very long time—minutes—for me to pass through the tunnel— I've begun to sweat inside my clothes—and there, finally, is our house: no lights on, a desolate place, abandoned. *I alone am alone, on this street. I am the lone person who is alone.* Because I haven't left any outdoor light on, or any lights inside the house to illuminate the walk to the courtyard, I have to grope my way inside. *The only person who must grope her way into her house. Who could be so ridiculous!* It isn't even the basilisk who jeers at me, but myself.

Weeks ago I might return home at such an hour, and there would be things left for me in the courtyard—a casserole still warm from a friend's oven, a tote bag of fruit drinks. Now it's the end of April and all that awaits me are UPS and FedEx deliveries. The dogwood tree is in bloom, a ghost tree in the shadows. By daylight I can't bear to see it.

Soon, the Korean dogwood at the front of the house, in front of my study, will begin to bloom. This tree, too, was one of Ray's favorites.

It is never an easy thing to return home to an empty house. Always when I step inside I am expecting—half-expecting—to see that damage has been done in my absence. Cushions thrown onto the floor, chairs overturned, lamps broken . . . My friend Lois has said to me *I worry about you, Joyce. In that house alone. It's so . . . accessible.*

In Detroit, in our first year in the house on Woodstock Drive, we'd returned one night to discover that the house had been *broken-into.*

Heedlessly and naively we'd walked into the house. Neither of us seemed to grasp that something was wrong. Seeing our two kitchen chairs out of place, kitchen drawers yanked open—the sliding door to the patio part-opened—we stared in silence as if confronted with a riddle too massive to be squeezed into our brains.

Then, we hurried upstairs. In our bedroom staring at bureau drawers overturned on the floor, clothing and pillows tossed about—*Has someone been here? What is this?* It is strange how slow to comprehend the situation we were, how literally slow-thinking, as if in slow motion, or underwater—it's said that this response is common when there has been a home burglary, the violation is so intimate it somehow can't be immediately registered.

And in my study, a small room at the rear of the house, in which there were few items of furniture—a card table on which I wrote, a chair, two or three small unfinished bookcases—for a long moment I stared before comprehending that my typewriter was missing. . . .

My typewriter! In this era before even electric typewriters, I had a manual typewriter, to which I was attached as a shackled slave might be said to be "attached" to shackles that had grown to fit the very contours of his limbs. It might be said, reasonably—*Joyce loves her typewriter! Joyce is utterly dependent upon that typewriter.*

Though I've always written by hand, always I've typed my work in its finished-draft form. Now burglars had taken away my typewriter, for what purpose we couldn't imagine—it wasn't new, it was far from an expensive model, surely it couldn't be sold? Pawned?

Ray called the police. Ray spoke with the police officers when they arrived. By this time it was late—past 11 P.M. The police officers looked through the house, asking us what was missing, and only vaguely, stumblingly, could we tell them—as if we'd been personally assaulted, we could not seem to think what was missing, apart from my typewriter and some silver-plated serving spoons and forks, that had been wedding presents; had we had money hidden anywhere, the police officers asked, and we said no, we had not; had we any firearms, the police officers asked, and we said no, we had not; were we insured, would we be filing an insurance claim, and we said yes, we supposed so.

The police officers addressed most of their remarks to Ray. Only perfunctorily did they appear to be taking notes. Clearly, in Murder City, USA, home burglaries like ours did not register heavily upon police consciousness. Their search of the house was quick and minimal. Before leaving they allowed Ray to know how dangerous it had been for us to go upstairs once we'd suspected that the house had been burglarized— "If they'd been upstairs, and there's no other way out for them, you and your wife could've been hurt, Mr. Smith." *Mr. Smith* was uttered just barely politely.

Man to man they were speaking. *Your wife* stood to the side. When they left, Ray was very quiet. And for days afterward, very quiet on the subject of the break-in.

By degrees I would realize *He was insulted by them. They spoke to him without respect. A man who'd behaved dangerously, stupidly—hadn't protected his wife.*

The glass house. How wise is this? No blinds, shutters—a single floor— "accessible."

In a glass house, by day or by night, there are unexpected reflections—ghost-images—shadowy figures moving in the corner of the eye. Deer are reflected in the glass, and their reflections reflected in another glass, or—is it a human figure?—*Is it Ray?*—for so often, over the years, of course it has been Ray; and the heart floods with . . .

Some sort of adrenaline-equivalent of *hope.*

Hope in the face of *common sense.*

To be insane is—this is a partial, improvised definition—to believe that something is what we wish to believe it is, in the face of knowing that it is not. To be not-insane is to acknowledge that one's deepest and most profound wishes have nothing to do with what is.

I conclude that I am not insane. Not just yet.

Maybe it is dangerous, living here alone. But the dangers are not likely to be from break-ins, serial killers.

I am thinking of the anonymous male worker-figures of Fritz Lang's *Metropolis* marching like zombies into the netherworld which is their abode.

I am thinking of a museum Ray and I had visited—possibly, the Louvre—a sinkhole of exhaustion—though containing "beautiful" things—"rare" things—in a wing of antiquities—walking together silently for we'd been silenced by the figures of long-deceased kings—their faces reduced to a few primitive features—some of the sculpted forms were armless, legless—headless—ancient Egypt, was it?—humanoid figures from an extinct species yet condemned to "exist"—in the museum; in that gray, diffuse light all meaning had drained from these blind, vacant figures—all meaning had drained from what we were doing there—bearing witness to what absurd claim of human identity, value? authority?

Ray took my hand—"Let's get out of here!"

Living alone it is very easy to become disembodied.

Thinking *I must stop taking these pills. I am being poisoned.*

(In New Jersey, it's said the air is polluted even in those parts of the state, like Princeton, in which the air is claimed to be not-polluted.)

(Sometimes, in any case, you can smell/taste the toxins—for instance a faint discoloration of the air not unlike the hue of dried cat urine on a death certificate issued by the State of New Jersey.)

Like his father—his father from whom he'd been emotionally estranged—Ray was once observed weeping. In his office, at his desk, and I'd come into the room utterly astonished, and concerned—asking what was wrong, what was wrong, oh what was wrong—for this was so utterly unlike my husband, as I'd known him; and Ray had turned away saying it was nothing, he'd been thinking about his father, that was all—nothing.

At this time his father had been dead perhaps a year or two.

Ray did not speak of his family often, or easily. But he'd told me

that more than once, he'd discovered his father weeping. Once, when
Ray had been quite young, he'd discovered his father hunched over, his
head on his arms. He'd been very frightened. It is frightening to see
your father crying. Frightening to see your father so seemingly helpless,
defeated. And another time when Ray was eighteen, and had ceased
going to mass on Sunday, his father had cried, his father had appeared
genuinely upset, anxious—*If you lose your faith I will be blamed. If you go
to hell. It will be my fault if you go to hell. I will be blamed.*

An adult man, crying! Frightened of hell! Telling me these things
Ray laughed. His lips twisted in a bitter sort of smile.

But did your father really mean this? I asked. How strange to me,
whose parents had never been devout or even very serious Catholics;
whose family would no more have spoken of God, Jesus Christ, Mary,
the Devil or heaven or hell than they'd have lapsed into a discussion of
higher mathematics. Somehow it seems, in Millersport, New York—a
rural crossroads community of a dozen houses—such "profound" issues
sound just plain silly.

Ray said yes. His father had meant it.

I asked how could anyone seriously believe . . .

Irritably Ray said that his father had believed. His father was a devout Roman Catholic and he "believed"—what Catholics believe.

But—

Let's drop the subject, Ray said. Please.

In a marriage, as in any intimate relationship, there are *sinkholes*.

Or maybe *minefields*.

You don't blunder into them. You don't make that mistake.

You don't make that mistake more than once.

To Ray, there was a sinkhole: his family.

The sinkhole was immense, covering many acres: his family, the
Church, hell.

This sinkhole nearly pulled him into it, to drown. Before I'd met
him, Ray said.

Or so I'd gathered, as a young wife.

My impression was that Ray had pulled himself out of the sinkhole at considerable cost—emotionally, psychologically. I could not ask him, as I could not ask him about his father. One of those bullets that are lodged too close to the spinal column, or the brain, to be removed by surgery.

In writing this, I feel that I am betraying Ray. Yet in not writing it, I am not being altogether honest.

There is no purpose to a memoir, if it isn't honest. As there is no purpose to a declaration of love, if it isn't honest.

For years we'd lived with no reference to Ray's past, for Ray's past was ever more distant in time. But at the start of our marriage, this past had been close, in fact this past intruded upon the present, for Ray's parents were both living at the time. (Ray's mother would live well beyond ninety—when she'd died, she had been a widow for forty years.)

How does a young wife respond to her husband's family? If her husband is on good, easy terms with them, there is no problem. If he isn't, there is likely to be a problem.

I am not comfortable criticizing others. Though I am not what you'd call a credulous person, I don't want to be, or even to seem, scornful, skeptical, dismissive of others' beliefs.

Especially fervently held religious beliefs.

And so, with the issue of Ray's family, I withheld any opinion. I did not press the issue of wonderment, that Ray's father should actually have believed that he would be accountable—to God?—if his son left the Catholic Church.

As Ray said *Drop it.*

Another time, when we'd first met, and were seeing each other every night in Madison, Wisconsin, in the head-on excitement of being what we'd have been far too shy to have designated *newly in love*—Ray had spoken hesitantly of his sister who'd been "institutionalized."

This was a coincidence! For my sister Lynn, eighteen years younger than me, had been institutionalized, too.

So severely autistic, Lynn could not be kept at home beyond the age of eleven. She'd become violent, threatening my mother. This was a heartbreaking interlude in my parents' lives, after I'd gone away to college; implicitly, I'd left the family, and Lynn was perhaps to have been my replacement.

Or perhaps my younger sister had been an accident. Accidentally conceived when my mother was in her early forties.

But Ray's sister wasn't autistic. Ray's sister Carol, as he recalled her, had not been mentally defective, but she'd been—"excitable"—"difficult"—"disobedient."

Of the four children in Ray's family, Carol had been the rebellious one. Carol had resisted following orders from her parents, and Carol had "over-reacted" to the religious climate of the household.

What did this mean? I asked.

She hadn't been a good girl—a good little Catholic girl. She hadn't been devout. She'd been loud, argumentative.

And what—what happened to her? I asked.

She was institutionalized. When she was about eleven. Like your sister. But for different reasons.

Beyond this, Ray would not speak. The subject was upsetting to him and I did not want to press it.

I would meet Ray's younger brother Bob, a very nice if reticent individual who would spend his life working in a Milwaukee post office branch—so very different from Ray intellectually, emotionally, and in every other way, one would never have guessed they were brothers. And I would meet Ray's older sister Mary, who'd married and moved away from Milwaukee and the strong gravitational pull of the Catholic family, years ago. Ray admired Mary for having made a "normal life" for herself.

"She escaped. Carol couldn't."

It might have been when we were living in Princeton, that Carol died suddenly, in the hospital, or "home," in which she lived in the Milwaukee area. Ray spoke on the phone with his brother and with his sister but did not go to the funeral, if there was a funeral; he did not wish to talk about his lost sister.

I should say—*lost* is not Ray's word. *Lost* is my word.

When Ray died, in the confusion of those terrible hours—days—I could not seem to locate Mary's address in Ray's address book. I'd been instructed by an officer of the probate court that I must write to all close relatives of my deceased husband, to inform them of his death so that they might see his will, if they wished to see his will; if they had claims to make against the will, they would have to make these claims now. It was my responsibility to send a registered letter to Ray's surviving sibling but I could not locate her address, and in desperation I looked through Ray's papers, documents, desk drawers and filing cabinets; when a journalist called me from the *New York Times*, on some entirely different subject, I took the opportunity to enlist aid in searching for the elusive "Mary Samolis"—a resident of somewhere in Massachusetts, I thought—unless it was Connecticut. Eventually, from another source, I did locate the address and wrote to my sister-in-law, belatedly.

How shocked she'd been, to learn that her younger brother Ray had died, and so suddenly! (Their younger brother Bob had died several years before.)

Yet, the other day, in the courtyard, when I'd been looking through Ray's much-thumbed address book, I discovered his sister's name and address—it had been there all along.

So often discovering things I hadn't been able to find. Certain that I had looked, and looked, and looked—yet, somehow I'd overlooked what I was seeking.

All this is new to me. This—dazedness.

Beginning with the rude note under the windshield wiper of our car—LEARN TO PARK STUPPID BITCH. That was the first—the first indication that I am not thinking clearly, and I am not behaving—normally. The first indication from the world—the world that doesn't give a damn about me, or Ray—that I have entered a new phase of my life from which there will be no return.

Wet, wadded tissues. But these are my own, scattered on the carpet beside the bed.

77

The Garden

Surely Ray's garden is a *sinkhole*. Surely it will be a terrible mistake for me to step inside.

Yet I am unlatching the gate, I am stepping inside. A flood of such emotion comes over me, I think that I will faint. When we'd last been in this garden together, in the fall—how utterly different the garden had been, and our lives . . .

There are the lightweight lawn chairs, we'd brought into the garden to sit in the sun and have lunch. Ray had been touched when I'd suggested this—the garden was always *his place*—he'd been happy when I came out to join him.

And the cats, too—seeing that I was in the garden with Ray, and that we were talking together, Reynard and Cherie might enter the garden as if oblivious of each other.

I want to think that Ray was very happy at these times. That he wasn't thinking about the magazine, or the Press; he wasn't thinking about financial matters, taxes or "maintaining" the house and property, a full-time occupation.

If Ray's spirit is anywhere—it's in this garden.

Painful to see how the garden has been ravaged by winter. Storm debris has fallen from nearby trees. I am trying to remember where Ray's marigolds were, and his zinnias—everything is broken, their bright colors faded. Broken and rotted shells are all that remain of the pumpkins. Desiccated tomato vines on tilted poles, like frayed nerves. A snarl of last year's cucumber vines entwined with the fence wire.

Amid the ruin of the garden are some fresh green shoots that don't appear to be weeds! These are what Ray called—(did he invent the term, himself?)—"volunteers."

Flowers that had reseeded themselves, and had survived the winter. Where everything else had died.

I can't identify these green shoots yet. In time, they will emerge as sweet william.

Of course, morning glories return every year. Pale blue and white morning glories, I may have planted myself several years ago. For I was not always a stranger to the garden, I had loved Ray's garden, too.

This is the time of year when Ray would have the garden plowed. The hard-packed earth tilled in preparation for setting plants in. He would begin with lettuce, arugula, sweet basil. *Would you like to come with me to Kale's* Ray would ask hopefully and in my study, at my desk I would murmur *No thank you, I'm busy with*—

Now, too late. My insipid *busy-ness* has expanded, like a malevolent gas, to contain my entire life.

Now in May 2008 my choice is: to allow Ray's garden to revert to weeds, or, what seems equally undesirable, for me to plant a garden in its place.

When an avid gardener dies, his family must make this choice. You will see gardens that have been allowed to go wild, for no one is equal to the challenge of maintaining them.

When we'd moved into this house the garden was uncultivated but surrounded by a ten-foot fence which Ray had reinforced. It wasn't a very sturdy-appearing fence but it has kept deer out. I am thinking *Really, I can't do this. I can't put in a garden. I don't know how, and I am not strong enough. I have not enough time. This will be another posthumous mistake I will regret.*

Another alternative is to pay someone to put in a garden. But how sad this is. How desperate.

Once, I'd teased Ray by bringing home a beautifully shaped squash, to insinuate in a muddle of squash vines at the rear of the garden. Some sort of ghastly zucchini-bore had devastated most of his squashes that had blossomed and began to form fruit then abruptly began to shrivel. And as a prank I'd insinuated a perfectly formed acorn squash.

Look! Ray had said, bringing the acorn squash into the kitchen.

I'd laughed—Ray saw my face, and knew—"That isn't funny," he'd said, frowning.

Truly my husband had been hurt. But he'd managed to laugh, too.

No more pranks! This is a bittersweet memory.

I feel that really, I have no choice. I can't let Ray's garden go wild— the irony is too painful. And our friends will surely see.

In fact, several friends have offered to come over with the intention of "helping you with Ray's garden"—for always the garden will be Ray's whether it is cultivated or not.

So, here I am on my way to Kale's. It's a sudden—impetuous— decision, I hope I won't regret. In Millersport, on our small fruit-orchard farm, I'd helped my mother with our vegetable garden and with a cornfield and a strawberry patch, as I'd helped feed the chickens and gather eggs and keep their terribly smelly coops reasonably clean, but I am not really a gardener, some crucial gene is lacking in me, like a gene for mathematics, or a beautiful soprano voice.

At Kale's I will ask for perennials, exclusively—where Ray planted only annuals. I will ask for perennials that are hardy as weeds, flowers that bloom for much of the summer—"Anything that requires a mini-mum of work and is guaranteed to survive."

In this way, unwittingly, and against the grain of her temperament, the widow has made a very good decision. The widow has made a brilliant de-cision. Instead of drifting about the house like a ghost in an ever-downward sinking the widow will take over her husband's abandoned garden and she will plant her husband's garden in a new way—hardy perennials and not perishable annuals, flowers and not vegetables, sinewy fast-growing Russian sage, swaths of black-eyed susans and Shasta daisies, hollyhocks, hostas, salvia, day lilies, peonies. Naively the widow had anticipated one or two visits to the garden center, in fact the widow will return to the garden center many times through the summer. Asked if she has an account with the garden center, giving her a 10 percent discount on her purchases, the widow says yes, her husband has an account—"Raymond Smith, 9 Honey Brook Drive."

78

The Pilgrimage

Now I am beginning to realize—this memoir is a pilgrimage.

All memoirs are journeys, investigations. Some memoirs are pilgrimages.

You begin at X, and you will end at Z. You *will end*—in some way.

At the outset, in the confused nightmare-days/nights following Ray's death, the (familiar) terrain through which I moved had become terrifying—unfamiliar. The very house in which I lived, that was "our" house—this was terrifying because, though utterly familiar, it was—it still is, at times—"unfamiliar."

What had drained from it, like color bleached by the sun, was meaning.

To be human is to live *with meaning*. To live *without meaning* is to live sub-humanly. Like one who has suffered damage to a part of the brain in which language, emotions, and memory reside.

In the early days, weeks, months of her new, posthumous life the widow must live *without meaning*—as in an ontological black-comedy in which others seem to be reciting from prepared scripts, actors linked to one another by the circuitry of an elaborate if invisible plot, while she, the widow, the one who has suffered some irrevocable loss, like a limb, or an eye, or the capacity to reason, must stumble through scenes, missing the vital linkage, the significance: Why?

Why?—the question asked only by the miserably unhappy, the marginal, disenfranchised, embittered, sickly, sorrowful, black-sludge-souled at the edges of the brightly lit social comedy.

Why?—the question that, if you ask it, like turning a flashlight onto your own contorted face, reveals the asker as deficient, wounded.

Why?—the question that has no answer.

Why did you fall in love with the one with whom you fell in love?

Why did you not fall in love with the many others with whom you did not fall in love?

Why did he/she love you in return?—is it possible, he/she did not know you, as you know you?

Why did he/she not know you?—is it possible, you hid your truest self from him/her? And why?

And why do you imagine—for certainly, we always imagine this—that you know the one with whom you fell in love?

This is the possibility of which the widow is frightened.

This is the possibility of which the widow doesn't want to think.

To lose her husband is devastating enough—how painful then to realize that she might not have known him, in the deepest and most profound way.

In Ray's garden, such thoughts come to me. These are not thoughts that would come to me elsewhere, I think—only in Ray's garden.

For I've hired a man to come and till the soil, as Ray did each year at this time. I've begun hoeing, digging, raking—I am wearing Ray's old garden gloves; I am using Ray's garden implements, and I will use Ray's garden hose if I can manage to affix it properly to the faucet outlet at the rear of the house.

Ray would like it, I think—knowing that I am here. Ray would think *I was so happy there! I wish that I could be with you now, there.*

In a corner of the garden is the bright-colored Victorian birdhouse on a pole, ravaged from winter and beginning to buckle. Ray would have forced the pole more securely into the ground but I don't seem to be strong enough. I will lean the birdhouse against the fence and hope it will remain upright.

In an untidy pile at the rear of the garden are sticks Ray used to support his tomato plants. The fence is covered with grapevines, morning glory vines, the desiccated remnants of last year's cucumber vines. Broken tree limbs have fallen onto the roof of the garden shed on the other side of the fence and seem to have dented it. It is so strange to think that I am in Ray's garden—and Ray is not here; as if someone were in my study, at my desk, going through my papers—but I am not there.

Absence is terrible enough. Extinction, unthinkable.

So I will choose to think *Ray's spirit is here.*

I will think *If Ray's spirit is somewhere, anywhere—it is here.*

At the garden center I'd bought a number of plants—too many, it seems. My head is beginning to hurt at the prospect of having to dig holes for all these plants, shake the plants out of their containers and place them in the soil, and lightly pack the soil about them. And water them. Ray would instruct *Just do as many as you want to, today. The rest will save. Be sure to water them.*

It was an anxious moment, at Kale's—when the cashier searched the computer for RAYMOND SMITH. For I feared he would say *There's no one here by that name. Sorry.*

Ray said: removing a plant from its pot, always cut the exposed roots with a hoe, mash the soil that has been impacted from the pot so that the roots can breathe. Somehow, though I would have said that I know virtually nothing about gardening, I remember this.

Ray said: be sure to make the hole deep enough. But not too deep.

Be sure to water the plant's roots thoroughly. But don't drown it.

If a widow is honest about her feelings she will acknowledge that she has been afraid, since her husband's death, of learning something about him—of having something thrust into her face, about him—of which she had no previous knowledge. The widow fears not having known her husband intimately—or, having known him intimately, not having known him in a more public sense, as others knew him.

For intimacy can be blinding. The closer you are, the less you can see.

For there is—in all of us, perhaps—in some of us, certainly—something unknowable, inaccessible. A stubborn intractable intransigent *otherness.*

Why Ray would speak so reluctantly of his father, and then with a strange, hurt, bitter twist of his mouth—why Ray would turn from me, if I wished to come too close—this is a mystery, it arises from his *otherness*.

A wife must respect the *otherness* of her husband—she must accept it, she will never know him fully.

Digging, hoeing, raking—protecting my hands from blisters by wearing Ray's soiled gloves—I am thinking these thoughts. There is a deliberation in my thinking, I mean to think something through. When you are in the thrall of psychotropic medication always you are trying to think—trying to break through a scrim—like a bird desperate to break through a net. And so I am doing two things: I am working in Ray's garden to save it from weeds, and to create a new garden, in Ray's memory; and I am working with my hands, and with my back, and my legs—for working in the soil is *working*. And so, as I am *working*, I am *thinking*—but the kind of thinking I am doing isn't anything like the kind of thinking I would do elsewhere, still less in bed, in the nest. This is a kind of *thinking* in tandem with *working*—some part or parts of my brain is roused, alive.

What I am doing, I think, is—preparing myself for reading *Black Mass*.

These weeks, months—I have been afraid to look at it. Ray's novel manuscript, left uncompleted. *Will I regret this? Would it be better for me to put the manuscript away, and never look at it again? Is there a story of Ray's secret life that he'd have wanted to keep secret? And yet—if this were so, wouldn't Ray have destroyed the manuscript long ago? Had he forgotten it? Outgrown it? Did he want me to see it—sometime? And is this the time? I am my husband's executrix—I am the only one.*

79

"You Looked So Happy"

In Windsor, Ontario, where we'd moved in the summer of 1968, and lived in a white brick house on Riverside Drive East on the Detroit River, looking across to Belle Isle. In Windsor where we both had teaching positions at the university and where each day, each afternoon, we walked together—along the crest of a long steep hill above the river, or along tree-lined residential streets in the Riverside district several miles from the university. Sometimes, we drove south along the Detroit River to Lake Erie and Point Pelee Park.

(I am looking at photographs taken from our car, of autumn cornfields in the vicinity of Amherstburg. Brilliant blue sky, rows of broken cornstalks, how this so-ordinary sight tears at my heart . . . I am wondering *Did I take these pictures? Was Ray driving? What were we talking about?*

Did we have lunch somewhere along the lake? And what was awaiting us, back in our Windsor house? What were the preoccupations of our lives, at this time?)

And there was a woman in Windsor of about my age, or just slightly younger—the wife of an English department colleague who'd been stricken with multiple sclerosis and who as he weakened, grew sicker and was finally forced to use a wheelchair, and was finally too ill to teach any longer, faded from our consciousness as from the memories of

his students; and when this woman encountered me at university func-
tions she would stare at me, so strangely—not obviously with hostility,
though not in a friendly manner, either; and I felt uneasy, and tried to
avoid her. And there came within a few years her husband's death, at a
quite young age—in his early thirties.

And at the memorial service at the university there was the wife,
the widow, surrounded by her friends, but staring at me, with a fierce
little smile—saying to me that she'd seen Ray and me walking along
the river the other day and we were holding hands—"You looked so
happy."

It was an accusation, a reproach. That fierce hurt widow's smile.

I could not understand then. But I do now.

80

BLACK MASS I

On the desk in front of me is Ray's unfinished novel-manuscript, in a soiled and tattered manila folder.

Years ago, he'd given me some of this to read. Several chapters, of which I remember just a little. Later, when we were living in Windsor, Ray worked again on the manuscript, but didn't show me what he'd written; like other subjects, the subject of *Black Mass* was not one that Ray cared to discuss with me.

Once I'd overheard Ray say to a friend that being an editor was nothing like trying to be a writer—"No one ever killed himself over 'editing.'"

Most of Ray's adult life is not represented here, in this tattered and much-annotated manuscript. *Black Mass* was written by a young man in his twenties whom I had not met—a highly intelligent, intellectual, yet insecure young man troubled by family issues, disturbed by religion—a "lapsed" Catholic who hadn't yet become comfortable with his new freedom *not to believe*.

For a Catholic, however, from a devout family, the issue isn't simply belief but the emotional pressure of the family, that one seem to believe; that one behave as if one believed, in the public sense.

Each Sunday the Catholic mass, each Sunday communion with the family.

All religions involve such rituals. When it is a family ritual, the wish to deny, to repudiate, to flee is bound up with the wish not to upset, disrespect, antagonize.

Ray's devout parents had sent all of their children to parochial schools—of course. *Give me a child before he's seven and I will have him for life*—so the Jesuits believe, without irony.

Ray had been highly impressionable, he'd told me. He was likely to believe what he was told by adults in authority. The Church, in Ray's lifetime, was characterized by the most intractable demands— the absolute obedience of all Catholics to the dictums of priest, bishop, archbishop, cardinal, pope. As young children Catholics were taught to believe that the slightest, most trivial of infractions (i.e., before the Church law was changed, eating meat on Fridays; breaking your fast before communion by allowing even a snowflake to melt on your lips; any use of "artificial" birth control) could constitute a sin for which the sinner would be damned to Hell.

Venial sins sent you to Purgatory, for an unspecified time. *Mortal sins* sent you to Hell, forever.

The Church teaches that you can work your way out of Purgatory, eventually. Like ascending steep steps up a mountain—it will take time, it might take years, but you can do it.

Also, if you are in Purgatory, your family can help you by praying to the Virgin Mary on your behalf, and by paying for masses to be said for the redemption of your soul.

Within its straitjacket of absurd canon law, by tradition the Church is curiously flexible, if not whimsical. To be prayed-over after your death is a kind of lobbying and, like lobbying, requires payment to individuals in authority. The Virgin Mary is the soft, feminine, maternal figure to whom you can pray for intercession with the stern, hyper-masculine paternal figure of God. In Ray's time Catholics believed that if God wished to detain you for a long time in Purgatory, it was possible for Mary to ease you out, into Paradise, through the *back door*.

Hence the football term, inexplicable to non-Catholics—*Hail Mary pass*.

The "Hail Mary" is the prayer that is exclusively to Mary: *Hail Mary, full of grace, the Lord is with Thee. Blessed art Thou amongst women, and blessed is the fruit of Thy womb, Jesus.*

How many hundreds—thousands?—of times had Ray uttered this prayer. How many times had Ray "crossed" himself—tips of fingers to his forehead, to his breastbone, to his left shoulder, and to his right shoulder.

How deeply imprinted these ritual-gestures. Far more deeply than anything in a Catholic's more "conscious" life.

Purgatory is not unlike life. Purgatory is life as a prison sentence, from which one might be redeemed. Hell is a different matter.

Once you are in Hell, you can't work your way out of Hell. Your family can't petition you out. No matter how many high masses your family purchases for you, you will never leave Hell.

You will suffer such torments in Hell!—physical, spiritual.

Much of parochial school religion in Ray's time focused upon the punishments of Hell. Paradise was a vague bright place overseen by God and populated by angels—Hell was a vivid place overseen by the Devil and populated by devils.

Each sinner could expect to be punished by his/her own devil.

For brilliantly imagined sadistic punishments to expect in the Catholic Hell, see James Joyce's *A Portrait of the Artist as a Young Man*. And recall that, for all his repudiation of the Church, and his disdain for such primitive superstition, Joyce's Stephen Dedalus concedes that he's still afraid there is a "malevolent reality" to what he no longer believes.

As it was the hope of most Catholics that at least one of their children might enter the religious life—take "holy orders"—so Ray's father expressed the hope that Ray would become a priest. After graduating from Marquette High School in Milwaukee—a Jesuit-run school with a reputation for academic excellence—Ray entered a Jesuit seminary in the area, at the age of eighteen.

In photographs, Ray Smith at age eighteen looks so very young—like fifteen, or fourteen.

Exactly what happened at the seminary, I don't know—Ray didn't speak of it except generally, obliquely—*Things didn't work out. I dropped out after a few months.*

Ray's emotions about the Church, thus about his childhood/boyhood in Milwaukee, were very complicated. A more aggressive wife—a wife who was closer to her husband's age—might have succeeded in getting him to speak more openly about it, and about his feelings for his parents; a more aggressive wife might have become better acquainted with Ray's parents.

Though Ray became very fond of my parents, as if he were a blood relative of theirs, I scarcely knew Ray's parents. He didn't encourage me, and we visited Milwaukee rarely.

My memories of Ray's parents are good ones. Seeing Ray with his family at the time—his father, his mother, his brother Bob—was to see the man I had fallen in love with in another context: son, brother. I did not feel that my claim upon my husband was greater than theirs and I feared—as many young wives do—that it was less.

After our first visit Ray said, "Did you see how my mother looked at you? Smiled at you? She couldn't stop touching you . . ." This was pleasing to Ray, and very nice for me to hear.

For this reason, I always felt close to Ray's mother whom I would see on only a few occasions in her lifetime. When she died at a very old age—it might have been ninety-nine—the way in which Ray grieved for her suggested that he'd never had any quarrel with *her*.

What is eerie, unsettling—as Ray grew older, the more Ray began to resemble his father, Raymond Joseph Smith, for whom he was named.

The more Ray began to dislike his photographs. The more Ray insisted upon being the one who took photographs, whose photograph was not *taken*.

In the first insomniac nights after Ray's death, when I lay dazed and exhausted and sleepless wondering what had happened to us, as the victim of an earthquake or a wreck must lay astonished and wondering what had happened quite apart from any physical pain or even any fear of what might happen again at any time, for some reason I was thinking of Ray and of his father—I was seeing Ray and his father, as if their faces had almost merged—I was thinking *Ray was older than his father when his father died. Ray should have forgiven his father.*

I had no clear idea what might have been "forgiven."

I would never have ventured such a thought to Ray.

Then, I remembered: it wasn't just that Ray had discovered his father crying, or even that his father had expressed a terror of being "damned" because of Ray; Ray was also upset by his father's habit of praying aloud when others could overhear, murmuring the ejaculation *Jesus, Mary, and Joseph!* which is, or was, a Catholic plea for the overcoming of temptation, or for forgiveness.

Seeing an attractive woman on television, for instance, Ray's father would quickly look away murmuring *Jesus, Mary, and Joseph!*—a way of blocking an unwanted/sinful sexual thought.

To have *impure thoughts* was believed to be a grave sin, in the Catholic cosmology. If a Catholic did not sufficiently confess his *impure thoughts* to a priest, and if he took the sacrament of communion, he would be committing a mortal sin and if he died in this state of mortal sin, he would be punished forever in Hell.

How ridiculous such notions seem to us! To some of us.

How crucial to life, to others. We must consider that most of the world's population "believes" in some sort of personal, often punitive God-relationship. The soil of the earth is steeped in the blood of those who have died for their religious beliefs as by those who have been killed by those who believe.

Ray's father had fought in World War I, as a young man. He'd been born Catholic and except for illness, he'd never missed a Sunday mass or a holy day of obligation in all of his life.

He was a car salesman in Milwaukee. Even through the Depression, he worked. Ray would say of him *He worked so hard. He never stopped working. He was always at the dealership, or he was on the phone. He never rested. He wore himself out. His only happiness was the Church—taking communion.*

I have no memory of Ray calling his father anything other than *my father.* I don't recall him addressing his father. Not once did I hear Ray utter the word *Dad, Daddy.*

I am thinking now that it was a mistake that I made no effort to urge Ray to be reconciled with his father. I seemed not to have given the possibility any thought. Very likely I took a kind of pleasure in it, that Ray was emotionally estranged from his family and therefore more dependent upon *me*.

While we saw my parents often, and were on the very best, friendliest terms with Carolina and Fred.

Seeing Ray with my parents, seeing how well we all got along, how happy we were together, I might have thought *He doesn't need anyone except us, as a family. He has us.*

This was a naive thought. It was a young-wife sort of thought, the jealousy of one who isn't altogether certain of herself.

Now that it's too late, in fact decades too late, I am sorry about this. I don't even know whether Ray loved his father, as well as being un-comfortable with him, and angry—and embarrassed. I don't even know whether Ray's father was upset about his son living at such a distance from him, seeing his parents so rarely. And there came the day in the late 1960s when Ray's brother called to say that Ray's father had died. And we went to the funeral in Milwaukee, and Ray was utterly stunned, silent; and whatever Ray felt, he did not share with me.

I was young then, and naive. I may have imagined, since Ray said so little about his father, that Ray wasn't grieving for him. That when I asked him how he was feeling, and he shrugged and said *All right*, that was a reasonable answer.

It's a fact, a man will love his father—in some way.

Snarled and twisted like the roots of a gigantic tree—these are the contortions of familial love.

Yet even now, if Ray were to return—could I ask him about his fa-ther? His family? Would I dare? Or would the slightest frown on Ray's part discourage me, and deflect the conversation onto another subject, as it always did?

As a wife, I had never wanted to upset my husband. I had never wanted to quarrel, to disagree or to be disagreeable. To be *not loved* seemed to me the risk, if a wife confronted her husband against his wishes.

And now, I am *not loved*. And what a strange lucidity this seems to bring, like disinfectant slapped on an open wound.

* * *

From Ray's notes, handwritten:

> BLACK MASS. Title: double meaning—requiem mass and Sa-
> tanic inversion of mass. V. working at a poem of this title at the
> time of her suicide, P. discovers it in her journal . . . The poem
> (incomplete) describes their sexual encounter in terms of a witch's
> black mass; her ironic projection of the guilt she imagines he felt
> . . . P. is about eight years older than V., a professor and a priest . . .

The manuscript *Black Mass* contains about one hundred typed pages, irregularly numbered. Included in the folder are numerous pages of notes and detailed outlines. Some pages are typed in red ink, others in black. Considering the age of the manuscript, the ink hasn't faded much, though there are paragraphs that have been x'ed out as if impatiently and the author's marginal notes are near-unreadable.

A kind of trance has overcome me, reading these notes of Ray's. The single-spaced typing gives Ray's writing an air of intensity, urgency. I feel as if I am overhearing Ray talking to himself and the sensation reminds me of the sensation I felt as a girl wandering onto rural property posted NO TRESPASSING.

There are two principal characters in *Black Mass*—V. (Vanessa), a poet (who bears some resemblance to Sylvia Plath?) and P. (Paul), who bears some resemblance, except for the fact that he is an ordained priest, to the young novelist Ray.

> V.'s poetry is sincere, with a distinct voice . . . Her writing gives her
> an identity; it is a psychological outlet. She sees with the poet's eye,
> continually assembling words in her head—"ordering the world."
> She meets Paul at Wisconsin. She meets him several times, once at
> a grad student Christmas party; he shows an interest in her writ-
> ing, encourages her . . .

Is this a coincidence? Only a coincidence—Ray and I met at a graduate student reception, not at Christmas but in October. And it can only
be a coincidence, Paul is eight years older than Vanessa. As I read further
it seems clear that Paul is Ray's alter ego, the center of consciousness of

the novel; the story is being related retrospectively, after Vanessa's death/ suicide, as Paul, at this time forty-one, a Jesuit, looks back upon their (not quite consummated?) love affair, which he'd broken off. Most of the notes focus on Paul:

> He comes from a middle-class family in Milwaukee, Irish mother, father discontented with the "burden" of wife and children . . . Paul's formal religious duties consist of saying mass every morning and saying his brievery [sic] . . . which have become mechanical to him . . . He feels that he functions "religiously" mainly when he helps other people . . . He is one of the "new" priests. Paul meets Vanessa in his fourth year when he is working on his dissertation . . . He thinks of her as superior to the other graduate students he knows and feels a certain protectiveness toward her. He is happy to read her poetry and offer criticism.

This, too, is coincidental—I think—for when Ray met me, he was in his fourth, final year as a graduate student, and he was writing his dissertation. Ray, too, volunteered to read some of my writing—not poetry, but fiction—including a story that had been published in *Mademoiselle* when I was nineteen. And I think that he felt "protective" toward me. . . .

What is fictitious about Paul is his career as a Jesuit academic: after leaving Madison, Wisconsin, he acquires a position at the University of Detroit (!) and later becomes chair of the English department at Fordham, a Jesuit-run university in New York. Vanessa, the troubled poet, drops out of graduate school after having failed her M.A. orals—she's too brilliantly independent-minded to give her questioners the answers they expect . . . (Surely this is a coincidence, though I didn't fail my M.A. orals in the spring of 1961 I was given a difficult time by my [male, smug] interrogators, and advised not to seek a Ph.D.; Ray was incensed on my behalf, more than I was, since I had not the slightest interest at the time in continuing the grim dull ordeal of graduate school.)

Reading Ray's notes, hearing Ray's voice—questing, questioning— the author addressing himself on the subject of his characters—(who are invariably as "real" as individuals in the "real" world, to the novelist)—

leaves me terribly moved. It's so clear that Paul *is* Ray—the Ray who'd lived out his father's hope for him, and became that most elite of Catholic priests—a Jesuit. (Among the Catholic religious orders, the Society of Jesus is the Brahmin caste. Perversely, Jesuits take vows of poverty, chastity, and obedience—but Jesuits have traditionally/historically moved in the highest social classes in both Europe and the United States and have exerted political influence disproportionate to their numbers. Among Ray's priest-friends were several Jesuits, my colleagues at the University of Detroit.)

It seems clear that Ray may have felt a strong attraction to the Church, despite his intellectual rejection of it; and that Ray identified with the "celibate" Paul, attracted to a young woman in defiance of his vows.

The crux of the novel is Paul's rejection of Vanessa, and Vanessa's subsequent suicide, not immediately but several years later. The present tense of the novel is the requiem mass Paul says for his former lover and his realization belatedly that he loved her—"If she could be brought back to life, would he leave the Church for her? Would he leave the priesthood to save her?" Amid much speculation is the blunt statement:

He has not left the priesthood for her. She is dead.

Paul and Vanessa are meant to suggest Abelard and Eloise, the fated lovers of medieval Catholic tradition, whose letters Ray had read and found deeply moving. Clearly there is a parallel also with the life and early death of Sylvia Plath, for Vanessa like Plath commits suicide by turning on a gas oven in a rented flat in London. (Recall that, when Ray was writing this novel in the late 1950s, the vogue for Sylvia Plath had only just begun and this material, far from being over-familiar as it would seem to us now, was quite daring for a novelist to explore.) Paul, however, is no Ted Hughes—his sexuality is self-conscious, thwarted. He's a Catholic steeped in a sense of sin, as Ray was, by his own account, in adolescence; when he feels desire for Vanessa, and gives in to that desire, he is inadvertently condemning her to death—suicide: "To what extent is P. implicated in V.'s suicide? He has encouraged her in her poetry, which was life-giving to her . . . But when he realized he loved her, he decides not to see her again. . . ." And, the final note in the first section: "What about the Journal? How does P. get hold of it? V.'s point of view—helps fill in last days. No answers here, however."

Following the typed notes are a dozen tablet-paper pages covered in Ray's handwriting, twenty-three numbered paragraphs. I am not able to read more than a fraction of this handwriting—I am beginning to feel dazed, disoriented—how sad it seems to me, that Ray worked so hard on this novel, cared so much for his characters!—who must have dwelt deep within him, for years. Isolated queries—"Have V.'s voice recorded some way????"—"Would it be too idealistic for V. to give P. up?—remove herself from *his* life?"

Heartbreaking to see so detailed an outline for the novel—twenty-six chapters indicated by place names (London, Madison, Madison, London, Detroit, London, New York, London, etc.) with intercalations from the poet's Journal ("poetry circuit in Midwest," "midnight walk on George Washington Bridge," "last days before suicide & poem 'Black Mass'")—chronologies of the lives of the characters—an obituary from the Sunday *Times* on the poet's death, and much, much more . . . There is even an alternative ending, in which V. only just attempts suicide, and P. hurries to her, in London: "How can I show Paul making his choice—partially by the fact that he's in London? Hopes she will recover, there won't be brain damage, wonders whether she'll be sorry she's alive" (This breaks off without a punctuation mark.) The novel begins *in medias res* with a densely typed page of which most has been crossed out, though I can read what has been crossed out if I peer carefully at it. The prose is flat, blunt, affect-less and reportorial in the Hemingway mode, as a means of creating subtextual tension, but the author must have been dissatisfied with this beginning because in a few pages the scene evaporates and he begins again from another perspective.

Astonishing, I discover a dream-account Ray had written! Here is my young husband writing in a way he'd rarely spoken to me:

DREAM

In the dream I visited Marquette High school—where my class-mates who'd become priests (about 1 dozen) were present . . . a sort of reunion?—dressed in "civilian" clothing—richly colored sport coats, suits and ties, each one different as if the colors matched per-

sonalities . . . Sitting on a sofa talking to my old friend upon whom
Jerry in the novel is based. I looked at him with the idea of how
to improve my description of Jerry's features, feeling a little guilty
about this. Later I was standing, talking to the Master of Discipline
Father Boyle who seemed pleased to see me. I talked to him in the
persona of the character Paul in my novel, telling him among other
things that I had been ordained two years ago. In contrast to the
others, I was not so richly dressed, but wore a sleeveless sweater
instead of a coat—my position (duties?) were different. I was in
an inferior position to them. How this is to be interpreted is puz-
zling. Fr. Boyle was wearing the usual cassock. Earlier I'd received
a letter from the former principal with a handwritten note: "This
Alumni Newsletter would like to hear about one Raymond Smith."
(The other Raymond Smith in my class is dead.)

There is no question but that the dream ties in with the novel!
The novel may be seen as a belated attempt to enter upon a "higher"
vocation, which would have pleased my father(s). It can be seen,
too, as demonstrating what would have been wrong with that path.
Paul is an alter ego—he is how I would have been had I entered the
Jesuits at 19 instead of having a nervous breakdown.

This is stunning to me . . . "Nervous breakdown."

In fact, Ray had told me when we'd first met—something about a
"breakdown" about ten years before—in our early, intense conversations
we spoke of things we would not speak of again. So in a sense I knew
this, though I would have said that I'd forgotten it.

I had known, too, that there was another "Raymond Smith" in Ray's
high school class, who'd become a priest, and who had died. He'd died
in some mysterious way, at a Jesuit residence in Ohio. Ray had said that
the two "Ray Smiths" had been friendly in high school but hadn't been
close friends; yet when "Father Ray Smith" died, when Ray was studying in Madison, he'd been very upset.

Not since the early days of our courtship had Ray and I spoken of
Ray's alleged "breakdown"—he'd confessed to me, and I told him that it
made absolutely no difference to me; I'd kissed him, and assured him—
which was true, of course—that whatever had happened to him, ten

years before, wasn't important to me and would not alter my feelings for him in the slightest.

As I'd told Ray about my "heart murmur"—"tachycardia"—and he'd said it made no difference to him, either.

All these years, these intervening decades—neither the "breakdown" nor the "heart murmur" had consequences in our marriage. But these were gestures of openness, confiding, intimacy at the start of our love for each other, that make me cry now, recalling.

From Ray's notes to himself, catechism-style, handwritten in fading blue ink:

"What function did the 'nervous breakdown' have?"

It lifted me right out of the situation I was in—the religious situation—the terrible guilt—kept me out of churches and away from anything religious—gave me a chance to see things more objectively . . .

"How did you contrive the 'breakdown'?"

I allowed myself to get run-down—inadequate food and sleep. Didn't keep up with my college subjects—unprepared for big chem. exam—didn't go to school that morning—kept worrying myself with moral hairsplitting—like breaking fast, bad thoughts, etc.

"What brought you out of it?"

"Love"—"affair" with young woman at the sanitarium—this gave me reason to live, gave me something to think of—a new obsession, as it were. Psychiatrist had referred to me as being "Love-starved." (Would Paul be love-starved?)

These words, I read over—and over: " 'Love'—'affair' with a young woman at the sanitarium" . . . "Psychiatrist had referred to me as being 'love-starved.' "

Ray had never told me this. In his account of his "breakdown" at nineteen he'd been brief, and vague; he'd seemed embarrassed, and ashamed; he'd appeared anxious, as if fearing that I might be repelled by what he was telling me. He'd told me virtually nothing about women with whom he'd gone out before meeting me; it was my impression that he'd never had an actual "love affair"—that I was the first woman/girl he'd loved. . . .

Of course, it should not surprise me: a young man of nineteen is certainly likely to fall in love, and to have a "love affair." It should not fill me with unease to learn this, after Ray's death; and so many years after it happened. *But he hadn't told me! It was his secret. He'd been "love-starved"—someone else had provided that love.*

I try to instruct myself: ten years later, when we met in Madison, Ray was a different person, and obviously he'd broken off with the young woman in the sanitarium, long before. It's ridiculous for me to feel such belated jealousy—on a May morning in 2008, reading of a love affair that had occurred in 1949 . . .

But I am beginning to feel light-headed. I have been trying to ignore a sort of stinging electric-current pain between my shoulder blades, exacerbated by the way I am leaning over my desk, reading the dense-typed pages. And I have been trying to ignore the curious blots and blotches in my eyes, like slow-drifting gnats in the corner of my vision.

Love-starved. How true this is. In May 2008 as in that long-ago season of breakdown 1949.

81

BLACK MASS II

Why didn't you finish your novel, Ray?

I set it aside and never went back. I became interested in other things.

So Ray told our friends, always with a smile. So Ray told anyone who knew he'd once been working on a novel.

Often adding *Bringing out a magazine is much more rewarding. You get to know new writers, each issue is new, each mail delivery . . . there are constant surprises.*

This is the way Ray began to feel, in time. Where originally he'd wanted to be a writer, eventually in the 1970s he shifted his creative instincts to editing/publishing. As he was revealed to be a born gardener with a gardener's zest for working in the soil with his hands, so he was revealed to be a born editor with a zest for working with writers, nurturing their work and publishing it. Many of his closest friendships were editor/writer relationships forged in the intimacy of letters, phone calls, faxes. With his Jesuit-trained scrupulosity for "perfection" Ray was an ideal line-editor and made it a principle to read, reread, and reread material—in manuscript, in galleys, and in page proofs.

Editors and gardeners are perennial optimists. No one steeped in a tragic sense of life can be either.

It was fortunate for Ray that he'd set his fiction writing aside. The Jesuit-trained scrupulosity that made him an excellent and enthusiastic

editor was a handicap in the writing of fiction which can become obsessive for such personalities, exhausting and claustrophobic. Those of us
who've been writers for most of our lives feel conflicted about urging
others to write—and relief at hearing that someone has "set aside" a
wish to write.

That Ray was working sporadically for years on a single novel without completing it suggests that, for all his impassioned identification with
his central character, he hadn't the artist's necessary instinct for finishing
a project and moving on. Essential as it is to be immersed in one's work
it is equally essential to move through it, and past it. It's a terrible thing
to be devoured by one's work—you must learn to leap free of it as one
might leap free of a raging fire.

Of course there are great writers who've been devoured by their
work, but not happily so—James Joyce is the most extreme example, in
his fanatic immersion in *Finnegans Wake* (his "monster" book) for more
than a decade.

But overall, the writer must beware of becoming mesmerized by his
material and lacking the perspective to organize it. It seems clear from
the fragmentary pages of *Black Mass* that Ray left behind that he was utterly mesmerized by his material, that so paralleled his own life. Lengthy
scenes of impassioned dialogue, densely packed passages of childhood
memories, exposition, analysis—chapters that break off abruptly, alternative sub-plots that are taken up, then discarded—the novel fragment
thrums with a vivid, felt life, an authentic *cri de coeur* of one wracked by
guilt for having escaped with his own life—*Black Mass* is fascinating to
me, to read yet would probably be impenetrable to someone else.

Initially, the (mad) thought had come to me—*Maybe I should finish*
Black Mass. *If it's near completion, I can complete it.*

Except that it isn't anywhere near completion. An entirely new work
would have to be erected on this shaky foundation. And to what purpose?

There is no point in thinking *Ray would want this*. Surely, *Ray would
not want this.*

Yet, the prospect of "completing" the novel hovers before me, tan-
talizingly. For my own writing moves with such excruciating slowness.

How much easier for me to be mesmerized by this material, and feel an intimacy with my lost husband of a kind I didn't have while Ray was alive.

For all that I knew Ray so well, I didn't know his *imagination*.

I knew his daily, hourly self. I knew his sweet, kindly, ever-thoughtful domestic self. And I knew him as a presence among others—his "social" self. But it can't be claimed that I knew anything of Ray's *imagination*, as evidenced by this fragmentary novel.

That Ray would create a priest-protagonist, for instance. That the "religious situation"—the "terrible guilt"—was so predominant in his life several years after he had left the Jesuit seminary and broken with the Church. Paul, Vanessa . . . The celibate Jesuit, the "brilliantly talented, troubled" poet . . . They seem to me immensely attractive people, quite vivid and "real" on the page.

As I read through the fragmentary *Black Mass*—trying to establish a probable sequence of scenes, though many pages are not numbered and much has been crossed out—it's as if I am inside Ray's head, magically—as if he hasn't died but is still young, and hopeful: typing these words rapidly on a manual typewriter in his quick-darting way—for he'd never taken time to learn to type, he'd used just one or two fingers of each hand.

On nearly every page I am likely to be startled by a nugget of memory, an incident about which Ray had told me years ago, long forgotten and now suddenly recalled:

One night Lucy [Paul's sister] told me about her fiancée. We were sitting out at the kitchen table . . . I was drinking a bottle of my father's beer. I had been in the seminary about four years and was home for a visit. "I gave in to him," she said. "Last night—I let him touch me—the two of us—so close. It's supposed to be a mortal sin. I don't think it's a sin when you love someone. I love him so." She was looking across the table, waiting for my judgment. I couldn't contradict her, give her a sense of guilt . . .

And, more jarring:

We sat across from each other at a table in the student cafeteria
with its panoramic view of the frozen lake [Mendota] white and
silent, the ice occasionally cracking like a rifle. Our coffee cups
were empty. The little magazine V. had handed to me—*Pacific
Review*—lay open on the table. I was reading the poem for the
second time trying to concentrate . . . In signing the poem V. had
used only her first two initials and surname. I thought this curious.

"Why the initials?" I asked.

"So the editor wouldn't know it's a woman," she said.

I looked up to see that she was watching me, seriously. Her thick
dark hair was brushed back from her shoulders.

"I don't understand," I said. . . .

"It's easier for a man to be published than a woman," she said
matter-of-factly, lighting her cigarette.

I looked doubtful.

"It's like that in every area of life," she said, a little heatedly. "All
else being equal, it's easier for a man than a woman. More is expected of a woman—a superior performance."

I saw that she lived in a world where women competed with
men. I had never thought of it that way before—of the two sexes
competing professionally. This kind of competition was absent
from the Church. Nuns did not compete with priests. Women
could approach the altar only as far as the communion railing.

This exchange, almost verbatim, was one Ray and I had had, in the
Wisconsin student union. We, too, had a table overlooking frozen Lake
Mendota. Ray, too, had expressed skepticism about my remarks—a sort
of playful, flirtatious skepticism—though he'd seemed sympathetic,
essentially. It's jarring that Ray should so casually state "nuns did not
compete with priests"—as if nuns were a sub-species, set beside their
male counterparts—but for me, more jarring to realize that, except for
the cigarette V. is smoking, the portrait of V. seems very familiar . . .

Is Ray writing about *me*?

Or maybe just partly—drawing upon Sylvia Plath, his young wife
Joyce, and his own imagination . . .

Another jarring thing: I am beginning to realize that much of *Black Mass* must have been written after Ray had met me, and not before. Always he'd led me to believe that the bulk of the manuscript had been written before 1960 and so could have nothing to do with our relationship, or with me, but judging from the chronological outlines, which take the narrative into the 1970s, Ray was certainly working on the manuscript as late as 1972, 1973, 1974.

One of the chapters brings Paul to London, where Ray and I had lived in 1971–1972. The streets Ray describes are streets we'd walked on, often, in Mayfair, where we'd lived in a flat overlooking Hyde Park; frequently we passed the massive American Embassy with its security guards in perpetual readiness against anti-American picketers. I am fascinated to see how Ray used this material, as background to his Midwestern love story; it had never been possible for me to set a work of fiction in London, though I'd loved the city, as Ray had.

Fascinating, too, to see what use Ray has made of the Modern Language Association meeting in Chicago, to which we'd gone from Beaumont, Texas; and what use he has made of Detroit; and of his own brief tenure as chair of the English department at Windsor. Whenever Vanessa enters the narrative, the tone shifts—Vanessa is the mysterious other, like Christabel in Coleridge's gothic poem: the (male) protagonist is drawn to her as if against his will, as she is drawn to him: the (forbidden) celibate priest.

Did Ray think of himself as a (forbidden) celibate priest, in his marriage?

Did Ray think of me, his wife, as a "mysterious other"?

Truly, I don't think so. I can't think so. There was much laughter in our marriage. *Black Mass* is a myth, not a literal replica of life.

I must keep that in mind. I must not upset myself, reading meanings into this material that might not be there.

Maybe the girl with whom he fell in love in the sanitarium. Maybe this is the "mysterious other"—who had saved him from despair, and whom he'd lost.

But Vanessa is a poet, allegedly a very good poet. And Vanessa kills herself, when Paul rejects her.

Paul rejects her because he has taken vows of celibacy, as a Jesuit priest. Paul does not reject her because he doesn't love her. Devoted as Vanessa was to her poetry, as Paul says: "Her poetry wasn't enough."

Lost love, a death sentence. It is said to Paul, by an angry friend of Vanessa: "You celibate. You bloody celibate. And now you want to write a book about her."

Now, I am writing a book about Ray.

I am writing a book about the (lost) Ray.

Black Mass isn't complete but there is an ending of a sort, a poem by Vanessa which Paul discovers after her death. The last words are *Rest in peace, rest in peace.*

What I wish: that Ray had shown me the manuscript of *Black Mass* after he'd worked on it further. That we'd spoken more openly about it. That I might have helped him. (I might have encouraged him.) Maybe, when he'd first shown me the manuscript, when we were first married, I hadn't known what to say, and had not said the right things. As a young wife married to an "older" man—a man with an air of authority, in matters in which I was naively inexperienced—I had so rarely expressed any opinion that was not intended to placate him, or to entertain or impress him; it was years before I summoned the courage to suggest to Ray that I did not really like some of the music he frequently played on our stereo—such macho-hectic compositions as Prokofiev's *Alexander Nevsky*, the chorale ending of Beethoven's *Ninth Symphony* with its relentless *joy joy joy* like spikes hammered into the skull, much of Mahler . . .

Now, I would be so happy to hear this music booming out of the stereo.

Mostly the house is silent, since Ray died. I have not played a single CD. Rarely do I turn on the radio in the kitchen, to which Ray listened when he prepared his breakfast or made coffee.

Ray's coffee: the package is still in the refrigerator. Since I don't drink coffee, it will never be touched again. Yet I can't bring myself to throw it away, as I can't bring myself to remove Ray's books from the coffee table . . . I am afraid that, when friends come to visit, over a period of months—years?—they will see these books in exactly the same place and feel pity for me ... *But I can't. I can't move Ray's books. If I take them away there will be emptiness there. I can't.*

As dusk comes on, the pain between my shoulder blades is gradually worsening. And there seem to be related pains, short vertical pains, around my rib cage. But I can't stop reading *Black Mass*, I am drawn into the melancholy tale of P. and V.—the celibate priest, the "brilliantly talented troubled poet" ... Almost, I can forget that this is fiction; it has the tone of memoir, to which fictitious elements have been added, like the light strokes of a watercolor brush.

Amid a section of unnumbered red-ink pages near the end of the novel there are several paragraphs crossed out, which I can decipher, barely. This seems to be a memory sequence—Paul recalling his sister's "rebellious behavior"—not the "good" sister Lucy but a "bad" sister Caroline—younger than Lucy—a girl of twelve who flares up in anger against the righteous father—refuses to say the rosary with the family— is obstreperous at mass—becomes personally messy, "smelly"—laughs "inappropriately."

"Caroline" is clearly Carol. Ray is writing about his institutionalized sister Carol. But the typed scene breaks off in the middle of a page.

Then, a few pages later, in scrawled handwriting there's a new memory sequence involving Caroline in which Paul's father summons their parish priest—the priest "prays over" Caroline who is believed to be "demon-possessed"—there is an "exorcism" conducted in the parents' bedroom—Paul (who is nine at the time) and Lucy are terrified and kept from seeing what is done to their sister; at a later time, Caroline is taken forcibly to a doctor/clinic—a "lobotomy" is performed on her brain, to "calm" her—when Paul sees his sister again, he doesn't recognize her at first. She will be committed to "St. Francis of Assisi"—a hospital, or a residence ...

This sequence, too, ends abruptly. The writing is flat, blunt, crude and Ray's handwriting is near-illegible.

Lobotomized! This must have been what was done to Ray's sister Carol, when he was a child.

The girl had been "lobotomized"—a portion of the frontal lobes of her brain cut out by a crude quasi-surgical procedure of a kind frequently performed in the 1940s and 1950s by self-styled practitioners. The stated purpose was to treat extreme behavior in schizophrenics and others suffering from mental illness, the unstated purpose to control individuals whose behavior was annoying, offensive, or rebellious—like Ray's sister.

In 1949, the "peak year" for lobotomies in the United States—forty thousand were performed!—the Portuguese Egas Moniz was awarded a Nobel Prize for having developed the procedure, which was to be discredited only a few years later. In the interim, many thousands of individuals were as much maimed by the operation as "helped"—if indeed any were "helped."

This was the shameful family secret of which Ray never spoke except obliquely.

This was the traumatic memory of Ray's childhood that had lodged as deeply in him as his early fear of sin and Hell.

In the fragmentary *Black Mass*, these vignettes involving "Caroline" are crossed out. Very little of Paul's family background is included, only just references to Paul's father that quiver with dislike and irony. Whenever Paul's father is evoked, Ray's writing becomes flatly ironic, sarcastic. The author couldn't seem to find a modulated tone in which to write about this painful material, as if sensing how it would eclipse the more conventional romance of the celibate priest and the beautiful woman poet.

If Ray had completed the novel, and if it were to be published—very likely he'd have excised this material. Not that it's too raw or unintegrated with the plot—revising and recasting could have remedied this—but rather, the material is just too personal. Both Ray's parents were living at the time he'd been writing the novel, as well as his sisters and brother.

Or maybe—I'm mistaken. Maybe, boldly and defiantly, Ray would have wanted the material included. Maybe he'd have wanted it included, in this posthumous and abbreviated manner, in what I am writing about him.

Through this turbulent night I'm awake though the room is darkened—I am not trying to read, or watch TV—sharp burning pains in my back, upper torso—can't find a comfortable position to lie in as if columns of red ants are marching across my skin—thinking of Ray, missing Ray so,

for there is no one to whom I can speak about what I have been reading, and what I've discovered—trying to remember what Ray told me
about his sister: Had Carol been subjected to "shock treatments" too?
Or had "shock treatments" been suggested for Ray himself, when he'd
been in the sanitarium? And what sort of "sanitarium" was this? Was it
a private hospital, or one associated with the Catholic Church? Ray had
never told me.

Had Ray seen his sister, often? While he was growing up? Had he
visited her in the institution in which she lived, and was she brought
back to the family home to visit?

Or am I thinking now of my own sister Lynn, whom my father
brought home to Millersport, on Sundays? It was said of Lynn that she
paid little attention to my parents but was eager to eat her favorite sweet
foods which my mother baked for her. My brother Fred said that the
visits were a "strain" for my mother but that my father "insisted" on
bringing Lynn home—Sunday after Sunday—for years. And to ac-
commodate my father's wishes, and my sister's exhausting presence, my
mother Carolina began taking tranquilizers—Xanax—to which she
would become addicted . . . For my soft-spoken mother could not oppose
my father in the smallest matter, let alone in this, his will was so much
stronger than hers.

My brother has told me, too, that each Sunday as it neared the time
when my father would take Lynn back to the residence in Amherst, she
became restless and eager to leave. *She doesn't feel comfortable anywhere
else. With people like herself, she seems—almost—to be happy.*

I wonder if Ray's sister Carol felt like this. If, though her life as a
normal woman had been destroyed by a medical folly, she had had some
measure of human happiness in "St. Francis of Assisi"—or its real-life
equivalent.

82

"Good Girl!"

We take turns throwing the stick into the field. It's a tree limb stippled with the dog's teeth marks and damp with the dog's saliva. As the dog rushes to retrieve the stick, we are admiring of the dog—a beautiful long-haired collie with exquisite fur—burnished-red, tawny-gold, snowy-white—her ears are sharply alert, her eyes are limpid-damp—almost, Trixi seems to be smiling at us—the wet eager smile of a creature for whom happiness is solely pleasing her master, her mistress.

"Good girl! What a *good girl* she is. . . ."

Roughly our friend strokes the collie's head, snatches up the stick and throws it again, out into the field—again Trixi rushes to retrieve it.

"Isn't she a *good girl* . . . Go, Trixi!"

Trixi trots back to us with the stick panting with joy, sides shuddering, tail wagging . . . though quickly the game of fetch begins to bore us, especially the game of fetch begins to bore Trixi's master and mistress who play the game of fetch often with Trixi in summer, in their country place.

"Maybe that's enough for now, Trix. *Good girl*—OK?"

We are visiting our friends who live in the Poconos, in Pennsylvania, in a sprawling old fieldstone house above a small lake. We will stay overnight in their guest room which has a fieldstone fireplace, bookcases crammed with interesting books, no doubt there will be a nest of spiders somewhere in the room for one of us to discover with a little cry of alarm which will evoke memories of Beaumont, Texas—the flying "palmetto" bugs—"Sure was glad to get out of there alive!"

Which summer this is, I am not certain. It might have been four years ago, or longer. For time passes so swiftly now. As if sun and moon whirl about, the eye stares dazed and uncomprehending. Our visit wasn't last summer and probably not the previous summer. Snapshots have been taken of us all at our friends' summer house for the past fifteen years but the snapshots are interchangeable if not precisely dated—one summer has blended into the next.

You would think we are the same people—unchanging. The snapshots must show a pattern of aging but it has been so gradual, we've seemed not to notice.

Except sometimes Ray will stare at a photo of himself which I've just had developed at the camera store in Pennington, amid a swath of new photos taken on a recent trip or at a recent party, with a look of dismay—if I'm not alert, and take it from his fingers, he might dispose of it.

Honey? What's wrong? I ask him. You look very handsome in that picture.

Handsome! Ray will wince, and laugh.

He isn't a vain person. Quite the contrary! Checking his appearance in a mirror, running his hands through his hair, he frowns, as if slightly embarrassed at what he's doing.

Your beautiful eyes. Blue-gray eyes.

Yet somewhat recessed eyes, so that, behind the lenses of his wire-rimmed glasses, the beautiful blue-gray eyes are not prominent; I am thinking that no one has really seen these eyes, gazed into these eyes, except his wife who loves him.

But Ray winces, seeing a photo of himself—the shadowy face of his father superimposed upon Ray's younger face.

(Not, oddly, in life. Only in certain photos, taken at certain angles.)

Once, we'd spent New Year's Eve with these friends at the home of other, mutual friends in Princeton. On the windowsill in my study is a photograph memorializing the evening. Eight of us in the picture—all very festive, smiling—my hair is longer, and curlier; Ray is standing at the rear, almost in shadow. I see that he's wearing the Unicorn Tapestry

necktie I'd bought for him at the Cloisters, years ago when we'd slipped
out of the very long May ceremonial of the American Academy of Arts
and Letters, amid the marathon announcements of literary awards, and
driven a few miles north to the Cloisters Museum which was one of the
places that made Ray very happy . . .

Ever more I am being pitched into the past, as into a roiling sea. I
think there is some danger that I will drown in this sea.

"Good girl!"—the call summons me back.

"Good girl—isn't she? But I think that's enough for now, Trix."

I will never be able to think of these friends whom we loved—who
loved us—without thinking of Ray and I will not be able to see them, I
think, without Ray.

Here is a shameful fact: when these friends called on the day following Ray's death, I could not lift the phone receiver.

I dared not lift it. That name in the caller ID—I could not answer.

Joyce? Hello? We've heard the—terrible news . . .

Will you call us? Please?

How are you doing? Should we drive to Princeton? We could be there
tomorrow afternoon.

Please call, let us know . . .

Joyce? Are you listening?

But this is the future—unimaginable now.

This summery late-afternoon in the Poconos. A grayish haze in the
mountains and dark thunderheads at the horizon but elsewhere, as if
from a supernatural source, there is a bright, brilliant light across the
hills—as in an eerily luminous—ominous—landscape by Martin Johnson Heade: *The Coming Storm.*

Trixi the collie was a rescued dog—a "shelter dog"—now in the
prime of life, a dynamo of energy, her eyes filled with adoration for her
master and mistress who are so kind to her—and very wonderfully Trixi
nudges her head against our hands also, eager to be petted, ears stroked,
the beautiful burnished-red fur admired, and the fast-wagging tail.
Though we are attentive to her, to a degree, yet we've ceased throwing
the stick for her to retrieve, which is disappointing to her, and is making her anxious—she barks, quick high yips like a child's whimpering,
a craving for more attention, immediate attention; for Trixi's doggy-life

is subservient to our human life, unimaginable without us—"Good girl! Go fetch! One last time! That-a-girl."

Again the saliva-dampened stick is tossed into the field, into a patch of Queen Anne's lace, and again Trixi bounds to retrieve it, now barking excitedly.

It is now that our friend astounds us by remarking, casually—"When Trixi passes on, we're going to get a smaller breed. To take on airplanes."

I am so surprised by this remark that I can't respond. I dare not even glance at Ray.

" . . . it's such a hassle, putting her into a kennel. And she's so agitated, and misses us so. If we're away even for a day or two . . ."

" . . . we try to take her with us, when we can . . ."

". . . when we can, but usually we can't, not—"

" . . . not very conveniently."

"Except if we're driving. . . ."

" . . . If we're driving, it's all right. Not ideal, but—"

" . . . it's all right. But a hassle. She's a lovely dog, she's a terrific dog and we love her, but—Trix! Put the damned stick down, girl. Enough for right now."

83

THE RESOLUTION

In the morning—in the mirror—my upper back is striated with vertical red welts throbbing with heat—*shingles?*—for a long moment I stare utterly astonished.

Thinking *But this is something real! This is visible.*

In my naiveté thinking—almost thinking—*This is good!*—*it will take my mind off the other.*

On the Internet I learn that shingles is a *painful, blistering rash caused by the chickenpox virus, that is believed to be activated by severe stress*; I learn that its clinical term is *Herpes Zoster* (great name for a Thomas Pynchon character); and that its symptoms include *red patches on the skin followed by small blisters that resemble early chickenpox . . . the blisters break, forming small ulcers that begin to dry and fall off in 2–3 weeks.*

Medication should begin within twenty-four hours of the onset of these symptoms, to prevent serious complications.

When Dr. M___ examines me, however, he says flatly that I don't have shingles.

I don't have shingles? But—

Dr. M___ asks me how I am sleeping, and I tell him that I am not sleeping very well; Dr. M___ asks me how the anti-depressant tablets have been working, and I tell him that I don't know—I don't really know . . . It is tempting to hide my face in my hands and cry *I don't know! I don't know how I feel! I think that I am—not right . . . I think that there is something very wrong with me but—I don't know.*

Dr. M___ refills my prescriptions for Lunesta and for Cymbalta. I have not the heart to tell Dr. M___ that I've stopped taking Lunesta out of a fear of becoming addicted and that I am frightened of continuing to take Cymbalta because—I think—the medication has been making me feel very strange—but I'm not sure. . . . I'm not sure of so many things, my brain feels as if it has been zapped or cut with an ice pick, the frontal lobes in which "feelings" reside.

And so, though I have been told by my primary care physician that I don't have shingles, or *Herpes Zoster*, and this knowledge should placate me, or have the ameliorative effect of a placebo, the reddened welts on my upper back continue to erupt, and after a miserable night of insomnia compounded by actual physical distress in the morning I see in the mirror that there are twice as many welts on my chest, and my rib cage—flaming itching unbearable!—and so in desperation I call Dr. M___'s office again, and make another appointment, and this time, with some chagrin, Dr. M___ examines my flaming throbbing upper torso that looks as if I've been whipped and concludes that yes, I do have shingles after all.

"The worst case I've ever seen."

But more than twenty-four hours have passed since the symptoms first began to erupt, at least forty-eight hours, and so the antiviral medication Dr. M___ prescribes for me will have a limited effect. Abruptly now I am suffering from shingles, *in medias res*, and can't imagine what my life was like before this—what happiness, to be freed of this violently itching burning encasement of frayed nerves! My pain-free life of only a few days ago seems idyllic to me now but it's a measure of my delusion that I am almost cheerful about this, for shingles is something real—"visible"—and not of the ontological status of the ugly lizard-thing urging me to swallow all the pills in the medicine cabinet, curl up and die.

Except that now, when I check the Internet, I discover that shingles isn't a matter of two to three weeks but a much more serious ailment:

Sometimes, pain may last for months, or years. The pain, *Postherpetic neuralgia* can be extremely severe. Complications may include blindness, if there are lesions in the eyes; deafness; infection, lesions in body organs, sepsis, encephalitis . . .

Suddenly I am frightened: is shingles so *serious*? What if the angry blisters erupt in my eyes? The posthumous life of the widow is narrow enough, but what of a life both posthumous and *blind*?

My remedy is to flee the house where too many thoughts bombard me as if I'm trapped in a spider's web. There are a number of perennials from Kale's which I haven't yet set in the ground and this effort demands my total concentration so that the shingles-pain isn't predominant. Digging holes for anemone—beautiful "wind-flowers"—and a half-dozen hostas—I am wearing Ray's gardening gloves, and I am using Ray's gardening implements. If I don't glance up, or turn around, I can imagine that Ray is in the garden with me and that we're working companionably together in silence, with no need to talk. I will hide from Ray the distressing fact that my upper body is striated with shingles—"lesions"—he would be too concerned. I will hide from Ray the distressing fact that Dr. M___, who'd prescribed too many antibiotics for him, had failed to recognize the obvious symptoms of shingles in his patient and had failed to prescribe the antiviral medication in time.

What Ray would be curious to see, here in his garden, is what I've been planting. I think he would admire what I've done—I have taken time to place the new plants in the soil carefully, and to keep the roots damp. These are purple coneflowers—"rugged prairie plants"—and hostas with white and purple flowers. And something new to me— Siberian iris. Half of Ray's garden is now planted. The Russian sage is thriving. Morning glories I'd planted from seeds are throwing up thin tender vines. Amazing to me, that I have managed to do so much in a few weeks, wresting some sort of order out of weedy chaos . . . I am reminded of a conversation I'd had with Ray about D. H. Lawrence's novella *The Escaped Cock/The Man Who Died* which I'd taught at the

University of Windsor, in a graduate seminar on Lawrence's prose and poetry—this highly poetic and provocative parable of Jesus' "true" resurrection in which the question is asked *From what, and to what, could this infinite whirl be "saved"?*

We'd agreed, there is no salvation, as there is no need for salvation. The world, like the garden, simply *is*.

In a garden it's an easy matter, to be happy. Or, to forget unhappiness, which comes to the same thing.

Next morning, the shingles-lesions are slightly more prominent on my back, chest, sides like quivering snakes. The tiny blisters are filled with watery pus, which I must wash away carefully, to prevent the infection from spreading. (Especially, I must take care not to touch my eyes.) Now I have a cleansing ritual which I will perform several times a day and now—as I work in the garden, in the late afternoon—I am suddenly resolved, since I am obliged to take the new, antiviral medication, that I will stop taking Cymbalta.

In the sunlight, in a garden, what need of an *anti-depressant?* Life looks very different from this perspective.

Friends who've had experience with powerful psychotropic drugs have warned me, one must not cease taking these drugs suddenly. There is the possibility of unleashing severe side effects, hallucinations, tremor, malaise—"suicidal ideation"—even convulsions. And so I will take a single 30 milligram tablet instead of the 60 milligram prescribed by Dr. M___ ; the next morning, I will cut a 30 milligram tablet in half, and take just that amount; each morning I will half the previous day's dosage, until I am finished with the drug, on or about June 1, 2008.

At least, that is my plan. My hope.

This resolution, that comes to me only here in Ray's garden.

"Did Ray Like Swing?"

Jeanne has written me:

> Today I'm listening to La Bohème in its entirety for the first time
> since my father died. On my way home from errands I stopped by the
> cemetery and opened all the doors of my car and played "Musetta's
> Waltz" for Ray. I had the mezzo-soprano from the Cathedral in
> Cleveland sing it at my father's funeral. Then when all the gray
> people filed out of the church, I played my dad's c.d. of the Glenn
> Miller Band playing Sing Sing Sing I & II, featuring Gene Krupa on
> drums.
> Did Ray like swing?
> XXOO
> Jeanne

"Title"

"This is hard. But I'll be with you."

My friend Susan has offered to drive me to the Department of Motor Vehicles on Route 1 in Lawrenceville to fulfill the last of the lengthy drumroll of death-duties—transferring the title of our 2007 white Honda to the "executrix" of Raymond Smith's estate.

At least, I think this must be the last of the death-duties. I am so very tired of these death-duties, my soul shrivels like a desiccated leaf tossed into the fire at the mere prospect of—"executrix"—"Joyce Smith"—"death certificate". . .

Shingles-lesions throb with especial virulence at such times. Itching rises to an aria of jeering in parts of the body difficult to reach and in any case not allowable, when the widow is observed by others.

Think of the lesions as exposed nerves. Mangled quivering exposed nerves. Something of the furious and maimed widow-soul pushing through the skin like shale through earth. And all secret, in a terrible silence.

Riding with Susan in her car, stopping by Quaker Bridge Mall for a half hour in JCPenney and Macy's, being in the company of a friend at this hour of the day—early afternoon—is an adventure for me; since I never shop any longer except for groceries, and then as infrequently as I can manage; since drifting through a store, a mall, in any public place where people are likely to be with relatives, is just too painful for me and in any case there is nothing that I want to buy.

Shopping alone forces me to think of not-shopping-alone—as I'd done for years as a girl, with my mother Carolina, for whom department-store-shopping was an adventure also, since she hadn't much money to spend and was obliged to choose purchases very carefully, after comparing prices in stores; and, for even more years, with Ray, whose object in entering any store was to exit the store as quickly as possible with or without having made the purchases for which the store was entered.

In some stores in the Princeton area, if I don't steel myself and look quickly away I am likely to see us—*ghost-Ray and ghost-Joyce*—ascending on an escalator, pushing a cart into the utterly depressing fluorescent-lit warehouse interior of Wal-Mart.

But shopping in Susan's company is easy, and fun. And Susan and I are temperamentally akin: browsing JCPenney/Macy's for nightwear bargains.

Susan has taken me to Hopewell on that Saturday in summer when the entire town turns into a flea market/rummage sale. Fortunately, Ray had no interest in such creative-bargain-hunting and so I have no painful ghost-memories of shopping in Hopewell with him.

How busy the Department of Motor Vehicles is, on this weekday afternoon! Dispiriting to see so many people—all the seats are taken—as in probate court in Trenton, weeks ago.

In this waiting room there are no *memory pools*. This is a place of utter expediency, soulless and grim.

In a steady stream new arrivals fill out forms for the clerks at the counter and take their places in the long lines. As the lines move slowly forward they become "sitting lines" in several rows of vinyl chairs.

Clutching my death-duty documents, I take my place in one of the lines. Thinking *Who are all these people? I had not thought that death had undone so many . . .*

Badly I would like to hide somewhere, in a restroom stall, and claw at my hot-itching shingles-lesions with my fingernails. I am willing to draw blood if that will assuage the itching but of course it would only exacerbate the condition, that is fueled by stress.

Suffer! Ray was worth it.

But I am not so sure. Not that Ray isn't worth suffering for—but the value of suffering itself. Physical pain, emotional and psychological pain—is there any purpose to it? The faces of many individuals in this waiting room—dark faces, Hispanic and Asian faces predominant among them—are drawn with stress of one sort or another; if not grief for the loss of someone beloved, then another sort of loss, and another sort of grief. Though I am writing this memoir to see what can be made of the phenomenon of "grief" in the most exactingly minute of ways, I am no longer convinced that there is any inherent value in grief; or, if there is, if wisdom springs from the experience of terrible loss, it's a wisdom one might do without.

It is now early June, and I am no longer taking Cymbalta. My method of halving the dosage each day seems to have worked for I haven't had any unusual or alarming symptoms nor do I seem to be more—or less— "depressed" than I'd been at the start.

Still, I must "self-medicate" if I want to sleep for even a few hours. To endure to the point at which I might naturally "fall asleep" after hours, hours, and hours of anxious wakefulness is just not possible and now with the shingles-lesions provoked by stress, I am afraid to take such chances.

I haven't told anyone about the shingles. I have passed through the contagion stage and would have thought that, after several weeks, the welts, blisters, and watery pus would have abated, as well as the worst of the burning pain, but that isn't so.

But how tired I am, of being *sick*. When people inquire how I am, always I say I'm feeling very good—"Much better."

And my friends say: "Joyce! You are looking much better."

And my friends say, to the point at which, if Ray could overhear, he would laugh with me, for this remark has become so frequent: "Joyce! You're looking so much *better-rested*."

(A backhanded compliment to the widow since it suggests how ravaged, how wretched, how really terrible-looking the widow has been, previously.)

When friends greet me with hugs, it's all that I can do to keep from screaming and recoiling with pain, when the shingles-lesions are forcibly touched. Tears running down my cheeks even as I am smiling, smiling to assure my friends *Yes truly, I am feeling much better.*

Yes truly, I am alive. For a while, there was some doubt!

Often my eyes well miserably with tears. Often and surreptitiously I wipe my eyes with my fingertips. Especially here at the Motor Vehicles Department in the grim task of acquiring "title" to the car I have been driving for years as if I were not in fact entitled to the car purchased out of the joint checking account I'd had with my husband. When the widow is interrogated on the subject of her widowhood the widow is likely to feel embittered, resentful. The widow is likely to feel very depressed. Fortunately Susan has gone elsewhere and isn't a witness to my near-breakdown when an unfriendly female clerk gives me a difficult time, for some reason—*Does she think that I am pretending my husband is dead? Does she think that I have printed up this death certificate as a ruse, to acquire his car?* Rudely I am made to wait as my documents are checked and double-checked.

Death certificate: "certified."

Certificate of Title.

Executor Short Certificate.

Driver's license. Car registration. Insurance card. Identification papers.

Widows, survivors. I wonder how many there are of us here. Single women, older women—more women than men in the waiting room. In this inhospitable place I am trying to recall Ray. Seeing him suddenly outside my study window in the courtyard waving to me—"Come outside and see the new car."

And I'd gone outside, and saw the white Honda in the driveway—"But it's just like the old car."

"Of course."

Except now I am thinking—if only Ray had thought to purchase the car in both our names, not in just his own. Now I would not be here in the Department of Motor Vehicles pressing a claim for the very car I've been driving since January 2007 when Ray brought it home.

Months later, in the fall, when I am stopped on Pretty Brook Road for "crossing the white line"—the narrow country road is very twisty, there are numerous blind turns—and the police officer asks to see my auto registration, the document which I hand to him will be invalid,

because incomplete. In my desperation I will search the glove compart-
ment again, futilely—the police officer will issue me a ticket for driving
without registration— it's then that I will remember the frowning clerk
at the Department of Motor Vehicles who'd removed part of the auto
registration document—a card-sized piece of paper—and must have
kept it instead of returning it to me with the other documents.

I will wonder—is this the clerk's petty revenge? But revenge for what?

I will wonder—was it just a mistake? The clerk had torn out the
registration card and simply forgot to return it and there was nothing
intentional on her part, no covert meanness that will result in my having
to appear in the Titusville traffic court early one Monday morning in
October, to forestall having to pay a fine of three hundred dollars . . . ?

The "Executor Short Certificate" is one of the documents I have
grown to hate. This document states that "Joyce Smith" is the *executrix*
of the estate of "Raymond J. Smith, Jr."—to glance at it is to know, in an
instant, that "Joyce Smith" is the widow/survivor and that "Raymond J.
Smith, Jr." is gone.

How wrong, how unnatural this is. Anyone who knew Ray would
know that he would not have gone away and left me.

He would not have gone away and left me to this *infinite whirl*,
alone.

Another document I hate is the "certified"—i.e., stamped with the
New Jersey State seal—death certificate of Raymond J. Smith, Jr.

Such words as *cause of death*: *cardiopulmonary arrest—pneumonia.*
Time of death: *2/18/08 12:50 a.m.*

After almost four months, I am able to read these words without feeling *I want to die. I should die.* Almost, I am able to read these words as if
they were ordinary words and not terrible words that chart so casually
and perfunctorily the end of my life as I'd known it.

When I am alone in the house in which Ray and I lived for so many
years, I fantasize of families—the happiness of families, which seems
always so much greater than any happiness of which I might be capable
myself; but when I am in public places, seeing individuals with relatives,
I don't feel at all that I would like to trade places with them . . . even in
fantasy. The melancholy fact is: these individuals linked by blood will
not remain linked for very long. Many are older, elderly—they will not

be living much longer. Seeing a woman of about my age with a much older woman, no doubt her mother, I am led to think *But you won't have her much longer. I have lost my mother, six years ago. I never thought that I would laugh or even smile again but of course . . . Of course I have.*

Susan, who used her time at the Department of Motor Vehicles to have her car inspected outside, returns and is surprised that I haven't yet received the title to my car; I am still waiting in line, though at the very front of the line now. "What! How can these people be so *slow*?"

Susan is one of my wonderful women-writer-friends, with a wonderful husband, and though I am sure that Susan understands how her energy, her confidence, her good humor and her zest for work are inextricably bound up with her husband and her marriage, I think that she can't quite realize the degree to which this is so. And it is good for Susan, and for my other non-widow-women friends, that they can't know.

Maybe they will never know. This is possible.

"We're not in any hurry," Susan says, squeezing my hand. "We can wait."

"Your Husband Is Still Alive"

Your life together was purely chance. You must not forget, it was a gift freely given you could not have deserved.

On a Sunday evening, in a gathering of graduate students at the University of Wisconsin, Madison, in a room of the fabled old Student Union overlooking Lake Mendota, he came to sit beside me.

Only fleetingly I had a sense of this tall slender dark-haired young man, at first. I did not want to stare at him. I was talking with others, others were talking with me, it was a social situation, we were all smiling.

We may have been lonely people, in our residence rooms.

We may have been very lonely people, some of us new to Madison and knowing virtually no one.

Yet we were here, we'd come to meet one another, and so he'd crossed the room to sit beside me, before even I had had a clear glimpse of his face I'd begun to think *But this is something—someone—special. . . . Maybe.*

Pointedly he'd pulled out a chair from the table, and brought it to me. And he was sitting beside me. He introduced himself—"Ray Smith." I told him my name. He told me something of himself—he was a Ph.D. student in English, completing his dissertation on Jonathan Swift, he had a fellowship and wasn't teaching this semester; when he asked about me I told him that I was an M.A. student in English, I had a Knapp Fellowship and was not teaching, either. He asked me what I was studying and I told him—I told him that I was having difficulty with Old English—he laughed and said, "But I can help you with the 'great vowel shift'"—and he asked me if I would like to have dinner with him that evening which was the evening of October 23, 1960, and I said yes—yes I would—and so it happened that night, and the following night, and the following night—dinner together in Madison—and one of these evenings, an impromptu dinner in Ray's little rented room on Henry Street—and we were engaged on November 23 and we were married—in Madison, in the sacristy of the Catholic chapel there—on January 23, 1961; and for forty-seven years and twenty-five days we would be together nearly every day and every night until the morning of February 11, 2008, when I drove my husband to the emergency room of the Princeton Medical Center; and we would speak together every day of those forty-seven years and twenty-five days until the early morning of February 18, 2008, when the call came for me, rousing me from sleep and summoning me to the hospital quickly! quickly!—"Mrs. Smith! Your husband is still alive."

THREE SMALL SIGHTINGS IN AUGUST

August 11, 2008. Last night the garden was suffused with light—a strange sort of sourceless sunshine that seemed to come from all directions. I could not see clearly but the garden seemed both my garden—ours—Ray's and mine—and a larger, less cultivated setting. And Ray was—somewhere?—Ray was close by—Ray was turned to me, though I could not see his face clearly—and I felt such relief, saying *You're all right, then. You're here.*

August 19, 2008. So strange!—mysterious!—yet utterly ordinary: how sometime after 11 P.M. in bed while reading, I began to feel sleepy; a sensation of sinking, dissolving, as into warm lapping water; a sensation I had not felt since driving Ray to the hospital, that had become unfamiliar to me and but dimly recalled as the chronically ill but dimly recall the days of their health; a sensation of such wonder, such sweetness, such comfort, for I had not (yet) taken anything to help me sleep; for I would take a single non-prescription reputedly non-habit-forming pill to help me sleep, at about midnight; and again, if/when I woke, a second pill at perhaps 4 A.M., for this was my usual night, for this was my usual strategy of enduring the night, lying in a carefully calibrated position amid the bedclothes, to minimize the hot-itching-

pain of the shingles-lesions which had begun to abate, and even to fade,
yet continued to exert a curious autonomous life—a "crawling" sort of
sensation—as if the ugly lizard-thing had burrowed into my skin—
leaving fissures, scars and discolorations like leering birthmarks; yet
the sensation of *sleepiness* overcame all else, the phenomenon of *sleepiness*
rose like dusk lifting from the earth; and I did not have time really
to comprehend what was happening, the strangeness of what was happening; scarcely time to close the book I was reading, or trying to read,
for I'd been rereading the same passage for some minutes, and place
the book on the bedside table, and fumble to turn out the light, and
fall asleep. And following this night, for most nights afterward I slept
without medication; I slept for as long as seven or eight hours, which
seemed to me a miracle; I did not speak of this to anyone, for fear that
the miracle would depart, as abruptly as it had come to me. I thought
Am I abandoning Ray?—what is happening to me . . .

August 30, 2008. Waking this morning, or part-waking—a sense of yearning, anxiety—that there must be some mistake, or misunderstanding—I
wasn't married any longer. And it seemed to me that I could remarry
Ray—I would do this, and a vast wave of relief came over me.

And then, waking more fully, I remembered—why I was not married to Ray any longer, and why I could not hope to remarry him.

I was stricken with loss, very depressed. As if this were all new to
me—that I'd lost Ray. As if until now I hadn't exactly known, how I'd
lost Ray. And now, I was being made to see the situation from another
perspective, like one who is traveling about a disaster site, viewing the
disaster from different perspectives. Now that my insomnia had lifted
and after all these weeks I was still alive and often happy, in the presence of friends at least—now that the final issue of *Ontario Review* was
printed, published and has made its way into the world as Ray would
have wished—cautiously I'd been thinking *Maybe I am all right now, it's
all right. Maybe I can do this.*

But the dream has told me *No. It is not all right.*

And later that morning at the rear of the driveway: seeing one of the
trash cans fallen onto its side, and the contents spilled out rudely onto

the driveway—raccoons, it must have been, scavenging for food scraps, or the possibility of food scraps; for, the previous night, my friend Ebet and I had hosted a dinner at my house, a small dinner for the Princeton philosopher Harry Frankfurt whose wife was out of town, and to this dinner had come a disjointed gathering of guests, individuals whose spouses were away at the end of August, or had abandoned them, or both; there were only six people, including me; and one of these guests was a stranger to me, a neuroscientist at Princeton University invited by Ebet; and I could not have guessed how, another time so purely by chance, as years ago in Madison, Wisconsin, it was purely chance that Ray had come to sit beside me, my life would be altered—*You must not forget it is a gift freely given you could not deserve.*

Kneeling in the driveway picking up things scattered about by the marauding raccoons—wadded napkins, paper towels, bits of tin foil, packages, yogurt containers, a crumpled aluminum pan in which Ebet had brought homemade pizza—and there, amid the litter, a gleam of something silvery—an earring!—which I'd believed that I had lost; this earring must have been set on the kitchen counter, and gathered with the trash, and thrown out, the previous night; both earrings I'd removed, to lay on the kitchen counter, after the guests had departed; unwittingly then I'd swept the earrings into the trash; and now, kneeling in the driveway I see the second earring a few feet away . . . These were favorite earrings of mine though of no great consequence or worth, nor had Ray given me these earrings, but I wore them often. And I thought *This is my life now. Absurd, but unpredictable. Not absurd because unpredictable but unpredictable because absurd. If I have lost the meaning of my life, and the love of my life, I might still find small treasured things amid the spilled and pilfered trash.*

THE WIDOW'S HANDBOOK

Of the widow's countless death-duties there is really just one that matters: on the first anniversary of her husband's death the widow should think *I kept myself alive.*

EVA HAGGDAHL

Ray Smith and Joyce Carol Oates at a garden wedding.